Experimental and Independent Italian Cinema

Experimental and Independent Italian Cinema

Legacies and Transformations into the Twenty-First Century

Edited by
Anthony Cristiano and Carlo Coen

EDINBURGH
University Press

Edinburgh University Press is one of the leading university presses in the UK. We publish academic books and journals in our selected subject areas across the humanities and social sciences, combining cutting-edge scholarship with high editorial and production values to produce academic works of lasting importance. For more information visit our website: edinburghuniversitypress.com

© editorial matter and organisation Anthony Cristiano and Carlo Coen, 2020, 2022
© the chapters their several authors, 2020, 2022

First published in hardback by Edinburgh University Press 2020

Edinburgh University Press Ltd
The Tun – Holyrood Road
12(2f) Jackson's Entry
Edinburgh EH8 8PJ

Typeset in Monotype Ehrhardt by
IDSUK (DataConnection) Ltd

A CIP record for this book is available from the British Library

ISBN 978 1 4744 7403 0 (hardback)
ISBN 978 1 4744 7404 7 (paperback)
ISBN 978 1 4744 7405 4 (webready PDF)
ISBN 978 1 4744 7406 1 (epub)

The right of Anthony Cristiano and Carlo Coen to be identified as the editor of this work has been asserted in accordance with the Copyright, Designs and Patents Act 1988, and the Copyright and Related Rights Regulations 2003 (SI No. 2498).

Contents

List of Figures vii
Notes on Contributors x
Acknowledgements xii

    Introduction 1
    Anthony Cristiano and Carlo Coen
1 Filmmaker and the Milanese Independent Cinema of the
    1980s and 1990s 41
    Donatella Maraschin and Paola Nasini
2 Light and Liminal: Marinella Pirelli's Cinema 68
    Matilde Nardelli
3 From Vertov to Cine-Journals: Cesare Zavattini's
    Experimental Journey 84
    Carlo Coen
4 Gianfranco Brebbia: The 'Absurd', Expanded Quality of
    Experimental Cinema (1962–73) 103
    Donatella Valente
5 Italian Family Films: The Case of the Archivio Nazionale
    di Bologna 131
    Laura Ceccarelli
6 Independence as Opposition? Redefining Political Cinema
    Through the Case of Mirko Locatelli 141
    Gloria Dagnino
7 Travelling the World: The Essay Films of Massimo
    Bacigalupo (1968–77) 158
    Donatella Valente
8 Tales of Courage: Trade Stories of Italian Independent Cinema 180
    Edward Bowen

9	Niccolò Bruna's Ethical Process as Social Engagement: Upholding Human Stories against a Backdrop of Globalisation *David H. Fleming and Filippo Gilardi*	202
10	The Paradox of 'Independence' in Cyberspace: The Case of Italian Experimental and Independent Cinema *Anthony Cristiano*	216

Index 264

Figures

2.1	From *Film ambiente* (1969) installation of 2013	69
2.2	From *Film ambiente* (1969) installation in Rome of 1969	74
2.3	Preparatory diagram for *Film ambiente* (c. 1968)	77
2.4	Detail from *Film ambiente* (1969)	79
4.1 and 4.2	*Idea assurda per un filmaker. Luna (An Absurd Idea for a Filmmaker. Moon*, 1969)	105
4.3	*Anno 2000 (Year 2000*, 1969)	106
4.4	*Extremity 2* (1968)	106
4.5 and 4.6	*Identificazione (Identification*, 1965)	109
4.7	*Bet* (1972)	110
4.8	*Bazar* (1973)	110
4.9	*Idea assurda per un filmaker. Luna (An Absurd Idea for a Filmmaker. Moon, 1969)*	111
4.10	*Dall'archivio di Gianfranco Brebbia (From Gianfranco Brebbia's Archive)*	112
4.11, 4.12 and 4.13	*Deserto in luce solare (Desert in the Sunlight*, 1969)	113
4.14 and 4.15	*Idea assurda per un filmaker. Luna (An Absurd Idea for a Filmmaker. Moon*, 1969)	114
4.16 and 4.17	*Idea assurda per un filmaker (An Absurd Idea for a Filmmaker. Ester*, 1969)	115
4.18 and 4.19	*Idea assurda per un filmaker (An Absurd Idea for a Filmmaker. Matilde*, 1969)	115
4.20	*Bet* (1972)	117
4.21	*Bazar* (1973)	117
4.22 and 4.23	*Ufo* (1968)	118
4.24 and 4.25	*Fumus Art* (1969)	119
4.26 and 4.27	*Terra (Earth*, 1971)	122
7.1	*60 metri per il 31 marzo (200 Feet for March 31st*, 1968)	162
7.2 and 7.3	*Versus* (1968)	163

7.4	*Her* (1968)	166
7.5	*L'Ultima Estate* (*The Last Summer*, 1969)	168
7.6	*Né Bosco (una conversation)* (*Nor Wood (A Love-dialogue)*, 1970)	168
7.7	*Migrazione* (*Migration*, 1970)	169
7.8	*Coda* (1970)	169
7.9	*Warming Up* (1973)	172
7.10	*Into the House* (1975)	173
10.1	From left to right: Futurists Luigi Russolo, Carlo Carrà, Filippo Tommaso Marinetti, Umberto Boccioni, Gino Severini. Paris, 9 February, 1912	220
10.2	CCI members photographed by Luca Maria Patella. From left to right: Gianfranco Baruchello, Rosa Foschi, Massimo Bacigalupo, Guido Lombardi, Luca Patella (at the moment of taking the fish-eye photograph), Giorgio Turi, Alfredo Leonardi, Celestino Elia, Antonio Vergine, Adamo Vergine	222
10.3	Fondazione Cineteca Italiana (Milano)	223
10.4	National Film Library, Rome. Archivio Fotografico Cineteca Nazionale. Centro Sperimentale di Cinematografia, Roma	225
10.5	*Tempo nel tempo* (*Time in Time*, 1964) by Bruno Munari, Marcello Piccardo	227
10.6	*E nua ca simu a forza du mundu* (*And We Who Are the Force of the World*, 1971) by Alfredo Leonardi, Anna Lajolo, Guido Lombardi	229
10.7	*Verifica incerta* (*Disperse Exclamatory Phase*, 1964) by Gianfranco Baruchello, Alberto Grifi	232
10.8	*La riappropriazione della città* (*The Re-Appropriation of the City*, 1977) by Ugo La Pietra, Centre Pompidou Edition	234
10.9 and 10.10	*60 metri per il 31 marzo* (*200 Feet for March 31st*, 1968) by Massimo Bacigalupo. The representation with zoetrope is from Max Ernst's 1930 illustrated book *Rêve d'une petite fille qui voulut entrer au Carmel* (*Dream of a Girl Who Wanted to Join the Carmelites*).	236
10.11	*Es-pi'azione* (*Ex-pi'action*, 1968), a directorial formulation by Adamo Vergine. The drawing is described and found in 'Adamo Vergine', in 'Il film sperimentale' by Bacigalupo	238
10.12	*Hilarisdoppio* (1973) by Paolo Gioli	240
10.13	Frame from *Dove incominciano le gambe* (*Where the Legs Begin*, 1974) by Piero Bargellini	241

10.14 *Stop Forgetting: The Films of Yervant Gianikian and
    Angela Ricci Lucchi* (2015) 243
10.15 Façade of 'Azzuro Scipioni Cinema' in Rome 244
10.16 Frame from *Egg One Egg Zero* (1972) by Cioni Carpi 246
10.17 Distribution of YouTube video views, 2018. Sourced
    from Pex, Medium © Statista, <statista.com>. 248
10.18 Distribution of Italian video views, 2018. Data is partly
    sourced from ISTAT 'Internet Italia 2018', and from
    average YouTube views over a 5-year period of several
    films reference in the anthology. 249

Notes on Contributors

Edward Bowen is an Advanced Lecturer of Italian at the University of Kansas. He specialises in Italian film history, exhibition and urban studies. He co-edited the volume *The Cinema of Ettore Scola* (Wayne State University Press, 2020) and he has published articles in *Studies in Documentary Film*, *Journal of Italian Cinema and Media Studies* and *Cinema e storia*.

Laura Ceccarelli specializes in Archival disciplines and is Head of European Projects Office of Experimental Center of Cinematography (Italy). She is a member of the Italian National Archive Association.

Carlo Coen holds a PhD in Italian Studies from the University of Toronto and has several publications to his credit on Italian and Indian Cinema. He has delivered lectures in Canada, Italy, the USA, India and Australia. At present he is the Director of Programming of the *Italian Contemporary Film Festival*.

Anthony Cristiano is lecturer in the Digital Media, Journalism, and Communication program at Wilfrid Laurier University. His research interests include media ethics and cultural history. He is the co-editor of *Millennials and Media Ecology* (Routledge, 2020), and the author of the forthcoming 'Artificial Intelligence and Ultimate Reality' (University of Toronto Press).

Gloria Dagnino is adjunct lecturer in Film Economics at the Institute of Media and Journalism of the Università della Svizzera italiana (USI—Lugano, Switzerland). She is also Equal Opportunities Officer at USI. Her research interests include the political economy of audiovisual media, advertising and media convergence, and contemporary Italian film industry.

NOTES ON CONTRIBUTORS

David H. Fleming is Senior Lecturer in Film at the University of Stirling, Scotland. His research interests surround the intersections of cinema, philosophy and technology. He is the author of *Unbecoming Cinema: Unsettling Encounters with Ethical Event Films* (Intellect, 2017), and co-author with William Brown of *The Squid Cinema from Hell* (EUP, 2020), and with Simon Harrison of *Chinese Urban Shi-nema* (Palgrave, 2020).

Filippo Gilardi is an Associate Professor in Creative Industries and Transmedia, the Head of the School of International Communications, and the Deputy Director of the Institute of Asia and Pacific Studies (IAPS) at the University of Nottingham Ningbo China. He is also a Principal Fellow of the Higher Education Academy and a Fellow of the Royal Society of Arts.

Donatella Maraschin is an independent researcher with expertise in Italian cinema, the development of storytelling on the digital platform and digital health. Her lengthy Faculty Member experience in British Higher Education Institutions includes the University of Reading and London South Bank University, where she taught as Senior Lecturer in Media and Film. Her publications include the book *Pasolini: Cinema e Antropologia* (Peter Lang, 2014).

Matilde Nardelli is a Senior Lecturer in the London School of Film, Media and Design, at the University of West London. She co-edited a volume on the artist and designer Bruno Munari for Peter Lang (2017), and her monograph *Antonioni and the Aesthetics of Impurity: Re-Making the Image in the 1960s* is forthcoming from Edinburgh University Press.

Paola Nasini earned her BA in History of Philosophy at Statale University in Milan, continuing her education at Utrecht University in Holland with a Masters in Cultural Studies from Multicultural Perspectives. Through twenty years of international cultural events production, documentaries and commercials, she has established a reputation as a skilled producer, with a keen eye for talent and a strong personal creative vision.

Donatella Valente is currently completing her doctoral thesis at Birkbeck, University of London. She teaches in Film Studies (BA) and Screen Media (MA). Her research focuses on film theory, screen media aesthetics and critiquing gender in cinema. She has published with, and co-edited for, a variety of academic publishers, including Intellect, Mimesis International, NECSUS, BUFVC and *Senses of Cinema*.

Acknowledgements

The work on this singular anthology would not have been possible without the research and critique carried out over many years by several other scholars of visual art and film. We gratefully acknowledge and thank Bruno Di Marino, Adriano Aprà and Sandra Lischi, for their kind correspondence. We wish to pay tribute to and acknowledge the entrepreneurship and career of Silvano Cavatorta – co-founder with Pedote of Filmmaker Coop – as well as those of Americo Sbardella and Enzo Ungari – who were among the founders of the Filmstudio. The composition and compilation of the various chapters in this anthology have greatly benefitted from the number of artists, cineastes, institutions and foundations who have kindly assisted us in various ways, particularly with the collection of still photographs that appear in several chapters. We therefore acknowledge and thank all of them, including Luca Maria Patella, Andrea Piccardo, Massimo Bacigalupo, Silvano Agosti, Giovanna Brebbia, Paolo Gioli and the critic Roberta Valporta, as well as the Ugo La Pietra Foundation, Marinella Pirelli Foundation, the Cineteca Nazionale – Centro Sperimentale di Cinematografia in Rome, and the several centres, institutions, professionals, curators and individuals, who have in various ways made the work on this volume possible and, if not effortless, at least easier to bring to fruition and complete. We thank the various scholars who contributed to the anthology, and who have undertaken to conduct research in this burgeoning field of study as well as, in several cases, carry out interviews with the artists and filmmakers whose work is herein discussed, and which constitutes a sample of a larger and rich tableau of Italian visual, documentary, and moving image arts. May we also remember our dear colleague Sara Iommi, who passed away prematurely, before she could bring to fruition her proposal for this anthology. We finally extend our appreciation and thanks to the various people at Edinburgh University Press and their associates, Gillian Leslie, Richard Strachan, Rebecca Mackenzie, Eliza Wright, Helena Heald and George MacBeth, for the kind assistance, sensitivity and professionalism they have shown throughout the publication process, which brings this very first anthology, in the English language on the topic, to the world.

INTRODUCTION
Anthony Cristiano and Carlo Coen

Forms of experimentalism and independence in the panorama of Italian cinema date back to the birth of cinema, and have continued to emerge and develop, with varying intensity, throughout the history of Italian filmmaking. Overall, the same cinematic, artistic and anthropological merits have been largely overlooked by the official academies of human and social sciences, both within and beyond the nation's borders. The historical avant-garde phenomenon of the Italian Futurists, with their excursions into various forms of art, are an exception, probably due to their provocative nature, systematic propositions and revolutionary intentions. Italian fringe-like work in the cinema has received institutional 'adoption', and subsequent attention by mainstream venues, only when its narrative has complied with marketable agendas – such is the case from the silent period to Rossellini's postwar films.[1] Forms of independence or experimentalism, which were deemed extravagant, idiosyncratic, or marginal, remained largely unnoticed and unappreciated, even by experts in the field of visual-arts. In recent decades, however, a number of Italian scholars, and scholars of Italian descent, have questioned the lack of attention, study and analysis, given to unconventional forms of Italian cinema, its peculiar character and practices. Other national histories have exhibited a similar pattern, as supported by cases such as that of P. Adams Sitney – one of the rare historians of neglected forms of American experimental cinema – who happened to also write in the 1990s about the crisis within Italian cinema. In Italy, an increasing number of film historians and scholars are picking up on the wealth and body of work of experimental and independent Italian cinema. The 'discovery' via cinema *d'essai* and *cineclub* festivals, as well as gallery and media-lab exhibits, of alternative forms of art and modes of dissemination, has led to systematic studies into and penetrating criticism of the significance and import of art expressions, and forms of independence, that mirror novel socio-cultural trends as well as alternative, innovative, or revolutionary worldviews. Italian cinema has been at the forefront of international film practices throughout several periods of cinematic history, for its originality and independence, as well as its ground-breaking styles, techniques and thematic concerns. Such has been the case since Giovanni Pastrone (1883–1959), through the lost films of the Futurists, to Roberto Rossellini (1906–77), Ermanno Olmi, Cesare Zavattini (1902–89),[2] Pier Paolo Pasolini (1922–75), Nanni Moretti[3] and Silvio Soldini[4] – to mention only a few names associated with a distinctive legacy of certain forms of experimentalism or independent praxis and attitudes within their respective milieus. Though scholars have acknowledged the interdisciplinarity of Italian cinematic tradition and of individual cineastes, the further cinematic legacy of 'underground' practices of experimental and independent cinema has been neglected. Furthermore, the subject matter is scarcely known in the English-speaking world, and thus has received little to no attention in English language literature and anthologies – even when these are devoted to socio-cultural histories and art criticism. No introductory monograph or systematic study on Italian experimental and independent cinema has been released in book format to the English-speaking world to this day. This volume therefore constitutes an initial attempt to supplant the lack of academic treatises in the English language and, thus, to provide a first and introductory study and collection of essays on the topic.

A look at the terminology adopted helps to place the experimental and independent cinema phenomena into a historical context and distinguish the characteristics which are peculiar to the Italian panorama. Scholars have regularly found forms of continuation between different cinematic epochs, for instance Antonio Costa, Bruno Di Marino and others who have identified a continuation of Futurist approaches in film practices of the 1930s and beyond.[5] Throughout the last century, a host of terms have been deployed to describe unconventional practices of filmmaking. They may refer to the procedures adopted and/or the peculiar nature and general aim of a single work, or body of work, in opposition to standards of mainstream practices. In Italy, as well as in European and North American contexts, scholars have referred to unconventional cinema as experimental, alternative, expanded, different, subversive, abstract, underground and so forth. For the purposes of this volume, we opted for the general designation of 'experimental and independent cinema'. The expression is meant to include a variety of practices and forms: art film, avant-garde, experimental, expanded, artisanal, political, low-budget, as well as unknown or neglected directors and artists – deserving of greater attention – controversial or otherwise extreme in their treatments and approaches. While the multiplicity of categorisations may underscore the need to indicate a given study's purpose or perspective, whether historical, anthropological, or aesthetic, there also appears to be an underlying common denominator in terms of atypical or pioneering procedures, their formal approaches and their content. The appropriateness of the words 'experimental' and 'independent' lies in the critical use of the terms, that is, the application of the historical, artistic and socio-cultural, notions summoned. Scholars have repeatedly detected, and enunciated on, forms of experimentation and independence regardless of categorisations, in both unconventional and mainstream film practices. Some have employed the term 'independent' and 'experimental' to refer to the Italian cinematic renaissance during the late twentieth century – as in Zagarrio.[6] The same terms[7] have been applied to several epochs and trends by Paolo Bertetto, Paolo D'Agostini, Bruno Di Marino, Sandra Lischi and several others.

Though useful, 'independent cinema', and 'experimental cinema', are very fluid and continuously debated notions – particularly by filmmakers themselves. Scholars and filmmakers adapt them to peculiar critiques and visions, at times antithetical to each other. To the new poetics involving the relationship between filmmaker and reader/spectator, is added the explorative relationship between filmmaker and art form. Maverick filmmakers (Gianfranco Brebbia, and Silvano Agosti, among several others) have come to hold idealistic views and have referred to independent filmmaking as a 'total devotion' to the art form, or 'total freedom' in matter of practices, or have sought 'purity' of form, concerns and style. It must be acknowledged that whilst the individual approach of independent artists to filmmaking practices may be quite different (especially in terms of concerns and style), several of them nonetheless share a totalising view of cinema as a creative process, from production, to distribution, to exhibition. Scholars interested in socio-cultural readings, have historicised or critiqued experimental and independent film as politically subversive or nonconforming, at other times they have been attracted by the self-reflexive and expanded nature and use of the medium. The field is immensely varied, and any attempt to encompass it into a single and constraining theoretical template is destined to fail. Experimental and independent cinema has been particularly and frequently used to designate the work and practices of *nuovi autori* (new *auteurs*), to refer to low budget productions, to denote the movements such as the Cooperativa del Cinema Indipendente (CCI, Co-operative of Independent Cinema), the *officina di ricerca* (experimentation labs) such as those of animation practices, as well as unconventional production, distribution and exhibition methods, and new technological developments within moving images, such as *videoarte* and *poetronica* (video-art and poetronics), and the like. What is more important is that the expression 'experimental and independent cinema' meets both the denotative and connotative requirements of a versatile lexis. Forms of experimentation, avant-gardism, unconventional approaches and techniques, innovative *modus operandi* or styles, all denote one or more forms of self-determining practices. All refer to the ability to identify irregular patterns, novel expressions, revolutionary methods and styles, whether they expand, challenge, or alter, one's expectations or preconceived notions of the nature and aims of art, and in the case in point of moving-image-arts, they are understood as a way of locating innovation and originality in artists and forms that stray from 'the given path' of traditional canons. For the artists it may amount to a claim of individuality and independence, or to the exploration of new aesthetic potentials and technical processes; the marking of uncharted territories, rather than conformity to, or the perpetuation of, habitual and 'safer' conventional practices.

From Legacies to Transformations

The transformations of Italian independent and experimental cinema are informed by the same cultural, socio-political and technological shifts and yearnings, informing the milieu of the periods in which they emerged. Within the 'western cinematic canon' – transposing a literary term to the art of moving-image – the underground and experimental scene of the late 1960s and onward, may have gained renown for its political and stylistic 'revolutionary' propositions, however its approaches and concerns are not entirely new, but are rather informed by preceding legacies and histories. Italian independent and experimental practices and cinema emerged very early within the history of world cinema, and have been much emulated eversince. They begin with the early film pioneers, gain explosive impulse with the Futurists and re-emerge, metamorphosed into new forms of artistry and craftsmanship, during the mid to late twentieth century. The artistic, performative and anthropological quality, of its approach and vision, are among the chief characteristic of Italian experimental and independent cinema. The field is offset by artists deemed *impegnati* (socially engaged) and *politici* (politicised), on one hand, and by those deemed 'lyrical' and 'abstract', on the other. The poetic and metacinematic function is counterbalanced by its antithesis, the storytelling and narrative thrust. The peculiar stock of the centenary-old Italian artistic tradition has informed the literary and visual art initiatives and movements throughout history as well as individual Italian artists' practices, in various fields. This includes the advent of moving-image arts, in a country renowned for its contribution to the screen-arts – along with counterparts such as French, German and Swedish, cinemas – since the birth of film.

Whether we look at *tematiche* (themes, motifs) or *qualità formali* (formal qualities), at historical avant-garde movements or at contemporary experimental practices, independent forms of Italian cinema have set the tone, *modus operandi* and concerns for many unconventional approaches since the dawn of the new medium, their attractive qualities and character. This is not only the case for the cinematic excursions of the *Futuristi* (Futurists) but also with many classic and neo-classic directors and movements as well. The inventiveness and openness to new ways of seeing and perceiving is found in different 'eras', or periods, within the development of Italian cinema and the history of the country. As Bernardi put it, speaking of the second wave of early Italian *auteurs*:

> [T]he 1930s group of auteurs and films referred to as formalism or calligraphism is an important episode in the history of cinema because, regardless of the aesthetic results that may be sometimes questionable, it presupposes or, even better, opens up a different way of watching the film, intending it as visual art and not as mere entertainment, and sets times and modes of vision very different from the classic ones.[8]

Early experimentation with the new art of cinema is detectable in emblematic figures such as the directors Giovanni Pastrone and Enrico Guazzoni (1876–1949), among other influential pioneers. Italian cinema is also known for its lavish scenography, and early use of colour. The results achieved by the Società Italiana Cines, in Rome, as seen in the 1906 *Le farfalle* (*Butterflies*), surpassed the stencil colouring of the renowned Pathé company in Vincennes, France. The Museo Nazionale del Cinema (National Museum of Cinema) in Turin prides itself for the preservation of pioneering works and artefacts. The Italian tradition in matters of screen arts enjoyed much verve and inventiveness since the *début* of the new art form.

From the late 1960s onwards, Italian experimental and independent filmmakers did not merely emulate their American counterparts, but rather drew inspiration from their own tradition of the arts and art movements: painting, theatre, music history, vanguardism and so forth. We are reminded that in the 1910s, and for several decades afterward, the Futurists' totalising vision incorporated the 'renovation' of film as an art, with provocative and exhilarating works. Among them the artists and directors, Anton Giulio Bragaglia (1890–1960), Arnaldo Ginna (1890–1982) and Bruno Corra (1892–1976), headed up some of the most innovative productions. The silent film *Thaïs*, directed by Bragaglia in 1917, and jealously conserved at the Cinémathèque Française in Paris, is a chief example of choreographic explorations. The painter Enrico Prampolini (1894–1956), devised for the film a series of geometric figures and patterns in a singular spatial-landscape construction of the set, which mirrors the turbulent cycles of the narrative along with the momentous quality of its characters. The achievement – culminating with the exhilarating symbolism in the concluding moments of the film – may be seen as the start of the imaginative flux of much anti-naturalistic cinema afterwards (beginning with German expressionism).[9] Millicent Marcus referred to it as the beginning of Futurist cinema, and noted its prototypic 'scenoplasticity'. Speaking of its innovation and legacy the scholar wrote that, among other things, the end of *Thaïs* can be seen as the culmination of the project to develop the filmic arts medium-specific powers of transcendence.[10] Brothers Ginna and Corra, whose Futurist films are unfortunately lost, are also recognised for their atypical and innovative work in the visual arts – preceding and influencing subsequent filmmakers such as Hans Richter and Walter Rittmann. Ginna, in particular, was an abstract painter, who as a Futurist sought in the ideal form of cinema – its composition, mechanism, dynamism, movement, musicality – the 'purest' expression of one's deepest sense, akin to chromaticism in music. Inspired by classical music, in his *cinepitture* (cine-paintings) shorts he applied unconventional techniques to 'translate' musical pieces into hand-coloured filmic symphonies – emulating his own canvas work, his 1908 *Nevrastenia*, the 1911 *La musica della danza* and other paintings. The undiluted 'transposition' of raw human emotions and moods into colour tonalities was seen as a primary function of the new medium of film. The multiform, polyvalent and plurally expressive, impetus of the Futurists, are a pivotal and provocative expression of revolutionary experimentation and independence. Their nonconforming and 'rebellious' rapport for various forms of media pave the way and set the tone for, several other artists and *auteurs* of subsequent periods, including the wave of much experimental and independent practices. In fact, such early characteristics recur in subsequent decades, including the late 1960s and early 1970s – the neo-futurism found in art, design and architecture, is well known and, among the work referred to in this anthology, Mario Schifano's own *Futurismo Rivisitato* (*Futurism Revisited*, 1965) represents a tribute to this historical movement. The independent studios and co-ops, as well as the practices of several individual Italian artists and filmmakers, throughout the mid to late twentieth century, are characterised by a propulsive movement forward and by an openness to the stimuli of the cultural and socio-political milieu of the counterculture – including their most paradoxical and superficial interpretations. It is the aesthetic quality and texture, the inventiveness, the performative nature, the musicality, along with the personal dimension, informed by a long and rich tradition of Italic arts in general that distinguishes experimental and independent Italian cinematic practices from their foreign counterparts – including in neighbouring France and, long-time followers of the development of the Italian scene, Germany and Britain.

During the 'underground' period, one London writer, on a visit to Italy, eulogised the abilities and visual achievements of Italian filmmakers who worked on 8mm – an 'inferior' film gauge – compared to their English counterparts, who could afford 16mm. Though he noted the political inefficiency in regard to the organisation and running of collective initiatives, he lauded its aesthetic prowess.[11] Perhaps suprisingly such 'anarchist' traits only appear to have contributed to the radical beauty and nature of much experimental and independent cinema. It may be that the very 'exhaustion' of such countercultural trends – among other dynamics – was one of the factors contributing to the demise of the self-run labs and co-ops of independent visual artists and filmmakers.

Within the history of Italian cinema, scholars have recognised a non-traditional tendency in style and language: the reference to periodic formal experimentations, in several Italian *auteurs* throughout the twentieth century, not only as an anti-realist vein running vis-à-vis the (controversial) 'realist cinematic tradition' of Italy, but moreover as an interpretative framework through which one may look at the world anew. If such a proposition proves true for narrative and generic forms of cinema, as expounded upon by Bertetto and Minuz in 'Le forme antirappresentative nel cinema italiano' ('The Anti-Representation Approaches/Forms of Italian Cinema'), how much more it ought to do so for counterintuitive, unconventional, or radical forms of moving-image making. Italian visual artists, storytellers and a number of artisanal-like minds, have veered towards filmmaking to explore new expressive avenues, mechanisms and forms. From a purely aesthetic standpoint, this has been the case with the classic vanguard movements such as the surrealists. The European and Italian cultural and political climate of 1968 intensified the trend in purely aesthetic terms rather than interrupting its forward movement – though no claims of continuity are made.

A systematic attempt to initiate collectives of Italian independent and underground cinema began in the late 1960s. One seminal event that contributed to paving the way towards the creation of co-ops was the exhibition of the New American Cinema in 1961, in Spoleto, followed by a number of other film festivals throughout the decade, in various cities, including Rapallo, Pesaro, Rome and Turin. Some of these saw several North American counterparts, such as Jonas Mekas, Gregory Markopoulos, Taylor Mead and Jack Smith, attend the screenings. They met with a number of Italian artists, some of whom found further inspiration in the American's radical, if not adamantly politicised, use of film equipment and cameras. Italian filmmakers, however, had background experience in theatre arts – though to different degrees. As Sergio Toffetti, writer of 'Before and After the Revolution: Experimental Cinema in Italy', recounts, the Living Theatre group also played an important role in shaping the vision of the Italian artist working in film:

> The impact of the Living Theatre – who later would be featured in an excellent film by Alfredo Leonardi (*Living and Glorious* 1965) – reinforces on the one hand the sense of the group, of the militant collective, and on the other the perception that the body is a medium, a fundamental intermediary for the encounter/clash between the inner self and outer reality, and thus for the political transformation of the world.[12]

Such trends in the arts are comparable to the ongoing search for new modes of expression; a new lens through which to look at the outer and inner realities of one's world. This is done via a melange of forms and modes, which encompass and borrow from a variety of other art forms, including performance, music and poetry. Unconventional, even popularising, practices of alternative cinema were nurtured in the co-ops, the cineclubs, *officine artistiche* (art labs) and *film studio* (film and exhibition centres). Some of which are discussed extensively in this volume. Within such centres the excitement, the debates and the 'labour of love' that went into producing the films were fostered, as well as promotion, distribution and exhibition initiatives and programmes. Scholars keen to explore the international film scene, also became the major researchers of Italian experimental and independent film practices. They emerge from the Italian collective phenomena of the late 1960s and beginning of 1970s; a new wave of art, performance and innovation, forms of unconventional and alternative film practices and works. A number of film scholars and exegetes, including Paolo Bertetto, Adriano Aprà, Antonio Costa, Vito Zagarrio, Flavio De Bernardinis, Bruno Di Marino, Enzo Ungari, Marco Meneguzzo, Vittorio Fagone, Patrick Rumble, Sandra Lischi, Marco Senaldi and Andrea La Porta, have offered their analyses of this unconventional and alternative, experimental and independent cinema. The artists and *auteurs*, who have received critical attention, include Luigi Veronesi, Bruno Munari, Paolo Gioli, Piero Bargellini, Gianfranco Baruchello, Anna Lajolo, Alfredo Leonardi, Guido Lombardi, Massimo Bacigalupo, Tornino De Bernardi, Pia Epremian De Silvestris, Pino Pascali, Franco Angeli, Ugo Nespolo, Mario Schifano, Ugo La Pietra, among several others. For study purposes two categories that have proven useful are those of narrative and abstract/lyrical forms of cinema.

In certain respects, forms of alternative cinema, that is, unconventional approaches to the functionality and consumption of the aesthetics peculiar to the new medium, along with different usages of moving-images' representative or anti-representative potentials, have been invested regularly within all phases of film-work, from inception to exhibition during the last century and into the new. Independence, whether economic or formalistic, is not necessarily regarded an artistic 'identity card' but rather a *modus operandi*, a style, a philosophical and political statement made against complacency and, especially, intended to reaffirm a sense of artistic/cultural liberation. The underlying philosophy of much low budget, unconventional and experimental and independent cinema may be understood through examining the techniques as well as the language and style adopted. On the 2005 occasion of the 'Giornate del cinema privato' (Days of Private Cinema), in Siena, Aprà spoke of low-budget narrative cinema in relation to the outcome of the technological transformations and seminal events of the latter part of the twentieth century, yet the notion equally applies to forms of experimentation.

> Whether it has to do with the high-cost movie [or the] low cost one, we are not confronted with different problems. . . .The cinema [has changed] with the mutation of recording equipment . . . The artist, though, is not conditioned by these things. [It's not that] the low-cost or high-cost production are [one less beautiful than the other] there are some ugly experimental films as there are some ugly narrative films. . . .Narrative cinema is in the third-person, but this represents a limit . . . whereas the narrative film in first-person has expanded the possibilities of 'storytelling', it opened broad fields so-to-speak. From the 1980s onwards this thing has spread rapidly. . . .The 'I' is more subconscious of the 'they' mode of speech.[13]

What transpires from such an understanding is a vision of the art of moving image as a vehicle of aesthetic, intellectual and socio-cultural, inquiry and pursuits. From the point of view of craftsmanship, of the nature of communicative iconic clues, the intent is more important than the wealth at the means at one's disposal. According to scholarly positions, such as quoted above, the change in perspective is not necessarily given by the independently produced work, the low-budget film, but rather afforded by a perceptual and cognitive 'metamorphosis'. It is a change of address, a change within linguistic paradigms. It amounts to a self-reflexive shift: from outward to inward, from the collective to the personal, from the public to the private and thus from the voice conveyed as 'objective' by the use of the third-person-plural, to that of the affirmative and 'subjective' mode of the first-person-singular regime. Although in anthropological and aesthetic terms the scholar must shift gears, the nature of independent and experimental cinema has continued to convey similar claims. What Aprà and others have observed is a levelling out of the field of artistic goals and endeavours and, in the case in point, one taking place within the transforming field of visual arts. In regard to the euphoric climate of the Sixties, the socio-cultural transformations of that period, along with the gradual adoption of new technologies, have not merely informed, but also 'unlocked', the individual artists' vision and simultaneously given the instruments to operate with increased degrees of freedom.

While there is no denying that the visits of American independent filmmakers and the screenings of their films have spawned analogous works and co-op centres in Italy, categorising the Italian independent and experimental phenomena of the late 1960s onwards as mere emulations omits and misrepresents the autochthonous nature and peculiar aesthetic of the Italian tradition. As discussed herein, such an analysis fails to differentiate from foreign ethnographies the socio-cultural traits which are typical of, and indigenous and endogenous to, the Italian peninsula. It overlooks the peculiar quality of a renowned aesthetic tradition, its painterly, performative, aesthetic, lyrical and even folkloristic character. When looking at the available independent work produced during the different periods, the conspicuous influence of such a tradition – on its intellectuals, poets, architects, painters, visual artists and now new *auteurs* of alternative cinema – is discerned. The indigenous, and unexplored, microcosmic histories, of a vast array of Italian independent and experimental work, is gradually emerging. The legacy of cinema forms, even the most short-lived, is being watched, researched and is gradually becoming the object of systematic study on different fronts and within diverse academic disciplines. Indeed, the fact that some periods and related activities have not received critical attention does not erase the traces of its history.[14]

Established and specialised festivals have devoted entire programmes to the screening of these films as well as retrospectives to the body of work of individual artists and filmmakers. Beginning in the late 1960s, several and frequent screenings of experimental films – works from both local and foreign artists – have been programmed at the well-known Filmstudio art centre in Rome (founded in 1967 by Americo Sbardella and Annabella Miscuglio), and some were then re-screened at the Montesacro Alto Cineclub in the mid 1970s. In 1980 the Roman Filmstudio ran a long season of screenings devoted to the Italian underground cinema that lasted fifteen days, from the 15 to the 28 of August, at the Massenzio Rassegna Cinematografica (Massenzio Film Festival) in Rome. During the same decade, other centres and festivals saw the programming of similar initiatives, such as the

Milanese *Filmmaker* group and, under the artistic direction of Aprà, the Salsomaggiore Film Festival, in the province of Parma. In 2003 Filmstudio organised an even greater event with the programming of 144 independent Italian films, dating from 1964 to 1984, and screening at the historic Roman location, on via degli Orti d'Alibert, from 17 November to 1 December. The same Filmstudio hosted the exhibition of (politically inspiring) foreign works, such as films by Robert Kramer, Jean-Marie Straub and Danièle Huillet – though the latter two made several of their films in Italy. More recently the Lucca Film Festival Europacinema, in Tuscany, offered a screening of independent films in its programme. The city of Pesaro has also set up programmes devoted to the Italian experimental and independent film scene for decades, since the mid to late twentieth century and into the first and second decades of the twenty-first century.

Several short and longer films, mentioned in this volume, can be accessed and viewed online on the webpages of Italian and European galleries, museums, and film archives, and moreover with the rise of the 'collaborative' culture of the Internet, on video-sharing platforms such as YouTube and Vimeo. The online prestigious sites hosting Italian works include the Museo Nazionale del Cinema, in Turin, the Austrian Film Museum, in Vienna, the Museum of Modern Art (MoMa), in New York, the Centre Pompidou, in Paris, the Deutsche Kinemathek, in Berlin, and others. Some of these host a selection of works on their eponymous YouTube and Vimeo channels. It is worth noting that Internet technologies may have played, and still play, an important role – in an era of bygone *cineclub* and *cinema d'essai* traditional circles – in increasing the exposure to and appreciation for experimental and independent cinema, in both the viewing public and the budding scholarly interest. Special, or late-hours, TV programmes have also showcased rare works or behind-the-scenes documentaries of some Italian independent and experimental filmmakers, including works by Alfredo Leonardi, Anna Lajolo, Guido Lombardi and Fortunato Frascà, among others. At its peak, and for a brief period, Italian experimental and underground cinema had its own literary magazine with the evocative title *Ombre elettriche*, which was founded and directed by Mario Ferrero in Turin.[15]

The Different Protagonists and Forms

If we were to identify two major trends of alternative Italian film artists and practices, two useful groupings could be: the painter/sculpture/architect/storyteller turned screen artist and the intellectually and socially *impegnato* (socially engaged) filmmaker who makes *film di denuncia* (exposé films).

Within the ranks of a shared battle against sterile forms of mainstream cinema, and the dominant forms of consumeristic mass-media, Italian independent filmmakers, similarly to their European and International counterparts – from Jean Cocteau and Hans Richter, to Peter Kubelka, Stan Brakhage, Michael Snow, Stephen Dwoskin, William Raban, Jonas Mekas, James Broughton, Gregory Markopoulos, Kenneth Anger, and Curtis Harrington, among several others – are likewise characterised by a wide variety of concerns, techniques, individual approaches and personal visions of 'art'. Some have channelled their oneiric and visionary sensibilities into an anti-narrative and pictorial tableau of images – at times even obsessively so. One of the early Italian pioneers who 'imprinted' movement into painterly work is the Italian visual artist Luigi Veronesi, who kept working till the late 1980s, and experimented with time and rhythm in his varied cinematic productions, such as in his 1941 work *Fantasia*. He mixed a very rigorous visual approach with an artisanal 'painterly film' practice. Artist Ugo Nespolo is a relatively more recent example of painterly approach and plurality of forms, with works such as *Le gote in fiamme* (*Cheeks on Fire*, 1967), *Le porte girevoli* (*Revolving Doors*, 1982) and *Film/a/TO* (2001). Roberto Capanna and Giorgio Turi made use of pre-existing material and added to it footage they filmed through documentary techniques. They looked at the *decadere delle cose* (the natural degeneration and decadence of things), the passage from childhood to adulthood and old age and the entropic nature of the material world, such as in the case of *Vo-yage* (1964). They also made political films, works of *impegno sociale* (social engagement) such as *Non-permetterò* (*I Will Not Permit It*, 1967): a depiction of tanks, and sounds, harmonised, or in a dialectical exchange with images such as flowers, instead of tensions and conflicts. The retrieval of archival footage, along with collage, montage, juxtaposition and other techniques, became very popular among artists and documentarians in multiple cinematic traditions the world over. In Italy, the couple Yervant Gianikian and Angela Ricci Lucchi, dig up little known, or wholly forgotten, archival footage and create contemporary 'narrative forms' with important historical echoes and relevance. They move their anthropological perspective to the spectator's gaze, one that involves a minute analysis of the texture of film along with 're-constructed' documentation of histories therein portrayed, including denarrativised records of oppression and enslavement. Their films have been screened at several international festivals and museums including MoMA, Centre Pompidou and Pirelli Hunger Bicocca, and include *Dal Polo all'Equatore* (*From the North Pole to the Equator*, 1986), *Prisoners of Wa*r (1995), *Oh! Uomo* (*Oh! Man*, 2005) and *Pays barbare* (*Barbarous Lands*, 2013).

The phenomenon of the film co-op-centres served various purposes, chief among which is the function of offering access to alternative means of production and distribution. The Cooperativa del Cinema Indipendente (CCI) founded originally in Naples in 1967 – the same year of the retrospective of the New American Cinema at the Mostra di Pesaro – and later transferred to the capital city, is only one of several artist-run centres in Italy, which opened the doors to new creative expressions – though members' talents, approaches and philosophies varied. Neapolitan brothers Adamo, Antonio and Aldo Vergine are the original founders, to whom were later added the Roman founders, such as Gianfranco Baruchello, Alfredo Leonardi, Guido Lombardi and Massimo Bacigalupo, among others. Engravers and painters such as Luca Maria Patella, Ugo Nespolo, Silvio Loffredo, Franco Angeli and Mario Schifano, enamoured by the kinetic nature of the medium of film, were persuaded by the possibilities of independently creating films of their own, transitioning their talents to the art of moving images. The works produced display the chiefly non-structuralist concerns of their visions, such as Bacigalupo's *60 metri per il 31 marzo* (*200 Feet for March 31st*, 1968), Schifano's *Souvenir* (1967) and Leonardi's *Se l'inconscio si ribella (If the Subconscious Were to Rebel*, 1967), among numerous others. Bacigalupo met up with friends that reject traditional film modes and language, to explore new lyrical paths, without the constraining requirement to convey 'a message'. They broke with such criteria and made lyrical films, which were meant to render or re-render the 'figurative idea' via the cinema, without human intervention or by reducing the intervening process to the minimum. It recalls the stance in opposition to films that required postproduction stages – such as elaborate editing – and in favour of self-making processes, the realisation of things that develop on their own: *happenings* (within and without the camera). In spite of the general disdain for structuralism, however, there are several exceptions to the rule. Films which are structuralist in tone or have an overall structuralist appeal include: Patella's *SKMP2* (1968), Angeli's *Schermi* (*Screens*, 1968) and even Baruchello and Alberto Grifi's anti-establishment and provocative piece *La verifica incerta* (*Disperse Exclamatory Phase*, 1964) made with the loose ends of several American feature films, which was meant to attack and deconstruct – if not outright ridicule – the 'language' and 'structure' of the Hollywood brand of dominant narrative cinema. Gianfranco Baruchello also created his *Tutto, tutto nello stesso istante* (*All, All at Once*, 1968) at the Roman cooperative – a painter with a penchant for assemblage and superimposition, among other techniques. Umberto Bignardi and Alfredo Leonardi are the makers of *Motion Vision* (1966–7), which is also considered structuralist in nature and style.

Bignardi is an artist who claims to have had a vision beyond the Pop Art movement, and to have been an imitator of Eadweard Muybridge insofar as he made films of *verifica* (verification), which were meant as investigations of spatio-temporal dimensions. Often the artist carried over the system, or systematised approach, from one medium to the next. Patella transferred the techniques and 'proclivities' peculiar to his profession to his film work, its genre, instruments and modes, through an innovative first-person approach. The 'science' of the new tools' mixes with the representational potential of new media to yield a picture of the subconscious nature of the world, that is, in sub-materialistic forms.

Several other self-run centres, *officine* and/or *laboratori*, have been created in other parts of the country. The Studio di Monte Olimpino (Mount Olimpino Studio Lab), in the province of Como, is a research and production laboratory, founded by the animation artists Bruno Munari and Marcello Piccardo in 1962. The activities lasted over ten years and the artists made films commissioned by various industries and, later on, animation projects aired on RAI, Italian national television. In the latter part of its existence the centre took on a pedagogical role with the initiative 'Il cinema fatto dai bambini' ('Cinema Fashioned by Children'). Their extraordinary talents brought a mastery of techniques and artistic-artisanal style to their work. Zavattini's vision was credited for their youth-project initiative made for television. Munari and Piccardo were also among the curators of Andy Warhol's film work at the Museo d'arte moderna di Torino (Turin's Museum of Modern Art). In his memoir *La collina del cinema* (*The Cinema Hilltop*), released by Nodo Libri in 1992, Piccardo recalls how research projects mixed with those meant, and made, for commercial purposes. *I colori della luce* (*The Colours of Light*, 1963), and *Tempo nel tempo* (*Time within Time*, 1964) and *Fiat ricerca N° 1* (*Fiat Research Project No. 1*, 1964), are early examples of industrial and research films – following the precursor Ermanno Olmi.[16] Experimental animation films were also created by artists who did not belong to any particular group or coop. Guido Lombardi is the co-founder, with Alfredo Leonardi, of the 1971 Videobase co-op.; Lombardi's early work is concerned with experimentation and conceptual films. In later years, in collaboration with Anna Lajolo they began a series titled 'L'alfabeto' ('The Alphabet'): a somewhat utopian project the aim of which was to re-think not only the cinema but the world entire. During the late 1960s and early 1970s, in addition to the Super8, videotape formats of 1-inch and 1/2-inch became available. Lombardi and others from the Videobase were attracted to the bursting and bristling social issues of their time. They began to film *nelle fabbriche* (in the factories) where the *contestazione ribolliva* (forms of protest erupted) and engaged with a militant or political activist ambience, whose performances and events they filmed. Lombardi speaks of *realtà cruda entrava nello schermo* (crude reality entering the screen) – as commented upon in Bruno Di Marino and Claudio Del Signore's documentary *Lo sguardo espanso: cinema d'artista italiano* (*The Expanded Gaze: Italian Art Cinema*, 2000–2013)[17] – but acknowledges the difficulty of editing the enormous amount of footage the videotape equipment made it possible to accumulate. The revealing legacy of documentary titles of the time, produced in collaboration with a number of other independent filmmakers, include among several others: *La casa è un diritto non un privilegio* (*Housing Is a Right and Not a Privilege*, 1970, co-authored with Alfredo Leonardi e Paola Scarnati), *E nua ca simu a forza du mundu* (*And We Who Are the Strength of the World*, 1971, co-authored with Alfredo Leonardi), *Il fitto dei padroni non lo paghiamo più* (*We Will No Longer Pay the Masters' Rent*, 1972), *Sotto le stelle, sotto il tendone* (*Under the Stars, Under the Tent*, 1972, co-authored with Alfredo Leonardi), *Quartieri popolari di Roma* (*Community Housing Quarters in Rome*, 1973), *Policlinico in lotta* (*Policlinico Hospital's Struggle*, 1973), *Lotta di classe alla Fiat* (*Class Struggle at Fiat*, 1974).

In Florence the long-running Scuola di Firenze centre (Lab of the Florence School) gathers a number of artists/cineastes, some of whom continued working at the centre throughout the 1970s and 1980s. The Florentine artists include Andrea Granchi and Arcangelo Mazzoleni, some of whose works received foreign recognition. Granchi's *La mano nell'occhio* (*A Hand in the Eye*, 1978), and Mazzoleni's *Aurélia* (1980), were screened at art centres and museums. Several other groups and co-ops remain to be investigated. This anthology includes an extended discussion of the Milanese Filmmaker co-op. The Milanese co-ops *Filmmaker* and *Studio Azzurro* came about in 1980 and in 1982 respectively, and were likewise fashioned with an alternative productive and distributive model that became the formative vehicle for a number of future directors, including Silvio Soldini and the younger Michelangelo Frammartino. The breaking point for the historical cooperatives may be due to the tug between aesthetical and ethical concerns: while authentic artists/*auteurs* wanted to devote themselves to forms of 'pure art-cinema', other members turned to political films, the so-called film of *impegno*. It must be noted that several artists and filmmakers kept coalescing the two fronts, so-to-speak, to acquiesce the differing political and private nature of their inspiration and work – the odd mixture of forms, style and concerns, found in Alberto Grifi and Paolo Brunatto, among others, being exemplary cases. In the aftermath of the 1968 uprisings – the demands for social change, the optimistic expectations and the turbulent years that followed – many began to make politically oriented films. For the same very reason, others began to feel disenfranchised and they turned to a freer and 'purer' form of cinema, free from any type of agenda, including experimental agendas, and the agendas of the official independent co-ops. Some of them were mere utopian films, films about doing and creating intuitively and/or lyrically, with a preference towards aesthetic enjoyment. The fact that the cooperatives' filmmakers were required to accompany their films, and give *indicazioni di lettura* (interpretative suggestions), in order to attract *cineclubs* or other festival venues' audiences to the screenings, contributed to the sense of alienation felt by some of them: poems are not 'explained' to one's readership, so why should the more immediate works of moving-images require explanation to one's viewership? The screening programmes of such experimental and independent cinema was seen by very few spectators. They were notoriously not a mainstream event, but the 'erudite' experience of *cineclubs* and co-op gatherings: the coming together of different minds and views, agreeably or as part of an intellectual confrontation. The public exhibition programmes of such works remained underground in nature, till most of their original activity disappeared altogether. In the present day it has re-emerged 'immigrated' online, thanks to the digital revolution, through screenings and other exhibition events in Italy and elsewhere continue thanks to the indefatigable work of artists such as Bacigalupo and scholars such as Di Marino, among others. In many respects, the Sixties and the Seventies set the tone for years to come. It was indeed an ebullient period, with art-house and experimental and independent forms of cinema that were interdisciplinary in nature. Like other trends and movements of the time, however, the same counter-cultural context and technological innovations, which contributed to the creation of the centres and co-ops, led to the obsolescence and demise of the original forms.

One important characteristic of the independent and experimental Italian film scene is the very interdisciplinary nature of its approach, enriched by talent, which funnelled into practices of moving image making. The number of Italian artists turned to moving images to explore new territory and experiment with alternative visual 'languages' and novel forms is testimony to the versatility of the various talent involved as much as the degree of pliability or plasticity found in the new medium. As it has been pointed out since its origins, artists who turned to filmmaking sought new ways of relating to the world and, thus, they often made the new 'language' of the cinema the focus of their inquiry.[18] It is hardly a coincidence that the Italian artists – particularly painters – turned filmmakers, are chiefly the ones who continue the independent practice into filmmaking even after the crisis, and demise, of the co-op centres. For them it also amounted to a departure from the confined, if not stifling, space of the gallery and studio/lab. The artist Cioni

Carpi worked in Canada and later in Italy, making films that coupled the investigation of the visual realm with that of one's inner cognitive processes; examples include *Un giorno un aereo* (*A Day an Airplane*, 1963), *55cm above Sea Level* (1972), *Egg One Egg Zero* (1974), and *Nero più bianco fa legge* (*Black Plus White Equals Law*, 1977). However, not all Italian artists who took up the practices of cinema joined a co-op. The aforementioned, painter Mario Schifano, did not relate to the independent co-ops initiatives. His turn to filmmaking was that of a painter's soulful approach. He broadened his perspective, travelled to America, befriended the director Marco Ferreri and sought to inject a broader socially oriented vision into his film work, referencing the relevant issues of the time. The 1967 films *Vietnam, Made in USA*, and *Voce della foresta di plastica* (*The Plastic Forest's Voice*), along with *Umano, non umano* (*Human, Non-Human*, 1969), constitute examples of such thematic and aesthetic concerns. Fortunato Frascà, a painter who worked as a professional scenographer with major Italian directors, including Luchino Visconti and Michelangelo Antonioni, was the co-founder with other Roman artists of the 'Gruppo Uno' ('Group One') in 1962. He turned to experimental and independent cinema to demystify canonical standards of filmmaking and overcome taboos which are typical within the industry. He was guided by a rational interest in the *analisi geometrica delle forme* (geometric analysis of forms), and made films that include forbidden items and practices, such as smoking cigarettes, and exposing production and narrative procedures that in regular productions are edited out as errors. His *Informazione Leitmotiv: L'informazione è ciò che conta* (*Information Leitmotif: Information Is What Matters*, 1968–9) with its cacophony of sounds and juxtaposition of signs is an early example of visual and auditory media saturation. Mario Masini – who later became the cinematographer of independent maverick Carmelo Bene – and Paolo Brunatto left the cooperative and made independent films of their own in 8mm or Super8, such as *Vieni, dolce morte* (*Come Sweet Death*, 1968). Other independent *auteurs*, such as Romano Scavolini, appear to have had no interest in the experimental vanguardist agenda or filmmaking. They were instead oriented towards a form of 'absolute cinema'. In Di Marino's documentary, Scavolini speaks of the *fluire spontaneo delle cose* (the spontaneous flow of things), which could not be interrupted, as if a sacred event had taken place. An example of such a perspective and approach is his 1970s experimental documentary *l.s.d.*. Other works, which attracted much attention from Italian censors, are *La prova generale* (*The Dress Rehearsal*, 1968), and *A mosca cieca* (*Blindman's Bluff*, 1966). Scavolini's further claim is that the cinema of the time was an *addomesticamento della coscienza* (taming of one's conscience), and in his view cinema had to head in the opposite direction, and 'wake up' and surprise the spectator. In his view, being unable to relate to what one was looking at on the screen amounted to a victory over the complacent attitude of standard, mainstream and commercial, cinema.

Several Italian independent filmmakers are artists who seek simplicity of transposition, purity of expression and spontaneity of presentation. Tonino De Bernardi is among the Italian independent filmmakers who finds inspiration in the self-made and self-determining approach of the American model. De Bernardi readily acknowledges his indebtedness to American independent cinema. He met his American counterparts in Italy, such as Jonas Mekas – and shared the vision that an artist need not rely on the industry. In De Bernardi's case, 'independent vision' meant a position countering the notorious industry formula originating from the capital city of Rome. The access to hand-held cameras, and the urge to tell stories from a personal point-of-view, led him to an idiosyncratic use of a sort of 'caméra-stylo' approach. Armed with a movie camera, he made atypical films, including 'family films', with friends, family members and actors willing to volunteer their talents. His notion of what is meant by independent cinema is very different from directors who sought public or private sponsorship and funds – some of whom made films during the late twentieth century when funding was secured through national and private TV networks and governmental aid and sponsorship programmes. De Bernardi openly admits of never having had a producer or production company sponsoring and funding him – though he was open to a possibility of such sort. He never concerned himself with distribution; but is proud of his friendship with Enrico Ghezzi, the producer of RAI's 'Fuori Orario' programme – a late hours show the National Broadcaster devoted to non-mainstream films and cinema *d'essai*. Lischi speaks of De Bernardi's work as simultaneously lyrical, classical and primitive.[19] De Bernardi is a low-key, often times overly long, but unassuming, and gentle *auteur* of 'marginal' cinema, whose suggestion to not let the lack of sponsorship hinder one's personal vision and career, is a statement to the free-spirit and subjectivity informing indigenous and undertone forms of independent Italian filmmaking. His films include *Vaso Etrusco* (*Etruscan Vase*, 1967), *Piccoli orrori* (*Little Horrors*, 1994) and the more recent *Accoltellati* (*Stabbed*, 2006). In other rare cases, forms of experimentation and independence within the Italian panorama led to documentary works elicited by a guttural response to the climate of the times. Massimo Sarchielli and Alberto Grifi are the creators of the film *Anna* (1972–5), a real and tragic story about a young and homeless single mother, Anna, and filmed in part on videotape and later transferred on 16mm film for exhibition. It was shown at the 1975 Venice International Film Festival, the Mostra Internazionale d'Arte Cinematografica, and thereafter at top film festivals internationally. This particular work appealed to the dire, disturbing and sensational climate of the times, a time of general unrest, public demonstrations, political resistance, militancy, and labour strikes. The documentary by Di Marino and Del Signore offers the following comment: 'it is a victory from a formal and technical standpoint . . . but it is a defeat from the purely social viewpoint; Anna, the authentic protagonist at the centre of the film, dies a year later, in a psychiatric hospital, forgotten by all'.[20]

The second half of the twentieth century seemed to have brought a heightened sense of awareness to the Italian art scene. Far from merely emulating their western peers, Italian filmmakers added a personal artistic vision and uniquely Italian imprint to their practices of visual arts. Champions of 'made in Italy' film and art, such as Paolo Gioli, Marinella Pirelli, Annabella Miscuglio, Piero Bargellini, Massimo Bacigalupo, Alfredo Leonardi, among others, pursue their vision apparently unhindered by any type of constraint – be it aesthetic, technical, or financial, in nature – and rather see in their peculiar contexts and conditions 'a call' to the exploration of new territories and fresher approaches. It must be noted that several artists began their journeys into practices of filmmaking before being exposed to the tour of American independent cinema; including Leonardi, Bagicalupo and others, some of the work of whom is discussed further in this anthology. A discussion of Pirelli's contribution to the experimental cinema scene is also included in the present volume. Included are also extraordinary examples of 'urban art' films, such as works by architect and experimental filmmaker Ugo La Pietra. Examples of his inner- and outer-city films, with commentary on the sociopolitical significance of the geographical (if not ideological) excursion include *La riappropriazione della città* (*The Re-Appropriation of the City*, 1977), *Recupero e reinvenzione* (*Restoration and Reinvention*, 1976), *Interventi pubblici per la città di Milano* (*Public Works for the City of Milan*, 1979), and *La casa telematica* (*The Telematic House*, 1981). His manifesto films are well calibrated and enlightening. They speak to issues of habitat and home, the need to create a space conducive to psychological and physical well-being. Sensitive matters of environmental adaptability and sustainability are tackled with professionalism, and moreover with a clever dose of irony. Of a different timbre, there are also meta-cinematic experimentalists, who question the processes in a minimalist fashion. Paolo Gioli is among the first of the vanguard artists and filmmakers to explore the camera's field-of-vision 'beyond the visible', so-to-speak. He is a man of multiple talents, a painter, a photographer, a filmmaker and a spontaneous inventor. One of his strategies is the use of self-made pinhole cameras, which may consist of boxes and tubes, used as camera chambers, in which the light is let in via pinholes in objects such as shirt buttons, pieces of metal, and other ordinary materials. Recently, David Bordwell wrote the following about him:

> When he needs a shutter, his fingers, or perhaps some leaves from trees, will suffice. He has embedded images within images without benefit of optical printers, and he has brought photos to frenetic life without animation stands. . . . Impresario of clamps and masking tape, he creates extraordinary films with equipment that looks distinctly knocked-together.[21]

Examples of Gioli's ingenious work include the 'cubic vision' of *Secondo il mio occhio di vetro* (*According to My Glass Eye*, 1971), the superimposed man to machine and viceversa in *Traumatografo* (*Thaumatrope*, 1973), and the more recent 'study' of vision and the physicality of the medium of film in *Quando l'occhio trema* (*When the Eye Flutters*, 1991). Gioli is indeed a unique case in the Italian panorama of independent film artists/creators/inventors, who brings a personal use of body-art and technique to his vision of experimental filmmaking and craftsmanship. A long time scholar of his work, Patrick Rumble, speaks of Gioli's cinema, as taking the viewer back to a time preceding 'the creation myth of protocinema'.[22] Gioli's approach, shared with friends such as Leonardi and Bargellini from the CCI, advocates a return to the origins, a reinvention of the cinematic experience altogether. The creative and ideological vision of such filmmakers was such that they opted for total independence. Their independence centred on their artistic approach and creativity. They exercised total control over every stage of production: the filming, development, editing, and release of the final prints of their work. Their artistic personalities emerge in their individual approaches and work, Gioli in his rather 'cold' approach and Bargellini in his 'warmer', domestic participations. The singularity of such experiences is evinced from their penchant for what could be thought of as a *reverse chronohistory of vision*. Like other independent Italian filmmakers, they are interested in the painterly and indigenous nature of their surroundings but with an eye to the past, to the history of 'sight and shadows'. In the 2013 documentary *Lo sguardo espanso: cinema d'artista italiano*, Aprà maintains that during the 1930s no Italian experimental film movement existed, and that neither did such a tradition exist during the silent period. For this scholar, the experimental and underground phenomena of the mid to late twentieth century represents a 'break' within the (preceding) 'break' with traditional mainstream canons – including notions of historical avant-gardes, realism, neorealism, *nouvelle vague*, *cinéma vérité* and so-forth. Aprà's position on Italian experimental and independent cinema is that: 'it was not emulating its

American counterpart, but rather it exhibited originality without complexes, that is, it was not merely relaying somebody else's cinematic experience, it represented a spontaneous impulse, one that saw the world as if for the very first time'.[23]

If the aesthetics of painting and that of film converged in the practices of several of the Italian independent and experimental artists mentioned above, the unique character of the Italian aesthetic tradition is also carried over in filmmakers who sought to attract a wider and mainstream audience while defending the peculiar 'freedom of expression' that characterises independent practice. Silvano Agosti and Franco Piavoli, are examples of filmmakers who conceive of independent cinema as a solitary endeavour, a single man's work, and yet the lyrical nature of their vision, coupled with the documentary content of their films, has nonetheless proven to make their work suited to broader audiences. Agosti's exemplary career as an independent Italian filmmaker stands out for its avowed total autonomy, *impegno* (social engagement), creativity, lyricism and overall anti-establishment narrative approach. He is the author of several narrative and documentary works that bear his signature lyrical style. They include *Il giardino delle delizie* (*Garden of Delights*, 1967), *Altri seguiranno* (*More Will Follow*, 1973), *D'amore si vive* (*Living on Love*, 1984) and *L'uomo proiettile* (*The Rocket Man*, 1995), among others. Though he laments a lack of appreciation in his native country of Italy, he has scored successes in several foreign lands, including Japan. From the point of view of cineastes such as Agosti and Piavoli, independent cinema does not, by definition, necessarily involve either the employment of a crew or other artists. The mainstream-industry model is not only frowned upon, it is pointed at as the source of much 'sterility'. Agosti maintains that 'the cinema which depends on the industry, has remained stagnant for seventy-eight years; it has nothing new to say . . . Independent cinema amounts to being free, not to depend on anyone, and on anything'.[24] Piavoli is, likewise, the author of much admired 'naturalist' documentaries and narrative features such as *Il pianeta azzurro* (*The Blue Planet*, 1982), *Voci nel tempo* (*Voices in Time*, 1996) and *Al primo soffio di vento* (*At the First Breath of Wind*, 2002). Such achievements belie the claim that independent filmmaking is merely restricted to niche audiences, and confirm the positions held by such cineastes: the insistence that independent filmmakers, though challenged by limited resources, reclaim 'unadulterated' forms of cinematic art with enlivened work, which has been denied to genuine spectators of cinema.

Experimentation and independence are not the phenomena of a single period or the prerogative of abstract or radical practices. Cineastes who aspired to break into the mainstream channels and thereby reach a broader audience while holding on to their independent approach and creative freedom, include Davide Ferrario, Giorgio Diritti, Vincenzo Marra, Gianfranco Rosi, Pietro Marcello and Giuseppe Gaudino, among many others discussed in several chapters herein. They have had greater success in having their films picked-up by standard distribution channels, and they have been viewed more widely. Theirs is a 'type' of cinema which is markedly of the narrative genre, but not in the modes and practices typical of mainstream productions. These filmmakers speak of independence in terms which are different from their experimental and one-man-crew Italian counterparts. They recognise the difference between the Hollywood machinery, and overall regimented modes of production peculiar to the United States, versus the irregular and anomalous production mechanisms in European countries. Whether or not Italy has an 'official film industry', its production system does constitute a network of entities, and a peculiar Italian production style, which for decades centred its artistic and ideological locus of operations on the geographical and political capital of Rome. Italian production firms have increasingly relied on public funding. Such institutionalised mechanisms and state of affairs has increasingly informed production initiatives elsewhere in the country, ideologically and logistically distant from the capital. The initiatives relied on public funds, and on collaborations and sponsorship with State TV and other Television networks, including foreign ones. Ferrario's independent work, if we are to apply the 'label' at all, falls into the category of filmmakers who began their careers thanks to such alternative production or procedural approach. The definition of independent films here refers to works by first time directors, so-called *début* films, which began to be conceived as original ideas, written and storyboarded independently, while seeking support for a possible production. While this category of independent filmmakers may appear to seek conventional legitimisation with some works of 'standard fare', it is not hard to detect a socio-political commitment rather than mere commercial glitter in their oeuvres. Ferrario is the maker of *La fine della notte* (*The End of the Night*, 1989), *Lontano da Roma* (*Far from Rome*, 1991), *Tutti giù per terra* (*We All Fall Down*, 1997), *Dopo mezzanotte* (*After Midnight*, 2004), set in Turin's 'Museo del Cinema', *Piazza Garibaldi* (2011) and the documentary *La strada di Levi* (*Primo Levi's Journey*, 2006) – among othe works – where Ferrario retraces the journey home of the writer after his liberation from Auschwitz. Diritti likewise directed works in which are mirrored peculiar socio-cultural milieux; his work includes *Il vento fa il suo giro* (*The Wind Blows Round*, 2005), and *L'uomo che verrà* (*The Man Who Will Come*, 2009) and the more recent *Volevo nascondermi* (*I Wanted to Hide*, 2020) a biopic of the naïf painter Antonio Ligabue. Marra directed *Vento di Terra* (*Earthbound Wind*, 2004), *Il grande progetto* (*The Big Project*, 2008), *Il gemello* (*The Twin*, 2012) and the award-winning documentary *L'amministratore* (*The Administrator*, 2013). Gaudino graduated from the Accademia di Belle Arti (Academy of Fine Arts) in Naples, a hotbed of talents, and his films include *Giro di lune tra terra e mare* (*Moons Spins between Land and Sea*, 1997), and the more recent *Per amor Vostro* (*For Your Love*, 2015). Pietro Marcello shares the same background as Gaudino (though he is younger). Marcello's films have been presented at several Film Festivals; the documentary *La bocca del lupo* (*The Mouth of the Wolf*, 2009) revealed his original approach to filmmaking, and *Bella e perduta* (*Lost and Beautiful*, 2015) gained several awards and nominations. His latest work, *Martin Eden* (2019), an original adaptation of Jack London's novel, has gained highly complimentary reviews both in Europe and North America. Gianfranco Rosi is the director of three multi awarded documentaries, *Below Sea Level* (2008), set in California, *Sacro GRA* (2013), exploring the daily routine of ordinary people in Rome's outskirts, and the much acclaimed and Oscar nominated *Fuocoammare* (*Fire at Sea*, 2013), capturing life on the small island of Lampedusa, at the frontline of the European immigrant crisis. Several independent filmmakers mirror in starker terms the psychological and political climate of Italy at the turn of the century – for which they have received the notable acclaim that launched their careers. Unlike the experimental filmmakers considered earlier, this 'variety' of independent cineastes/*auteurs* does not find dominant appeal in the painterly, abstract – or in rare cases 'pretentiously' structuralist – films of their 'purely' artistic compatriots. These are storytellers, chroniclers of topical subject matter, who see in the history of the country and its socio-political milieu a number of untold tales and larger stories in need of a narrative voice.

Summary of Key Points

Rather than being limited to the late 1960s and early 1970s, practices of independence and experimentation are detectable at different times and in different contexts, according to the varied definitions attributed to given filmmakers by critics and/or artists and cineastes themselves. What appears to be a common denominator, however, is the spontaneous need to detach oneself from routine practices and conventional approaches, and seek artistic and ideological freedom, political and economic contentment, in forms of independent filmmaking; an urge to exploit the potential of, and access to, new ideas and new means of production, to give voice to one's artistic and ethnographic identity and vocation. Independent practices are likewise a statement as to the 'pliability' of the medium of moving images, its swerving developments, its self-critique and study. Artistically and, thus, in aesthetic and philosophical terms, independent filmmaking may ultimately amount to: 1) interdisciplinary forms of artistic practice the multiplicity of which, in turn, translate praxis of individual (or collective) forms of cultural liberation, even if only metaphysical, 2) the unhindered exploration or investigation of one's own identity, history, tools of communication and environmental surroundings, and 3) an alternative form of self-determination and human connection, even if in resistance or rebellion to dominant political, social, or artistic, regimes. From the legacies of the early pioneers and avant-garde movements to the transformations of the mid to late twentieth century, Italian cinema practices have reaffirmed their peculiar brand of aesthetic sensibilities and unique Italic identity. If in philosophical terms independent and experimental filmmaking amounts to an instantiation of political and cultural forms of autonomy, in the case of Italy it is further nurtured by its uniquely boisterous civilisation and superlative tradition of art, classic and modern. The collection of this volume attests to the same plurality of voices, talents and variety of approaches that define Italian independent and experimental cinema: its productive modes and practices along with the philosophical and ideological substratum that has nurtured and propelles it forward, with new impetus, to this day. It locates, and re-frames, an Italian brand of experimental and independent cinema at the intersection of European and international craftsmanship of innovative forms of art practices, and pivotal socio-cultural narrative trends.

Chapters in this Anthology

In the chapter '*Filmmaker* and the Milanese independent cinema of the 1980s and 1990s', Donatella Maraschin and Paola Nasini provide a detailed historical analysis of the Milanese co-ops centres, and in particular the activities of the 1980s and 1990s collectives *Filmmaker* and *Studio Azzurro*. They begin by looking at the history of the independent groups in juxtaposition to the centralised film industry originating in the capital city of Rome and, in opposition to it, outline the peculiar traits of the independent Milanese scene. These include the prominent features of its embeddedness in the urban fabric and the interdisciplinary nature and links which marked the *impegno* (social engagement) and cultural output of the group. One precious feature of this chapter is the recent interviews conducted by the authors, and which in retrospect offer a nuanced historical recollection of the collectives through the eyes of its principal protagonists, such as the *Filmmaker*'s founders Gianfilippo Pedote and Silvano Cavatorta. The chapter reviews the centres' activities and experimentalism, and how they advanced the significance and social function of the arts of moving images. Notable outcomes include a catalogue of indigenous perspectives and works and the engendering of a variety of film talent, some of whom have gone on to pursue international careers, such as directors Davide Ferrario and Marco Tullio Giordana. Maraschin and Nasini's chapter offers a 'documentary' window into the socio-political and cultural dynamics of the city's art hubs, and how these affected independent film productions; how the local, provincial and indeed national climate bore, reflected, and refracted, the incandescent events of the preceding decades – the 1970s in particular. A further important feature of this chapter is the discussion of the self-mandated festival role of the independent film and video centres, a role that served to popularise the seminal and relevant nature of the groups with an increasingly wider audience. The interviews conducted by Maraschin and Nasini are an invaluable resource for understanding the unique periods and protagonists, and the import of the urban setting. This is a singular study that sets the template for any subsequent research. The films considered in the chapter include *Giulia in ottobre* (*Giulia in October*, Silvio Soldini, 1985), *L'osservatorio nucleare del signor Nanof* (*The Nuclear Observatory of Mister Nanof*, Paolo Rosa, 1985), *Fame chimica* (*Chemical Hunger*, Antonio Boccola, 2003) and *La casa delle belle addormentate* (*The Home of the Sleeping Beauties*, Michelangelo Frammartino, 1997), among others. Maraschin and Nasini draw some important conclusions from the history of the Milanese independent film centres, and ones that bear enlightening observations into the political, artistic and even metaphysical, dimensions and dynamics, of moving-images' arts, and which continue to inform much contemporary international practices.

In 'Light and Liminal: Marinella Pirelli's Cinema', Matilde Nardelli offers an absorbing study of Pirelli's cinema – which is overdue, particularly in the English language. While a number of Italian males working as independent filmmakers have been the subject of attention and critical study, the same can hardly be claimed for female protagonists in the moving-image arts. Nardelli's study includes an investigation of the gender gap via the aesthetic and operative strategies deployed by Pirelli as mirrored projections and liminal 'positions', to the filmmaker's advantage. Pirelli's career spans the pivotal years of the 'official' experimental and independent phenomenon of the 1960s and 1970s. It gave birth to a body of work, and it bestowed a legacy, which await the study and recognition they deserve. The three-dimensionality and ideological implications of Pirelli's experimentalism are both engrossing and ground-breaking.

The installations summon the 'spectator' into the process and onto the screened image, confronting its enduring perception and significance. The panorama of Italian experimental practices, owes part of its important artistic advancements to such daring visions. Pirelli's inventive, artisanal and diaristic approaches to experimentation belong to the seminal and paradigmatic strand of ground-breaking artistic practices. Her sculptural installations become precursors of 'participatory' forms of moving images: the 'sculpting' of time through space, onto light rays and patterns, which summon a haptic experience with the 'screen'. Nardelli probes the aesthetic and technical facets of Pirelli's legacy with painstaking accuracy and offers an illuminating examination of the performative dimensions of her cinema, in relation to the physical environment and metaphysical space for which the mythic surface of the screen stands. Greater attention is devoted to the key work of *Film Ambiente* (*Environmental Screen*, 1968), its critical reception and overall socio-cultural significance; other works include *Luce e movimento* (*Light and Movement*, 1969), *Il tempo dell'uomo* (*The Times of Man*, 1970), and *Sole in mano* (*The Sun in One's Hand*, 1973). The chapter positions Pirelli's legacy at the axial point of Italy's innovative art practices, its art history, and of the broader international discourse on the ontological significance of moving-images.

The chapter 'From Vertov to Cine Journals: Cesare Zavattini's Experimental Journey' by Carlo Coen, on one of the 'fathers' of Italian Cinema, stems from the exigency to identify an experimental and independent stream in the socio-cultural and theoretical history of Italian cinema – which is generally considered 'classic'. Zavattini, the writer of the greatest masterpieces of Italian Neorealism, was however – and above all – an inexhaustible promoter and organiser of radical and long-sighted projects; a forerunner who conceived of an organic and harmonious multimedia system, in which cinema, television, written language and other forms of media, would all contribute to a deeper understanding of the political, social and moral, challenges of contemporary life. Zavattini's world is one of commitment and humanism, and one that can be explored deeply through the audiovisual medium. The chapter identifies some ascendants of Zavattini's thought: Dziga Vertov primarily, but also the documentary waves of Flaherty and Grierson, together with certain suggestions of the post-war French and Canadian cinemas (Astruc and his *camerá-stylo* theory and the Canadian filmmakers of the National Film Board). The core of the discussion, however, is found in the analysis of the main themes of Zavattini's 'grand', chaotic, yet coherent, project: relying entirely on the very nature of the cinematographic medium, its 'eye', capable of exploring the world of people and of penetrating below the surface of reality, in order to eventually participate actively in the civil, social and political life of the times. Coen takes into consideration those films that best exemplify the sense of Zavattini's thought in relation to the notion of independent cinema: his 'collective' films, those for which he played the role of coordinator and organiser, from *L'amore in città* (*Love in the City*, 1953), to *I misteri di Roma* (*The Mysteries of Rome*, 1963), and up to the series of political newsreels realised in the years of the student struggles and the so-called 'Hot Autumn' of 1968–9. The understanding is that the vast corpus of works created by Cesare Zavattini constitutes a single large-scale project, supported by a theoretical effort of equally great breadth. As pointed out by historian Lino Miccichè, Zavattini's work is acknowledged as the most important and advanced theoretical contribution ever developed in Italy on the function and sense of cinema.

At the centre of the chapter 'Gianfranco Brebbia: The "Absurd" and Expanded Quality of Experimental Cinema (1962–73)', by Donatella Valente, are Brebbia's practices of experimentalism in juxtaposition to the analysis of the filmmaker's relationships with the artistic avant-gardes of his time. Influenced by the New American Cinema and by the Italian experimental trends of the post-war period (the 'Spatialist Movement', the 'Concrete Art Movement' and 'Arte Povera'), Brebbia actively participated in the most significant and advanced experiences of the times. The initiatives he took part in include the 'Cooperative of Independent Italian Cinema'. Brebbia's cinematic dream amounted to conceiving a medium with which it is possible to express the most complex and daring vision. The chapter dwells on important details in this regard, especially when beginning to describe and comment on the main elements of Brebbia's poetics. Valente examines numerous works by Brebbia – though they constitute only part of his vast filmography of over 100 films. It is through this probing description that the reader comes to appreciate the techniques used by Brebbia; through which he delved into forms of experimentalism that enlarged one's horizon beyond habitual/familiar surroundings and practices and into uncharted territories. The proximity, and commonality of intent, between Brebbia and the initiators of the 'Arte Povera' movement, for example, led him to the targeted use of recycled materials in the composition of his films. The recycling of pre-existing audiovisual materials, was followed by Brebbia's technical strategies characterised by experiments he carried out directly on film (the 'film-scratch' approach), which connects him to the experiences and work of Stan Brakhage, among others. These constitute the cameraless films. The conceptual notions characteristic of Brebbia's art are 'expansion', centred on the use of several and different techniques combined with each other, and the 'absurd', a word that recurs repeatedly in the titles of many of his filmic works, and which indicates the juxtaposition of real and oneiric elements. The author has met the daughter of Gianfranco Brebbia, and as a result the chapter is also accompanied and complemented by numerous stills, authorised by her, and by documents and testimonies that further illuminate the eclectic figure and work of Brebbia.

The chapter on 'Italian Family Films: The Case of the *Archivio Nazionale di Bologna*' by Laura Ceccarelli constitutes an exclusive inclusion to this anthology offering a survey and study on a topic in need of critical attention. Ceccarelli introduces the topic by outlining its theoretical underpinnings and, thus, the socio-cultural relevance pertaining to discourses of identity and nationhood. Subsequently, she explores the *Archivio Nazionale di Bologna* (National Archive of Bologna), and gives an absorbing 'tour' of the curatorial and institutional practices along with the varied type of documentary material stored in its collections. Particular attention is given to the contextualisation of the significance, value and use, of 'family films' (also known as 'home movies'). Sourcing such material has increasingly become a major concern for historians and archivists. Whereas the 'badly', or imperfectly recorded and stored family-event (or reunion) film may initially have been guided by personal memory and enjoyment purposes, it soon became evident that such audiovisual material is invested with greater historical and ethnographic significance and value. The category of 'family films' represents a record of endogenous culture, communities and the visual history of an entire nation's nucleic textures. The author gives invaluable information on the curatorial efforts aimed at sourcing, gathering and classifying such material, along with the types of centres and institutions that are equipping themselves for the delicate procedures involved in such tasks. The review of the Archivio Nazionale dei Film di Famiglia (National Archive of Family Films) includes a consideration of the *archivi femminili* (women archives). Moreover, the Fondi (Collections) of the City of Bologna includes a number of diverse women amateur cineastes. Such material has enormous importance. For research purposes, they may be studied in a multiplicity of disciplines and fields, including departments of Gender Studies, Sociology and Anthropology. Though the biographies may be quite different, the women's activities underscore the shared desire to narrate their life stories through film and video recordings, and thus voice their personal situatedness and sentiment. Ceccarelli's study is of particular interest due to its scoio-cultural and national (if not international) appeal with a variety of people and professionals. The chapter ends by examining the varied use to which 'family films' have been put, and the necessity to acquire the proper sensibility and skills required to handle such delicate material.

Gloria Dagnino is the author of the chapter 'Independence as Opposition? Redefining Political Cinema Through the Case of Mirko Locatelli'. The chapter is particularly relevant for the epistemic contribution it makes to the definition and understanding of theories of Italian independent cinema, which have been long debated but are often misconstrued. The chapter begins by tracing the historical roots of the problematic construct, to the theoretical and socio-cultural discourse on the anti-fascist movement of *La Resistenza* (anti-German and anti-Fascist Resistance Fighters' Movement of the Second World War). The chief trait of the Italian talent is supposedly evinced through the theoretical notion of 'Italian difference', which posits a conflictual, or oppositional, stance as the key characteristic of much Italian canon and thought, including the development of forms of independent cinema. Dagnino counteracts this recurring motif by seeking and offering an alternative perspective in one important practitioner's viewpoint, that of filmmaker Mirko Locatelli and scriptwriter and producer Giuditta Tarantelli. The chapter is intelligently organised into sections, which aid and lead forward the discussion and understanding of the notion of 'independence', in the cinema, as a statement to creative, personal and expressive freedom. Dagnino delves deeper into the issues with the first-person testimony of filmmakers Locatelli and Tarantelli, whom she interviewed for this particular study. The chapter offers valuable insights into contemporary independent filmmaking procedures in Italy, its legalistic, economic, technical and logistic facets, making important references to Italy's national cinema, as well as those of other European national cinemas, movements and trends. The unconventional paths pursued by individual Italian filmmakers and producers are exemplified in the careers of Locatelli and Tarantelli and, particularly, through an admirable defence of their authorial, aesthetic and ethical commitments and visions. The filmography under consideration includes the feature films, *Il primo giorno d'inverno* (*The First Day of Winter*, 2008), *I corpi estranei* (*Foreign Bodies*, 2013) and *Isabelle* (2018).

Donatella Valente's chapter 'Travelling the World: The Essay Films of Massimo Bacigalupo (1968–77)' is a study of the work of one of the central figures of the experimental and independent wave of filmmakers of the late Sixties and onward. Bacigalupo is one of the founders of the Cooperativa del Cinema Independente (Cooperative of Independent Cinema), and a spearheading figure of those pivotal events and years. He is the author of the introductory premise or 'unofficial manifesto' of the movement – if we are allowed to retroactively refer to the events of the collective initiative in such terms – which appeared on the pages of the Italian cinema journal *Bianco e Nero*: 'Il film sperimentale' (The experimental film). Valente reviews Bacigalupo's formative years and travel periods and offers a composite picture of the rich tableau of referents alluded to in films such as *60 metri per il 31 marzo* (*200 Feet for March 31ˢᵗ*, 1968) and *Versus* (1968). The chapter articulates in theoretical terms the distinctive subjective lyricism of Bacigalupo's work. The quality of his films is given by the background and perspective of the artist's persona, one which is informed by an explorer's soul and a probing mind. Bacigalupo 'paints' onto his films the subtle shades and tones of his memories and travels like a writer would onto an inseparable notebook. Valente's sensitive study conveys the inspirational drive that animates the period from 1968 to 1977 in the filmmaker's activities and life. She critically examines the subjective persona in rapport to the camera-eye and situates the filmmaker as part of the larger critical-theoretical perspective pertaining to the history of the medium. The chapter offers a detailed analysis of single projects, such as the films *Her* (1968) and *Fiore d'eringio* (*Eryngium*, 1969–70). Valente's comprehensive analysis includes a review of films such as *Warming Up* (1973), as well as Bacigalupo's 'family film' *Into the House* (1975) – which in the case in point, they are also informed by the dexterity of the singular maker, whose knowledge of art and film techniques is remarkable. The result is a revealing chapter on the artist's career and seminal work, and of the cultural heritage to which it belongs.

In the chapter 'Tales of Courage: Trade Stories of Italian Independent Cinema', Edward Bowen examines the history of Italian independent cinema through both relevant documentaries and the largely unexamined testimonies found in DVD bonus material. Bowen expands on Jonathan Gray's theory of media paratexts and John Caldwell's 'trade stories' approach in order to show the important role played by the 'against-all-odds' stories in practices of independent Italian filmmaking. The chapter chiefly focuses on productions carried out in the new millennium, and offers insightful and instructive tales on the most pragmatic and challenging phases of the making of independent feature films: the practices of organising a production, of securing funds, shooting on unusually low-budgets and in very short periods of time and finally initiating a theatrical run for the film. The chapter examines the pros and cons of releasing such first-person-narrator's tales of success, and/or frustration, about the inspirational drive and hardship involved in making independent feature films, and draws important conclusions regarding the unexpected results of including such chronicles in DVD bonus material. Bowen's research and charming penmanship engage, and challenge, the reader to look into the details of many 'acts of courage', along with the unexpected 'acts of friendship' and unspeakable sense of growth and achievement, resulting from such life experiences and from the monumental effort of giving birth to an independent feature-length film – some of which are fortunate enough to end up in mainstream exhibition venues. The chapter sheds much light into contemporary practices of independent feature film-production and their social role – and thus of great value to unsuspecting film talent, who might have shied away from bringing to fruition their dream projects and stories. It is a story of bravery, which in literary terms might be regarded as a sort of neoclassical allegory worthy of the heroic Latin stock. Bowen's contribution is a refreshing and timely study of the socio-cultural function of artisanal practices of independent Italian film production within Italy's contemporary political climate of the increasing *fai da te* (DIY, do-it-yourself) culture. The production tales of documentaries and films examined include *Gli invisibili: Esordi del cinema italiano 2000–2006* (*The Invisibles: Debuts in Italian Cinema 2000–2006*, 2007) to whose concept Vito Zagarrio contributed, Federico Rizzo's *Fuga dal call center* (*Escape from the Call Centre*, 2008), Marco Chiarini's *L'uomo fiammifero* (*The Thin Match Man*, 2009), Valerio Jalongo's *Di me cosa ne sai* (*What Do You Know about Me*, 2009), Gregory Fusaro and Massimiliano Vergani's *In Via Savona al 57* (*At 57 Savona Street*, 2013) and Emanuele Caruso's *E fu sera e fu mattina* (*And There Was Evening and There Was Morning*, 2014), among others.

The chapter 'Niccolò Bruna's Ethical Process as Social Engagement: Upholding Human Stories Against a Backdrop of Globalisation' by David Fleming and Filippo Gilardi is dedicated to Niccolò Bruna's work viewed in light of the ethics of *impegno* (social/political engagement). All of Bruna's documentaries are examined in detail, from both narrative and stylistic viewpoints. Bruna's independent approach is informed by his personal form of humanism. The authors find the essential feature of his work in the filmmaker's Marxism, expressed through the exploration of complex relationships. The themes of exclusion, challenges that problematise one's identity and displacement, are seen as the logical outcome of Bruna's ideological stance. Fleming and Gilardi emphasise the filmmaker's 'polycentric' view, corroborated by a style that favours an ethical detachment or withdrawn approach, which allows for the 'unabridged' voices of the characters to be heard in all their nuances, while delivering 'a range of perspectives onto various national and international social issues'. The chapter includes Bruna's direct testimonies and descriptive comments on his films, summarising the development of his career. One of the most relevant points raised by the authors when reporting on Bruna's own positions is the focus on the filmmaker's sense of responsibility. Bruna's films are deeply influenced by Werner Herzog's 'perspectivism'. The idea of introducing 'various different perspectives' is a powerful notion turned into a tool that Bruna deploys in his 'multi-perspectival filmmaking techniques'. Bruna's political and social commitment stands precisely on this attempt to use the camera in the most open minded and 'democratic' fashion. The analysis of Bruna's films is carried out along these guidelines and is therefore presented with penetrating insight, which unveils the unifying principle behind each work. Human relations take the forefront, essentially because Bruna believes they are the ultimate emotional and political explanation of the stories told in his films, humans as ends and not as means. Bruna's films share the same principle, defined by the authors as evidence for a 'unique human interest for human plight', the essence of the corpus of his work.

The last chapter, 'The Paradox of "Independence" in Cyberspace: The Case of Italian Experimental and Independent Cinema', by Anthony Cristiano, examines the migration online of the Italian filmic legacy, specifically the use which experimental and independent cinema artists and scholars have made of digital technologies. While Italian cinema has enjoyed much success over the years, and the country's talent is emulated and summoned by industries the world over, the new era of digital media, and the political economy of cyberspace, pose unprecedented challenges to alternative, and scarcely known, film work and legacies, to the point of endangering their very identity and survival. In times of crisis, practices of independent cinema have notoriously had an advantage over mainstream productions, for by definition they are known to rely on their own ingenuity and industriousness. The author investigates such a definition in light of the technical and socio-political dynamics presented by the new scenario of cyberspace. New media raise a host of new questions. The questions tackled by Cristiano include: whether Italian experimental and independent cinema is enjoying a new renaissance online, or whether it is being met by a greater paradox that threatens its survival? Whether the 'immigration' online has boosted or weakened the dissemination efforts and appreciation of unknown legacies? The chapter traces the underpinning philosophy and the practices of independence beginning with the historical avant-garde, and through the independent cooperatives' of the late 1960s and onward. It subsequently re-evaluates the legacy of its objectives and modalities vis-à-vis the algorithmic regime imposed by cyberspace. What emerges is a paradox: the promise of independence online is tied to relinquishing a significant part of it to strict protocols. The chapter offers a survey of the work and thrust of several independent artists, and the meaning of their presence or absence in online platforms – from Luigi Veronesi to Ugo Nespolo, to Marcello Piccardo and

Bruno Munari, and from Alfredo Leonardi to Piero Bargellini, Ugo La Pietra and several others. It includes a discussion of the online activities of national galleries and museums, aimed at establishing and promoting cinematic and cultural heritage via cyberspace. The leading concern pertains to the viability of notions of independence, in conjunction with cultural identity, vis-à-vis the onslaught of corporate interests via technocratic codes.

Notes

1. Besides the sharp decline of film production starting in the early 1920s, and lasting until the foundation of the Direzione Generale della Cinematogrfia (General Directorate of Cinema), headed by Luigi Freddi, the strict control over all aspects of cultural products (including film) by the Fascist regime also contributed significantly to the downgrading of independent and experimental endeavours.
2. Zavattini's exemplary case – cursorily labeled as 'screenwriting work' by the uniformed – is discussed in one of the chapters of this volume.
3. Nanni Moretti's independent practices are acknowledged beyond his early films. Of *Caro Diario* (*Dear Diary*, 1993) it has been said: '*Caro Diario* rappresenta l'elogio dell'*one man show*, l'estremizzazione della produzione indipendente cui dedicano un attento paragrafo Bordwell e Thompson nel citato *Film Art. An Introduction*. . . .' [English original: '*Caro Diario* stands as an acclamation of the *one man show*, an extreme form of independent production on which a careful word is found in Bordwell and Thompson's *Film Art. An Introduction*.'], Zagarrio (2011), p. 162.
4. See Zagarrio (2005b), pp. 6, 16, 25–6, 29.
5. See Costa (2002), p. 207; Di Marino (2006), pp. 145–76.
6. Zagarrio (2005b), pp. 19–26.
7. See Bertetto (2011), pp. 139–45; Paolo D'Agostini (2005), pp. 222–4; Di Marino (2008), pp. 422–34; Sandra Lischi (2017), pp. 461–5.
8. My translation. Original quote: '[I]l gruppo di film e di autori degli anni '30 che va sotto il nome di formalismo o di calligrafismo costituisce un episodio importante nella storia, poiché, indipendentemente dai risultati estetici a volte discutibili, presuppone o, meglio, addirittura inaugura un modo differente di guardare il film, intendendolo come arte visiva e non come intrattenimento, e imposta dei tempi e delle modalità di visione molto differenti da quelli classici'. Bernardi (2011), p. 287.
9. A recent comment on *Thaïs* is found in Paulicelli (2016), pp. 23–4.
10. Marcus (1996), p. 79.
11. Extract from 'Further Notes from Italy', see Collins (2015), pp. 14–15.
12. Toffetti (2015), pp. 18–19. The same is recalled by the mime street theatre led by Claude and Julian Chagrin in Antonioni's *Blowup* (1966).
13. My translation. Original quote: 'Con il film ad alto costo [. . . o quello] a basso costo non mi pongo problemi diversi. . . . Il cinema [è cambiato . . .]

con la variazione delle tipologie di registrazione . . . Anche se l'artista non si è mai lasciato condizionare da queste cose [. . . Non è che] il cinema a basso costo o ad alto costo sia [l'uno meno bello dell'altro . . .] ci sono i brutti film sperimentali come ci sono i brutti film narrativi . . . Il cinema narrativo è alla terza persona, ma è un limite . . . mentre parlare in prima persona ha allargato la possibilità di dire, si sono aperti dei campi vastissimi. Dagli anni 80 in poi questa cosa si è diffusa. . . . L' "io" è piu inconscio del discorso del "loro"'. Aprà (2005).
14. In this case scholar's documented reactions, such as Aprà's, seem to betray a nostalgic, or utopian, rather than a lucid foresight; see Aprà (2006), pp. 177–91.
15. *Bianco e Nero* 35 (1974): 152–8.
16. Between 1954 and 1958 Ermanno Olmi made several films for Edison; see Benedetta (2008), and Olmi (2009).
17. The documentary film is available online, on YouTube at: <https://www.youtube.com/watch?v=Xt-8AQ9YwT0>, last accessed 14 July 2017.
18. Fagone (1977).
19. Lischi (2017), p. 352.
20. My translation. Orignal quote: 'è una vittoria dal punto di vista del linguaggio e delle tecniche . . . è una sconfitta del punto di vista sociale; la vera Anna muore un anno dopo, in un ospedale psichiatrico, dimenticata da tutti.' Di Marino, Del Signore (2013).
21. Bordwell (2016).
22. Rumble (2009), p 16.
23. My translation. Original quote: 'quello italiano non imitava quello americano, ma era originalità senza complessi, non era un cinema di riporto, è fatto con spontaneità, come se vedessero le cose per la prima volta'. Di Marino, Del Signore (2013).
24. My translation. Original quote: 'Il cinema che dipende dall'industria è fermo da settant'otto anni; non dice niente di nuovo . . . Far cinema indipendente significa essere liberi, non dipendere da nessuno, e da nessuna cosa.' *660secondi* (*600 Seconds*, 2012).

Works Cited

Agosti, Silvano (2003), *Il semplice oblio: romanzo*, Rome: L'immagine.

Agosti, Silvano (1987), *Uova di garofano: romanzo breve*, Rome: Edizioni L'immagine.

Allegretti, Elisa, and Giancarlo Giraud eds. (2001), *Ermanno Olmi: L'esperienza di Ipotesi cinema*, in collaborazione con CGS, Cinecircoli giovanili socioculturali, Recco (Genoa): Le mani.

Apollonio, Umbro ed. and trans. (1973), *Futurist Manifestos: The Documents of 20th Century Art*, New York: Viking Press.

Aprà, Adriano ed. (2013), *Fuori norma. La via sperimentale del cinema italiano*, Venice: Marsilio Editori.

Aprà, Adriano (2006), 'Cinema sperimentale e mezzi di massa in Italia', in Cosetta Saba ed., *Cinema video internet. Tecnologie e avanguardie in Italian dal Futurismo alla Net.art*, Bologna: CLUEB, pp. 177–91.
Aprà, Adriano (2005), Interview, 'Giornate del cinema privato (Days of Private Cinema)', Siena, 28 April 2011, at: <https://www.youtube.com/watch?v=Pagn5vHajzo>, last accessed 12 July 2017.
Aprà, Adriano (1986), *New American Cinema: il cinema indipendente americano degli anni Sessanta*, Milan: Ubulibri.
Aprà, Adriano (1976), *Cinema sperimentale e mezzi di massa in Italia*, Milan: Fondazione Angelo Rizzoli.
Bacigalupo, Massimo (2003), 'Quarant'anni dopo' in Catalogo *Il cinema indipendente italiano 1964–1984*, Rome: Filmstudio, 17 November to 1 December 2003, pp. 15–17.
Bernardi, Sandro (2011), 'L'inquadratura e il quadro. Presenza della pittura nel cinema italiano', in Paolo Bertetto ed., *Storia del cinema italiano. Uno sguardo d'insieme*, Venice: Marsilio, Edizioni di Bianco e Nero, pp. 279–300.
Bertetto, Paolo ed. (2011), *Storia del cinema italiano. Uno sguardo d'insieme*, Venice: Marsilio, Edizioni di Bianco e Nero.
Bertetto, Paolo, and Andrea Minuz (2011), 'Le forme antirappresentative nel cinema italiano', in Paolo Bertetto ed., *Storia del cinema italiano. Uno sguardo d'insieme*, Venice: Marsilio, Edizioni di Bianco e Nero, pp. 117–46.
Bertetto, Paolo ed. (1983), *Il cinema d'avanguardia: 1910–1930*, Venice: Marsilio.
Bolpagni, Paolo, Andreina Di Brino, Chiara Savettieri, eds. (2011), *Ritmi visive. Luigi Veronesi nell'astrattismo europeo*, Lucca: Edizioni Fondazione Ragghianti.
Bordina, Alessandro, and Antonio Somaini, eds. (2014), *Paolo Gioli: The Man without a Movie Camera*, Sesto San Giovanni (Milan): Mimesis.
Bordwell, David (2016), 'Paolo Gioli, Maximal Minimalist', *David Bordwell's website on cinema*, 19 April, <http://www.davidbordwell.net/blog/2016/04/19/paolo-gioli-maximal-minimalist/>, last accessed 7 July 2017.
Bordwell, David, and Kristin Thompson (1997), *Film Art. An Introduction*, New York: McGraw-Hill, pp. 26–7.
Cantini, Maristella ed. (2013), *Italian Women Filmmakers and the Gendered Screen*, New York: Palgrave MacMillan.
Cappabianca, Alessandro (2012), *Carmelo Bene: Il cinema oltre se stesso*, Cosenza: Luigi Pellegrini.
Casetti, Francesco (2011), 'l cinema italiano e la modernità. L'apertura degli orizzonti discorsivi, geografici e ideologici', in Paolo Bertetto ed., *Storia del cinema italiano. Uno sguardo d'insieme*, Venice: Marsilio, Edizioni di Bianco e Nero, pp. 381–93.
Censi, Rinaldo (2015), 'Tychic Motifs and Hidden Details: The Work of Yervant Gianikian & Angela Ricci Lucchi', *Journal of Film Preservation*, 93 (October): 33–40.

Censi, Rinaldo (2006), '*Piero Bargellini: (as)salto al cielo*', in Catalogo Generale del 24° Torino Film Festival, pp. 291–3, on occasion of the 'Piero Bargellini Retrospective' by Fulvio Baglivi.
Cincinelli, Sonia (2009), *I migranti nel cinema italiano*, Rome: Kappa.
Coco, Attilio (2008), 'Film sperimentali per la TV', in Flavio De Bernardinis ed., *Storia del cinema italiano. Volume XII – 1970/1976*, Venice: Marsilio, Edizioni di Bianco e Nero, pp. 414–21.
Collins, John (2015), etract from 'Further Notes from Italy, 1970', in *Tate Film – If Arte Povera Was Pop: Artists' and Experimental Cinema in Italy 1960s-70s*, Tate Modern Starr Auditorium, (23–25 October): 13–14, <tare.org.uk/film>, last accessed 7 July 2917.
Comer, Stuart, ed. (2009), *Film and Video Art*, London: Tate Publishing.
Corra, Bruno (1973). 'Abstract Cinema – Chromatic Music 1912', in *Futurist Manifestos Futurist Manifestos: The Documents of 20th Century Art*, Umbro Apollonio ed. and trans., New York: Viking Press, p. 67.
Corsi, Barbara (2001), *Con qualche dollaro in meno. Storia economica del cinema italiano*, Rome: Editori Riuniti.
Costa, Antonio (2002), *Il cinema e le arti visive*, Turin: Einaudi.
Costa, Antonio (2012), 'Otto frammenti di un discorso lacunoso: Il film d'artista nel contesto del cinema italiano', in Di Marino, Bruno, Marco Meneguzzo, Andrea La Porta, eds., *Lo sguardo espanso. Cinema d'artista italiano 1912–2012*, Cinesello Balsamo (Milan): Silvana Editoriale, pp. 42–5.
D'Agostini, Paolo (2005), 'Gli albori del "nouvo cinema" anni '90', in Vito Zagarrio ed., *Storia del cinema italiano. Volume XIII – 1977/1985*, Venice: Marsilio, Edizioni di Bianco e Nero, pp. 222–4.
De Bernardinis, Flavio ed., (2008), *Storia del cinema italiano. Volume XII – 1970/1976*, Venice: Marsilio, Edizioni di *Bianco e Nero*.
De Bernardinis, Flavio (2008), 'Ipotesi per nuovi modelli di produzione e distribuzione. 1970–1976: appunti per una mutazione', in Flavio De Bernardinis ed., *Storia del cinema italiano. Volume XII – 1970/1976*, Venice: Marsilio, Edizioni di Bianco e Nero, pp. 478–85.
De Cuir, Greg Jr., and Miriam De Rosa (2016), 'A Treatise on the Apparatus and the Artistic Yield of Yervant Gianikian & Angela Ricci Lucchi', *Millennium Film Journal* 64 (Fall): 68–75.
De Palo, Gianluigi, and Federico Pontiggia (2004), *I sogni dei giovani*, Cantalupa (Turin): Effata Editrice.
Di Marino, Bruno (2015), 'Cinema d'artista in Italia. Gli anni 1960–'70', *Artribune* (31 October), <http://www.artribune.com/attualita/2015/10/cinema-artisti-italia-anni-60-70/>, last accessed 8 September 2017.
Di Marino, Bruno (2014), 'Lo sguardo, la tela, lo schermo. Gli anni Sessanta a Roma e dintorni ovvero: l'âge d'or del cinema d'artista italiano', *Flash Art* (maggio-giugno): 1–6, <http://www.flashartonline.it/article/lo-sguardo-la-tela-lo-schermo/>, last accessed 10 July 2017.
Di Marino, Bruno, Claudio Del Signore (2013), *Lo sguardo espanso: cinema d'artista italiano*, Rome: Karadel, 2000–2013, video narration, YouTube, <https://www.youtube.com/watch?v=Xt-8AQ9YwT0>, last accessed 10 July 2017.

Di Marino, Bruno, Marco Meneguzzo, Andrea La Porta, eds. (2012), *Lo sguardo espanso. Cinema d'artista italiano 1912–2012*, Cinesello Balsamo (Milan): Silvana Editoriale.
Di Marino, Bruno (2008), 'Oltre l'underground. Il cinema di ricerca, il videotape, e l'animazione d'autore', in Flavio De Bernardinis ed., *Storia del cinema italiano. Volume XII – 1970/1976*, Venice: Marsilio, Edizioni di *Bianco e Nero*, pp. 422–34.
Di Marino, Bruno ed. (2007), *Tracce, sguardi e altri pensieri*, in booklet with DVD *Studio Azzurro*, Milan: Feltrinelli Real Cinema.
Di Marino, Bruno (2006), 'Con (e senza) macchina da presa. Estetica e tecnologia dagli anni '30 agli anni '70', in *Cinema Video Internet: Technologie e avanguardia in Italian dal Futurismo alla Net.art*, in Cosetta Saba ed., Bologna: CLUEB, pp. 145–76.
Di Marino, Bruno (2002), *Interferenze dello sguardo. La sperimentazione audiovisiva tra analogico e digitale*, Rome: Bulzoni.
Di Marino, Bruno (1999), *Sguardo inconscio azione. Il cinema underground e d'artista a Roma (1965–1975)*, Rome: Lithos editrice.
Editorial (2015), *Tate Film – If Arte Povera Was Pop: Artists' and Experimental Cinema in Italy 1960s-70s*, Tate Modern Starr Auditorium (23–25 October): 1–32, <tate.org.uk/film>, last accessed July 2017.
Editorial (1967), in *Ombre elettriche* (dicembre), reprinted in *Bianco e Nero* (May–August 1974): 152–3.
Fagone, Vittorio (2004), *Arte del video: il viaggio dell'uomo immobile. Videoinstallazioni, videoproiezioni*, Lucca: Edizioni Fondazione Ragghianti Studi sull'Arte.
Fagone, Vittorio ed. (1977), *Arte e cinema: per un catalogo di cinema d'artista in Italia, 1965–1977*, Venice: Marsilio.
Fagone, Vittorio (1976), *In the Wake of the Italian Artisan: The Traces of Material Culture*, Milan: Silvana Editoriale.
Fallerini, Paola (1999–2000), 'Le forme dello spazio inosservato': I. (1 December 1999), II. and III. *Fucine Mute Magazine* (1 January 2000), <http://www.fucinemute.it/1999/12/le-forme-dello-spazio-inosservato-i/>, last accessed 8 September 2017.
Fanchi, Mariagrazia, and Federica Villa (2011), 'Sapere sociale, cinema e produzione di nuovi immaginari', in Paolo Bertetto ed., *Storia del cinema italiano. Uno sguardo d'insieme*, Venice: Marsilio, Edizioni di *Bianco e Nero*, pp. 433–44.
Farassino, Alberto (1979), 'Aspetti del cinema sperimentale italiano', in catalogo *Cine qua non. Giornate internazionali del cinema d'artista*, (Florence), Andrea Granchi ed., (12–23 December): 133–4.
Filmstudio Mon Amour, documentary directed by Toni D'Angelo, 16:9HD, Francesco Antonio Castaldo prod., International Madcast, 2015.
Gnoli, Antonio (2016), 'Tonino De Bernardi: "Il mio cinema undergraound sparito, io ho perso, ma non mi sento un fallito"', *La Repubblica*, 5 January.
Hoefert de Turégano, Teresa (2015), 'European Union Initiatives for Independent Film', in Doris Baltruschat and Mary Erickson eds., *Independent Filmmaking around the Globe*, Toronto: University of Toronto Press.

Lajolo, Anna, and Guido Lombardo (1994), *L'isola in capo al mondo*, Turin: Nuova ERI.
La Pietra, Ugo (2019). 'Abitare è essere ovunque a casa propria', Fondazione Ugo La Pietra, pp. iii–vi.
La Polla, Franco (2011), 'L'americanizzazione del cinema italiano', in a cura di Paolo Bertetto ed., *Storia del cinema italiano. Uno sguardo d'insieme*, Venice: Marsilio, Edizioni di Bianco e Nero, pp. 170–91.
Leonardi, Alfredo (2006), *Occhio mio dio: il new american cinema*, Bologna: CLUEB.
Lischi, Sandra (2017), 'Independents, Experimentalists: A Premise', in Frank Burke ed., *A Companion to Italian Cinema*, Hoboken, N.J.: John Wiley & Sons, pp. 340–60.
Lischi, Sandra (2005), 'Senza chiedere permesso: il videotape e il cinema militante', in Vito Zagarrio ed., *Storia del cinema italiano. Volume XIII – 1977/1985*, Venice: Marsilio, Edizioni di Bianco e Nero, pp. 91–102.
Marcus, Millicent (1996), 'Anton Giulio Bragaglia's *Thaïs*; or, The Death of the Diva + the Rise of the Scenoplastica = The Borth of Futurist Cinema', *South Central Review* 13.2–3 (Summer-Autumn): 63–81.
Meneguzzo, Marco (2012), 'Il territorio mutante. Il film d'artista nel contesto dell'arte italiana: i primi cento anni', in Di Marino, Bruno, Marco Meneguzzo, Andrea La Porta, eds., *Lo sguardo espanso. Cinema d'artista italiano 1912–2012*, Cinesello Balsamo (Milan): Silvana Editoriale, pp. 36–41.
Miccichè, Lino (1998), 'Testimonianze e memorie degli anni 80', in Lino Miccichè ed., *Schermi opachi: il cinema italiano degli anni '80*, Venice: Marsilio, pp. 343–92.
Miccichè, Lino ed. (1998), *Schermi opachi: il cinema italiano degli anni '80*, Venice: Marsilio.
Morsiani, Alberto, and Serena Agusto eds. (2011), *Il cinema di Franco Piavoli*, Milan: Il Castoro.
Olmi, Ermanno (2009), *Gli anni Editon. Documentary e cortometraggi 1954–1958*, book and DVD, Milan: Feltrinelli.
Patella, Luca Maria (2002), 'Interview by Angela Madesani', in Angela Madesani ed., *Le icone fluttuanti. Storia del cinema d'artista e della videoarte in Italia*, Milan: Bruno Mondadori, pp. 182–200.
Paulicelli, Eugenia (2016), *Italian Style: Fashion & Film from Early Cinema to Digital Age*, New York: Bloomsbury.
Piccardo, Marcello (1992), *La collina del cinema*, Como: Nodo Libri.
Quaglietti, Lorenzo (1980), *Storia economico-politica del cinema italiano. 1945–1980*, Rome: Editori Riuniti.
Rees, Alan Leonard (2009), 'Movements in art 1912–40', in Stuart Comer ed., *Film and Video Art*, London: Tate Publishing, pp. 26–65.
Rees, Alan Leonard (1999), *A history of experimental film and video*, London: Tate Publishing.
Restany, Pierre, and Maurizi Vitta (1991), *Ugo La Pietra*, Barcelona: Gustavo Gili Editorial S.A.

Rumble, Patrick (2009), 'Free Films Made Freely: Paolo Gioli and Experimental Filmmaking in Italy', *CineAction* 78 (Winter): 10–16.
Saba, Cosetta ed. (2006), *Cinema Video Internet: Technologie e avanguardia in Italian dal Futurismo alla Net.art*, Bologna: CLUEB.
Sbardella, Americo (2003), 'Introduzione', in catalogo *Il cinema indipendente italiano 1964–1984*, Rome: Filmstudio, (17 November to 1 December): 5–11, <http://www.activitaly.it/immaginicinema/indipendente/cinema>, last accessed 10 September 2017.
Sbardella, Americo (2000), *Cinema e spiritualità: istanze etiche, trascendenza e rappresentatione cinematografica*. Rome: Semar.
Senaldi, Marco (2012), 'The Italian Job: Il cinema d'artista nel contesto internazionale', in Di Marino, Bruno, Marco Meneguzzo, Andrea La Porta, eds., *Lo sguardo espanso. Cinema d'artista italiano 1912–2012*, Cinesello Balsamo (Milan): Silvana Editoriale, 46–51.
Silvestri, Roberto ed. (1993), *Il cinema contro di Alberto Grifi, Atripalda*, Atripalda (Avellino): Edizioni Laceno.
Sitney, P. Adams (2000), '*Il cinema d'avanguardia*', in Gian Piero Brunetta ed., *Storia del cinema mondiale*, Volume Secondo, *Gli Stati Uniti*, Tomo Secondo, Turin: Einaudi, pp. 1569–1603.
660secondi, Silvano Agosti Il cinema indipendente (660seconds, Silvano Agosti The Independent Cinema) (2012), YouTube, <https://www.youtube.com/watch?v=49J0HQBI4uU>, 1 September 2012 accessed August 2017.
Subrizi, Carla ed. (2004), *Baruchello e Grifi. Verifica incerta. L'arte oltre i confini del cinema*, Rome: Derive Approdi.
Tempesta, Manuela ed. (2008), *Alberto Grifi: oltre le regole del cinema*, Atripalda (Avellino): Edizioni Laceno.
Terzano, Enzo Nicola (2011). *On the Birth of Experimental Cinema*, Nina Robinson trans. Toronto: Guernica Editions.
Tobagi, Benedetta ed. (2008), *I volti e le mani*, Milan: Feltrinelli, volume with DVD *Gli anni Edison. Documentari e cortometraggi 1954–1958* by Ermanno Olmi.
Toffetti, Sergio (2015), 'Before and After the Revolution: Experimental Cinema in Italy', Saverio Piccolo trans., in Editorial, *If Arte Povera Was Pop: Artists' and Experimental Cinema in Italy 1960s-70s, Tate Film* (October): 18–19.
Ungari, Enzo (1978), *Schermo delle mie brame*, Florence: Vallecchi.
Ungari, Enzo (1975), *Imagine del disastro: cinema, shock e tabù*, Rome: Arcana.
Youngblood, Gene (1970), *Expanded Cinema*, Richard Buckminster Fuller intro., New York: Dutton.
Zagarrio, Vito ed. (2011), 'I modi di produzione', in Paolo Bertetto ed., *Storia del cinema italiano. Uno sguardo d'insieme*, Venice: Marsilio, Edizioni di Bianco e Nero, pp. 147–66.
Zagarrio, Vito ed. (2005), *Storia del cinema italiano. Volume XIII – 1977/1985*, Venice: Marsilio, Edizioni di Bianco e Nero.

Zagarrio, Vito ed. (2005), 'Dopo la morte dei padri. Dagli anni della crisi agli albori della rinascita', in Vito Zagarrio ed., *Storia del cinema italiano. Volume XIII – 1977/1985*, Venice: Marsilio, Edizioni di Bianco e Nero, pp. 3–42.

Zagarrio, Vito ed. (2005), 'Documenti. Nuove forme del consumo cinematografico: cineclub, cinema d'essai, Massenzio', in Vito Zagarrio ed., *Storia del cinema italiano. Volume XIII - 1977/1985*, Venice: Marsilio, Edizioni di Bianco e Nero, pp. 601–622.

Zambetti, Sandro (2003), 'L'affermazione del cineclubismo', in Gianni Canova ed., *Storia del cinema italiano. Volume XI – 1965/1969*, Venice: Marsilio-Edizioni di Bianco e Nero, pp. 446–55.

CHAPTER 1

Filmmaker and the Milanese Independent Cinema of the 1980s and 1990s
Donatella Maraschin and Paola Nasini

Introduction

The Milanese cinema represents one of the many traditions of Italy's independent cinematic culture, which developed in various parts of the country, often in antithesis and in a subaltern position to the national film industry based in Rome – where it had been merged since Mussolini's policies of the 1930s, and where it has been further centralised after the Second World War when the American funds of the Marshall Plan flooded into the country.[1]

Traditionally, the Milanese cinematic culture is defined by a number of important traits: (1) its aspiration to counter the often commercial nature of films produced in Rome and their mode of production; (2) its strong association with the local industries and the industrial culture typical of the region; (3) its tendency to produce films which are intrinsically embedded in the Milanese urban fabric as well as in Lombardia's regional landscape; (4) its fruitful collaborations and interdisciplinary links with intellectuals, professionals and artists from very different fields (including literature, theatre, publishing, architecture, performing and traditional arts, advertising and so forth); and, finally, (5) its idea of a cinema oriented towards meaningful social issues with which the younger generation of viewers, in particular, can identify. These themes emerge as early as the themes pertaining to the theoretical debates surrounding cinema, which appeared in film and cultural journals printed in Milan during the 1930s[2] and, thereafter, continued to define the Milanese independent cinema movement for many decades.

In this chapter we discuss how the 'politics of locations'[3] affected the development of some specific traits of the Milanese independent cinema. We decontextualise here a well-known concept coined within the context of feminist theory to stress the importance of the influence and the specificity of place when countering gender generalisations. Our analysis addresses the extent to which, given the absence of state infrastructures to regulate the development of a film industry locally, the socio-cultural-political milieu of Milan during the 1970s, 1980s and 1990s, shaped the specificity of both the cinematic culture and production modes of the film scene in the city.

One line of investigation examines the political *impegno* (commitment/engagement), which infiltrated Milanese society during the 1970s, and its influence on both social interactions and on the output of cultural products. We address the long-standing impact of such political *impegno* on the cinema produced in the city during the decades that followed. To do so, we focus in particular on *Filmmaker*, an independent Festival of Film and Video founded in 1980 by Salvatore Cavatorta and Gianfilippo Pedote, which also acted as an enterprise via the production company Studio Equatore and the distribution company Indigena, and operated as a lab for the development of young talents.

The chapter is based on research we conducted in *Filmmaker*'s archive and on interviews with key players of the Milanese independent film scene of the 1980s and 1990s. *Filmmaker*'s contribution – during such decades – to the promotion of an alternative cinematic culture and to a positive image of Italian cinema abroad, to date has not been sufficiently studied and, moreover, has mainly attracted research limited to Milan's micro-histories, which were published solely in Italian. The purpose of this chapter is to shed some light on this submerged cinema.

Some Historical Considerations

The Milanese independent cinema sits at the cusp between commercial cinema, documentary film, industrial cinema, video art and art cinema. Over time, the Milanese cinema has uniquely been able to provide an alternative pole of production, although for brief periods, to the Roman national hegemonic film industry by producing films that gained national and international recognition.

ICET (Industrie Cinematiche e Teatrali – Cinema and Theatre Industries) and its progressive evolution, by 1960, into Cinelandia Milanese[4] reflects the aspirations and determination of Milanese film circles to break away from their subordinate position to Rome. The absence of film equipment rental facilities and infrastructures, and of specialised technicians, were some of its major pitfalls. With the development of studios in the suburban area of Cologno Monzese, which were able to offer all the services needed by the film industry, the city was finally able to make films entirely produced in Milan. Amongst them were films such as *La notte* (*The Night*,

Michelangelo Antonioni 1960), *Rocco e i suoi fratelli* (*Rocco and His Brothers*, Luchino Visconti 1960), *La vita agra* (*It's a Hard Life*, Carlo Lizzani 1964) and *Achtung banditi!* (*Achtung: Bandits!*, Carlo Lizzani 1968).

Nonetheless, the history of the Cinelandia studios is emblematic of the challenges that the Milanese cinema faces to date. This history is powered by the problematic relationship between two realities which are at once intertwined and antagonistic: the advertising industry, television and commercial cinema, on one hand, and on the other the underlying inclination towards a cinematic culture driven by non-commercial works, socially committed films related to art cinema and to documentary practices. As such, whilst Cinelandia was created to support and develop Milan's film industry, the studios in the 1960s were mainly used to produce industrial films, television programmes and television advertisements. No less than 80 per cent of the RAI's national Carosello (the only advertising platform of Italian Television at the time) was produced here, with one studio exclusively and permanently rented by General Film – the biggest advertising Italian production company at that time. These commercial and non-cinematic productions transformed the Cinelandia studios into a viable business model, turning away the attention and investments from those high-quality films engaged with social critique which defined the ICET productions of the 1940s and 1950s, including *Gente del Po* (*People of the Po Valley*, 1943–47) and *Nettezza Urbana* (*Sanitation Department*, 1948) both films by Michelangelo Antonioni, as well as films produced in the Milanese studios with investments from Rome, such as *Miracolo a Milano* (*Miracle in Milan*, Vittorio De Sica 1950), *Lo svitato* (*The Nut*, Carlo Lizzani 1955), *Gli sbandati* (*The Wayward*, Francesco Maselli 1955) and *Il prigioniero della montagna* (*The Prisoner of the Mountain*, Luis Trenker 1955). As a result, when the Carosello was suspended in 1977, television programmes progressively took over from the advertising productions in the studios. In 1983, Berlusconi's Finivest bought ICET's Cinelandia studios and transformed them into 'Tivulandia',[5] which comprised almost exclusively television studios while it retained small studios for the production of television advertising and small budget movies.

During the 1980s, Berlusconi's Reteitalia – the company of the Gruppo Finivest devoted to the production of feature films, which in the 1990s became known as Silvio Berlusconi Communication, and later on as Mediaset and Medusa – produced in its Milanese studios mainly low-quality films, with few exceptions. These include Carlo Vanzina's and Neri Parenti's films, who during the 1980s and 1990s directed 1 or 2 films per year, feeding into the long-lasting phenomenon of the 'cinepanettone'.[6]

Outside of these circuits – though in some cases, with funding raised through the aid of Berlusconi's film production enterprises – the Milanese independent film industry was nonetheless able to produce quality films, some of which gained international recognition. With limited access to institutional production facilities, the Milanese directors and producers had to invent productive channels, often led by informal networks emerging from the city's cultural, militant and art circles. It is this state of confinement, together with other factors dealt with in the ensuing discussion – including the osmotic mechanism the cinema circles of Milan continued to establish over the years with both the film industry in Rome and the local advertising industry – that defines the independent cinematic culture of Milan, one that represents a sort of force of resistance. The independent filmmakers active in Milan during the 1980s and 1990s included: Davide Ferrario, Gianluca Fumagalli, Adriana Monti, Gianni Martuzzi and Massimo Mazzucco, Enzo Monteleone, Michele Soavi, Michele Sordillo, Maurizio Zaccaro and Marco Tullio Giordana.[7]

Another relevant but failed attempt by the Milanese cinematic circles to counter the Roman monopoly over the production of feature films is Ermanno Olmi's and Bruno Janni's production company 22 Dicembre (22 December). Founded in 1961 with 51 per cent of investment from the Edison Group firm, it aimed at developing alternative and innovative modes of production, oriented towards documentary, industrial films, content for television and low budget films.[8] The history of 22 Dicembre highlights a key feature of the Milanese cultural fabric of the 1950s and 1960s, often driven by a cultured and enlightened elite of industrial dynasties interested in supporting and sponsoring cultural projects of high social impact. During these optimistic years of economic growth the industry saw cinema not only as a form of investment, in terms of promotion, business communication and public relations – especially in the case of industrial cinema – but also as a form of social enterprise, by endorsing cultural events for the firm's community and the wider society.

The aim of the 22 Dicembre initiative was to develop low budget films of young up-and-coming film directors and to act as a film school, intended as a hub for nurturing innovative approaches to cinema. Olmi and Janni's idea of cinema was: '*not a commercial* cinema, as it is usually understood, but rather a kind of cinema that somehow was close, without commercial preconditions, to the problems of our time'.[9] Soon 22 Dicembre became 'the destination for Milanese intellectuals interested in cinema'[10] and produced films such as *I basilischi* (*The Basilisks*, Lina Wertmuller 1963), *I ragazzi che si amano* (*Youngsters in Love*, Alberto Caldana 1963), *La rimpatriata* (*The Reunion*, Damiano Damiani 1963), *Il terrorista* (*The Terrorist*, Gianfranco De Bosio

1963), *I fidanzati* (*The Fiances*, Ermanno Olmi 1963), as well as the serial TV documentary by Roberto Rossellini, *L'età del ferro* (*The Iron Age*, 1963).

However, problems of distribution, limited returns due to the production of non-commercial cinema, and clashes between Olmi and Janni brought the activities of 22 Dicembre to an end. Nonetheless, in many ways the cinema project of 22 Dicembre, despite its short-lived activity, continued to remain at the heart of the cinematic culture of Milan for decades to follow. As will be seen, the culture of nurturing up-and-coming film directors, producing low budget non-commercial films and the didactic approach of the lab, continued to define the mandate of *Filmmaker*, which voiced and embodied this philosophy in the 1980s and 1990s. Moreover, the links between the industry and the Milanese cinematic culture are long-lasting and will remain central to the city's independent film productions in the decades that follow.

Formal Experimentalism

Two specific features of independent Milanese cinema – its links with industry and the industrial film, and the synergies it established with video and various forms of art – are traditionally rooted in, as we have mentioned, the fabric and the history of the city. The industrial film and the art film made some important achievements during the 1980s and 1990s thanks to the workings of the production company Metamorphosi and the art collective Studio Azzurro. Although these two entities produced some fiction films, the bulk of their activities resided outside this mainstream film category. In many ways, they both contributed considerably to the formal experimentalism and expressive concerns of the independent Milanese cinema and of *Filmmaker*.

Metamorphosi more than any other production enterprise in Milan, inherited and reinvented the tradition of the industrial film,[11] which runs through the history of the Milanese cinema due to the city's links with many sectors of the industry. Founded by Marco and Andrea Poma during the surge of production companies that in the 1980s gravitated around *Filmmaker*, Metamorphosi produced video content commissioned by the local industries, the local businesses (music companies, architecture studios and the like), and local institutions (Provincia di Milano – Province of Milan – Triennale Museum, Swiss Radio Television and others).

Susanna Schoenberg,[12] who has collaborated with Metamorphosi since 1989, explains how these commercial commissions amounted to the chief source of revenue, which was converted into investments for the production of fiction projects. By working on these commissions, Metamorphosi and its collaborators defined new formal frontiers and reinvented the industrial cinema of the earlier decades. One example of this is the competence that Metamorphosi developed in producing films based on talking heads and testimonials, anticipating formal strategies now well established in documentary. Soon Metamorphosi became the platform for the production of public relation content for the prolific architecture and music industry of the city.

While initially Metamorphosi worked mainly in film – as Schoenberg[13] recalls, by seeking leftover film stock from the local production companies working in the advertising industry – with the advent of video the production company created post-production studios which could be used free of charge by their collaborators or rented out. During the 1980s and 1990s the production company nurtured a new generation of filmmakers by commissioning from them the production of commercial videos for their clients, and thus progressively developed the skills of those filmmakers. At the time, Metamorphosi allowed the filmmakers the use of the production and post-production facilities to produce their own independent projects. Conversely, by working with Metamorphosi both on their own and commissioned projects, these filmmakers brought more business to the production company by renting Metamorphosi's facilities on behalf of external clients.

Schoenberg,[14] now an acclaimed video artist based in Cologne, Germany, recognises the impact Metamorphosi had in building her professionalism. In its studios, filmmakers learned to develop different abilities, including writing, filming, editing, cinematography and so forth. In many ways, experimentalism became an outcome of the access to technologies, as the culture of Metamorphosi and of its collaborators was driven by artistic aspirations and forms of expressionism. According to Schoenberg[15] Metamorphosi's drive to develop the technical skills of the new generation of filmmakers was not dictated purely by financial needs – so as to have a pool of people with whom one could produce commercial content and generate income – but was also shaped by the idea that hardware needs experimentalism to continue to evolve. The strategy of free access to technology for up-and-coming filmmakers was part of an overarching plan, to invest in quality work and nurture an experimental cinematic culture in the long run.

The work of Studio Azzurro, especially in the field of art installation, is world-renowned.[16] The collective of artists – formed in different fields of the arts – includes, amongst others, Paolo Rosa, Fabio Cirifino, Leonardo Sangiorgi and the duo Armando Bertacchi and Gianni Rocco who collaborated together since 1969. The collective produced their first fiction film in 1979, with *Facce di Festa* (*Merry Faces*). The artistic and political background of the city of Milan is crucial in defining the works of

Studio Azzurro. Their works interpolate video with other media, including photography, theatre and architecture. Cirifino[17] explains how the collective saw video as 'a spongy element that sucks everything and what comes out is no longer what it has absorbed. Cinema absorbed by video returned something other than the original medium, in a metamorphic movement'.[18] In this sense, Studio Azzurro's approach to video and cinema reproduces the Milanese cultural scene, defined by its interdisciplinary exchanges between different fields of arts.

The fluidity of the mélange and relations between media is the trademark of the collective's prolific activity over time, and it includes films, videos, installations, 'sensitive environments' and 'theme museums'[19] – and it is so fertile and diverse that it exceeds the remit of this investigation. It is worth noting, however, that amongst this wide range of art fields, the collective widely contributed to the Milanese independent cinema scene. As will be seen, some of Studio Azzurro's films are intrinsically connected to the genesis and the history of *Filmmaker*. Within this context, Studio Azzurro played a central role in expanding the use of technologies amongst the Milanese independent circles of cinematic art, especially in relation to video.

Political *Impegno* (Engagement)

Another important feature of the Milanese independent cinema is its long-standing interest in tackling social issues. This is also reflected in the genesis of *Filmmaker* and in the cinema project that it represents. To understand the *impegno politico* (political engagement) that dominated the Milanese independent cinematic culture of the 1980s and 1990s, we need to look back at the 1970s and at the generational aspirations of the young directors and producers who grew up during that decade.

The idea of political commitment or engagement has led to many theoretical debates, and has been defined by its historical context. In the 1970s the idea of engagement was underpinned by the belief in a single conceptual framework. As Alfonso Berardinelli explains:

> The logic of *engagement* ... starts from knowing with certainty that one's own political-literary conscience of the present is the principle from which to deduct *only one* historical correct way to solve one's own relationship held between social reality, political imperative, and literary forms.[20]

Jennifer Burns points out that the monolithic idea of commitment linked to a Marxist ideology started to reveal its limitation in the 1950s.[21] This progressively led the notion of commitment linked to one single social agenda to a fragmentation and diversification from which emerged a number of specific issues. However, according to Pier Paolo Antonello and Florian Mussgnug, the rejection of universalism and metanarratives doesn't mean 'the end of *impegno* (commitment/engagement), or indeed of modern emancipatory politics'.[22] We argue that in many ways the genesis and development of *Filmmaker* encapsulates the (difficult) journey of a group of filmmakers, producers and intellectuals, into new forms of *impegno*.

When Pedote and Cavatorta founded *Filmmaker*, they were 27 and 32 years of age respectively. As adolescents, they grew up in a highly charged political culture, dominated by ideological polarisations not only between catholic, conservative and liberal frames, but also between political ideas rooted in the history of post-war Europe. The dichotomy between the extreme Right and extreme Left that distinguishes the 1970s found a fertile terrain in Milan. This was particularly felt by the generation of the baby-boomers – as a result of Italy's economic boom of the 1960s – who as young adults experienced the political tensions and clashes which were splitting the public opinion of the country during the *anni di piombo* (years of the bullet). This decade also witnessed traumatic terrorist acts which scarred the cultural memory of the country, of the city and of this generation in particular. These included the bomb planted at the National Agrarian Bank in Piazza Fontana on 12 December 1969, which killed 17 people and wounded 88; the detainment and fall from the window of the Questura of Milan of Giuseppe Pinelli in 1969; the kidnapping and killing of the President of the Christian Democratic Party Aldo Moro in 1978; and the killing, also in 1978, of Fausto Tinelli and Lorenzo Iannucci (known as Fausto e Iaio) metres away from the Centro Sociale Autogestito Leoncavallo (Squat of Leoncavallo).

Growing up in Milan during those years meant that young people had to choose a political alignment. Friends often shared similar political ideas, and it was a common practice to act upon such ideas together by taking part in political activities, including *collettivi* (political collectives), *occupazioni* (squattings), sit-ins, assemblies, demonstrations and the like. Universities took an active role in leading political activism, in particular the Università Statale (State University), the Accademia di Brera (Brera Academy) and the *licei* (*Lyceums* or high schools) made known their political alliance, which often led to violent clashes between teenagers attending neighbouring schools. A common motto of those years: *Chi non occupa preoccupa* (literally: the one not squatting is a concern) shows the extent of peer pressure and the currency attached to political activism at that time.[23]

Many artistic and cultural initiatives that took place in Milan in the 1970s were led by leftist groups – with the exception of some led by catholic circles – that saw culture and the arts as a tool to counter the dominant catholic-liberalist culture of the political and media establishment. With growing social tensions generated by the labour and the student movements, during the 1970s many groups concerned with political debate and activism formed spontaneously outside the fabric of the mainstream economic structures. Political and cultural activities were conceived as two sides of the same coin. For example, the Centro Sociale Leoncavallo (Squat of Leoncavallo) was a popular point of reference not only for organising political demonstrations, squattings and political rallies, but also for music and theatre events.

Within these circles, led by ideas derived from the extra-parliamentary left, cinema was seen as a tool for propaganda and civic dissent. Milan saw the formation of the Collettivo di Cinema Militante (Militant Cinema Collective), which was mainly led by students. The Collective became the hub for the production of 8mm low cost propaganda films, chiefly documentaries, which were distributed in schools, factories, cultural centres and so forth. Amongst these were films such as *Totem*, *Le lotte di via Tibaldi* (*Struggles in via Tibaldi*), *Lotte a Milano* (*Struggles in Milan*), *La città del capitale* (*The City of Capital*), *Feda Fargos*, *No alla tregua* (*No to Truce*), *Pagherete caro, pagherete tutto* (*You Shall Pay Dearly, You Shall Pay All*) and *Il capital* (*The Capital*). As De Berti has pointed out, the Collective also ran cultural debates mainly focussed on the critique of traditional cinema production and distribution modes, as well as on the role of cinema as trigger-agency and its ability to elicit an active intervention in the social sphere.[24] Another idea promoted by the Collective was the use of emerging video analogue technologies and by shifting traditional mode of productions and distributions, it represented an opportunity for the democratisation of cinema. In many ways, as will be seen, the concerns raised by the Collective align with the work carried forward by *Filmmaker* in the decades that followed.

Other symbolic loci of the 1970s, which contributed to forging the Milanese independent cinematic landscape of the following decade, were: (1) the Cineclubs and Cineforums – clubs with a limited number of members, and which offered retrospectives of, and debates around, American and art cinema – such as the Cineclub Brera, the Obraz Cinestudio and the Centro Studi Cinematografici (Centre for Studies of Cinema) that comprised around thirty clubs, including the catholic group Centro S. Fedele; (2) and the *Cinema d'essai* (*Art house cinemas*) – amongst which were the Arti cinema, the FAC (Film, Art and Culture), and the cinema

Argentina. These initiatives were specifically designed to promote a cinematic culture that ran outside mainstream circuits as well as a critical understanding of film.

Amongst these alternative cinemas, the Cinema Anteo has continued over several decades to represent a hub and a leading force for the discovery and dissemination in the city of quality films peripheral to commercial cinema. The Cinema Anteo was already active in the 1940s, when it hosted the activities of the Circolo del Cinema Mario Ferrari (Cine Club Mario Ferrari). Thereafter, under the direction of the MusiCineTeatro – a collective of young cinema lovers lead by Lionello Cerri and Maurizio Ballabio – in 1979 the cinema became 'an alternative pole in the way cinema was presented'.[25] The MusiCineTeatro offered retrospectives of past films not yet screened to the public, new European art cinema and American independent films that were likely to generate commercial interest, and an open lab delivering popular classes and courses with leading film scholars, including Francesco Casetti.[26]

Another crucial factor that shaped the independent Milanese cinema scene of the 1980s and 1990s is the popular local left-wing radio station Radio Popolare (Popular Radio). *Filmmaker*'s founders Pedote and Cavatorta worked at the radio in the late 1970s. Pedote describes the radio station as a *'catalizzatore di energie'* (energy catalyst) and explains how it became a soundboard for the cultural and cinematic initiatives and events of the city:

> The end of the 70s was a time of particular curiosity and proactivity in the small cinema world of Milan. What emerged was a great desire to work in a new and freer way, and one open to the encounter with other experiences . . . This effervescence finds its voice in Popular Radio, which collected and disseminated the best ideas that were circulating in town. . . . *Filmmaker* was born in connection to the radio . . . and was the point of confluence of all those cinematographic energies.[27]

At the radio Pedote and Cavatorta, together with Daniele Maggioni and Gianluca Fumagalli, curated film reviews and debate programmes, which focussed on experimental, low-budget, cinema engaged in social critique. Pedote recalls the popularity of buzzwords at the radio, words such as *cinema indipendente* (independent cinema) and *documentario sociale* (social documentary).[28] The film team also launched radio campaigns in support of new independent films and they collaborated with the art house cinemas Anteo and Cristallo in promoting as well as in managing their film screening programmes. It is within this setting that Pedote and Cavatorta organised the first edition of *Filmmaker* in 1980.

Milano da bere? (Milan to Drink?)

While the political engagement of 1970s forged the cultural frames and political ideas of Pedote, Cavatorta and of many of the intellectuals, artists, producers and filmmakers who were engaged in the cinematic culture of Milan at that time, during the 1980s the cultural climate of the city changed drastically and the socio-political tensions of the previous decade eased. The economic and financial crisis of the 1970s saw many factors that contributed to this shift. They include: (1) a process of partial de-industrialisation with the closure of many local factories; (2) the growth of the tertiary sector (especially banks and finance), of the luxury brand industry and of the television and advertising industry; and (3) the emergence of the signs of a postindustrial society. One of the effects of the emergence of the new political, cultural and financial landscape, was the freeing of creative and experimental tendencies that had somehow been constrained by the orthodox ideology of the 1970s.

The shifting cultural framework of the city is reflected in the public relations campaign driven by the Socialist Party and its Milanese Mayor Ugo Tognoli (1976–86), who aimed at promoting a positive image of the city. During the 1980s and the *Craxismo* – Italian Socialist Party leader Bettino Craxi's liberal-socialist ideas – Milan was chosen as the epicentre of the new political power and became associated with an image of prosperity, yuppies, beauty, style and fashion. The idea of promoting Milan as a *città vetrina* (shop-window city) projecting a cosmopolitan, trendy, upbeat and glamorous image is mirrored in the famous advert made by the liqueur Amaro Ramazzotti's advertising campaign, '*Milano da bere*' ('*Milan to drink*').

These radical changes also affected the Milanese production and consumption of cinema. As explained by Pavesi: 'This complex social, cultural, and economic landscape of transition triggers the "open" crisis of cinema, and the data . . . also confirm a crisis for the cinema exhibitors within the city'.[29] One indicator of such crisis is the number of filmgoers in Milan. The number went from 20,998 million in 1976 to 11,311 million in 1980.[30]

To counter the diminished interest of the public in watching films at cinema theatres, and in line with the ongoing campaign aimed at promoting a confident image of the city, the local authorities (both the City of Milan and the Province of Lombardia) offered a prolific string of cinematic and cultural initiatives at low cost. These led to what Pavesi describes as a *surplus culturale* (cultural surplus) with an excess of, and with repetitive, offers.[31] Amongst these initiatives we remember the following: (1) *Le vie del cinema*

(*The Ways of Cinema*) – created in 1980 with a different title as a window for 10 films presented at Mostra del Cinema di Venezia – quickly became a very popular event and brought to the city almost a hundred films; (2) retrospectives of films in the original language, and an increased number of cinemas offering quality films – including the cinemas De Amicis, Arcobaleno, Centrale, Angelicum, Paris, e Dal Verme; and (3) special summer programmes such as Arianateo organised by the Cinema Anteo.

It must be noted, however, that even if the departure from the previous decade's idea of Milan as a sort of moral capital succeeded in setting new forms of social interactions and new aspirations in some city circles, it did not eradicate the strong sense of social commitment of many Milanese intellectuals and filmmakers. We argue that to some extent the many tensions amid different cultural and political realities of the city – the new Left of the Socialist Party, the rise of the new Right, which brought together the party La Lega (The North League) and Silvio Berlusconi, the advertising industry, the television industry and so forth – helped intellectuals, artists, filmmakers and producers, who felt that they did not fit in the emerging social and ideological categories, to gather together and to create an alternative common platform, such as *Filmmaker*.

Filmmaker Festival of Film and Video

It is in the complex and contradictory Milanese landscape across the 1970s and 1980s that *Filmmaker* began its journey. It was founded by Silvano Cavatorta and Gianfilippo Pedote to 'support research, experimentation, innovation in Italian audiovisual production',[32] and during the 1980s and 1990s *Filmmaker* led the Milanese independent cinema scene by bringing together the city's filmmakers and producers who were operating outside the commercial circles. It certainly was not an easy task. Armed with an ideology of social commitment and with political ideas that were increasingly seen as uncomfortable and outdated by a society in rapid transformation, the filmmakers, producers and scholars who associated with *Filmmaker* tried to promote a cinematic culture that in terms of themes and production modes did not fit in with the mainstream industry and culture.

In a recent interview with us, Gianfilippo Pedote emphasised the political dimension of the city in the 1970s, and recognised in the '*impronta generazionale*' (generational footprint) of the young adults of the 1970s – such as himself – the matrix of *Filmmaker*'s identity and mission: '*Filmmaker* reflects the political commitment of the 1970s, as there was a desire not only for political reflection but also to intervene and drive social changes'.[33]

The very history of *Filmmaker* gives a sense of the collective's rapid success and growth.[34] As mentioned earlier, in 1980 at the Cinema Cristallo, Pedote and Cavatorta organised the first edition of Filmmaker Festival of Film and Video, for which they received a small grant from the Provincia di Milano (Province of Milan). They named the festival after Jonas Mekas' New American cinema and *Filmmaker*'s cooperative – who is considered the godfather of American avant-garde cinema.

At the first edition of the film festival, *Filmmaker* did not have a director; it was *autogestita* (self-managed) and it was modelled on the idea of the 1970s' collectives. It was the brainchild of a network of people who gravitated around Radio Popolare, and who were passionate about innovative ways to conceive cinema. This first event was the product of the strong, personal and generational, bond amongst the coordinators and the filmmakers represented. Pedote recalls that the programme was organised 'on trust, without having previewed the films'.[35] It showcased a very small number of films, by artists such as Bruno Bigoni, Mario Canali, Giancarlo Soldi and work from the collective Studio Azzurro represented by Paolo Rosa, and it was a success. Many films in the programme engaged with the 'end of an era' (the 1970s) theme and the conflicts and struggles of a generation in crisis and were experimental in their use of the cinematic apparatus and language. As Pedote highlights, the first edition of the festival was organised more with the intent to promote a new idea of cinema than to showcase films.[36] As a result, in the interim between the first and second edition of *Filmmaker*, Pedote and Cavatorta created Studio Equatore, a production company intended to create a platform for the production of films. From this moment onwards Pedote took up the role of Executive Producer of Studio Equatore, while Cavatorta focussed on the curation of the festival. Pedote explains that Cavatorta for over thirty years has relentlessly continued to act as the spiritual guide of *Filmmaker* until 2011, when he passed away.[37]

The second edition, in 1982, was organised by Studio Equatore, and Pedote and Cavatorta officially became the Artistic Directors of the festival, thus changing the collaborative paradigm of the previous event. This edition showcased a very high volume of heterogeneous films from Italy and from abroad, including commercial films, videos, non-professional and professional independent films, documentaries, and the like.

It is with the third edition in 1984 that *Filmmaker* introduced a prize system. Through Studio Equatore and with investments received from Provincia di Milano, AGIS of RAI and the Swiss Radio Television Company, the move resulted in the production of ten films. They include the work of Studio Azzurro, Silvio Soldini, Bruno Bigoni, Tonino Curagi and Kiko Stella. The Centre Pompidou in Paris validated the success of this event by showcasing the films produced by *Filmmaker*. With this edition *Filmmaker* not only took on its characteristic role of producing films – rather than solely showcasing them – but also introduced another feature that will define its mandate: educating a new generation of filmmakers through the added means of workshops and debates led by key players of the independent American cinema and European art film scene. Examples of low-budgets 16mm films produced include: *Giulia in ottobre* (*Giulia in October*, Silvio Soldini, 1984 – 19 milion Lire/8 thousand Euros); *Rosso di sera* (*Red Evening*, Kiko Stella, 1984 – 25 million Lire/17.5 thousand Euros); *Osservatorio nucleare del Signor Nanof* (*Mr. Nanof's Lunar Observatory*, Paolo Rosa, 1985 – 50 million Lire/25 thousand Euros). With the fourth edition, in 1988, the investment for the production prize grew to 50 million Lire – which in post-Lira times is equivalent to roughly 25 thousand Euros – for films developed from original scripts by contemporary writers.

When the fifth edition was held in 1991, the production efforts were extended to nineteen projects. Between 1994 and 1997, however, *Filmmaker* did not produce any films. This was mainly due to Pedote's departure, the driving force of the production enterprise linked to the festival, who had in 1993 joined the creative hub Fabrica of Benetton, with film director Goffrey Reggio. Without Pedote, *Filmmaker* was no longer be managed by Studio Equatore, and become an independent cultural association, directed by Cavatorta alone.

The 1995 edition included a full retrospective on the essay-film, which marked the festival's increasing interest in the documentary genre, and which resulting in workshops and master classes with world-leading documentarians. The festival continued its efforts to promote Milanese and Italian cinema abroad. Amongst such initiative we note a collaboration with the Locarno Film Festival in 1995 on a retrospective of Italian short films. When in 1997 *Filmmaker* fully resumed its production activities, some of the films gained national and international acclaim. Such works include: *Fame chimica 1* (*Chemical Hunger 1*, a short film by Paolo Vari and Antonio Bocola, produced in collaboration with Centro Sociale Giambellino, 1997) and *Dolce stil novo* (*Dolce Stil Novo*, Giovanni Maderna, 1998).

It is important to note that the initial success of *Filmmaker* was partly due to the fact that within the social fabric of the city resided the type of audience which the films produced by *Filmmaker* attracted. Such an audience was comprised chiefly of the numerous creative minds and the intelligentsia of Milan, and in turn its shared culture, age and background, with the young film directors that *Filmmaker* showcased. Pedote recalls:

> With the massive participation in what actually might have seemed just a small festival for short films, this public, so curious and involved, seemed to declare its desire to be able to recognize and mirror themselves in the films – something that was not easy to do at the time with Italian cinema, which was culturally backward by one generation compared to them. . . . It was an audience made up of people who were experiencing some of the profound social and cultural transformations of the city.[38]

As a result of the buzz and confidence – created by *Filmmaker* – for the marketability, though limited, of independent films, since the 1980s a number of small production companies were created in Milan. These include: (1) Bilico (thereafter Monogatari), by Silvio Soldini, Daniele Maggioni and Luca Bigazzi; (2) Electric Film, by Kiko Stella and Bruno Bigoni; (3) Metamorphosi, by Marco and Andrea Poma; and (4) Bambú Cinematografica, by Maurizio Nichetti and Ernesto di Sarro. This positive climate also led to the creation of the distribution company Indigena, directed by Minnie Ferrara and Bruno Bigoni, to guarantee the promotion and distribution of the films outside the festival. Many of these companies, often founded by film directors to aid the production of their own work, covered a range of productions, including art video, industrial film, documentaries, film genres and styles, installations and low-budget feature films. Video art and art installations became a trademark of the Milanese creative scenes in 1980s and 1990s. In many ways, Studio Azzurro led the way and played a prominent role in influencing the cinematic language of the independent films produced in those years through *Filmmaker*.

As has been attested above, over time *Filmmaker* established itself as a multidimensional enterprise, which challenged the mainstream Italian film industry on many fronts. Firstly, the festival promoted cinematic experimentalism by showcasing an eclectic array of formats and genres, including: (1) the feature film – mainly in 16mm but also in video; (2) the short film – including fiction, video art installations, animation films, industrial films, computer graphic and theatre installations; (3) and, since 1995, documentary. Secondly, as a production enterprise, it provided a consistent, although limited, pool of funding, creatively generated through the support of various sources. These include: (1) the local authorities, such as Comune and Provincia di Milano (City and Province of Milan) and Regione Lombardia (Lombardy Region); (2) the local industry – including advertising – and, in the new millennium, the local bank Cariplo;[39] and (3) some support from the Roman film industry. It also stimulated a surge in production companies in the city and, via Studio Equatore, it produced low-budget films of international appeal – including works by Studio Azzurro, Silvio Soldini, Alina Marazzi, Michelangelo Frammartino, Marco Bechis and others. Thirdly, as a professional training hub *Filmmaker* succeeded in educating a new generation of filmmakers, via the delivery of cutting-edge professional training by world-renowned independent American and European filmmakers – among whom were Giuseppe Bertolucci, Jon Alpert, Wim Wenders, Vittorio De Seta, Errol Morris and others. And fourthly, it established a promotion and distribution system which validated *Filmmaker*'s success at both the local and international levels – locally via the promotion of Radio Popolare and the distribution in the Cinema Anteo, as well as in other Milanese art cinemas, and internationally via linking with cultural institutions such as the Centre Pompidou and the Cinémathèque in Paris, the Locarno Film Festival and the Berlin Film Festival.

For a short period of time *Filmmaker* created an autonomous industry, which in many ways reproduces – in a different technological context – ICET's efforts in the 1950s and 1960s to create an alternative pole to the Roman monopoly for the production, distribution and showcasing of films. As such *Filmmaker* embodies the city's cinematic and cultural breeding-ground developed over decades: (1) its 'in-betweeness' amid the national film industry based in Rome and the television and advertising cultures of Milan – something which had already emerged in the 1950s and 1960s with the growth and epilogues of ICET and 22 Dicembre; (2) the intent to develop low-budget films for up-and-coming film directors as well as the pedagogic goal of nurturing innovative approaches to cinema – which years earlier drove the short-lived adventure of Olmi's 22 Dicembre; (3) the passionate interest in new technologies, especially with the advent of video – which stems from the experimental projects of the Militant Cinema Collective; and (4) the fruitful osmotic exchanges with sectors of the theatre and the advertising industry, allowing the expertise of skilled operators from other creative fields to enrich film productions with their competencies and professionalism – which recalls the rather eclectic mix of artists, industry people and intellectuals that since the 1930s have gravitated around the Milanese circles of cinema. As De Berti suggests:

> The cultural environment and the city's art life are the fertile soil in which the different expressive needs mature. In the absence of 'institutional' production centres in which the stages that lead to the completion of the film are already set

and somehow encoded, the Milanese directors must, from time to time, invent productive paths, learning the-art-of-getting-by; but since the making of a film is part of a team work, as there were no official pre-formations to draw from, the aggregation is informal, even unpredictable, and it inevitably creates a closer relationship with the city, within the cultural circle, within the critical and militant experience, within the theatre and television activity: the city turns into a breeding ground for incentives, initiatives, fruitful exchanges. It is here, it seems, that the film directors are rooted in the fabric of the Milanese city.[40]

However, by the end of the 1990s the Milanese administration started losing interest in the cinema projects and, overall, public investments by local authorities in the arts began to decrease. Pedote recalls that, as one of the main reasons for the weakening of *Filmmaker* in the 1990s the fact that 'everyone was forced to fend for themselves and strive for survival'.[41] Notably, as we have mentioned, between 1994 and 1997 *Filmmaker* did not produce any films. As a consequence, the network of production companies, that emerged and collaborated together during the 1980s, failed to act as a united front in the following decade, and soon a competitive environment emerged. While the success of *Filmmaker* resided in the ability of a group of people from different fields and with different skills to collaborate with each other and create an environment in which innovative production modes and cinematic language emerged, the limited collaborative efforts of the 1990s redirected *Filmmaker* towards new frontiers.

With the emergence of the new generation of filmmakers – among them, Paolo Vari and Antonio Bocola, Alina Marazzi, Michelangelo Frammartino, Anna Negri, to mention only a few – *Filmmaker*'s collective framework built on the osmosis between organisers, producers and filmmakers, with similar experiences, expectations and aspirations, started to shrink. Pedote evokes with some nostalgia *Filmmaker*'s strong sense of identity and of belonging of the 1980s.[42] The generational gap introduced new dynamics: as the organisers had gotten older the younger members now related to *Filmmaker* as a training and support centre, where interpersonal relations were driven by formative experiences rather than by collaborative projects. Furthermore, in conjunction with this generation of filmmakers, new themes were introduced and the formal strategies of their filmmaking approaches became more conventional. At the same time, the new generation of filmmakers broadened the festival's interest by venturing into new areas, such as art installations, and by developing a greater passion for the documentary genre – the programmes of which included retrospectives and workshops on/by Frederick Wiseman in 2000 and Errol Morris in 2001. The generational gap grew even further in the new millennium. This is exemplified by the introduction of a new funding system, with selected projects undergoing a mentoring system delivered by older generations of experts, and which led to the selection of a few projects to be developed into films, and the establishment of a prize for best film. This practice, which is well established in many international film festivals, marks a philosophical shift from the collaborative paradigm, typical of the first editions of *Filmmaker*, to a hierarchical model characterised by a sort of master-and-pupil dynamics.

Moreover, other factors contributed to substantial differences between the first editions of *Filmmaker* during the 1980s and those of the following decades. Firstly, we mention the new digital technologies, which partly changed the production modes. Though *Filmmaker* was involved with video technologies since its first edition, the advent of high definition video and digital formats engendered a different technological landscape. Secondly, many seminal Cineclubs, which forged the cinematic culture of Milan in the 1970s and 1980s, closed down due to the advent of VHS home videos; this included the influential Obraz Cinestudio. In response to this, the new generation of Milanese film lovers, in addition to the short-lived (1989–91) Circolo Creativo ISU (Creative Circle ISU) in Porta Romana, which among other novelties offered workshops by film critic Morando Morandini, founded the Associazione Pandora in 1995. Many of the remaining Cineclubs turned into Film Festivals, given that the local authorities only injected funding into festivals – a trend still found in today's Milanese cinema landscape. Moreover, during the 1990s some of the historical Milanese schools which trained many film directors associated with *Filmmaker*, started to lose their kudos. These included the Scuola Civica of Milan, and I.T.S.O.S., Istituto Tecnico Statale a Ordinamento Speciale (State Technical Institute with Special Orientation) of via Pace in Milan. The latter was particularly affected by the departure in 1997 of one of the school's founders, Nuccio Ambrosino, and by its relocation, from the city centre to the suburbs. Academia di Brera, however, retained its leading role within the field.

Closing Comments

This analysis suggests that *Filmmaker* nurtured a cinematic culture that on many levels aligns itself with that of global art cinema and the transnational New Waves.[43] As Pedote has pointed out, art and experimental films from around the globe – including American director John Cassavetes, the New American cinema, the *Nouvelle Vague*, the New German cinema, which emerged from the Oberhausen manifesto – were great sources of inspiration for the *Filmmaker* circle.[44] For instance, *Filmmaker*'s cinematic modus operandi, which contrasts drastically with the high level of division of labour and specialisation common to the mainstream national cinema industry, echoes the production modes of art cinema. The development of low-budget films by young up-and-coming film directors, the nurturing of innovative modes of production, the passionate interest in new technologies, and the promotion of the idea of the artist/director in control of all stages of the production process are also considered as defining traits of art cinema.

Moreover, some of the themes that recur in films produced by *Filmmaker* echo core concerns which film historians have identified in the transnational New Waves of the past half century.[45] These include: (1) the investigation of societies on the cusp of fast economic, cultural and technological changes; (2) the attention to the youth's adaptation to these changes; (3) the focus on the youth and young adults as agents of social and cultural transformation; and (4) the use of urban landscape as a prototype for the re-conceptualisation of society. Naturally, alongside thematic patterns, *Filmmaker*'s cinematic framework is also connected to that of the New Waves by virtue of its investment in aesthetic dynamism and technological experimentation as well as the international circulation of their films via art house cinemas and at international film festivals.

However, compared to the established New Waves that flourished globally in the past half century, *Filmmaker* did not develop a strong identity as a movement and failed to establish a long-lasting presence in the industry as far as its viability as a commercial venture was concerned. Reflecting a posteriori, Pedote openly expressed his frustrations at *Filmmaker's* partial failures:

> We should ask ourselves why the relationship between Milan and the cinema cannot evolve beyond a string of fragmented experiences, sometimes very interesting, at others even innovative and big, but nonetheless incapable of settling and of forming a base on which continuity can ensue, constructively. Surely, the Milanese initiative did not develop as an industry (given that the centralised position it assumed in Rome, apparently sufficed) and yet, neither as an instrumental experience through which the city could 'reveal' itself, and its way of life in our times.[46]

Filmmaker's inability to develop into a self-sufficient industry can be explained by the historically fragmentary nature of the Milanese independent cinema scene, which, as we have mentioned, manifested itself well before the adventure of *Filmmaker*. As a result, the city has traditionally played an important role in launching the career of several film directors who began by making films in Milan, but subsequently continued directing and producing films in Rome, or even abroad. These include Antonioni, Lattuada, Olmi, Comencini, Risi, Salvatores and Soldini.

The Milanese independent cinema, and *Filmmaker*, testify to how the crisis of cinema can sit paradoxically 'out' of cinema.[47] Some concomitant factors contributed to both the success and failures of the city's independent cinema: (1) the city's internal political and cultural polarisations; (2) the prominent presence of an eclectic creative industry; (3) the absence of institutional production facilities; and (4) the reliance on a fluctuating level of local funding – including the local authorities, the local industry and local banks.

Nonetheless, it must be noted that an important achievement of Pedote and Cavatorta, and of the group of filmmakers and producers that contributed to *Filmmaker*, is their ability to have repurposed and reinvented over the years – though perhaps without being conscious of it – the concept of political *impegno* (engagement) from which the initiative originated in the first place. As has been mentioned, this *impegno* initially informed *Filmmaker* via: (1) the idea of the collective and of the collaborative (rather than hierarchical) framework; (2) the social critique embedded in the films produced; and (3) the democratic forms of production modes. Nonetheless, during the 1990s the *impegno* of the past morphed into new frameworks and meanings – no longer directly derived from a Marxist ideology, which by then was rather old-fashioned – and was able to take on forms which were meaningful to the emerging generations. Pedote admits how, along with Cavatorta, he struggled at that time to understand the socio-cultural-political shifts that were taking place.[48] However, the fact that *Filmmaker* has continued to sustain itself over the years as a viable cultural reference and platform for filmmakers at the margin of Italian cinema's institutional pathways, testifies to its ability to reconfigure itself into new forms of commitment through time, without losing its grip on experimentalism and social critique. The essence of this metamorphic commitment resides, according to Pedote, in Cavatorta's leadership and in an internal 'tension oriented towards that which is new, towards research, and towards that which could undo conventional practices, and moreover in an interest and a rare ability to identify and develop the talent of young people'.[49] The significant success the festival had with the public over the years constitutes one important proof of this.

The peripheral place traditionally occupied by the Milanese cinema (both in terms of volume and scale of production as well as in the geographical sense) has nevertheless been anything but negligible within the landscape of Italian cinema. If, as Pedote points out, *Filmmaker* has failed in its ambition to change and reinvent the national film industry,[50] the quality of the films that it produced have succeeded in renewing the interest in Italian cinema both at the national and international levels. Within Italy, *Filmmaker* challenged mainstream Italian cinema and some of its formulaic clichés by providing an alternative model with the ability to address audiences with unconventional stories and aesthetics. Meanwhile, at the international level it renewed interest in Italian cinema worldwide producing the work of filmmakers such as Salvatores, Soldini and Frammartino, among several others.

Notes

1. Brunetta (1982), p. 44.
2. Anderi (1996), pp. 191–201.
3. See Braidotti (1994).
4. See De Berti (1996), pp. 262–4.
5. Ibid., p. 264.
6. On 'cinepanettone', see O'Leary (2013). Films produced by Reteitalia/Silvio Berlusconi Communication/Mediaset/Medusa during the 1980s and 1990s include: *Signori e signore* (*Ladies and Gentlemen*, Tonino Pulci 1984), *Via Montenapoleone* (Carlo Vanzina 1986), *Il camorrista* (*The Professor*, Giuseppe Tornatore 1986), *Rimini Rimini* (Sergio Corbucci 1987), *Soldati – 365 all'alba* (*Soldiers – 365 at Dawn*, Marco Risi 1987), *Caramelle da uno sconosciuto* (*Candies from a Stranger*, Franco Ferrini 1987), *I miei primi quarant'anni* (*My First Forty Years*, Carlo Vanzina 1987), *Angel Hill – L'ultima missione* (*Last Platoon*, Ignazio Dolce 1988), *La cintura* (*The Belt*, Giuliana Gamba 1989), *La maschera del demonio* (*Black Sunday*, Mario Bava 1989), *Il sole buio* (*The Dark Sun*, Damiano Damiani 1990), *Le comiche* (*Slapstick*, Neri Parenti 1990), *Stanno tutti bene* (*Everybody's Fine*, Giuseppe Tornatore 1990), *Johnny Stecchino* (Roberto Benigni 1991), *Mediterraneo* (Gabriele Salvatores 1991), *Volere volare* (*To Want to Fly*, Maurizio Nichetti 1991), *Caldo soffocante* (*Suffocating Heat*, Giovanna Gagliardo 1991), *Cin Cin* (*A Fine Romance*, Gene Saks 1991), *Hornsby e Rodriguez – Sfida Criminale* (*Mean Tricks*, Umberto Lenzi 1992), *Infelici e contenti* (*Unhappy and Content*, Neri Parenti 1992), *Dellamorte dellamore* (*Cemetery Man*, Michele Soavi 1993), *Il silenzio dei prosciutti* (*The Silence of the Hams*, Ezio Greggio 1994), *Facciamo paradiso* (Looking for Paradise, Mario Monicelli 1995).
7. See De Berti (1996), pp. 269–73. Independent films produced in Milan during the 1980s and 1990s include: Maurizio Nichetti's *Ratataplan* (1979), *Ho fatto splash* (*I Made a Splash*, 1980), *Domani si balla!* (*Tomorrow We Dance*, 1982), *Ladri di saponette* (*The Icicle Thief*, 1989), *Volere volare* (*To Want to Fly*, 1990) and *Stefano quantestorie* (*Stefano Manystories*, 1993), all of which gained national acclaim. Gabriele Salvatores, co-founder of the Teatro dell'Elfo, directed *Sogno di una notte d'estate* (*A Summer's Night Dream*, 1983) and later on with Colorado Film *Kamikaze, ultima notte a Milano* (*Kamikaze: Last Night in Milan*,

1988), *Marrakesh Express* (1989), *Mediterraneo* (1991) – which earned an Academy Award for Best Foreign Film – *Puerto Escondido* (1992), and *Sud* (1993). Amongst Silvio Soldini's films, we remember *Giulia in Ottobre* (*Giulia in October*, 1985), *L'aria serena dell'Ovest* (*The Peaceful Air of the West*, 1990), *Un'anima divisa in due* (*A Soul Divided in Two*, 1993) and the episode *D'estate* (*In Summer*) for the multi-direct – which included Mario Martone and Paolo Rosa – film *Miracoli, Storie per corti* (*Miracles: Stories for Shorts*, 1994). Paolo Rosa with Studio Azzurro directed *Osservatorio nucleare del Signor Nanof* (*Mr. Nanof's Nuclear Observatory*, 1985), *La variabile Felsen* (*The Felsen Variable*, 1988), *Dov'è Yankel?* (*Where's Yankel?*) for *Miracoli, Storie per corti* (*Miracles: Stories for Shorts*, 1994), and *Il mnemonista* (*The Mnemonist*, 2000), and Armando Bertacchi and Fabio Cirifino directed *Facce di Festa* (*Merry Faces*, 1980).
8. Olmi's relationship with the industry dates back to the early 1950s and his work with the industrial film at the Sezione Cinema Edisonvolta (Cinema Section Edisonvolta) till the end of the 1950s; see Boledi and Mosconi (1996), pp. 299–301.
9. My translation. Original quote: '*non* il cinema *commerciale*, come normalmente inteso, bensì del cinema che in qualche modo si accostasse, senza pregiudiziali commerciali, alle problematiche del nostro tempo'. Olmi in De Berti (1996), p. 265, emphasis in the original.
10. My translation. Original quote: 'la meta di tutti gli intellettuali milanesi interessati al cinema'. Janni in De Berti (1996), p. 266, emphasis in the original
11. On the Milanese industrial film see Boledi and Mosconi (1996), pp. 295–311.
12. See Schoenberg (2016).
13. Ibid.
14. Ibid.
15. Ibid.
16. The literature on Studio Azzurro is copious and is published in many languages. For a brief overview of their work, see the bilingual volume by Di Marino (2010).
17. Interview by the authors; Cirifino and Sangiorgi (2016).
18. My translation. Original quote: 'il video sia un elemento spugnoso, che risucchia tutto e ciò che esce non sia più ciò che ha assorbito. Il cinema assorbito dal video restituiva qualcosa di diverso dal medium iniziale, in un movimento metamorfico'. Cirifino e Sangiorgi (2016).
19. Cirifino and Sangiorgi (2016).
20. My translation. Original quote: 'La logica dell'*engagement* . . . parte dalla certezza che la propria coscienza politico-letteraria del presente è il principio da cui dedurre *un solo modo* storicamente corretto di risolvere il proprio rapporto fra realtà sociale, imperativi politici, forme letterarie'. Berardinelli (2007), p. 66, emphasis in the original.
21. Burns (2001), p. 1.
22. Antonello and Mussgnung (2009), p. 3, our emphasis.

23. Young activism continued to develop during the 1980s. On this see De Sario (2012), pp. 117–38.
24. De Berti (1996), p. 267.
25. My translation. Original quote: 'un polo alternativo nel modo di presentare il cinema'. Pavesi (1996), p. 345.
26. On cinema Anteo, see AA. VV. (2004).
27. My translation. Original quote: 'La fine degli anni '70 fu un momento di particolare curiosità e propositività per il piccolo mondo del cinema a Milano che si traduceva in un grande desiderio di lavorare in modo nuovo, più libero, aperto al confronto con altre esperienze . . . Questa effervescenza trova la sua voce in Radio Popolare, che riusciva a raccogliere e diffondere le idee migliori che circolavano in città. . . . *Filmmaker* nacque intorno alla radio . . . e fu il punto di confluenza di tutte quelle energie "cinematografiche"'. Pedote (2016).
28. Ibid.
29. My translation. Original quote: 'Questo complesso panorama sociale, culturale, ed economico di transizione innesca quindi la crisi "manifesta" del cinema e i dati [. . .] trovano conferma anche nella crisi cinematografica dell'esercizio cittadino'. Pavesi (1996), p. 334.
30. Ibid.
31. Pavesi (1996), p. 348.
32. My translation. Original quote: 'sostenere la ricerca, la sperimentazione, l'innovazione nella produzione audiovisiva italiana'. Pedote (1998).
33. My translation. Original quote: 'Filmmaker rifletta l'impegno politico degli anni Settanta, poiché c'era un desiderio non solo di riflessione politica ma anche d'intervento sul sociale'. Pedote (2016).
34. For *Filmmaker* and the Milanese independent film see also Pasciulli (1998), Bertozzi (2003), Bertozzi (2008), Palazzini and Raimondi (2009).
35. My translation. Original quote: 'sulla fiducia, senza aver neanche visto i film'. Pedote (2016).
36. Ibid.
37. Ibid.
38. My translation. Original quote: 'Con la partecipazione massiccia a quello che in realtà poteva apparire solo un piccolo festival per piccoli film, questo pubblico così curioso e coinvolto sembrava voler dichiarare il suo desiderio di potersi riconoscere e rispecchiare nel cinema, cosa che allora non era facile col cinema italiano, culturalmente indietro di una generazione rispetto a loro. . . . Era un pubblico fatto di persone che stavano vivendo alcune profonde trasformazioni sociali e culturali della città'. Pedote (1998).
39. Since 2012, Cariplo has continued to sponsor Filmmaker and since 2013 the Milan Film Network, an association of seven Milanese film festivals. However, amongst these the only local festival that has consistently invested in a production unit is *Filmmaker*, whilst the Milan Film Festival has only sporadically funded its own productions.

40. My translation. Original quote: 'In questo senso l'ambiente culturale, la vita artistica cittadina costituiscono il terreno fertile in cui giungono a maturare le diverse esigenze espressive. In mancanza di strutture produttive 'istituzionali' nelle quali le tappe che portano alla realizzazione del film sono già scandite e in qualche modo codificate, per i registi milanesi occorre di volta in volta inventare dei percorsi produttivi, imparando l'arte di arrangiarsi; ma poichè l'opera filmica è anche un lavoro di squadra, laddove non esistono formazioni ufficiali alle quali attingere, l'aggregazione è informale, anche imprevedibile, e si crea inevitabilmente in un rapporto più stretto con la città, nel circolo culturale, nell'esperienza critica e militante, nell'attività teatrale e televisiva: la città è un vivaio di fermenti, di iniziative, di scambi proficui. È qui che si insinua, ci sembra, il radicamento dei registi nel tessuto milanese'. De Berti (1996), pp. 260–61.
41. My translation. Original quote: 'ognuno era costretto a pensare a sé e alla propria sopravvivenza'. Pedote (1998).
42. Pedote (2016).
43. Some global New Waves which emerged during the 1980s and 1990s include: New German Cinema – Rainer Werner Fassbinder, Werner Herzog, Wim Wenders, Margarethe Von Trotta; New Taiwanese Cinema – Edward Yang, Te-Chen Tao, I-Chen Ko, Yi Chang, Hou Hsiao-hsien; Hong Kong New Wave – John Woo, Wong Kar-wai, Ann Hui, Mabel Cheung, Alex Law; *La Movida Madrileña* (The Madrilenian Scene) – Pedro Almodóvar, Juan Antonio Bardem, Carlos Saura, Julio Médem; Taiwanese second wave – Ang Lee, Tasi Ming-liang, Stan Lai, Wei Te-sheng; *Nuevo Cine Mexicano* (New Mexican Cinema) – Alfonso Cuarón, Alejandro G. Iñárritu'; Korean New Wave – Park Kwang-su, Jang Sun-woo, Chung Ji-young, Lee Myung-se; Danish 'Dogme95' – Lars Von Trier and Thomas Vinterberg.
44. Pedote (1998) and (2016).
45. Tweedie (2013).
46. My translation. Original quote: 'C'è da chiedersi perché tra Milano ed il cinema le cose non riescano ad andare al di là di un susseguirsi frammentato di esperienze, a volte molto interessanti, a volte addirittura innovative e grandi, eppure incapaci di sedimentarsi e di formare una base su cui costruire con continuità. Milano sembra non aver mai veramente creduto nel cinema. Certamente non come industria (da quando si è concentrata lì, Roma bastava) ma neanche come strumento attarverso il quale "rivelare" se stessa e i suoi modi di vivere il nostro tempo'. Pedote (1998).
47. Pavesi (1996), p. 332.
48. Pedote (2016).
49. My translation. Original quote: 'una incredibile vivacità intellettuale, una tensione per il nuovo, per la ricerca, per quello che poteva rompere gli schemi convenzionali, e poi un'attenzione e una capacità rara di individuare e valorizzare il talento dei giovani'. Pedote (2016).
50. Ibid.

Works Cited

AA. VV. (2004), *Anteo 1979–2004: Venticinque anni di cinema a Milano*, Milan: Feltrinelli.
Anderi, Giuseppe (1996), 'Il cinema fra le due arti nella Milano degli anni Trenta', in Raffaele De Berti ed., *Un secolo di cinema a Milano*, Milan: Il Castoro, pp. 191–213.
Antonello, Pierpaolo, and Florian Mussgnug eds. (2009), *Postmodern 'Impegno': Ethics and Commitment in Contemporary Italian Culture*, Oxford: Peter Lang.
Berardinelli, Alfonso (2007), *Casi critici: Dal Postmodernismo alla mutazione*, Rome: Quodlibet.
Bertozzi, Marco (2003), *L'idea documentaria*, Turin: Lindau.
Bertozzi, Marco (2008), *Storia del documentario italiano*, Venice: Marsilio.
Boledi, Luigi, and Elena Mosconi (1996), 'Il film industriale', in Raffaele De Berti ed., *Un secolo di cinema a Milano*, Milan: Il Castoro, pp. 295–311.
Braidotti, Rosi (1994), *Soggetto Nomade. Femminismo e crisi della modernità*, Rome: Donzelli.
Brunetta, Gian Piero (1982), *Storia del Cinema Italiano 1945–1980*, Rome: Editori Riuniti.
Burns, Jennifer (2001), *Fragments of Impegno: Interpretations of Commitment in Contemporary Italian narrative, 1980–2000*, Leeds: Northern University Press.
Cirifino, Fabio, and Leonardo Sangiorgi (2016), Interview by Donatella Maraschin and Paola Nasini, 4 December.
De Berti, Raffaele (1996), 'Da cinelandia a "tivulandia": la produzione cinematografica dal 1945 a oggi', in Raffaele De Berti ed., *Un secolo di cinema a Milano*, Milan: Il Castoro, pp. 259–73.
De Sario, Beppe (2012), 'Cambiamento sociale e attivismo giovanile nell'italia degli anni Ottanta: il caso dei centri sociali occupati e autogestiti', in *Cahiers d'études italiennes*, 14: 117–38, <http://cei.revues.org/416>, last accessed 5 January 2017.
Di Marino, Bruno ed. (2010), *Tracce, sguardi e altri pensieri*, Milan: Feltrinelli.
Filmmaker Festival of Film and Video's website, <http://www.Filmmakerfest.com/>, last accessed 2 January 2017.
O'Leary, Alan (2013), *Fenomenologia del cinepanettone*, Soveria Mannelli: Rubbettino.
Palazzini, Marco, and Mauro Raimondi (2009), *Milano films 1896/2009*, Genoa: Fratelli Frilli Editore.
Pasciulli, Ettore (1998), *Milano cinema prodigio. Anticiapzioni e primati in un secolo di avventure*. Venice: Canal & I Nodi.
Pavesi, Matteo (1996), 'Consumo ed esercizio cinematografico dal secondo dopoguerra ai giorni nostri', in R. De Berti ed., *Un secolo di cinema a Milano*, Milan: Il Castoro, pp. 312–59.
Pedote, Gianfilippo (1998), 'Il sogno indipendente: "Filmmaker" una nota di presentazione', in E. Pasciulli ed., *Milano cinema prodigio. Cento anni di cinema a Milano*, Venice: Canal & I Nodi.

Pedote, Gianfilippo (2016), Interview by Donatella Maraschin and Paola Nasini, 15 November.
Schoenberg, Susanna (2016), Interview by Donatella Maraschin and Paola Nasini, 15 December.
Tweedie, James (2013), *The Age of the New Waves: Art Cinema and the staging of Globalisation*, Oxford: Oxford University Press.

Filmography (List of films produced by *Filmmaker*)

1984
Ave... Maria, film, directed by B. Conti Rossini, 16mm, col., 5'
Foglie Morte (*Dead Leaves*), film, directed by F. Del Bosco, video, col., 29'
I Volti dell'Altro Luogo (*Glances from the Other Place*), film, directed by E. Inetti, video, col., 30'
Accendi la Tele (Videogag) (*Turn on the TV (Videogag)*), film, directed by M. Lombezzi, video, col., 10'
Kamera, film, directed by M. Pratesi, video, col., 18'
Polsi Sottili (*Thin Wrists*), film, directed by G. Soldi, 16mm, col., 50'
Rosso di Sera (*Red Evening*), film, directed by K. Stella, 16mm, col., 20'
L'Osservatorio Nucleare del Sig. Nanof (*The Nuclear Observatory of Mr. Nanof*), film, directed by P. Rosa, 16mm, col., 60'

1985
Le Mille Cose Infinite (*The Infinite One-Thousand-Things*), film, directed by T. Curagi e F. Ilacqua, 16mm, b/n, 65'
Rifiuti (*Rubbish*), film, directed by S. Francalanci, video, col., 30'
Giulia in Ottobre (*Giulia in October*), film, directed by S. Soldini, 16mm, col., 60'

1988
La Metamorfosi (*The Metamorphosis*), film, directed by L. Mugnai, 16mm, col., 29'
My Sweet Camera, film, directed by R. Sodi, 16mm, col., 30'
La Variabile Felsen (*The Felsen Variable*), film, directed by P. Rosa, 16mm, col., 30'
Viva gli Sposi (*Hurray to the Newly Wed*), film, directed by G. Del Re, Super 16mm, b/n

1991
L'America me la immaginavo (*I Dreamed of America*), film, directed by A. Marazzi, 16mm, col., 22'
La Confessione di un Maniaco (*The Confession of a Maniac*), film, directed by G. Fumagalli
Nothing Compares to You, film, directed by G. P. Rizzo, video, col., 17'
Il Congedo del Viaggiatore Cerimonioso (*The Farewell of the Ceremonious Traveler*), film, directed by G. Bertolucci, video, col., 35'

1994
Siamo Tutti Innamorati (*We Are All in Love*), film, directed by M. Spada

1997
La Casa delle Belle Addormentate (*The House of the Sleeping Beauties*), installazione, curated by M. Frammartino, video, col
Girotondo (*Ring a Ring o' Roses*), film, directed by M. Pellegrini, 16mm, col., 14'
Fame Chimica 1 (*Chemical Hunger 1*), film, directed by P. Vari e A. Bocola, video, col., 60'

1998
Il Dolce Stil Novo (*The Sweet New Style*), film, directed by G. Maderna

1999
Pompeo (*Pompeo*), film, directed by P. Vari e A. Bocola, video, col., 31'
Vietato Scappare (*Running Away is Forbidden*), film, directed by G. Carella, video, col., 45'
Garage Olimpo (*Olympus Garage*), film, directed by M. Bechis, 16mm, col., 98'

2000
Isban (*Isban*), film, directed by G. Carella, video, col., 47'
Orario d'Apertura (*Opening Hours*), film, directed by C. Tassin, video, col., 30'

CHAPTER 2

Light and Liminal: Marinella Pirelli's Cinema
Matilde Nardelli

Introducing Pirelli's Cinema

We are looking at a photograph of a three-dimensional structure (Figure 2.1). It is not quite a cube; geometrically, it would be defined as a rectangular cuboid, since its height is obviously shorter than its other two dimensions. It sits within an enclosed built space of which the walls are visible. The presence of a human figure makes it relatively easy to gauge a sense of the structure's scale. Its dimensions suggest something *between* an object – a sculptural object, perhaps, like the cubes of 1960s minimal art – and architecture. As an object, even as a sculptural cuboid of Minimalist inspiration, it is relatively large. However, as an architectural structure, even though its height would be able to accommodate comfortably the person who seems to be stepping inside it, it is fairly modest, nested within the larger enclosed space that hosts it. It is solid, material; yet it also has an ethereal and evanescent quality to it. Indeed, what is perhaps most striking is the fact that the structure appears, one wants to say, to be filled with light. So much so that light spills out from it onto the surrounding walls and bathes the body of the onlooker, making his clothes appear as if dyed by the work's coloured light. If the structure seems to be *between* – or, perhaps, both – sculpture and architecture, other kinds of in-betweenness come to one's lips in the attempt to describe it. Focussing on the light and the human silhouette visible inside it (an actual person, a cut-out or a shadow?), the structure appears somewhat between cinema and theatre; or perhaps, again, as a bit of both. Is the illuminated cuboid a stage within the larger architecture, or a giant unruly projector – throwing patterns of coloured light all around the space?

Film ambiente (*Environmental Screen*, 1969) is one of the most complex and richest intermedial achievements of the Italian artist-filmmaker Marinella Pirelli (1925–2009), whose practice is characterised by a pursuit of cinema which, as we will see, seeks to exceed and transcend the traditional

Figure 2.1 from *Film ambiente* (1969) installation of 2013.

experience of cinema. In the late 1960s and early 1970s, when it was first exhibited, *Film ambiente* was the main result of Pirelli's endeavour to 'free' the process of projection, to give it, as she put it, 'real freedom'.[1] If *Film ambiente* took projection beyond the two-dimensionality of the flat surface of the rectangular screen, as we shall see in more detail further on, it also took cinema beyond itself by bringing it into contact – actually mixing it – with the categories of sculpture, architecture and theatre. As such, *Film ambiente* is both representative and, as I will argue, exemplary of the radical moment of 'intermediality' and dialogue between art and cinema, which spans from the mid-1960s to the mid-1970s. The key redrawing of boundaries within and across these disciplines which took place in this period still profoundly shapes contemporary arts and culture.

Pirelli's installation was shown at various venues across Europe in the late 1960s and early 1970s. These include the important Italian show *Al di là della pittura* (*Beyond Painting*) of 1969, in which experimental filmmakers such as Gianfranco Baruchello and Luca Patella participated, but also experimental musicians including Vittorio Gelmetti (who composed the electronic music for Michelangelo Antonioni's *Il deserto rosso* (*Red Desert*, 1964), and *Prospekt 1971: Projection*, in Düsseldorf. The latter saw the participation of artist-filmmakers such as Hollis Frampton, Robert Smithson, Andy Warhol and Marcel Broodthaers, and the event contributed to establishing cinematic projection and film installation as modes of exhibition in contemporary art.[2] In this context, *Film ambiente*'s partaking of the attributes of sculpture, architecture, cinema and theatre, testifies to the generative porosity and dialogue between the arts characteristic of the cultural atmosphere of those years. As Fluxus artist Dick Higgins declared in 1966, mocking the rhetoric of separation of modernist critics such as Clement Greenberg, who advocated clear divisions between individual artistic disciplines as well as between the fine arts and mass media: 'Much of the best work being produced today seems to fall *between* media'.[3]

Ironically for a work so overtly based on light, *Film ambiente* fell into obscurity in the mid-1970s, as did Pirelli herself who, while not giving up her artistic practice, withdrew from the public eye following a family tragedy. It is only in the last decade or so that *Film ambiente* and Pirelli's practice more broadly have regained some visibility, as interest in experimental and artist cinema has been renewed and fostered by the increased accessibility to this type of work offered by digital media platforms and the 'cinematic turn' of contemporary art. A number of events in recent years, including a rare film screening at London's Institute of Contemporary Arts (ICA) in 2015 and a full retrospective with a re-installation of *Film ambiente* in Milan's Museo del Novecento (Museum of Twentieth Century Art) in 2019, are contributing to the rediscovery of Pirelli's work.[4] As one of very few women artists and filmmakers working in Italy at the time, and in view of her intermedial approach to cinema, a fuller critical study of her work, and its peculiarities, is of historical and critical importance. Such a study would contribute to the mapping of a period, the 1960s and 1970s, and a field, that of experimental cinema and moving-image art, which have not been fully explored and studied from either a specifically Italian or more global or transnational perspective.

Pirelli came to experimental filmmaking via both painting and working in the film industry proper. She performed animation work for the production company, *Filmeco*, in the 1950s, and worked as an extra at Cinecittà. She produced a varied body of work which includes single-screen 16mm films, among which are the performances for, and with, the camera in *Narciso* (1966) and *Sole in mano (Appropriazione, a propria azione, azione propria)* (*Sun in One's hand (Appropriation, A-Proper-Action, Action-Proper*, 1973), as well as the installations and objects centred on light, projection and movement such as *Il tempo dell'uomo* (*The Time of Man*, 1970) and the series of *Meteore* and *Pulsars* (*Meteors, Pulsars*, 1970–72), which consists of composite, yet intentionally primitive, mechanical sculptures with small motors and light bulbs.[5] Moving in the peripheral orbits of several practices of the period, Pirelli produced work that seems equally in dialogue with the kinetic installations and environments of Gianni Colombo, the research films of Bruno Munari, the experimental projections and para-cinematic works of Fabio Mauri and the technologically artisanal, if not purposefully rudimentary, films of Paolo Gioli. In this respect, her practice can be studied not only as a fragment of a fragmentary – and fragmentarily-known – Italian experimental cinema but also, as this chapter sets out to show, through a focus on *Film ambiente*, as an active and original voice in the expanded-cinema movements that developed in the US, Europe and Japan, between the mid-1960s and the mid-1970s.[6]

Coinage of the expression 'expanded cinema' is generally credited to Stan Vanderbeek, who, having built his own 'Movie Drome' for multimedia shows in upstate New York in 1965, used the term in an essay published in 1966 in *Film Culture*, titled 'Culture: Intercom and Expanded Cinema', to outline and promote his vision of a future multimedial expansion of cinema into a global audio-visual network.[7] However, the term is used to describe a heterogeneous range of experimental filmmakers, including those who emerged from the seemingly opposed tendencies of 'structural' or minimal cinema, and who may at first sight not partake of the visionary enthusiasm of VanDerBeek himself. Indeed, artists such as Tony Conrad, Paul Sharits and Anthony McCall in the US, or William Raban, Malcolm Le Grice and Gill Eatherley in the UK, whose formally stripped-down work focussed on cinema's constitutive, if not essential, elements, might be seen to pursue a path of 'reduction' of cinema, rather than expansion. Yet, even this more circumscribed focus on the specific material, on the mechanical and institutional characteristics of the medium – often pursued as a transgressive critique of cinema as such from outside its mainstream institutions – yielded an intermedial opening and expansion, albeit different from Vanderbeek's networked multimedia ideal.[8] Mention could be made of, for example, Conrad's *The Flicker* (1966) and McCall's *Line*

Describing a Cone (1973), where the reduction of cinema to its minimum requirements (all-but-imageless film, projector and screen) paradoxically brings the works within the domain of other disciplines. In *The Flicker*, the stroboscopic effect produced by the alternation of frames of black and white leader illuminates the architectural setting in which the film is being shown, thus revealing it and redoubling it at the same time; while in *Line Describing a Cone* the beam of light from the projector gradually emerges as a sculptural presence – a definite, yet ethereal, conical shape. Or again, we could point to Le Grice's *Horror Film 1* (1971) and Eatherley's *Aperture Sweep* (1973), where cinema's cutback to minimal shadow play simultaneously takes the medium into the realm of theatre and performance.[9]

Expanded cinema's varied strategies and modalities constituted a pursuit of cinema which, ultimately, aimed at transcending cinema itself: whether aesthetically, in its orthodox materiality and mechanics, or as a social protocol and cultural apparatus moulded by (dominant) ideology. In this respect, it resonates strongly with Pirelli's work. Furthermore, just as Pirelli's work sought ways to subvert and exceed the institutionalised modalities of cinematic production and reception, it also shared with these practices the pursuit of both intermediality and in-between-ness, if not liminality. Indeed, if in the male-dominated cultural scene of Italy at the time her gender almost inevitably confined her to a marginal position, Pirelli seems to have pursued in-between-ness and liminality as a kind of critical strategy. She intentionally situated herself and her work at the threshold between cinema and art, the industrial and the artisanal, commercial animation and experimental cinema, single projection and sculptural-architectural installation, object and performance. While this is manifested throughout much of her work, it is most cogently encapsulated in *Film ambiente*.

Screen, Space and Performance

If we were in the room with Pirelli's illuminated structure, we would be able to see a projector outside of the cuboid, which is not shown in the photograph above. The coloured light, then, does not come from a source internal to the structure but is projected onto it. While in recent reconstructions, including at the Museo del Novecento retrospective, the projector has been a digital one, with a slideshow of still abstract images on a loop, in its original incarnation in the late 1960s the work was based on the projection of one of two 16mm films.[10] On the one hand, then, this makes the cuboid a screen, as *Environmental Screen* also suggests, and this is the English title Pirelli herself chose for the work for its exhibition at *Prospekt 1971*. Yet, it is not the type of screen one is ordinarily accustomed to think of in relation to cinema: a basically flat, generally rectangular, surface that functions as the 'end' of projection, the place where the beam of light emitted by the projector is intercepted and 'stopped' to give us the image.

In fact, as a screen, *Film ambiente* is not simply three-dimensional. It is rather a complex structure composed of a modular dark frame, with each unit in particular recalling in size and height a doorway that supports a series of see-through sheets. Even in photographic reproduction, it is possible to see that the sheets are not only on the outer perimeter of the cube: they line most of the internal rectangular subdivisions engendered by the frame. So, as a screen, the work is a very particular one indeed. For it is not simply like the three-dimensional objects used as projection surfaces by Mauri in the 1960s and 1970s, and Tony Oursler in the 1980s, but it is also an *ambiente*, an environment: a complex architectural structure, a kind of labyrinthine room that can be entered by viewers, who can make their way through it by lifting some of the see-through sheets, which are movable and made of a flexible plastic material. In the very same years in which the philosopher Stanley Cavell, in *The World Viewed: Reflections on the Ontology of Film* (1971), was engaged in theorising the screen as a 'barrier', Pirelli's *Film Ambiente* enticed the viewer with a way *into* the screen: not beyond it (as viewers were sometimes be promised would happen with a particularly gripping story, or a particularly well-wrought diegetic world), but *literally* inside it (Figure. 2.2).[11]

The way in which *Film ambiente* turns the screen – the projection surface – into an inhabitable space brings to mind the unrealised visions of 1920s and 1930s avant-gardes artists such as László Moholy-Nagy, El Lissitzky and Theo van Doesburg. In an essay of 1929, 'Film as Pure Form', van Doesburg advocated cinema's abandonment of the two-dimensional screen: the 'projection surface' reminiscent of an 'enframed canvas' should be superseded.[12] Indeed, the ideal development that van Doesburg goes on to describe, in the future tense, might seem to find a fairly close realisation in Pirelli's structure:

> Instead of a painterly setting, an architectural one will first be necessary. Then the newly mastered medium will make possible a new light architecture . . . [T]he spectator space will become part of the film space. The separation of 'projection surface' is abolished. The spectator will no longer observe the film, like a theatrical presentation, but will participate in it optically and acoustically.[13]

Van Doesburg's aspirations to abolish the 'projection surface' helps to bring into relief an important aspect of Pirelli's work. This concerns the position offered to the spectator. Unlike in traditional cinema, in the

Figure 2.2 from *Film ambiente* (1969) installation in Rome of 1969.

spatially developed cinema that van Doesburg envisioned the spectator is not merely inside it but also part of it: he or she 'participate[s] in it optically and acoustically'. On entering *Film ambiente*, one can similarly be at once inside it *and* part of it, viewer and performer at the same time, adding one's own body and shadow to the work. In the early presentations of the late 1960s, this performative contribution of the audience was further underlined by a live soundtrack. Obtained by converting into sounds light variations inside the structure produced by bodies moving within it, this soundtrack functioned as a sort of aural demonstration of the public's intervention on the work.[14]

The participatory, if not performative, role of the audience was evident to Italian art critic Tommaso Trini. Reviewing the piece in 1969 Trini presented it as a cinematic elaboration of what a couple of years earlier Richard Schechner had come to define as 'environmental theatre': a radically 'open' theatre where the audience itself, made to share the same space as the actors and to participate in the performance, becomes actor.[15] Not incidentally, Schechner's 'environmental theatre' also described Julian Beck and Judith Malina's legendary Living Theatre company. In exile from New York, the Living Theatre was travelling through Europe and Italy in the late 1960s, where it proved inspirational for many artists, including Pirelli.[16] Indeed, in virtue of its potential openness and inclusiveness, 'theatre' became a key tool not only for the inclusion of the viewer into the work, but also in the radical attempts to break down distinctions between disciplines. 'The arts', as Susan Sontag wrote at the time, with theatrically-driven events such as *Happenings* and *9 Evenings: Theatre and Engineering* (1966) in mind, might 'eventuate in one art'.[17] It is on the 'openness' of theatre that experimental and expanded cinema often drew to off-set, and challenge, the 'closeness' of cinema. If artists such as Le Grice and Eatherley, mentioned above, turned cinema's conventional screening event into a live performance in a space shared with the audience, then Pirelli's accessible screen threw open cinema's conventionally impenetrable barrier and handed it over to the viewer. Ironically, modernist critic Michael Fried's famous condemnation of 'theatre', in his essay 'Art and Objecthood' (1967), understood cinema to be protected from theatricality. Fried attacks 'theatre' as a force which works against separation, both between distinct art disciplines, and between the autonomous art object and its public. Yet cinema, according to Fried, 'escapes theatre' and that which for him is the deeply unwelcome prospect of a loss of distinction and separation, precisely because the screen acts as a 'barrier' which seals film off from the spectator.[18] This, of course, is precisely what *Film ambiente* puts into question.

Furthermore, as a bath of light, *Film ambiente*'s elements of participation co-exist with, or even rely on, a condition of immersion. Such co-existence and interdependency are interesting. 'Immersion' in the spectacle provided by cinema and other mass media is generally understood in negative or pejorative terms, as a condition of passivity and a-criticality, if not 'deception', as Theodor Adorno and Max Horkheimer put it in their well-known scathing condemnation of what they termed the 'culture industry'.[19] Yet, while they might have often been animated by a scepticism or disapproval of *certain* immersive spectacles, many artist-filmmakers associated with experimental and expanded-cinema movements pursued immersion precisely as a means to viewers' participation, *critical* participation even. In the case of *Film ambiente*, physical 'immersion', being *inside* the work, seemed precisely to be what Pirelli relied on to encourage reflection *on* the work. As with van Doesburg's envisioned 'light architecture', Pirelli's *Film ambiente* invited the viewer not inside a film but a structure. The point of Pirelli's structure is not to take viewers inside, or beyond, the screen figuratively (for example, by bringing them into the story, making them feel part of the representation) but, precisely, to put them in the screen in a *literal* sense. In a way, overcoming the 'barrier' of the screen is to enter part of cinema's apparatus and acquire a vantage point from which to observe and think about its ordinary material functioning along with its cultural function.

Trini (one of the most perceptive art critics in Italy at the time) in part alluded to this in the title of his piece on *Film ambiente*, which reads 'M' illumino di film'.[20] Hard to translate in English, the expression can mean both 'I lit up with film' and 'I am enlightened through film'. In its emphasis on light, and on a sense of both body and mind being 'illuminated' by film, it functions as a succinct, if cryptic, description of Pirelli's cinematic installation and the way in which physical immersion co-exists or, more strongly, is the conduit for, mental apprehension. While Trini saw the work as an enlightenment *through* film, I want to suggest that the object of such enlightenment is, indeed, film – or cinema itself. With its simple, open structure, the spectacle of *Film ambiente* lies in the way in which it takes on cinema: not only in the sense of adopting (and adapting) elements of it, but also in the sense of confronting it.

Screen/Projection

In the economy of the work, it is neither exhaustive nor accurate to describe Pirelli's complex structure as a screen. More in-between-ness – or, can one dare say, 'both-ness' – is needed here to explore it further. For this cuboid structure which we have come to see as a screen, as a resistance or obstacle, which by intercepting the projector's beam of light functions as the 'end' of projection, at the same time acts as a source of projection. Again, this is a result of the complexity of its seemingly minimal structure. Though partly transparent, the sheets are screen-printed with a fine pattern that also makes them in part opaque and reflective. In this way, the multi-coloured light – sequences of more or less abstract imagery, in fact – from the projector can be transmitted by means of transparency across sheets found

MARINELLA PIRELLI'S CINEMA   77

along its path, but, thanks to the opaque pattern on the sheets, it can also be reflected off and onto other sheets, including those outside the cone of projection. To this is added the arrangement of the sheets themselves within the structure (some of them, obviously, stand at 90 degrees to each other) and the positioning of the projector, which is placed not frontally but along the diagonal axis of the cuboid (Figure 2.3), all of which contributes to engendering the radiant quality of *Film ambiente*: the effect of light being projected from within the cube, filling it with such luminous effect that

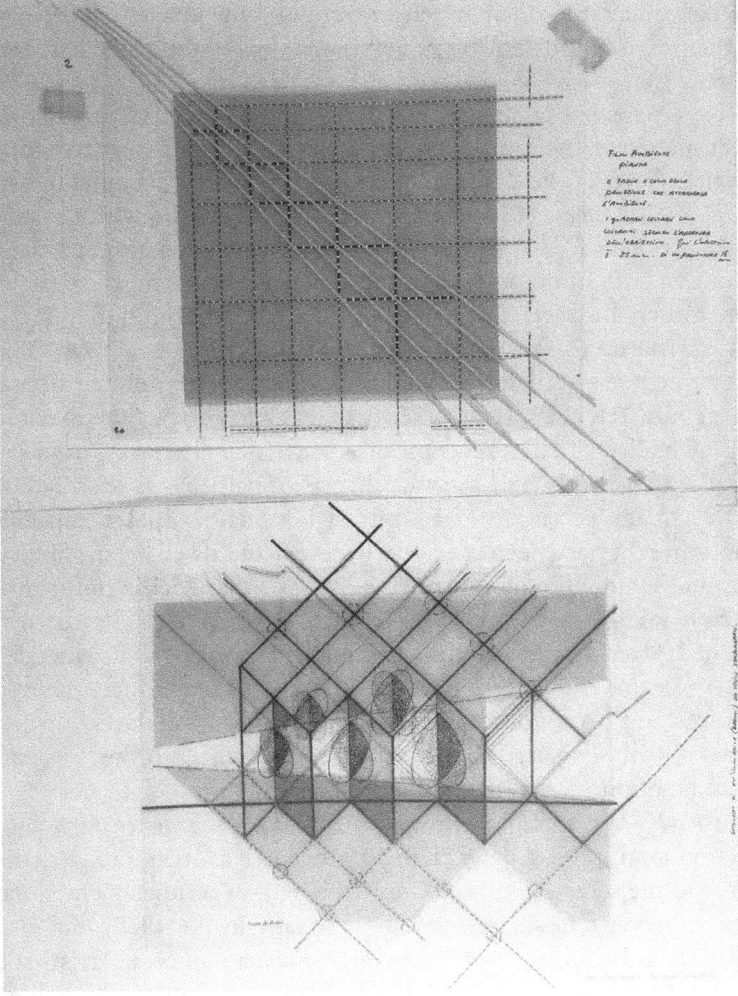

Figure 2.3 Preparatory diagram for *Film ambiente* (c. 1968).

spills out onto the surrounding walls, ceiling and bodies. So, in addition to its being a screen receiving projection from an external source, the structure itself also functions as a kind of projector. Furthermore, the projection effect generated by *Film ambiente*'s meticulously planned system of sheets has a three-dimensional quality. At the 90-degree intersections between sheets, the images projected off the sheets themselves superimpose to create an illusory volume, or, as Pirelli called them, 'virtual images' in the space *between* the sheets.[21] 'Thus, from a single projection', as Pirelli summarised the combined effects of *Film ambiente*, 'a multiplicity of images is generated, at different points in space, and the viewer can move among – and feel inside, rather than merely in front of – the images', as s/he would be if they were simply looking *at* a screen, as in a traditional cinema set-up (Figure. 2.4).[22]

It is perhaps not incidental to Pirelli's emphasis on virtuality that the subject matter of the films she initially projected onto her structure was sculpture. Such is the case with the kinetic objects documented in her film *Luce e Movimento* (*Light and Movement*, 1968) and with the perspex cuboids in *Nuovo Paradiso* (*New Paradise*, 1969) by arte-povera artist Gino Marotta. In both films, the sculptural objects are not so much represented, but are rather 'abstracted' into moving coloured light through framing and shooting. Marotta's static but translucent sculptures in *Nuovo Paradiso*, for example, were hung from a wire, and filmed as they rotated after being spun around. Yet, at the same time, virtuality and abstraction do not imply a lack of reality, or the exclusion of a sense of materiality, even if only dealing with a reality and a materiality as impalpable as those conveyed by light. In the evocation of a contrast between sculpture and cinema, the point might have been precisely to reveal and dwell on the alternative reality and materiality of cinematic light. As Jonas Mekas put it in 1965, '[t]here is no abstract cinema: all cinema is concrete'. 'The cinema', he continued, 'even at its most ideal and abstract, remains in its essence concrete; it remains the art of motion and light and color. Once we leave our prejudices and preconditionings outside, we open ourselves to the concreteness of pure visual and kinaesthetic experience, to the "realism" of light and motion, . . . to the matter of cinema'.[23]

In many ways, Pirelli's enthusiasm for how *Film ambiente* would free projection, multiplying it and taking it into space as such, rather than confining it to the screen, recalls not only the light experiments envisioned or practiced by van Doesburg and Moholy-Nagy in the 1920s, but also the fascination and curiosity that drove early-cinema pioneers. Artists such as Louis Le Prince and Georges Méliès explored such potentialities at a time in which the technical and cultural parameters of the new medium were still

Figure 2.4 Detail from *Film ambiente* (1969).

unfixed, and the sense of possibility of the new technology was at its highest. Pirelli was fascinated by the phantasmatic and illusory qualities of cinema, but, like these pioneers, she was also very interested in the way in which such qualities were the result of specific materials and precise mechanics. As with the cinema pioneers, there is something of the inventor, at once artisanal, industrial, and even entrepreneurial, in Pirelli's approach to her work. Mass-produced materials and machines are adopted, but uniquely adapted and, as is the case with *Film ambiente*, which took over two years of preparation and meticulous calculations, protected by a patent.[24]

Pirelli's dedication to developing a structure that generates and projects 'virtual images' is itself part of her exploration of the cinematic medium, where its magic and illusion might be studied not with a view to dispelling or eliminating such attributes, but with a view to re-deploying and re-articulating them. Let me return, here, to the expression Trini coined to describe *Film ambiente*: 'M'illumino di film'. Though not an idiomatic expression in Italian, oddly meaningful and nonsensical at the same time, to an Italian reader the title of Trini's review would have most likely called to mind a 1917 poem by the modernist poet Giuseppe Ungaretti, 'Mattina' (Morning), well-known also particularly because of its extreme brevity.[25] Indeed, Trini's title *is* the poem, but for the fact that he swapped 'film' for 'immensity'. In Ungaretti's poem, made up of just four, short, words, the 'I' lights up not with 'film' but with 'immensity'. The apparent contrast between brevity and extension (even, indeed, infinite extension), and simplicity of means and complexity of meaning, at work in Ungaretti's poem, is also at work in Pirelli's installation. *Film ambiente* is a very simple structure made of steel, plastic sheets, and projector. Yet, even on a purely phenomenological level, the effects it generates exceed this simplicity: quite a lot is achieved with very little, so to speak, as the play of projection and reflection creates a complex, intricate environment. The fact that Trini's title bears the echo of Ungaretti's evocation of space – in fact, the paradoxical spatial dimension of infinity – contributes, in its turn, to bringing into focus the crucial strategy at the core of Pirelli's work: a sense of boundlessness conjured within a bounded environment. As it does so, Pirelli's complex screen also endows projection with a tangibility of sorts. Even if light remains ungraspable and impalpable to the sense of touch, its projection is a material component of the work, the very phenomenon viewers are invited at once to wander through and wonder at. What is on show is the very ambivalence of projection, at once physical and illusory, material and phantasmatic, as is the way in which such ambivalence is so fundamental to cinema as both bare technology and cultural apparatus. We are looking, then, at a photograph of a curious structure: a screen-space where projection does not 'end' but, in a way, begins, and where cinema is at once an object of exploration, if not critique, and a point of departure.

Notes

1. Marinella Pirelli, untitled artist statement, in Gallery Denise René brochure, see René and Mayer (1971), n.p. The statement appears in German, English and Italian. The English version offers 'substantial freedom' for 'libertà reale', which is the expression Pirelli uses in Italian.

2. Marucci, (1969); Fisher, Jürgen and Strelow (1971).
3. Higgins, (1996), n.p., my emphasis; Greenberg, (1940), pp. 296–310.
4. See 'Now You Can Go: Marinella Pirelli Screening', ICA, London, 5 December 2015: <https://www.ica.org.uk/whats-on/now-you-can-go-marinella-pirelli-screening>, last accessed 29 July 2019; *Luce Movimento. Il cinema sperimentale di Marinella Pirelli*, Milan, Museo del Novecento, 22 March to 25 August 2019, for which an exhibition catalogue is published by Electa, Milan. See also: *Marinella Pirelli: Pulsar,* Teatro dei Filodrammatici, Milan, 21–25 May 2015: <http://www.domusweb.it/it/notizie/2013/05/21/marinella_pirelli_pulsar.html>, last accessed 29 July 2017.
5. See Gualdoni (1997), esp. pp. 53–102.
6. For an overview of Italian experimental cinema in the 1960s and 1970s, see Di Marino (1999); and Sbardella (2003). For expanded cinema see in particular Rees, White, Ball and Curtis (2011); and Uroskie (2014).
7. VanDerBeek (1966), pp. 15–18.
8. On expanded cinema as pursuing yet transcending, if not transgressing, cinema, see Raban (2011), pp. 98–107.
9. On the idea of an expanded cinema via reduction or contraction, see Iles (2009). For a take on 'intermediality' and expanded cinema as sculpture see Baker (2006), pp. 92–125.
10. The films presented kinetic sculptures exhibited at the show *Luce e movimento* at the Ariete Gallery in Milan in 1967, and a series of colour Perspex cuboids by Arte-Povera artist Giorgio Marotta titled *Nuovo paradiso* (*New Paradise,* 1968) respectively.
11. Cavell (1971), p. 24.
12. van Doesburg (1966), pp. 8–9.
13. Ibid., 11.
14. Gualdoni (1997), p. 76.
15. Trini (1969), p. 36; Schechner (1967).
16. Pirelli (2006).
17. Sontag, (1966), p. 35.
18. Fried (1967), pp. 148–72, esp. p. 164 and 171.
19. Adorno and Horkheimer (1944), pp. 94–136.
20. Trini, 'M'illumino di film'.
21. Marinella Pirelli quoted in René and Mayer (1971).
22. Ibid.
23. Mekas (2016), p. 227.
24. Gualdoni (1997), p. 74.
25. The poem with the definitive title was published in Ungaretti (1919).

Works Cited

Adorno, Theodor W. and Max Horkheimer, (1944), 'The Culture Industry: Enlightenment as Mass Deception', *Dialectic of Enlightenment: Philosophical*

Fragments, Edmund Jephcott trans. (2002), Stanford: Stanford University Press.
Baker, George (2006), 'Film Beyond Its Limits', *October* 25 (Fall):92–125.
Cavell, Stanley (1971), *The World Viewed: Reflections on the Ontology of Film*, Cambridge: Harvard University Press.
Di Marino, Bruno (1999), *Sguardo, inconscio, azione: cinema underground e sperimentale a Roma (1965–1975)*, Rome: Lithos.
Fisher, Konrad, Jürgen Harten, Hans Strelow (1971), *Prospect 71: Projection*, Düsseldorf: Art-Press Verlag.
Fried, Michael (1967), 'Art and Objecthood', in *Art and Objecthood: Essays and Reviews*. Chicago: The University of Chicago Press, 1998, pp. 148–72.
Greenberg, Clement (1940), 'Towards a Newer Laocoon', *Partisan Review* 8.4 (July-August): 296–310.
Gualdoni, Flaminio, ed. (1997), *Marinella Pirelli*. Milan: Skira.
Higgins, Dick (1996), 'Intermedia', *The Something Else Newsletter*, 1.1 (February): n.p.
Iles, Chrissie (2009), 'Inside Out: Expanded Cinema and Its Relationship to the Gallery in the 1970s', conference paper, *Expanded Cinema: Activating the Space of Reception*, Tate Modern Starr Auditorium, London, 17–19 April, <http://www.rewind.ac.uk/expanded/Narrative/Tate_Doc_Session_2_CI.html>, last accessed 25 June 2017.
Marucci, Luciano, ed. (1969), *Al di là della pittura*, Florence: Centro Di Edizioni.
Mekas, Jonas (2016), 'There Is No Abstract Cinema: All Cinema is Concrete', 9 December 1965, *Movie Journal: The Rise of the New American Cinema, 1959–1971*, New York: Columbia University Press.
Mekas, Jonas (2016), *Movie Journal: The Rise of the New American Cinema, 1959–1971*, New York: Columbia University Press.
Pirelli, Marinella (2006), 'Estratto da biografia leggera: tra Roma e Milano, 1948–1970', typescript, 19, Archivio Marinella Pirelli.
Raban, William (2011), 'Reflexivity and Expanded Cinema: A Cinema of Transgression?' in Alan Leonard Rees, Dunca White, Steven Ball, David Curtis, eds., *Expanded Cinema: Art, Performance, Film*, London: Tate Publishing, pp. 98–107.
Rees, Alan Leonard, Dunca White, Steven Ball, David Curtis, eds. (2011), *Expanded Cinema: Art, Performance, Film*, London: Tate Publishing.
René, Denise and Hans Mayer (1971), *The Environmental-Screen of Marinella Pirelli*, Gallery Denise René brochure for *Prospekt 1971: Projection*, Düsseldorf, 7–15 October, n.p.
Sbardella, Americo (2003), *Il cinema indipendente italiano 1964–1984*, <http://www.activitaly.it/immaginicinema/indipendente/cinema%20italiano%20indipendente.htm >, last accessed 25 June 2017.
Schechner, Richard (1967), 'Six Axioms for Environmental Theatre', in *Environmental Theatre* (1994), New York: Applause, pp. 41–64.
Sontag, Susan (1966), 'Film and Theatre', *The Tulane Drama Review*, 11.1 (Autumn): 24–37.

Trini, Tommaso (1969), 'M'illumino di film', *Domus*, 477 (August): 36–9.
Ungaretti, Giuseppe (1919), *Allegria di naufragi*. Florence: Firenze Vallecchi.
Uroskie, Andrew V. (2014), *Between the Black Box and the White Cube: Expanded Cinema and Postwar Art*, Chicago: Chicago University Press.
van Doesburg, Theo (1966), 'Film as Pure Form' (1929), Standish D. Lawder trans., *Form*, 1 (Summer): 5–11.
Vanderbeek, Stan (1966), 'Culture: Intercom and Expanded Cinema. A Proposal and Manifesto', *Film Culture* 40 (November): 15–18.

Filmography*

Aperture Sweep, film/performance, directed by Gill Eatherley, 1973.
Film ambiente (*Environmental Screen*), film installation, directed by Marinella Pirelli, 1969.
Horror Film 1, film/performance, directed by Malcolm Le Grice, 1971.
Line Describing a Cone, film installation, directed by Anthony MacCall, 1973.
The Flicker, film, directed by Tony Conrad, 1966.

* Detailed data on independent film productions is sparse and often uncertain; several of these works are by definition not constrained by 'duration'.

CHAPTER 3

From Vertov to Cine-Journals: Cesare Zavattini's Experimental Journey
Carlo Coen

> Our eyes see very little and very badly – so people dreamed up the microscope to let them see invisible phenomena; they invented the telescope... now they have perfected the cinecamera to penetrate more deeply into the visible world, to explore and record visual phenomena so that what is happening now, which will have to be taken account of in the future, is not forgotten
>
> Dziga Vertov[1]

> As far as the history of cinema proper is concerned, Zavattini's immediacy places itself along an illustrious and heroic series, finding its origins in Vertov's *Kino-Glaz*, passing through Siegfried Kracauer's *Theory of Film: The Redemption of Physical Reality*, and continuing, beyond the important stage set by our author, into *cinéma-verité*, and the *underground*.
>
> Renato Barilli[2]

Introduction

Cesare Zavattini crossed the entire history of Italian sound cinema, from the 1930s until his death in 1989. If one can conceive of an Italian 'independent-*auteur* cinema', that is, a cinema capable of relating to experimentalism, attempting to free itself from traditional production modes and, at the same time, renewing the authors' intellectual rapport with their audience, Zavattini was certainly a key, if not unique, figure in such cinema.

His importance and his contribution are gathered not only from the 80-plus films of which he was the screenwriter– often breakthrough scripts when compared to contemporary ones – but also by dwelling with utmost attention on the profound coherence of his entire body of work. In fact, Zavattini cannot simply be considered a brilliant scriptwriter and the major and most lucid theoretician of Italian neorealism. His work, in addition to the aforementioned, includes short stories and novellas, articles, papers and even paintings, all of which constitute an inseparable wholeness, created with the greatest curiosity for the new, with the most profound and heartfelt humanism, with long-sightedness and enlightening anticipations of the future of media. Most probably because of the multitalented persona and wide-ranging scope, his works are not always immediately clear and perfectly structured, and yet are perhaps among the major contributions to the understanding of the culture of the twentieth century. This is due to the fact that they span across a broad spectrum of insights and explorations, in a relentless search for all that could be significant: from considerations on human nature to the boldest proposals aimed at acquiring the deepest possible knowledge of such nature through the medium of cinema; from political battles, fought to give voice to the voiceless, to the identification of the most appropriate artistic expressions. The thrust appears to be that of a utopian-like broadening of the political and social sense of awareness of the Italian nation, her people; a vision motivated by a sense of disappointment, among other things, generated by the incomplete fruition of the democratic process begun after the war.

The sense of the present chapter is therefore found in the conviction that in the history of Italian cinema one can identify a tendency, experimental in its form and style, and independent in its constant search for production modes alternative to traditional ones. Such trends were unequivocally pursued by Cesare Zavattini, who never directed a film (with the exception of his 1988 *La veritaaaà / The Truuuuth*), and who was never simply a screenwriter, but incessantly the promoter and the coordinator of a wide range of projects. The fact that his projects did not yield satisfactory results (according also to Zavattini's own opinion) is still an unsolved critical issue, especially if we consider the width and the magnitude of the critical literature dedicated to him.

The history of the Resistance against Nazism and Fascism, besides being the major historical event behind neorealism, was also an inexhaustible source of oral history, and likewise the source of numerous attempts to lay the foundations for an independent cinema. Productions financed by the ANPI[3] and other Partisans' Associations were important endeavours aimed at overcoming the old production modes and patterns. It would suffice to cite *Giorni di gloria* (*Days of Glory*, 1945), a collective work directed by Luchino Visconti, Giuseppe De Santis, and Marcello Pagliero, together with *Il sole sorge ancora* (*The Sun Rises Again*, 1946) by Aldo Vergano, *Pian delle Stelle* (*The Plain of Stars*, 1946) by Giorgio Ferroni, and *Achtung banditi!* (*Achtung: Bandits!*, 1951) by Carlo Lizzani. Later on, Lizzani also directed *Cronache di poveri amanti* (*Chronicles of Poor Lovers*, 1954) with funds gathered from the Cooperativa Spettatori Produttori Cinematografici (Cinema Spectators Producers Cooperative), the same that had produced *Achtung banditi!*. Moreover, *La terra trema* (*The Earth Trembles*,

1947) by Luchino Visconti, and *Luci del Varietà* (*Variety Lights*, 1950) by Alberto Lattuada and Federico Fellini, could be classified as important films produced through self-financing or the principal contributions of political associations.

In terms of depth and width, however, Cesare Zavattini's contribution to a truly independent Italian cinema goes well beyond the input given through the above-mentioned films. Zavattini explores the entire array of issues relevant to cinema as a medium, draws outcomes affecting the present and the future, connects to the best of the avant-garde experience and paves the way to new elaborations.

> In Zavattini Neorealism shapes itself as an attitude, a way to place oneself before the world, people, things, social and cultural systems: it is a critical disposition that can be applied to all realms, to journalism, to songs and music, to television and radio, to comics, to modern mass media, wherever technological progress reduces distances and allows large scale communication. . . . In Zavattini there is bold enthusiasm for the printed press, the news magazines, films, radio broadcast, TV; there is this direct immersion into mass media, feeling their electrifying fascination and endless communicative and expressive potential.[4]

Zavattini's New Vision of the Cinema

Zavattini's focus on the potentials of the camera eye and its ability to reproduce reality 'directly' (as he often states) leads to a much broader view, transcending the limits of the debate on neorealism of those years. The term 'neorealism' is in fact used very sparingly by Zavattini, who rather insists on the term 'cinema' in his writings; the two terms eventually coincide and form one unit, which is both conceptual and practical. Therefore, Zavattini should be regarded as the precursor of several experimental and avant-garde theories and practices, rather than simply as the theoretician of neorealism. Zavattini considers neorealism as the best possible epiphany of cinema, intended as the best possible medium to harmonise the exigency of a deep analysis (involving the audience in a direct manner) with the urgency of a redeeming action.

Critical literature has accurately highlighted the origins and the influence of his thought. First of all, Dziga Vertov is an essential reference point. As Lino Miccichè noted, Zavattini's 'vertovism' 'was partial, disorganised and, above all, he was not totally aware of it'.[5] When Zavattini described the camera's relationship with the human eye, concluding that the cinematic medium allowed a more analytical view of reality than any other previous medium, the knowledge of Vertov's texts and theorisations in Italy was scarce and second-hand. Zavattini's lack of acquaintance with Vertov's works does not detract from the fact that, by admission of Miccinché himself, it is anyway 'conspicuous'.[6] In fact, it does not matter whether or not Zavattini had read Vertov's texts, or how he managed to acquaint himself with any of Vertov's elaborations: the closeness and the similarity are unmistakable.

Others, as shown below, have delved further into the theme of experimentalism found in Zavattini's theories: reference has been made to Flaherty and Grierson, to *ciné-verité*, even to Cubism, with critical considerations that connect Zavattini's thought to the most advanced experiences of the historical avant-garde:

> The path Zavattini points to, in order to 'discover' this true meaning of facts and actions, even the most ordinary (especially the most ordinary), is an analytical use of cinema, capable to render on the screen the diverse viewpoints from which the object may be examined. Here too, the analogy with the main characteristics of the artistic avant-garde of the twentieth century is clear, in particular with the visual arts, with the phenomenological approach of Cézanne and Cubism. As in the cubist works by Picasso and Braque, Gris and Delaunay (both in the so-called 'analytical' and 'synthetic' cubism), the three-dimensional object explored along multiple perspectives is reproduced on the canvas through a process that is contradictory to the concept of painting as 'a window on the world' (linked to the illusion of the perspective), and in favour of a concept of painting intended as the knowledge of the deepest truth of things (a truth literally unfolded on the plane of the canvas). Therefore, Zavattini's analysis overturns all the standards of the cinematic narrative, favouring a dynamic de-composition of every day actions and gestures; such de-composition, actualized by the cinematic camera, is re-actualized phenomenologically on the screen for the purpose of triggering the perceptive and intellectual intervention of the spectator.[7]

Once some of the origins of his elaboration are defined, one must add that such elaborations also contain several elements that differ from the basis of their theoretical sources:

> Finally, Zavattini is not far from Flaherty when he advocates fleeing from studios and novel-like narrative, and his predecessors are also John Grierson and his school – which would have been unthinkable without the foundational lines passed on by the director of *Nanook of the North* and *Man of Aran*. However, neither Grierson nor Flaherty, and not even Vertov, assign to fantasy, as Zavattini does, the role of provocation in a genre that is actually supposed to reject it. . . . It is within the French or the Canadian *cinéma-vérité* of the Sixties that it is possible to retrace certain suggestions coming from Zavattini.[8]

The role of what he calls 'fantasy' is in fact prominent in many of his writings; it is undeniable that Zavattini never conceived cinema as a medium of pure representation of reality – despite being accused of this on many occasions, especially by the followers of Lukàcs and the supporters of the 'passage from neorealism to realism', led by Guido Aristarco. Actually, the introduction of a fantastic dimension by the author leads precisely to that deeper understanding of the human condition observed through the camera-eye, and which constitutes the ultimate purpose of any audiovisual endeavour.

Zavattini introduces another element that must be considered fundamental to the new vision of cinema he had in mind, that of the insistence of the camera's gaze, which constitutes a central moment of his elaboration. Zavattini's position in this regard is extremely clear and radical:

> In the future, realism will find other forms, but now it must *know*, even through cruel means, and enable human beings to take resolutions. Let us ask an unemployed man to stand still before the camera, and then let us nail the audience for five minutes in front of that image on the screen. Nobody wants that. Shouts will be heard: 'Editing!' – for images must roll fast and the awareness of the audience made superficial, to avoid delving into the truth. I say an unemployed man, but I could say anything else requiring urgent intervention, issues for which our *duration* of attention is always lower than the actual need to really know them.[9]

The article titled 'Tesi sul Neorealismo' (Thesis on Neorealism), published in the magazine *Emilia*,[10] dates back to 1953 and is remarkably similar to what Roland Barthes would say, approximately 27 years later, about Michelangelo Antonioni in his open letter 'Cher Antonioni'. Barthes further radicalises the meaning of the insistence of the gaze by attributing to Power, to the 'established order', the rush, the superficiality identified in those who shout 'Editing!'. Even more remarkably, Barthes shares with Zavattini the recognition of the essence of the 'persistent gaze' in the very nature of the cinematic medium:

> Another aspect of fragility for the artist, paradoxically, is the firmness and insistence of his look. Power of any kind, because it is violence, never looks; if it looked one minute longer (one minute too much) it would lose its essence as power. The artist, for his part, stops and looks lengthily, and I would imagine you became a film-maker because the camera is an eye, constrained by its technical properties to look. What you, like all film-makers, add to these properties is to look at things radically, until you have exhausted them.... This is dangerous, because to look longer than expected (I insist on this added intensity) disturbs established orders of every kind, to the extent that normally the time of the look is controlled by society; hence the scandalous nature of certain photographs and certain films, not the most indecent or the most 'poised'.[11]

L'amore in città (*Love in the City*, 1953) is one of the few completed films that can be classified as following the lines of Zavattini's wider vision and project. According to Zavattini, its segmented structure should not have followed the formula which had been already used and which would be overused in the following years, but was meant to take on the form of a proper cine-journal, with all its recognizable sections.

> This collective work produced by Cesare Zavattini, Riccardo Ghione and Marco Ferreri for Faro Film of Messina is still interesting today, not much and not only for its aesthetic results, but chiefly as a test for the most advanced theories of Zavattini. Mixed and heterogeneous, strongly hybrid in its blend of documentary and fictional stances, at the crossroad between testament and reconstruction, story and essay, this film translates in forms which are precursors of investigative TV reports, *cinéma vérité*, and *direct cinema*, the 'author's' reflections on the so-called 'flash-film', considered the ideal development of neorealism.[12]

It is essential, therefore, to cite the very words of Zavattini on the concept created by him, that of 'flash-film' ('film-lampo'), a definition that sheds an important light on Zavattini's intentions:

> This kind of film, that is, a film that reproduces a news item in the very location where it occurred, and is re-interpreted by those who were the principal protagonists of the event, stems from my old desire to employ cinema to know what happens around us in a direct and immediate way, while the other way, the one based on fictional narratives, is an indirect and mediated way.[13]

Such a manuscript, probably drawn up around 1952, shows that Zavattini had already begun to reflect on the different roles of different media at that time; in it we find the reiteration of his profound confidence in the peculiar nature of cinema. Noteworthy is his consideration on the potential of television, expressed even before its official introduction in Italy, which took place in 1954:

> There is no hierarchy of facts, more or less worth cinematographing, but all facts are worth to be reconstructed, worth of such a collective work, . . . that only cinema can deliver in a complete way (that radio can deliver in a smaller measure and that television will be able to deliver in a larger measure than cinema), because it is the medium which leaves the least room for imprecision and non-objectivity.[14]

The directors involved in the operation are those whose names in the next few years will rise to the level of *auteur*: first and foremost, Federico Fellini and Michelangelo Antonioni, but also Dino Risi, Francesco Maselli and Carlo Lizzani, side by side with established names such as Alberto Lattuada. The criticism of *L'amore in città* – soon after its release and in later years – seems to be almost unanimous in pointing at the film's characteristic discontinuity, at its scanty cohesion and, consequently, in regarding it as a failed attempt. It is not relevant to this context to elaborate on whether or not Fellini's segment, *Agenzia matrimoniale* (*Marriage Bureau*), constitutes a very important moment in the career of the Riminese director – who is already thinking of (and probably already writing) *La strada*, a milestone film that has changed not only his career forever, but the whole panorama of Italian cinema. Likewise it is irrelevant to dwell on whether, apart from Antonioni's insistence on the subject of suicide – which will be found also in *Le amiche* (*The Girlfriends*, 1955) – and in any case on the theme of the 'defeated ones',[15] *Tentato suicidio* (*Attempted Suicide*) is the only segment to deeply explore the urban landscapes – a trait which will characterise Antonioni's later work – or on whether or not other segments of *Love in the City* turn out to be as visually outstanding. The central segment is in fact *Storia di Caterina* (*Caterina's Story*), conceived in the smallest detail by Zavattini himself and shot by Francesco Maselli. Caterina was a very poor woman who had attracted the attention of the media, after having abandoned her few-month-old son on a bench in a Roman parkette, and, regretting her extreme gesture, had gone back to retrieve him. This is evidently an ideal daily event for Zavattini's theories: daily chronicles become history; reality is told as if it were a story;[16] cinema performs its in-depth analysis on downtrodden human beings. Unfortunately for Zavattini, the woman called to play herself, greatly complicated the production of the episode, to the point of putting into question the very essence of the Zavattinian elaborations. Instead of 'catching life in the act' *Storia di Caterina* clearly reveals its character of reconstruction and, as such, its being subjected to re-elaborations and mediations which are incompatible with the 'purest' aspects of Zavattini's project.

Therefore, Lino Miccichè, in his commentary on *Love in the City* – a contributed essay in De Giusti's eighth edited volume *Storia del cinema italiano* (*History of Italian Cinema*) collection – highlights the poor results obtained and examines the core of the contradictions of neo-realism in the doldrums in which the film ended up.[17] Furthermore, Vitella concludes his article with poignant considerations hinting at the end of the movement which Zavattini had contributed to creating, while paving the way towards the prospects of a new, perhaps more coherent vision:

> In an extreme attempt to reassign to cinematographic neorealism its glorious mandate, Zavattini's film ends up with the admission of its demise, and acknowledges, in the wake of the resounding commercial success of illustrated news magazines and the progressive "industrialisation" of the image of neorealism, the novel social role played by photography, with its ability to "examine", "re-imagine", and "bear witness to" the visible world.[18]

A Transformative Legacy

Love in the city is, however, only one of the many projects Zavattini tried tirelessly to put on film in those years. It is worth mentioning at least two more among them: *My Italy*, conceived probably in the same period (1953), or perhaps a year earlier, and *The Mysteries of Rome*, made ten years later, in 1963.[19]

My Italy is an incomplete project, among the many that were conceived in the 1950s, and it did not see the light.[20] Had it been shot, the film could have had a significant impact. Much more than the reasons for its failure, it is again worth discussing the spirit behind the project: one of the most ambitious 'flash-films', focussed entirely on the discovery of the countless faces of Italian social reality, in total conformity to Zavattinian theories. It is very important to consider that unrealised works are potentially much more interesting than those which actually appeared on the screen. In a 1953 article, Zavattini sums up the idea he repeated on countless occasions at the height of neo-realism's popularity: cinema 'must tell reality as if it were a story'.[21] The director of the film was supposed to be Vittorio De Sica but, due to earlier commitments, his long-time friend and collaborator was unable to accept the invitation. Following the pass on De Sica's part, Zavattini contacted Roberto Rossellini, but the film failed to take off. What remains are the long and detailed descriptions of the project addressed to both De Sica and Rossellini: a film made of daily episodes of extreme simplicity.

> The film unfolds through a series of episodes or moments in different places without the need to name them. It is always Italy, the protagonists are always Italians. From two youngsters, caught ten minutes before their love encounter – the first episode – whom we see respectively and alternately during the anxious preparations for this meeting, at home at the one end, and at office at the other, we then move to the portrayal of an Italian family as a documentarian would depict it; then to the departure and arrival times at large stations, small stations, and ports; from a popular dance on the Po plains to a quarrel between poor people within a large community housing complex; to the bricklayers who work at a construction site, caught in the moment between rest and resumption of work, with their words, their minimal acts, and the world around them.[22]

In his letter to De Sica, Zavattini reminds him of other projects, clearly discussed together on previous occasions, insisting on the immediacy of the film he expected him to direct. His distinction between 'episodes' and 'moments' emphasises research and exploration as the core features of *My Italy*:

> We will come upon a village whose name is known by maybe a few hundred people. We will stop for a few minutes. I mean, it will look like we've stopped for

a few minutes; instead we will stop the time necessary to put together those few minutes of film. (More than a film of 'episodes' it will be a film of 'moments'). We will catch more moments than episodes, just as if we were to cross Italy in a car.[23]

In the letter to Rossellini we can even find a very precise description of how important the theories about 'flash-film' are, and the process through which the real life of the country becomes an exciting and spectacular story to tell.

We will see, and I am rather simplifying here: a man praying; a girl waiting for her boyfriend; people who do not know each other, e.g. from different villages, put together by the author to observe their reactions on a given subject; a roadman who speaks with the author who met him along the road; the stages of a birth; a lunch of peasants in the Cassinese; the Redeemer's Holiday in Venice or Piedigrotta in Naples. . . . The facts must obey the necessity to be represented with rapidity, simultaneity and extension in time and space, with the precise function of linking each attempt with each subsequent fact – to convey synthetically the meaning of an entire country or of a single man by capturing images revealing the human side of our people.[24]

It is unimportant, in this context, to get into the enlightening details of this Zavattinian text; I believe, however, that the impact that such a film would have registered in Italy in those years would have been unprecedented. The idea at the basis of *My Italy* leaves an important legacy when in 1964 Pasolini decides to embark on a very similar journey for the making of his most 'Zavattinian' work: *Comizi d'amore* (*Love Meetings*). As in the project of Zavattini, Pasolini makes a film in which 'the protagonists are always Italians' and which, eleven years after *My Italy*, embodies a courageous and renewed exploration of contemporary Italy.

Ten years later, Zavattini ultimately coordinated *I misteri di Roma* (*The Mysteries of Rome*), a 'flash-film' involving fifteen directors. In a long and detailed script that appeared in the volume dedicated to the film as part of the 'From the Script to the Film' series published by Cappelli, and curated by Francesco Bolzoni, Zavattini further elaborates his theories and, above all, provides the reader with numerous interpretative keys to his thinking. There are many technical aspects mentioned by Zavattini in his writings that describe *The Mysteries of Rome*, but behind the apparent technicalities it is not difficult to capture a visionary element that looks to the future, towards a much wider audiovisual universe:

In some of our procedures there are similarities with television, and in this kind of cinema this is not surprising. In comparison to television, however, we will have a greater range of possibilities and freedom and, from a stylistic point of view, a greater intensity of expression. The narrative fabric of a television inquiry program is often quite loose, whereas here it must be very tight and every moment must be expressed with the essentiality, even plastic, of a 'fiction' movie, with the difference that it has from beginning to end the rigour and the characteristic of the things that are really happening.[25]

Elsewhere, when describing the film from a different point of view, Zavattini clarifies the nature of *The Mysteries of Rome* as a 'flash-film':

Our 'film-inquiry', which will be about four thousand metres, intends to convey a 'one-day' portrait of Rome . . . We are not going to capture our Rome – a twice-capital city – in its official moments, but in the most daily ones, hour by hour and sometimes minute by minute, with its heroes pervading the chronicles, not the history, though the history comes out every now and then from our daily lives. . . . Our film intends to be sincere, free, and mobile as a diary, and will therefore express itself with all its open-minded variation of techniques and languages that the identification of truth from time to time will involve: from telephoto-lens to cameras, or sound devices, hidden here and there as traps; from the 35mm camera to the 16mm one, to the 18mm; and even photography, in some exceptional circumstances, will be able to offer us data and images otherwise inaccessible . . . And sometimes we will need not one camera, but ten, twenty cameras for one event, for which we can all be mobilised.[26]

The series of very distinctly political newsreels that Zavattini co-ordinated from 1968 to 1970 deserves special attention. In these years, Zavattini became the protagonist, as a screenwriter, co-ordinator and initiator of 13 newsreels focussed on the political and labour union struggles of those years, and oriented decisively in favour of the rising student movement as well as the labour strikes of the 1969 so-called 'hot autumn' and the short period that followed thereafter. The 2009 volume *Hidden Zavattini* (*Zavattini sottotraccia*), edited by his collaborator Ansano Giannarelli remains the most comprehensive source in this respect. As has already been pointed out many times earlier, however, what is most interesting is Zavattini's insistence on the communicative role of the cinematographic medium once again. He was increasingly convinced of such power, enthused by its immediacy, by its unmatched ability to analyse political and social reality, in a way in which neither the written word of literature nor of traditional journalism had been able to do.

It is in this lucid and radical consciousness of the potential deployment of the medium that Zavattini connects with the most advanced experiences of the history of the audiovisual, and in this sense his immense and often confused, but always extremely rich, work of organiser and creator amounts to a contribution that cannot be compared to any other experience found in the Italian cinema scene. On the other hand, the cinema conceived by Zavattini invoked a totally different production method, alternative to the one prevailing in the years in which he was fighting his battles. The advent of the digital, and even the opening up of the new horizons made possible by the World Wide Web, would have certainly aroused his enthusiasm.

The cineaste who shared with Zavattini such vision and openness, the one whose audiovisual universe could overcome the productive and expressive conventions of traditional cinema, was undoubtedly Roberto Rossellini. It would suffice to remember what Rossellini hoped for, after a long encounter with the young French intellectuals who worshipped him and were close to the entourage of *Les Cahiers du Cinéma*:

> I was preaching to those young men something with which I had always been obsessed, something I myself had always tried to achieve: getting rid of huge industrial structures and making films with a very low budget, even by using less expensive technical equipment. We never had theoretical discussions, whether to make realist or non-realist, or even surrealist films, etc., because what mattered the most to me was to promote the blooming of very small productions, which could succeed in drawing the attention of the public to emerging new voices.[27]

It is striking how 'Zavattinian' is this stance by Rossellini, just as striking as the fact that the two filmmakers have shared – in spite of recurring disappointment and rethinking – a deep confidence in the renewal of the audiovisual system, to be pursued within the outlook of a profound humanism. As with Rossellini, the older he became the bolder Zavattini became in his experiments.[28]

Concluding Thoughts

The question that remains to be solved, and which is far from being secondary or irrelevant, is the contrast, so evident in Zavattini, between theory and results, and above all between original projects and achievements.

'I think it's one of my little tragedies, my drama, this wanting to create an investigative cinema, with all its new formulations, and so forth, and falling again into a narrative cinema'.[29] According to Lino Micciché, this contradiction has played a fundamental role not only in the work of Zavattini, but also and above all in the evolution of cinema, which owes him the legacies of masterpieces like *Sciuscià* (1945), *Bicycle Thieves* (1948) and *Umberto D.* (1952) – in spite of the recriminations and the admission by Zavattini to have re-proposed compromising works. It amounted to the hiatus emphasised by Zavattini himself and meant to provide meaning both to the films and to his own theoretical elaborations. It should be appropriate, therefore, to end this contribution by quoting Micciché on the exceptional importance of Cesare Zavattini's 'proposals', notwithstanding (or thanks to) the contradiction between the narrative cinema he contributed to creating and renewing, on the one side, and the attempt to envision a completely different concept of the medium, on the other.

> Without such a – so to speak – "theoretical contradiction", film culture would not have had one of the most intense proposals aimed at going beyond the existing cinematic communication and the traditional social use of cinema; no one has yet reconstructed or identified completely and exhaustively the "systematic" aspect of such proposals. Yet, they are the only – and in any case the widest – systematic reflection ever elaborated by an Italian cineaste within the entire history of our cinema.[30]

Notes

1. Available at: <http://sensesofcinema.com/2003/great-directors/vertov/>, last accessed 29 September 2019.
2. My translation. Original quote: 'per quanto riguarda la storia cinematografica propriamente detta, l'immediatezza zavattiniana si situa lungo una serie illustre ed eroica, che ha alle sue origini il *Kino-Glaz* di Vertov, passa per le concezioni di Siegfried Kracauer, del *Film come ritorno alla realtà fisica*, continua, oltre la tappa importante assicurata dal nostro autore, nel *cinéma-verité*, nell'*underground*'. Barilli (1992), p. 83.
3. Associazione Nazionale Partigiani d'Italia (National Association of Italian Partisans).
4. My translation. Original quote: 'In Zavattini il neorealismo si configura come una attitudine, un modo di situarsi dinanzi al mondo, agli uomini, alle cose, ai sistemi sociali e culturali: è una disposizione critica applicabile in ogni ambito, nel giornalismo, nella canzone e nella musica, nella televisione e nella radio, nel fumetto, nei moderni mass media, ovunque il progresso della tecnologia abbrevi distanze e permetta di comunicare su larga scala. . . . C'è un baldanzoso entusiasmo in Zavattini per la carta stampata, il rotocalco, i film, le trasmissioni radiofoniche, la TV, una sua diretta immersione nei mass media, di cui sente il fascino elettrizzante e l'enorme virtualità comunicativa ed espressiva'. Argentieri (1992b), p. 165.
5. My translation. Original quote: 'fu parziale, disorganico e, soprattutto, inconsapevole'. Micciché (1992), p. 242.
6. Ibid. In the original: 'vistoso'.
7. My translation. Original quote: 'La via che Zavattini indica per 'scoprire' questo senso vero dei fatti e degli atti, anche i più quotidiani (proprio i più quotidiani) è un uso analitico del cinema, capace di restituirci in successione

sullo schermo i tanti diversi punti di vista dai quali l'oggetto può essere esaminato. Anche qui è ben evidente l'analogia con le grandi linee delle avanguardie artistiche del Novecento, in particolare, nelle arti figurative, con la linea fenomenologica cézanniana e con il cubismo. Come nelle opere cubiste di Picasso e Braque, Gris e Delaunay (tanto nel cosiddetto cubismo "analitico" quanto in quello "sintetico") l'oggetto tridimensionale riguardato secondo molteplici prospettive è restituito analizzato sulla tela, con un processo che contraddice il concetto di pittura come finestra sul mondo (legato all'illusione della prospettiva) a favore di una pittura come conoscenza della verità più profonda delle cose (una verità dispiegata letteralmente sul piano della tela); così l'analisi zavattiniana capovolge gli standard della narrazione cinematografica a favore di una scomposizione dinamica di atti e gesti del quotidiano che, attuata dalla cinepresa, è riattualizzata fenomenologicamente sullo schermo per l'intervento percettivo e intellettuale dello spettatore'. De Vincenti (1992), pp. 253–4.
8. My translation. Original quote: 'In definitiva, Zavattini non è distante da Flaherty nell'esortare alla fuga dai teatri di posa e dal romanzesco, e a precederlo v'è anche John Grierson e la sua scuola, impensabili se non vi fosse stato il regista di *Nanouk* e de *L'uomo di Aran* ad anticipare alcuni fondamentali lineamenti. Ma né Grierson, né Flaherty e neanche Vertov assegnano, come fa Zavattini, alla fantasia un ruolo di provocazione in un genere peraltro che parrebbe opporsi ad essa. . . . È nel *cinéma-vérité* francese o canadese degli anni sessanta che sarà possibile riacciuffare certe suggestioni che sono state proprie di Zavattini'. Argentieri (1992a), pp. 107–8.
9. My translation. Original quote: 'Nel futuro il realismo troverà altre forme, ma intanto deve *conoscere*, anche con mezzi crudeli, per mettere in grado gli uomini di prendere delle risoluzioni. Mettiamo un disoccupato fermo davanti alla macchina da presa, e poi inchiodiamo il pubblico per cinque minuti davanti a quell'immagine proiettata sullo schermo. Questo non si vuole. Si grida: "Montaggio!", perché le immagini scorrano veloci e la conoscenza del pubblico resti superficiale, e la verità non venga approfondita. Dico disoccupato ma potrei dire qualunque cosa che richieda urgenti interventi e per la quale la nostra *durata* di attenzione è sempre inferiore alla necessità di conoscerla veramente'. Zavattini (1979), p. 118, emphases in the original.
10. Zavattini (1953c).
11. Barthes (1980), n. p.
12. My translation. Original quote: 'L'opera collettiva prodotta da Cesare Zavattini, Riccardo Ghione e Marco Ferreri per la Faro Film di Messina – interessa oggi, soprattutto, non tanto e non solo per i suoi esiti propriamente estetici, quanto come storico banco di prova delle più avanzate teorie zavattiniane. Composito ed eterogeneo, fortemente ibrido nella sua commistione di istanze documentarie e finzionali, all'incrocio tra testimonianza e ricostruzione, narrazione e saggio, il film traduce in forme precorritrici dell'inchiesta televisiva, del *cinéma vérité* e del *direct cinema* le riflessioni

del suo "autore" sul cosiddetto "film-lampo", quale ideale "sviluppo del neorealismo"'. Vitella (2017), p. 213.
13. My translation. Original quote: 'Questo tipo di film, cioè un film che riproduce un fatto di cronaca nei luoghi dov'è realmente avvenuto e che interpretano coloro stessi che ne sono stati i principali protagonisti, nasce dal mio vecchio desiderio di adoperare il cinema per conoscere ciò che succede intorno a noi, ma in modo diretto e immediato, mentre l'altro modo, quello dei racconti inventati, è un modo indiretto e mediato'. Zavattini (1979), p. 89.
14. My translation. Original quote: 'Non vi è neanche una gerarchia di fatti più o meno cinematografabili, ma qualunque fatto è degno di essere ricostruito, degno di quest'opera collettiva, . . . che solo il cinema (e che la radio dà in piccola misura e che la televisione potrà dare in misura maggiore del cinema) può dare in un modo completo in quanto è il mezzo che lascia il minor margine alla imprecisione, alla non-obiettività'. Ibid., p. 90.
15. See also *I vinti* (*The Defeated Ones*), a film in three episodi set in France, Italy and England shot in 1952.
16. Zavattini (1953b), p. 68.
17. Micciché (2003), p. 507.
18. My translation. Original quote: 'Nell'estremo tentativo di riconsegnare al neorealismo cinematografico il suo glorioso mandato, il film di Zavattini finisce suo malgrado per ammetterne il tramonto, riconoscendo altresì, nel quadro della clamorosa affermazione commerciale dei rotocalchi illustrati e della progressiva "industrializzazione" dell'immagine neorealista, il nuovo ruolo sociale interpretato dalla fotografia, nella sua capacità di "perlustrare", "rifigurare" e "testimoniare" il mondo visibile'. Vitella (1992), p. 218.
19. In 1961 Zavattini coordinated another project entitled *Le italiane e l'amore* (*Italian Women in Love*), which was directed by several filmmakers and addressed how Italian women were dealing with love.
20. For a wider study on the unfinished projects of these years, see Carpi (1958).
21. Zavattini (1953b), p. 68.
22. My translation. Original quote: 'Il film continua a snodarsi attraverso una serie di episodi o di momenti, in luoghi diversi senza neppur bisogno di nominarli. È sempre l'Italia, sono sempre gli italiani i protagonisti. Da due ragazzi colti dieci minuti prima di un loro convegno amoroso, il primo, e che vediamo alternativamente durante l'ansioso prepararsi a questo convegno nel seno della famiglia l'una e dell'ufficio l'altro, passiamo al ritratto di una famiglia italiana come lo farebbe un documentarista; a momenti di partenza e di arrivo nelle grandi stazioni, nelle piccole stazioni, nei porti; da un ballo popolare sulle strade della pianura a una lite di poveri in un grande casamento popolare; ai muratori che costruiscono una casa, colti nel momento in cui dal riposo passano alla ripresa del lavoro, colle loro parole, i loro atti minimi e il mondo che hanno intorno'. Zavattini (1953b), p. 628.
23. My translation. Original quote: 'Capiteremo in un paesino di cui forse poche centinaia di persone sanno il nome. Ci fermeremo pochi minuti. Voglio dire

che apparirà come se ci fossimo fermati pochi minuti; invece ci fermeremo il tempo necessario per mettere insieme quei pochi minuti di pellicola. (Più che il film degli "episodi" sarà il film dei "momenti"). Coglieremo più momenti che episodi, proprio come se attraversassimo l'Italia su un'automobile'. Ibid.
24. My translation. Original quote: 'Vedremo così, tanto per esemplificare: un uomo che prega; una fanciulla che aspetta il fidanzato; persone che non si conoscono, di differenti paesi ad es., messe insieme dall'autore per osservarne le reazioni su un dato argomento; un cantoniere che parla con l'autore che l'ha incontrato per via; le fasi di una nascita; un pranzo di contadini nel Cassinese; la festa del Redentore a Venezia o di Piedigrotta a Napoli. . . . I fatti debbono obbedire alla necessità di essere rappresentati con rapidità, simultaneità ed estensione nel tempo e nello spazio in funzione precisa del tentativo continuato con ogni fatto susseguente – di dare sinteticamente il senso di un paese o di un uomo cogliendo quelle immagini che svelano il lato umano del nostro popolo'. Ibid.
25. My translation. Original quote: 'In qualche nostro procedimento ci sono delle parentele con la televisione, e in un certo tipo di cinema come questo non c'è da stupirsene. Ma nei confronti della televisione avremo tematicamente un maggior raggio di possibilità e di libertà, e dal punto di vista stilistico una maggiore intensità d'espressione. Il tessuto narrativo di un'inchiesta per televisione è spesso piuttosto allentato quando invece qui deve essere strettissimo e ogni momento espresso con la essenzialità, anche plastica, di un film 'fiction' con la differenza che ha dal principio alla fine il rigore e la caratteristica delle cose che stanno realmente avvenendo'. Zavattini (1963), p. 32.
26. My translation. Original quote: 'Il nostro "film-inchiesta", che sarà di circa quattromila metri, intende dare il ritratto di "una giornata" di Roma . . . Noi non abbiamo intenzione di cogliere la nostra Roma, due volte capitale, nei suoi momenti ufficiali, ma in quelli più correnti, ora per ora e qualche volta minuto per minuto, con i suoi eroi che riempiono la cronaca e non la storia, anche se la storia balena ogni tanto dietro le nostre quotidiane vicende. . . . Il nostro film intende essere sincero libero e mobile come un diario, e perciò si esprimerà con tutta quella spregiudicata variazione di tecniche e di linguaggi che la identificazione del vero di volta in volta comporterà: dal teleobiettivo alle macchina da presa, o sonore, nascoste qua e là come trappole; dalla macchina a trentacinque millimetri a quella a sedici millimetri, a diciotto millimetri; e perfino la fotografia, in qualche circostanza eccezionale potrà offrirci dati, immagini, non altrimenti captabili . . . E a volte non di una macchina da presa avremo bisogno, ma di dieci, di venti per un solo avvenimento, per il quale potremo essere mobilitati tutti'. Ibid., pp. 14–15.
27. My translation. Original quote: 'Io predicavo a questi ragazzi una cosa che mi aveva sempre assillato e che io stesso avevo cercato in un certo senso di rendere effettiva: di liberarsi dalle grandi strutture industriali e di fare dei film a bassissimo costo, anche attraverso l'impiego dei mezzi tecnici meno costosi. Non abbiamo mai avuto discussioni di carattere teorico, se cioè bisognasse fare film

realisti o non realisti o film surrealisti ecc, poiché quello che mi sembrava più importante era promuovere questa fioritura di minuscole produzioni che riuscissero perlomeno a proporre all'attenzione del pubblico delle forze nuove'. Rossellini (1987), p. 310.
28. As noted by Martin Scorsese in his documentary *My Voyage to Italy* (1999).
29. My translation. Original quote: 'Credo sia una delle mie piccole tragedie, dei miei drammi, questo desiderare di fare un cinema-inchiesta con tutte le sue formulazioni nuove eccetera, e il ricadere in un cinema affabulato'. Gambetti (1986), p. 136.
30. My translation. Original quote: 'senza la "contraddizione" – diciamo così – "teorica", la cultura cinematografica non avrebbe avuto alcune tra le più intense proposte di superamento della comunicazione filmica esistente e del tradizionale uso sociale del cinema, proposte di cui nessuno ha finora completamente individuato ed esaurientemente ricostruito l'aspetto "sistematico", ma che pure sono la sola – e comunque la più ampia – riflessione sistematica che un cineasta italiano abbia prodotto nell'intera storia del nostro cinema'. Miccichè (1992), p. 252.

Works Cited

Argentieri, Mino (1992), 'Inchiesta', in Guglielmo Moneti ed., *Lessico zavattiniano*, Venice: Marsilio, pp. 104–8.

Argentieri, Mino (1992), 'Neorealismo', in Guglielmo Moneti ed., *Lessico zavattiniano*, Venice: Marsilio, pp. 161–8.

Barrili, Renato (1992), 'Evento', in Guglielmo Moneti ed., *Lessico zavattiniano*, Venice: Marsilio, pp. 78–85.

Barthes, Roland (1980), Dear Antonioni', *Cahiers du Cinéma*, 311, <http://shihlun.blogspot.ca/2015/07/dear-antonioni-roland-barthes-1980.html>, last accessed 29 September 2019.

Carpi, Fabio (1958), *Cinema italiano del dopoguerra*, Milan: Schwarz.

De Giusti, Luciano ed. (2003), *Storia del cinema italiano. Volume VIII – 1945–1953*, Venice: Marsilio.

De Vincenti, Giorgio (1992), 'Sperimentalismo', in Guglielmo Moneti ed., *Lessico zavattiniano*, Venice: Marsilio, pp. 253–60.

Gambetti, Giacomo (1986), *Zavattini mago e tecnico*, Rome: Ente dello Spettacolo.

Giannarelli, Ansano ed. (2009), *Zavattini sottotraccia*, Arcidosso (Gorizia): Edizioni Effigi.

Kracauer, Siegfried (1997), *Theory of Film: The Redemption of Physical Reality*, Princeton: Princeton University Press.

Miccichè, Lino (2003), 'Un film "teorico": *L'amore in città*', in Luciano De Giusti ed., *Storia del cinema italiano. Volume VIII – 1945–1953*, Venice: Marsilio, pp. 506–7.

Miccichè, Lino (1992), 'Soggetto e sceneggiatura', in Guglielmo Moneti ed., *Lessico zavattiniano*, Venice: Marsilio, pp. 241–52.

Moneti, Guglielmo ed. (1992), *Lessico zavattiniano*, Venice: Marsilio.
Parigi, Stefania (2003), 'Il pensiero di Zavattini', in Luciano De Giusti ed., *Storia del cinema italiano. Volume VIII – 1945–1953*, Venice: Marsilio, pp. 502–13.
Rossellini, Roberto (1987), *Il mio metodo*, Venice: Marsilio.
Vertov, Dziga (1926), 'Provisional Instructions to Kino-Eye Groups', cited in Jonathan Dawson, 'Vertov, Dziga', <http://sensesofcinema.com/2003/great-directors/vertov/>, last accessed 29 September 2019.
Vitella, Federico (2017), 'Strategie di "autenticazione"', in *L'amore in città*, *Fata Morgana*, <http://fatamorgana.unical.it/numero19/indice19.htm>, last accessed 29 September 2019.
Zavattini, Cesare (1979), *Neorealismo ecc.*, Milan: Bompiani.
Zavattini, Cesare (1963), *I misteri di Roma*, Francesco Bolzoni ed., Bologna: Cappelli.
Zavattini, Cesare (1953), '*La Rassegna del Film*. 16 marzo - 13 aprile', in Luciano De Giusti ed., *Storia del cinema italiano. Volume VIII – 1945–1953*, Venice: Marsilio, pp. 627–33.
Zavattini, Cesare (1953), 'Some Ideas on the Cinema', *Sight and Sound*, 23.2: 64–9, <http://www.f.waseda.jp/norm/Realism11/Zavattini.pdf>, last accessed 29 September 2019.
Zavattini, Cesare (1953), 'Tesi sul neorelismo', *Emilia*, 53 (novembre).

Filmography

Nanouk of the North, DVD, directed by Robert J. Flaherty. Scr.: Frances Flaherty, Robert J. Flaherty. Prod.: Robert J. Flaherty, 1922.
Man of Aran, DVD, directed by Robert J. Flaherty. Scr.: Robert J. Flaherty. Prod.: Gainsborough Pictures, 1934.
Giorni di gloria (*Days of Glory*), DVD, directed by Giuseppe De Santis, Marcello Pagliero, Mario Serandrei, Luchino Visconti. Scr.: Umberto Barbaro and Umberto Calosso. Prod.: Fulvio Ricci for ANPI (Associazione Nazionale Partigiani d'Italia), 1945.
Sciuscià (*Shoeshine*), DVD, directed by Vittorio De Sica. Scr.: Sergio Amidei, Adolfo Franci, Cesare Giulio Viola, Cesare Zavattini. Prod.: Paolo William Tamburella for Società Cooperativa Alfa Cinematografica, 1946.
Pian delle stelle (*Plain of Stars*), VHS, directed by Giorgio Ferroni. Scr.: Giorgio Ferroni, Vittorio Metz, Indro Montanelli, Rodolfo Sonego. Prod.: Corpo Volontari della Libertà, 1946.
Il sole sorge ancora (*The Sun Still Rises*), DVD, directed by Aldo Vergano. Scr.: Guido Aristarco, Giuseppe De Santis, Giuseppe Gorgerino, Carlo Lizzani. Prod.: ENIC, 1946.
La terra trema (*The Earth Trembles*), DVD, directed by Luchino Visconti. Scr.: Giovanni Verga, Antonio Pietrangeli, Luchino Visconti. Prod.: Universalia Film, PCI,1947.
Ladri di biciclette (*Bicycle Thieves*), DVD, directed by Vittorio De Sica. Scr.: Luigi Bartolini, Oreste Biancoli, Suso Cecchi D'Amico, Vittorio De Sica, Adolfo

Franci, Gherardo Gherardi, Gerardo Guerrieri, Cesare Zavattini. Prod.: Produzioni De Sica, 1948.

Luci del varietà (*Variety Lights*), DVD, directed by Federico Fellini, Alberto Lattuada. Scr.: Federico Fellini, Ennio Flaiano, Alberto Lattuada, Tullio Pinelli. Prod.: Federico Fellini and Alberto Lattuada for Capitolium, 1950.

Achtung banditi! (*Achtung: Bandits!*), DVD directed by Carlo Lizzani. Scr.: Carlo Lizzani, Rodolfo Sonego, Ugo Pirro, Giuliani De Negri, Giuseppe Dagnino, Massimo Mida, Enrico Ribulsi, Mario Socrate. Prod.: Cooperativa Spettatori Produttori Cinematografici, 1951.

Umberto D., DVD, directed by Vittorio De Sica. Scr.: Cesare Zavattini. Prod.: Amato Film, Produzione Films Vittorio De Sica, Rizzoli Film, 1952.

I vinti (*The Defeated Ones*), DVD, directed by Michelangelo Antonioni. Scr.: Michelangelo Antonioni, Suso Cecchi D'Amico, Giorgio Bassani, Turi Vasile. Prod.: Film Costellazione, SGC, 1952.

L'amore in città (*Love in the City*), DVD, directed by Michelangelo Antonioni, Federico Fellini, Alberto Lattuada, Carlo Lizzani, Francesco Maselli, Dino Risi. Scr.: Aldo Buzzi, Luigi Chiarini, Luigi Malerba, Tullio Pinelli, Luigi Vanzi, Vittorio Veltroni, Cesare Zavattini, Michelangelo Antonioni, Federico Fellini, Alberto Lattuada, Carlo Lizzani, Francesco Maselli, Dino Risi. Coordinated by Cesare Zavattini. Prod.: Marco Ferreri, Riccardo Ghione and Cesare Zavattini for Faro Film, 1953.

Cronache di poveri amanti (*Chronicles of Poor Lovers*), VHS, directed by Carlo Lizzani. Scr.: Vasco Pratolini, Sergio Amidei, Giuseppe Dagnino, Carlo Lizzani, Massimo Mida. Prod.: Cooperativa Spettatori Produttori Cinematografici, 1954.

La strada (*The Road*), DVD, directed by Federico Fellini. Scr.: Federico Fellini, Ennio Flaiano, Tullio Pinelli. Prod.: Ponti-De Laurentiis Cinematografica, 1954.

Le amiche (*The Girlfriends*), DVD, directed by Michelangelo Antonioni. Scr.: Cesare Pavese, Michelangelo Antonioni, Suso Cecchi D'Amico, Alba de Cespedes. Prod.: Trionfalcine, 1955.

Le italiane e l'amore (*Italian Women and Love*), DVD, directed by Gian Vittorio Baldi, Marco Ferreri, Giulio Macchi, Francesco Maselli, Lorenza Mazzetti, Gianfranco Mingozzi, Carlo Musso, Piero Nelli, Giulio Questi, Nelo Risi, Florestano Vancini. Scr.: Baccio Bandini, Lorenza Mazzetti, Carlo Musso, Enrico Muzii, Giulio Questi, Piero Nelli, Daniela Parca, Gabriella Parca, Cesare Zavattini. Coordinated by Cesare Zavattini. Prod.: Magic Film, Pathé, 1961.

I misteri di Roma (*The Mysteries of Rome*), VHS, Directed by Gianni Bisiach, Libero Bizzarri, Mario Carbone, Angelo D'Alessandro, Lino Del Fra, Luigi Di Gianni, Giuseppe Ferrara, Ansano Giannarelli, Giulio Macchi, Lorenza Mazzetti, Massimo Mida, Enzo Muzii, Piero Nelli, Paolo Nuzzi, Dino B. Partesano, Giovanni Vento. Coordinated by Cesare Zavattini. Prod.: Spa Cinematografica, 1963.

Comizi d'amore (*Love Meetings*), DVD, directed by Pier Paolo Pasolini. Prod.: Arco Film, 1964.

La veritaaaà (*The Truuuuth*), VHS, directed by Cesare Zavattini. Scr.: Cesare Zavattini. Prod.: RAI, Reiac Film, 1982.

My Voyage to Italy, DVD, directed by Martin Scorsese. Scr.: Suso Cecchi D'Amico, Raffaele Donato, Kent Jones, Martin Scorsese. Prod.: Media Trade, Cappa Production, Paso Doble Film, 1999.

CHAPTER 4

Gianfranco Brebbia: The 'Absurd', Expanded Quality of Experimental Cinema (1962–73)*

Donatella Valente

Introduction

In *Underground Cinema Today* (1974), experimental and independent filmmaker Sirio Luginbühl stated that Gianfranco Brebbia 'used his camera as if it was a machine-gun that scratches, burns, erodes the film to incandescence and a multitude of explosions of magnificent force and energy, like only a gentle and civilized man can when crying out to the entire world his desperate wish for a revolution'.[1]

This encapsulates Brebbia's persona; a creative energy and an independent intellectual drive to find innovative ways of deploying media, were the features of a strong personality which shaped his vision as an artist in a highly idiosyncratic style. His films – between 1962 and 1973 he made 109 experimental films in 8mm and H8[2] – are the result of what one could term as an 'alchemical fusion' between polished analysis and an instinctive, creative approach to materials and techniques testing the boundaries of film as an expressive medium.

Especially relevant to the study of Brebbia's films are the Historical avant-garde, and the post-WWII film avant-garde with the Cooperativa del Cinema Indipendente (Co-operative of Independent Cinema) and the filmmakers of the New American Cinema.

In *Cinema sperimentale e mezzi di massa in Italia* (*Experimental Cinema and the Mass Media in Italy*), film historian Adriano Aprà argued that Italian experimental cinema had no history and no critical context. He wrote:

> One could argue that there was no *underground* in Italy – though films, catalogue lists, and even a critical text, constitute evidence of its existence. This is due to two reasons: these films did not circulate widely, even in parallel or alternative exhibition circuits; and, moreover, they did not receive much critical attention. . . . Born not to be seen, they were neither aristocratic nor assertive as their American counterparts; they did not aspire to the museum venues, perhaps merely exhibited

in domestic spaces in everyday circumstances; given that they were never born they neither died.[3]

For this reason, the task of this chapter is to explore Brebbia's artistic vision in an attempt to provide some historical and critical material that is relevant to bridge a cultural gap in the history of Italian experimental and independent cinema. It will map onto the historical landscape of the film avant-garde some of his films, which are expressions of an overlooked epistemological approach to an expanded practice with a range of media, which include film, photography, and painting. This will also cast some light on how his inventive approach to media technologies and materials formed not merely a subjective vision but, rather, a language that had an innovative scope in cinematic terms. The latter was the result of opposite yet complementary expressions: a subjective practice, ideally always fluid and dynamic, and an objective and scientific practice, both operating within the cultural limits of which Brebbia was aware he was working.

Influences: The New Italian Avant-garde and the New American Cinema

Brebbia found inspiration for his experimental art films beyond his study of classical literature. He highly respected Dziga Vertov's avant-garde reflexive documentary, from which he learned how to shape a personal vision of the world through a subjective camera-eye, to create montage and image juxtapositions, and dissolves. He also admired Michelangelo Antonioni's and Federico Fellini's sophisticated and visionary cinematography. Among Brebbia's greatest sources of inspiration for experimental approaches to filmmaking was Jonas Mekas, however, with whom he shared the idea that the camera could be used as a notebook with which to gather subjective impressions of everyday life. He met Jonas Mekas in Italy, and wrote him a letter in New York, in 1968,[4] in which he discussed his visions for a new cinema and passion for filmmaking. For Brebbia, cinema as an experimental practice had to start again, from the beginning. He also shared his ideas and creative cinematic visions in his correspondence with fellow independent filmmaker and friend Alfredo Leonardi.[5] These experiences were the inspirational motivation behind his affiliation to the Cooperativa del Cinema Independente between 1968 and 1969.

Brebbia also drew on the avant-garde practice of 'found footage' based on the aesthetic of re-shaping old film material – a practice that harks back to the early cinema era. In his book *Film Begets Film*, Jay Leyda claimed that compiling found footage allows the filmmaker to create new 'actuality' films. In this respect, in *Recycled Images*, William C. Wees argued:

> Compilation films may reinterpret images taken from film and television archives, but generally speaking, they do not challenge the representational nature of the images themselves. That is, they still operate on the assumption that there is a direct correspondence between the images and their profilmic sources in the real world.[6]

Brebbia's use of archival footage taken from home movies and documentaries, as well as television reportages of the first Moon landing, transcends the representational nature of found footage. He turns his found footage materials into an amalgam, that is, a lyrical meditation on the social reality of that period and the cultural appeal of television in the domestic space (Figures 4.1 and 4.2).

Brebbia was a member of the Cooperativa del Cinema Independente, which was established at the end of June 1967 in Naples by the brothers Antonio and Adamo Vergine, with the support of independent and experimental filmmakers from Turin and Rome, and at a time when other film co-operatives were being established in Belgium, Switzerland, Britain and elsewhere in Europe. The catalysing factors for the founding of this initiative were not only the films the New American Cinema exhibited in Italy between 1961 and 1966, but also the organisational model of the New York Filmmakers' Co-operative, which was founded by Jonas Mekas in 1962. The first film season of the Cooperativa del Cinema Indipendente took place in the legendary independent art space in Rome, Filmstudio '70, in March of 1968.[7] By the end of the same year, however, the group had already lost its momentum, moving its activities to Rome and dismantling its juridical apparatus.

Figures 4.1, 4.2 *Idea assurda per un filmaker. Luna*
(*An Absurd Idea for a Filmaker. Moon*, 1969).

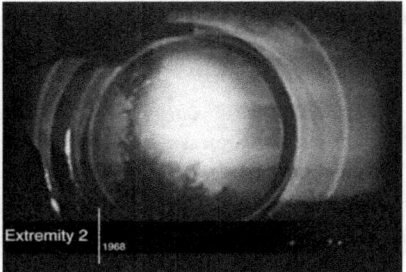

Figure 4.3 *Anno 2000* (*Year 2000*, 1969). **Figure 4.4** *Extremity 2* (1968).

During an evening of September 1969, on the occasion of the event 'Manifestazione–31' – a series of screenings dedicated to Independent Cinema – Brebbia screened his film *Polemizzando in bianco e nero* (*Polemics in Black and White*, 1967), and *Anno 2000* (*Year 2000*, 1969) (Figure 4.3). These were shown as part of the Cooperativa del Cinema Independente, alongside the work of other experimental filmmakers such as Gianfranco Baruchello,[8] Guido Lombardi, Giorgio Turi and others. Also in 1969, in San Marino, at the second event 'Rendez-vous Des Cinémas d'Art et D'Essai'[9] he screened his *Extremity 2* (1968) (Figure 4.4) under the name of the independent film group, while an entire film programme, titled 'dedicata a G. Brebbia della Cooperativa Cinema Indipendente di Roma' ('Dedicated to Gianfranco Brebbia, a member of the Cooperative of Independent Cinema of Rome'),[10] took place in the Northern town of Varese, where he was born and lived.

With his films, Brebbia attempted to share his profound insights and long-term experimental projects with his collaborators. The ethos of the group was founded on values such as equality and freedom of expression, as the film *Tutto, tutto nello stesso istante* (*All, All at Once*, 1969), the 'swansong film' of the Cooperativa del Cinema Indipendente, testifies.

Like most members of the Cooperativa del Cinema Indipendente, Brebbia's filmmaking style was steeped not only in the American cinematic counterculture of the Beat Generation, considered as a model to emulate and often to dream of, but also in the avant-garde practices of the New American Cinema. As a study conducted by Pablo Eucharren and Claudia Solaris testifies:

> Also in Italy, the spirit of the American Beat generation movement contributed to the founding of a model for a new micro-society, based on such values as solidarity and equality. This would be an alternative to dominant cultural values, which aimed at realising a direct conflict with institutional apparatuses, and which,

nevertheless, were criticized. It also lay the groundwork for a real, parallel community, characterised by its own habitat where everybody can follow one's own individual and artistic inclinations.[11]

In addition to this, Brebbia's creative sensibility must have also been influenced by earlier art forms, such as, from the late Forties, the *Movimento spazialista* (*Space Art Movement*), with Lucio Fontana's expanded media works, and *Movimento arte concreta* (*Movement Concrete Art*), founded in Milan in 1948 by artists, among others, Bruno Munari and Gillo Dorfles. By engaging with the legacies of the Bauhaus and Constructivism, the latter explored abstract and geometrical configurations as the primary constituents of matter and meaning.[12] The objectives of the *Movimento arte concreta* was exactly that of creating a 'concrete language' that is, one that could translate the artist's intuitions into concrete images, a pure interplay between colours and shapes which would enhance their rhythm and formal interaction, hence freeing them from any figurative reference and symbolic meaning.[13]

Arguably, however, many of Brebbia's films are also steeped in the ethos of the Italian art school *Arte Povera* (*Poor Art*), which prided itself on working 'around the notion of energy fields using "*poor*" materials, both natural and artificial. These artists deployed simple techniques and processes to generate significant experiences; their artworks were informed by both phenomenological and empirical perspectives'.[14] Its founder, Germano Celant, argued that they 'could serve as models, or even catalysts, of real social change'.[15]

Brebbia's working methodology revealed film's specific materiality through photographic over-exposure, or under-exposure: the coarse and grainy unrefined properties of the medium, its ragged surfaces. By a process of disclosure, his experimental cinema laid bare the texture that formed it. For Brebbia, the process of creative freedom entailed a commitment to effecting cultural changes through formal innovation. This was the inherent ethos of working with film and other media during a period of profound social and artistic changes.[16]

Experimenting with Media: Brebbia's 'Expanded' Cinema

Prior to making experimental films, Brebbia was primarily interested in documentary. While he was a war refugee in an internment camp in Switzerland, between 1943 and 1947, he started documenting his life by taking photographs. He refined his photographic skills during the following decade, especially when he returned to Italy and met his future wife Adele.

In the early Sixties, he started making home movies and participating in regional amateur filmmaking competitions. In 1962 he made his first film, *Go Kart*—with a Bolex Paillard Reflex H8–which was a transformative experience.[17] It even caused him what he saw as 'a crisis', something like an epiphany, an artistic rupture that compelled him to experiment. Everyday visual perceptions and phenomena inspired his sensibility, which became a receptacle of fleeting impressions. He took to writing poems, impressionistic notes that could be seen as a form of primer for his overall filmmaking process, helping him channel his life experiences and perceptions into film. He wrote: 'Perhaps writing suddenly freed my vision from those images'.[18] His deep engagement with the sensory world invoked his intuitions and creative instincts.

He made *La legge è uguale per tutti* (*All Are Equal before the Law*, 1964), which is something like a fairy tale with a good ending, shot at home, and with his daughters, Giovanna and Paola, as the only protagonists. With this film he participated in regional and national amateur film competitions, such as the '*Concorso nazionale della federazione nazionale cineamatori di Torino il fotogramma d'oro*' ('National Competition of the National Home Movies Federation of Turin, The Golden Photogram'), where he won the Special "Ferrania" Home Movie Award in Varese, in 1964, for the category of 'Best Family Film'. He won additional prizes for the category of 'cineamatori' ('home-movie filmmaker'), in regional and national Cine Clubs, and earned further critical acclaim from audiences and the press, which spurred on his research on cinematographic experimental techniques.

In 1965, the periodical *La Prealpina* (*The Pre-Alps Journal*) wrote that, as a young filmmaker, Brebbia's distinctive style was characterised by 'an independence of spirit and by an ongoing search for new effects, at times making use of techniques which are completely different from the more conventional ones'.[19]

While frequenting cultural events organised by cinema and theatre critics, he started to become acquainted with international art practices such as Fluxus, Happenings, the Living Theatre and Pop Art.[20] He was also very much aware of the *Arte Povera* practitioners, especially after meeting with Marisa and Mario Merz and the art historian and critic Daniela Palazzoli. In the mid Sixties, he was introduced to artists who also shared his visions and deployment of sophisticated spatialised forms. Indeed, inspired by *Arte Povera*, he took-up painting in the late Sixties, and created very original, idiosyncratic, artworks by using recycled materials such as glue, resins, acrylics, metal, and glass, thus achieving fantastic, three-dimensional, mixed media results.[21]

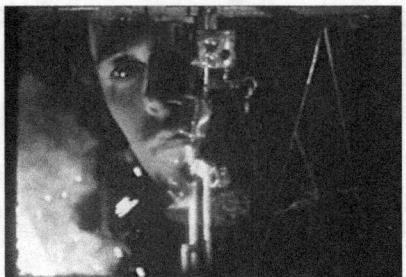 

Figures 4.5, 4.6 *Identificazione* (*Identification*, 1965).

According to an interview conducted by his daughter Giovanna Brebbia with painter and friend Sandro Uboldi in March 2014, the filmmaker found inspiration in Angelo Pozzi's sculptures around the imaginary relationship between objects and the surrounding space; Pozzi used to collect metal waste and arrange it according to abstract compositions.[22] (Figures 4.5 and 4.6) According to Uboldi, Brebbia was a pioneer in experimental film because of his remarkable curiosity for different artistic disciplines. For instance, his meticulously executed hand-coloured films created suggestive effects during projection, which recalled abstract and informal paintings in movement.[23] Uboldi argued that Brebbia handled the camera like a painter of the New York school, and reminded him of Franz Kline or Willem de Kooning. Indeed, this might be the case. Brebbia used his camera to trace bold and fluid spatial brushstrokes within more conventionally controlled tracking shots. He made a film like a sculptor would patiently attend to a sculpture, that is by moulding the primary matter; Brebbia used to 'sculpt' film, as it were, by directly and patiently scratching the emulsion layer of the film surface in order to not only create shapes and images, but also to invoke narratives and coherent visions. This artisanal methodology was enhanced by his frequent treatment of the film medium as a canvas, on which to paint by hand, rather than deploy the film camera as a medium through which the filmmaker photographically impresses images on film. These techniques recall American experimental filmmaker Stan Brakhage, whose several films, especially *Mothlight* (1963), and *The Garden of Earthly Delights* (1981), were also made as impressionistic, camera-less, and scratched and hand-painted film-poems (Figures 4.7 and 4.8).

In another interview conducted in 2014, the painter Vittore Frattini argued that 'Brebbia deployed a new language, with definitely unusual techniques. It was part of that cinematographic research which characterised the

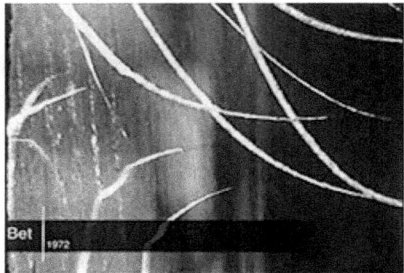 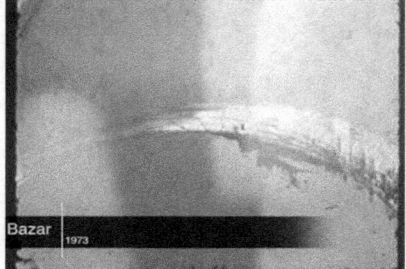

Figure 4.7 *Bet* (1972). Figure 4.8 *Bazar* (1973).

period between 1968 and 1969, when films became authentic "experimental cinema"'.[24] During this time, Brebbia was also influenced by other independent avant-garde initiatives. He became a member of the *Club nuovo teatro* (*New Theatre Club*) in Milan, which was the first film studio for artists' and underground cinema and, alongside other alternative spaces in Milan, screened films of the New American Cinema and English Free Cinema.[25]

For him, experimenting with art materials meant also expanding life-experience in its creative and imaginative dimension. Thus, his creative process involved a phenomenological re-creation of life as art experience. This was also characteristic of the Expanded Cinema tradition, which involved the creative use of space and media to enhance human sensory perception. As Gene Youngblood famoulsy explained in his 1970 book *Expanded Cinema*:

> We intuit that the human condition has expanded since yesterday, but the popular arts aren't telling us. The human condition does not stop with what we know about ourselves. Each genuinely new experience expands the definition of the human condition that much more. Some are seeking those new facts, those new experiences, through the synaesthetic research of expanded cinema.[26]

As posthumously published in the film journal *Bianco e Nero*, Brebbia's writing on an imaginary and experimental cinema envisioned bold new horizons in the attempt to expand human sensory thresholds and gain a different level of life awareness. He thus wrote: 'Throughout the immensity of the Universe, and the grandness of movement, it has been possible to trace abstract connections among ostensibly living beings'.[27] As I will examine later in this chapter, Brebbia's imaginative project of placing a multiplicity of projectors in space to expand human beings' consciousness in everyday life is one example (Figure 4.9).

The expanded quality of Brebbia's trademark experimental cinema was also steeped in his research on astronomy, which infused his poetic

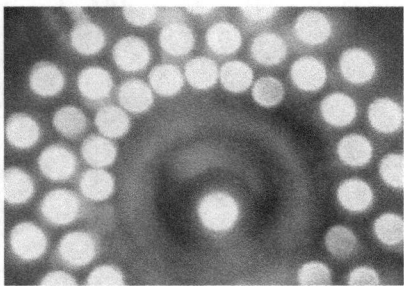

Figure 4.9 *Idea assurda per un filmaker. Luna (An Absurd Idea for a Filmmaker. Moon*, 1969).

writing with the idea of the artist's 'celestial' task and aim of propagating movement. He inspired his poet friend Claudio Panini to dedicate one of his poems to him, which started with the line 'To G.F.B (Gian Franco Brebbia) researcher of the Universe'.[28] His ability to fuse art and science can be seen in his use of pioneering techniques, through which he could foreground the plasticity of the filmic medium in shaping abstract imagery – imaginary, celestial visions of extra-terrestrial planets. Professor Fabio Minazzi, a scholar in the philosophy of applied and theoretical sciences, wrote about Brebbia's scientific approach to the arts and the creative process. For Brebbia, the relationship between abstract imagery and the physicality of the medium was alchemical. Minazzi writes that the filmmaker even felt as though he was 'immersed in the astral infinite, a creation of new worlds, not seen by anybody, yet'.[29] Ironically, the 'abstract-ism' of his visions of an expanded cinema was the result of both his 'sculpture' and 'painting' practices onto film as artefact. This process had a cultural value as it was devoted to creating an environment for the re-awakening of social consciousness. In this cathartic and mystical role of the avant-garde artist, as it were, Brebbia had the ability to propagate his imaginary alchemical fusion of spiritual and material energy in the surrounding space, and to his audience.[30]

In 1968, Brebbia experienced what he defined as a 'miracle', which took place after he decided to make films without a camera.[31] He mounted an orthodontic drill, which alternated up to 24 different sizes of very sharp small blades made of steel, on the base of an electrical toothbrush. With this customised creative tool, he applied the 'scratch-film' technique to his first camera-less, hand-coloured film *Stein* (1967). He scratched the Kolor film emulsion, which was successively coloured with a pen and India ink (Figure 4.10).[32] The projector infused movement to it, thus animating the abstract shapes created by the light etchings. With this experimental style,

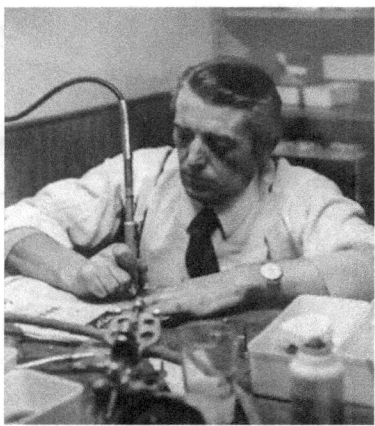

Figure 4.10 *Dall'archivio di Gianfranco Brebbia* (*From Gianfranco Brebbia's Archive*).

Brebbia created abstract formal compositions while foregrounding their expressive materials.

The hand-colouring and photographic manipulation of the film medium were first implemented by the historical avant-garde artists of the early twentieth century, from Len Lye's direct-animations to Man Ray's 'abstract/pure cinema', and Viking Eggeling's and Hans Richter's 'absolute' films. Also, the later generation of avant-garde filmmakers, from the 1950s onwards, experimented with the kinetic and plastic properties of the medium, and with its chromatic images, from Stan Brakhage to Malcolm Le Grice.

It could be argued that with his first camera-less film *Stein*, Brebbia accomplished his first step towards accomplishing an innovative, subjective vision of a 'cosmic' cinema, which entailed the projection of a more intense light onto the world in order to depict new forms and objects in space. Aiming to radically expand a cinematic perception of the world, Brebbia even envisioned projectors becoming like satellites circumnavigating the earth, bringing forth expanded optical experiences, and unveiling extraordinary new realms inhabiting a 'heavenly' space. Much of his writing was also abstract and lyrical. In the film journal *Bianco e Nero* he wrote:

> To have the privilege to switch off the sun . . . To replace every pre-existing thing on earth; to transform the location, dimension, form and colour of all objects . . . To create a completely new film, and think about a new vision for the human being, situated around the year 2150. To place a thousand billion cinema projectors in the stratosphere . . . To turn the switch connected to them and transform the night into the brightest imaginable spectacle.[33]

Clearly, his futuristic cinematic visions of the world were as much exceptionally original and lyrical as they were extravagantly imaginative. Brebbia's synaesthetic approach to light and primary materials can also be seen in *Deserto in luce solare* (*Desert in the Sunlight*, 1969), one of the films of the Cooperativa del Cinema Indipendente di Roma. It mostly consists of close-ups on a finger running through oil colours and heaps of coloured pigments, while tracing patterns through them. The interweaving of light and shadows with matter, combined with the sensual properties of the pulverised colours, mostly evoked by the close-ups, generate intricate new patterns, which might appeal to the human sensorium. *Deserto in luce solare* foregrounds Brebbia's experimental research into the creative process potentially activated by a sensorial engagement with the film's materials. As the distance of the camera from the objects being filmed narrows, it could be argued that *Deserto in luce solare* has a symbolic meaning; its foregrounding of the inherent grain of matter and strains reveals the irregular patterns of the imaginary (Figures 4.11–4.13). This is formally similar to some of the experimental films made by Bruno Munari and Marcello Piccardo of the Studio di Monte Olimpino, such as *I colori della luce* (*The Colours*

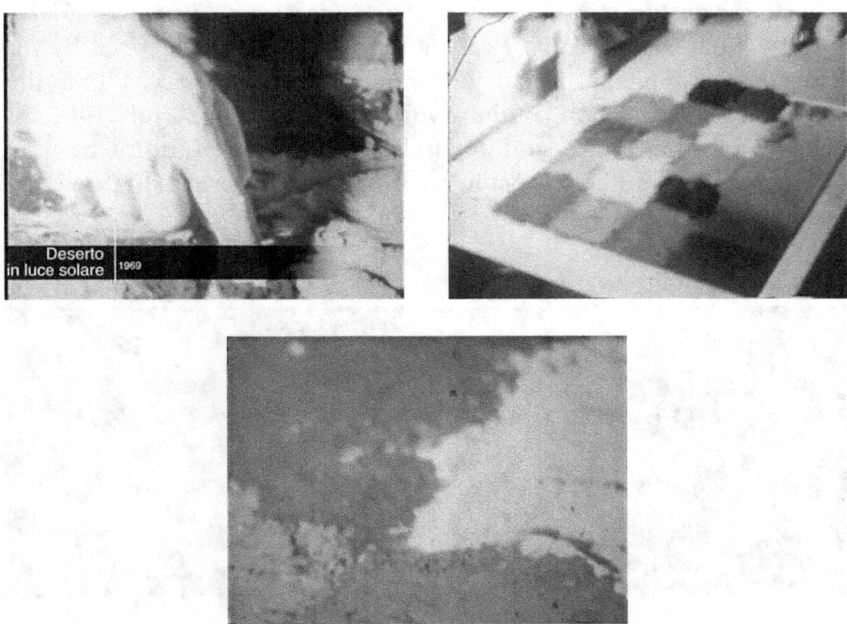

Figures 4.11, 4.12, 4.13 *Deserto in luce solare* (*Desert in the Sunlight*, 1969).

of Light, 1963) or *Moiré* (1964), which centres on the experimentation with light and pure colour.[34]

Deserto in luce solare is also about stretching and subtracting solidity from the wholeness of the original composition – as if expanding the field of vision into highly subjective dimensions – hence only leading us to see or perceive something that is, on a fantastic dimension, recreated by one's mind's eye. As images of these close-ups play at a faster rate (18 fps), the camera widens its angle, and reveals heaps of dyes neatly laid out on a mirror surface coming through beneath them. Because of its varying degrees of closeness to the photographed objects in *Deserto in luce solare*, the camera looks as if it was poised to tease out the ambivalent structures of the images, both the real and the fantastic. Here, the dual structure of the film language is also facilitated by the juxtaposition of colours alternating with light-play and accompanied by electronic music with ancient tribal rhythms. This polysemic texture reminds us of not only Bauhaus painter and photographer Làslò Moholy Nagy's 1930 film *Light-play: Black-White-Gray*, but also of *Lichtspiel Opus 1–4* (1921–5), the first abstract film made by Walther Ruttman, which illustrated the interaction between light-play, movement and geometrical patterns.

The exploration of space in its wider significance is central to *Idea assurda per un filmaker. Luna* (*An Absurd Idea for a Filmmaker. Moon*, 1969), which suggests that Brebbia may have been influenced by the Space art movement and Lucio Fontana's work on space.[35] The film draws on the first moon landing, which took place on 20 July 1969. As it made a strong impression on Brebbia's artistic sensibility, he used some footage from the television recordings of this event (Figures 4.14 and 4.15).

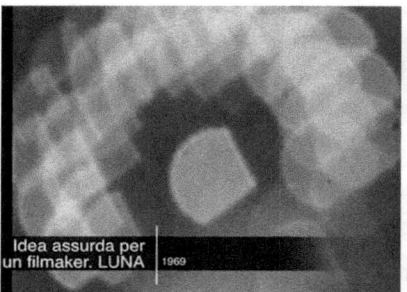 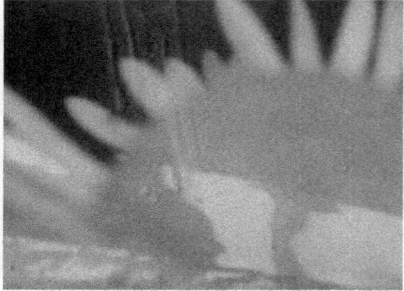

Figures 4.14, 4.15 *Idea assurda per un filmaker. Luna*
(*An Absurd Idea for a Filmmaker. Moon*, 1969).

The 'Absurd Idea' of Experimenting with Film

Perhaps it is no coincidence that in 1969 Brebbia made a cycle of four films whose title directly addresses the 'absurd idea' of filmmaking, implicitly relevant to the nature of wonder in scientific and technological advances, and supposedly meant to represent the progress of civilisation. One film, as just mentioned, was dedicated to the moon, the other films to three women: *Idea assurda per un filmaker. Matilde* (*An Absurd Idea for a Filmmaker. Matilde*), *Idea assurda per un filmaker. Ester* (*An Absurd Idea for a Filmmaker. Ester*), and *Idea assurda per un filmaker. Germana* (*An Absurd Idea for a Filmmaker. Germana*) (Figures 4.16–4.19).[36]

The genesis of the notion '*absurd idea*' may be traced both to his extraordinary interest in and enthusiasm for the cosmos, the stars and poetry. He wrote a long poem *Idea assurda per un filmaker* which he published in the eponymous article in the local paper the *Prealpina* on 14 July 1969, as the final sequence of the film also illustrates. Thus, this film cycle conveys the idea of 'absurdity' through a montage which connects

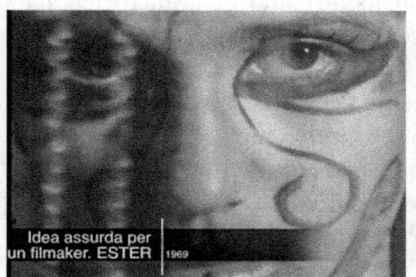 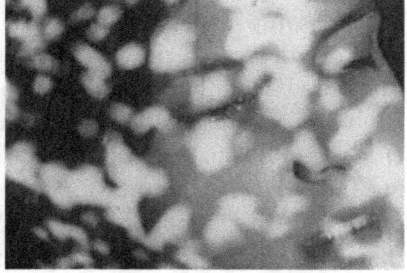

Figures 4.16, 4.17 *Idea assurda per un filmaker* (*An Absurd Idea for a Filmmaker. Ester*, 1969).

Figures 4.18, 4.19 *Idea assurda per un filmaker* (*An Absurd Idea for a Filmmaker. Matilde*, 1969).

science and technological progress to artistic experimentations with moving images – archival materials, colour filters, interspersed close-ups and superimpositions between the moon-landing footage and various other imagery, flowers, barbed wire, stones, naked feet and his *'idea assurda'* poem published in the newspaper. The statement inferred at the time was: what an absurd idea for a filmmaker to experiment so boldly, and extravagantly, by aiming to correlate the most disparate kind of media. Brebbia's poem in itself maps out an imaginary scenario where he envisions a potentially expanding media-ecology engaged in a concern for the human being's confinement in a fragile ecosystem.

It could be argued that Brebbia might have reached the apex of his artistic maturity by 1969, because of his conscious irony in using the concept of *'absurdity'* through which he seems to evoke the ambivalent nature of humankind. On the one hand, he celebrated technological progress, and on the other hand, he marginalised unusually visionary films for showing equally *'absurd'* ideas – such as the utilisation of unconventional media and materials in film.

For all that it is a reflexive film, which is to say one that stages its materials alongside people as protagonists, it could be argued that *Idea assurda per un filmaker. Luna* is also a conceptual artwork. The film makes visible both creative process and materials; he shows the camera, its colour filters and zoom lenses, along with the plastic and transparent materials. Brebbia's original instructions were to screen two films (15 minutes each) contemporaneously and in parallel: one showing the human being moving forward, reaching out for the moon, and viceversa, one showing the movement in the opposite direction.[37] Thus, while experimenting with these materials, and deploying them as the expressive semantics of his film language, he also forged conceptual connections. For instance, a montage illustrates television footage of the extraordinary moon-landing event through a red/blue filter, the human being associated with nature and the ordinary, as images of daisies are juxtaposed in large scale on the footage. The correlation is between the phenomenal aspect of scientific discovery and creativity – the human eye imagines itself in the stratosphere as it 'sees' the moon and the stars. This conceptual linkage is also underpinned by the poem's evocation of wonder in relation to the human sensorium – shaped as it is in day to day life.[38]

The concept of the 'absurd' idea of a filmmaker continues in the three portrait-films of three women. Each portrait holds in close-up a woman's face with the natural landscape as the background, often seen through tinted filters, out-of-focus and through photographic superimpositions. It could be argued that these female portraits, although figurative, may look

Figure 4.20 *Bet* (1972).   Figure 4.21 *Bazar* (1973).

like lyrical paintings in movements, given that Brebbia used his H8 camera as if it were a paintbrush. By tracing space with vigorous, fast and angular camera movements, he fragments the spatial dimension, thus recalling cubist kinetic paintings and their multi-perspectival representation of space, evoking the movement of still images. Brebbia was a visionary artist capable of synthetising avant-garde experimental ideas with modern media.

In 1972, Brebbia went back to making camera-less scratch films with *BET* and in 1973 with *Bazar* (Figures 4.20 and 4.21). As in *Stein*, both films' surfaces are scratched by an orthodontic drill and hand-coloured with India ink. *BET* is completely non-representational; an abstract film that experiments with geometric shapes and rhythm to the sound of tribal music. It resonates with such early abstract films as Len Lye's *Trade Tattoo* (1937) and Oskar Fischinger's *An Optical Poem* (1938). Though it may be very similar to *BET* for its abstract composition of shapes in movement, in the final part *Bazar* contains footage from Sirio Luginbhül's *Amarsi a Marghera* (*Love in Marghera*, 1970), which stylistically contrasts with the rest of the film, as it is figurative. It portrays a naked couple, standing, in each other's arms, pitted against the desert, with paparazzi taking their photos. With this Brebbia may have suggested the theme of unjust and unwanted attention, but also more broadly the expressive and creative freedom afforded by film.

The lyrical, visionary and 'expanded' quality of Brebbia's films can be seen also in *Ufo* and *Fumus Art* (*Smoke Art*, 1969) which document Happenings. While it formally differs from the rather abstract cameraless film *Stein*, *Ufo* (1968) retains the filmmaker's trademark vision of otherworldly realms, realised through experimentation in documentary-making and performance. It also shares with *Stein* a reflexive style in its manifest intent of awakening the audience's response to the pro-filmic

Figures 4.22, 4.23 *Ufo* (1968).

event, and to provoke thinking about social life as performance. It portrays a Happening called *UFO, oggetti volanti* (*UFO, Flying Objects*), which, with irony, refers to the unidentified flying objects of science fiction. This Happening took place on the hill of Monte Olimpino (a small town near Milan) in 1968. Brebbia met with experimental filmmaker Bruno Munari who, with Daniela Palazzoli, had organised the event (Figures 4.22 and 4.23).

From the opening sequence, we are plunged into a darkened room, where Brebbia, sitting at a table, directly looks into the camera, explicitly drawing our attention to the art magazine *BIT*, and to an advertisement of a call for artists to participate in the 'First International exhibition of Kites, Fire-balloons and Objects that lift themselves off the ground or move through the air',[39] which was the Happening he would be filming. His friend Claudio Panini wrote to Giovanna Brebbia that he had the natural, gestural, movements of an actor.[40]

The photographic effects used in staging the opening sequence, the glaring light reverberating from the desk lamp, the mercurial zooming-in and out of Brebbia's image, and his playful gestuality anticipated the tone of the performance event the film was about to exhibit. This ironic approach to the Happening was his way of communicating his perspective of life as a performance, where the experience of the everyday hinged on the interplay between imagination and reality. The frequently frantic mobility and the accelerated frame rate of the camera, while following the people's movements, also demonstrate his idea that the camera is an extension of the human body, while the film foregrounds the obtrusive presence not only of objects but also of people, treating them equally as outlandish and unknown. Towards the end, a bemused camera's gaze frames a cluster of white balloons with dangling letters forming the word '*potere*' ('power') flying up into the sky. Thus, the film playfully engages with the idea of the 'extra-terrestrial', the ordinary turned into the extraordinary. It also showcases the participatory nature of performance art partaking in the spirit of Happenings.

Stylistically, *UFO* also resembles some of the *Arte Povera* films, which trace the relationship between earth and human beings; hence, it draws the attention to the difference in scale and size between individual and place. For example, in his *Terra Animata* (*Animated Earth*, 1967), the *Arte Povera* painter, Luca Patella also choreographed the human body within the natural environment in order to investigate either the harmony or the alienation of the individual in relation to a specific place. As with Patella's creative use of industrial materials, Brebbia enjoyed re-inventing inverted images and accelerated animations through camera movements. Many of the camera's close-ups on textual imagery also demonstrate his interest in primary materials and flying objects. The film's conceptual and performative character was concerned with the portrayal of the human being in the landscape, celebrating creativity in the open space, a characteristic of another conceptual art practice, Land Art, which was an offshoot of *Arte Povera*.[41]

Brebbia's *Fumus Art* is also a Happening film. While it is made from a subjective perspective (by using expressive techniques such as unstable hand-held camera, jump cuts, photographic solarisation and so forth), process and performance are its central themes. It could be argued that the making of this experimental film is an expanded variation of conceptual art, as artificially coloured smoke, together with gigantic cylindrical props are used to also playfully engage with the concept of different degrees of ephemerality, while also evoking, with irony, psychedelic art populated by imagery of hallucinogenic experiences and dreams of escapism (Figures 4.24 and 4.25).

The films examined so far are the exemplification of Brebbia's cinema shaped by the contrasting yet generative relationship between reality and imagination, real objects, people and reveries. His friends, the artists

Figures 4.24, 4.25 *Fumus Art* (1969).

Massimo Crevani and Claudio Panini, were both of the opinion that what informed his art was something close to an alchemical reaction amongst such materials as 'wax, Indian ink, coffee powder, and a crystal', among others.[42] Film theorist Francesco Casetti also commented on the magical properties of the imagination in filmmaking. In his *Teorie del cinema 1945–1990* (*Theories about Cinema 1945–1990*), he wrote: 'Cinema is presented to us like something coetaneous with the aeroplane'.[43] Then he continues by citing Edgar Morin's anthropological approach to cinema, which explores the structures of the imaginary

> ... that has been launched, higher and higher, towards a dream cycle, towards infinity where the stars are . . . If therefore the imaginary is opposed to reality, this is not because it is false or a lie . . ., if it leads us to glimpse at the other side of the actual world it is not because it simply is its counterpart . . . The imaginary is that multiform and multidimensional afterlife in which we are equally immersed. It is the infinite virtual outcome accompanying what is actual, that is, what is singular, limited and finite in time. It is the antagonistic and complementary structure of what is said to be real, and without which, doubtlessly, there would be no sense of reality in man, or rather, no human reality altogether.[44]

By applying Casetti's and Morin's perspectives to the structures of the imaginary – both contradictory yet also complementary – to Brebbia's abstract films, but also to his experimental documentaries *UFO* and *Fumus Art*, the flying art objects, the dyes, the light and the scratches, are the actual, multidimensional and materialised forms of Brebbia's imagination. With him, the experimentation with film as an art medium can be deemed to be located between what is concrete and real, the subjective and the fantastic.

In the same years, other Italian independent and experimental filmmakers who applied scientific research to creative endeavours worked with (audio)visual experiments. For instance, with his film *Scusate il disturbo* (*Apologies for the Interruption*, 1968), Giorgio Turi worked around the theme of human's bungled reception of technology by setting out the separation of audio-visual signifiers intersecting across different media, such as television and film. Another example is Roberto Capanna's *Voy-age* (1964), made in collaboration with Turi, which forms another expression of the textual materiality of film – a structural interest that was typical of the Sixties and a prominent characteristic of many of the widespread independent film cooperatives, both in the United States and throughout Europe.[45]

These films share a formal interest with Paolo Gioli's films such as *Commutazioni con mutazione* (*Commutations with Mutation*, 1969), which deals with film as an art medium, and yet is the result of a composite, multiform structure. The 16mm film is the single support of three co-existing formats: Super8, 16mm, and 35mm. Gioli explains: 'The abovementioned formats were glued together, one at a time, fragment on top of fragment, using transparent adhesive tape'.[46] It could be argued that these structural aspects of filmmaking constitute another form of 'expanded' cinema, where film formats, as much as the various materials and tools deployed in the filmmaking process, are the expanded expressive possibilities of the cinematic apparatus.

To his friend Alfredo Leonardi, Brebbia wrote that he considered the camera as the extension of his own body:

> In my opinion, while filming, the camera must form an integral part of the human body. Thinking will therefore remain separate from the mechanical medium, yet already the spectator of the film that is being made. . . . I also believe that everybody in the future will use the camera as if it was an everyday STYLO PEN, as today we are still using it as if it was a quill pen.[47]

This suggests a predilection for a personal filmmaking style informed by technical expertise and an enthusiasm for experimental ideas. Not only painting, but also 'writing' with his personal camera, for Brebbia entailed that thought and creative processes were joined as one force.

This creative approach to filmmaking, is obviously reminiscent of the forefather of the French New Wave, Alexandre Astruc and his 1948 article 'Naissance d'une nouvelle avant-garde: la caméra-stylo' ('The Birth of a New Avant-Garde: The Camera Stylo'). The idea of the camera stylo, as a means for an innovative form of creative 'writing', is also present in Brebbia's visionary films: the camera's ocular mechanism as an extension of the human body and thought. It could be argued that Brebbia's films express a style that Paul Arthur defined as: 'a meeting ground for documentary, avant-garde, and art film impulses'.[48]

Concluding Thoughts

The films that I have analysed in this chapter form an eclectic combination of the abstract, the lyrical and the meditative, based on ordinary, real-life, events, and always perceived through a painterly and compositional sensibility. As with Brakhage's film-poems, one is reminded of the romantic figure of the artist as an alchemist (Figures 4.26 and 4.27).[49] Brebbia's enthusiasm for unusual techniques situates him as avant-garde artist within the wider national and international independent film practices of the Sixties and Seventies.[50]

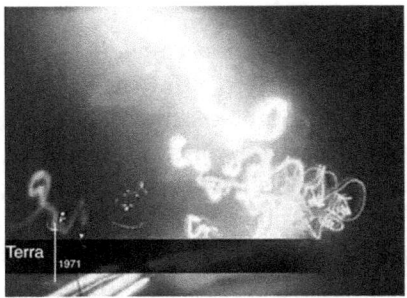 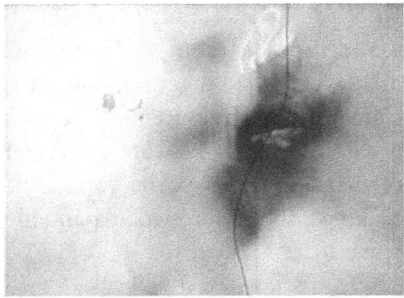

Figures 4.26, 4.27 *Terra* (*Earth*, 1971).

It could be argued that the 'absurd' expanded quality of Brebbia's cinema was based on his experimental and innovative techniques: from the 'free brushstroke' of his hand-coloured films, to his camera-less filming and film-scratching technique with the orthodontic drill. Born within the modernist era of the avant-gardes, which aspired to foster cultural changes through the arts, cinema was regarded as a particularly innovative practice. Brebbia's experimental filmmaking was steeped in this belief.

* All technical details concerning the films mentioned in this chapter are sourced from Gianfranco Brebbia's archive as published in Giovanna Brebbia's 2015 book *Idea assurda per un filmaker. Gianfranco Brebbia e il cinema sperimentale degli anni sessanta-settanta* (*An Absurd Idea for a Filmmaker: Gianfranco Brebbia and Experimental Cinema of the Sixties and Seventies*).

Notes

1. My translation. Original quote: '[Gianfranco Brebbia] ha usato la cinepresa come una mitragliatrice graffiando, bruciando, erodendo la pellicola in mille esplosioni di forza e di energia, come solo può fare un uomo mite e civile per gridare al mondo intero la sua disperata voglia di rivolta'. Brebbia (2015), p. 241.
2. Brebbia in Bacigalupo (1974), p. 62.
3. My translation. Original quote: 'Si potrebbe dire che l'*underground* in Italia non c'è stato, anche se restano dei film, dei cataloghi e perfino un volume a ricordarlo. E questo per due motivi: perché questi film hanno circolato pochissimo, anche nei circuiti paralleli o alternativi; e perché non hanno sollevato un discorso critico . . . Questi film, nati per non essere visti, sono privi dell'aristocraticità americana oltre che della sua assertività; non avevano

alcuna ambizione al museo, semmai alla casa e allo spazio del quotidiano; per non essere mai nati, non sono neppure morti'. Brebbia (2015), p. 146. Aprà (originally published in 1976 in limited print-run) in Saba (2006), pp. 177–97. Cited by Bursi in Aprà (2013), p. 15.
4. Bacigalupo (1974), p. 60.
5. Brebbia (2015), p. 157; originally in Biondi (1973).
6. Wees (1993), p. 36.
7. Bursi and Causo (2010), p. 148.
8. With experimental filmmaker Alberto Grifi, Baruchello co-directed the found footage film *Verifica incerta* (*Disperse Exclamatory Phase*) in 1965.
9. 'Art and Essay Film Club Association'. My translation.
10. Brebbia (2015), p. 79.
11. My translation. Original quote: '[I]l mondo beat Americano contribuì a fondare anche da noi il modello di una nuova microsocietà basata sui valori di solidarietà ed egualitarismo, alternativa a quella dominante, che si prefiggeva tanto di arrivare a uno scontro finale con gli apparati istituzionali, che comunque venivano criticati, quanto di instaurare una comunità reale, parallela, dotata di un suo habitat in cui ciascuno potesse seguire le proprie inclinazioni individuali e artistiche'. Echaurren and Salaris (1999), in Brebbia (2015), p. 145.
12. The *Movimento arte concreta* (*Concrete Art Movement*) was founded in Milan and explored abstraction and geometry, engaging the legacies of the Bauhaus and Constructivism'. Celant (1969a), p. 25.
13. Fondazione Angelo Bozzola, 'Gli anni Cinquanta e il Movimento Arte Concreta', available at: <http://www.fondazioneangelobozzola.it/angelo-bozzola/biografia/gli-anni-cinquanta-e-il-movimento-arte-concreta/>, last accessed 10 December 2018.
14. *Arte Povera* was coined by art critic and curator Germano Celant in 1967. Christov-Bakargiev (2001), p. 21.
15. Lumley (2001), p. 56.
16. He shared this approach with experimental filmmaker Guido Lombardi who argued: 'Film is determined within physicality. The absent images ultimately are part of a space that still needs to be construed as film wants to have the shape and time to grow'. My translation. Original quote: 'Il film ... è determinato nella fisicità. Le immagini assenti alla fine sono uno spazio ancora da costruire perché il film vuole avere la forma e il tempo di una crescita'. Brebbia in Bacigalupo (1974), p. 136. In 1971, together with Alfredo Leonardi, Lajolo and Lombardi formed a small video-documentary collective, called *Videobase*, through which they implemented the pertinence of media technologies to chronicling social discontents.
17. Brebbia (2015), p. 51.
18. My translation. Original quote: 'Forse lo scrivere d'improvviso mi liberava l'occhio che era sollecitato da quelle immagini'. Brebbia in Bacigalupo (1974), p. 59.

19. My translation. Original quote: '[U]no spirito di indipendenza e per la continua ricerca di effetti nuovi usando a volte una tecnica totalmente opposta a quella usuale'. Brebbia in Bacigalupo (1974), p. 59.
20. Brebbia, Gervasini, Minazzi (2015), p. 156.
21. His daughter Giovanna Brebbia described her father's long-time passion for painting that made him dream of one day having an entire exhibition dedicated to his artworks. Painting will complement his artistic expressive range mainly devoted to filming exemplary situations and moments in the everyday. Brebbia (2015), p. 248.
22. Ibid., p. 66.
23. Ibid., p. 67.
24. My translation. Original quote: 'Brebbia aveva utilizzato un linguaggio nuovo, con una tecnica certamente inusuale. Faceva parte di quella ricerca cinematografica che esplose tra il 1968 and 1969, allorquando i film divennero autentico "cinema sperimentale"'. Ibid., p. 70.
25. Ibid., p. 71.
26. Youngblood (1970), p. 68. Also relevant to Brebbia's 'expanded' use of film in combination with other media is Youngblood's statement: 'Expanded cinema has been expanding for a long time. Since it left the underground and became a popular avant-garde form in the late 1950s, the new cinema primarily has been an exercise in technique, the gradual development of a truly cinematic language with which to expand further man's communicative powers and thus his awareness. If expanded cinema has had anything to say, the message has been the medium'. Youngblood (1970), p. 75.
27. My translation. Original quote: 'Nell'immensità del creato, nella magnificenza del movimento, è stato possibile il collegamento astratto di esseri apparentemente viventi . . .'. Brebbia in Bacigalupo (1974), p. 59.
28. From Gianfranco Brebbia's archives, his daughter Giovanna published a poem by Claudio Panini, written in 1970. Brebbia (2015), p.179.
29. My translation. Original quote: 'immerso nell'infinito astrale. Una creazione di mondi nuovi mai visti da chicchessia'. Minazzi (2015), p. 18.
30. In an article published in the regional newspaper *La Prealpina* on 20 April of 1968, titled '*Con tre pellicole di un varesino astrattismo cinematografico al Cine Club*' ('*With Three Short Films by a Filmmaker from Varese, Abstract Cinema at the Cinema Club*', my translation), the author 'Emmedi' (name incomplete) argues that 'for having reached his apex with painting and sculpture, abstract art had expanded into the new territories of the short film: the abstract language of Brebbia's films had ventured into the most paroxysmal, extreme, and neurotic form, even verging on hysteria'. My translation. Original text reads: '[L]'astrattismo ha trovato un nuovo campo di espansione nella cinematografia a passo ridotto, avendo raggiunto il suo acme nella pittura e nella scultura: l'espressione astratta, nella enunciazione filmistica di Brebbia, è arrivata all'estremismo, al parossismo, alla nevrosi che rasenta l'isterismo'. Brebbia (2015), p. 73.

31. Brebbia in Bacigalupo (1974), p. 59.
32. Brebbia (2015), p. 162.
33. My translation. Original quote: 'Avere il privilegio di girare un interruttore e spegnere il sole. . . . Avere la possibilità nel frattempo di sostituire ogni cosa preesistente sul globo; trasformando collocazione, dimensione, forma e colore di ogni oggetto. . . . Creare un film inedito, completamente nuovo, opinando la percettività visiva dell'uomo stabilizzato sulla terra intorno al 2150. Disporre mille miliardi di proiettori cinematografici, involticizzati nella stratosfera . . . Girare l'interruttore collegato a questi apparecchi e trasformare la notte nel più luminoso spettacolo immaginabile. 23 marzo 1968'. Brebbia in Bacigalupo (1974), p. 60.
34. Munari was also known for having in 1962 founded, alongside Marcello Piccardo, a laboratory of scientific research called Lo Studio di Monte Olimpino where science and art converged to study and experiment with potential formal patterns across the spectrum of light, colour and movement. See bibliography for *Lo Studio di Monte Olimpino*.
35. In an experimental television programme broadcast in 1952 by the national television channel RAI, Lucio Fontana projected *Immagini spaziali in movimento* (*Images from Space in Movement*), which is based on the concept of space. This projection is accompanied by the *Manifesto del movimento spaziale per la televisione* (*A Space Movement Manifesto for the Television*. Madesani (2002), pp. 54–5. Fontana envisioned perceptual interconnections among new technologies such as radio, television and radar, thus expanding visual representations of space and the universe that prevailed in the mass media. Fontana stated that while the 'Space artist' did not foreground any figurative theme, the viewer was encouraged to create her or his own subjective, otherworldly dimensions, which were based on his or her own sensations and perceptions evoked by the moving images projected into space. The aesthetics of the 'Space movement' envisaged to set the painting free from the frame, the sculpture free from its materiality and the written page free from its typographical constraints. Fontana's, as much as Brebbia's, research into spatial dimensions in art can be likened to Suprematist Kazimir Malevich's abstract paintings, which prefigure spatial depth and extraterrestrial satellites through geometrical blocks of colour, as in the case of his pictorial composition 'Airplaine Flying' (1915).
36. Brebbia (2015), p. 132
37. A title card at the end of the film explains this film's structure.
38. Brebbia (2015), pp. 175–79.
39. The text of this advertisement's was originally in English. This source can be found on the DVD titled *Gianfranco Brebbia. Il Filmmaker che cadde sulla terra* (*The Filmmaker Who Fell to Earth*) authored by Giovanna Brebbia and distributed by MIC (Museo Interattivo del Cinema), 2016.
40. Brebbia (2015), p. 86.
41. In 1967, British conceptual artist Richard Long made the film *A Line Made by Walking* inspired by Land Art's interest in manifesting the generative

relationship between art objects and the landscape in which they are placed triggered by the artist's performance.
42. My translation. Original quote: 'la cera, l'inchiostro di china, caffè in polvere, un cristallo'. Brebbia (2015), p. 171.
43. My translation. Original quote: 'Il cinema ci viene presentato come qualcosa coetaneo all'aeroplano.' Casetti (2004), p. 51.
44. My translation. Original quote: '. . . che si è lanciato, sempre più in alto, verso un ciclo di sogno, verso l'infinito delle stelle . . . Se dunque l'immaginario si contrappone al reale, non è perché rappresenta il falso e la bugia . . . se ci porta ad intravvedere l'altra faccia del mondo effettivo, non è perché ne sia il semplice rovescio . . . L'immaginario è l'aldilà multiforme e pluridimensionale della nostra vita, nel quale siamo egualmente immersi. È l'infinita scaturigine virtuale che accompagna ciò che è attuale, vale a dire singolare, limitato e finito nel tempo. È la struttura antagonistica e complementare di ciò che si dice reale, e senza la quale, indubbiamente, non ci sarebbe reale nell'uomo, o meglio, realtà umana'. Morin (1982), p. 26, and (1963), p. 84. Casetti (2004), pp. 51–5.
45. The denomination of 'Structural Filmmaking' was first formulated in 1974 by P. Adams Sitney in relation to American avant-garde filmmaker Maya Deren, and later used to categorise the New American Cinema from the late Forties until the Sixties. Filmmakers such as Michael Snow, Hollis Frampton, Paul Sharits, Joyce and Paul Weiland, to name only a few, incorporated the analysis of the filmic text into the shape and structure of their films, hence the content advanced the idea of anti-illusionism and the study of the filmic apparatus. In 1976, Peter Gidal enriched this view with his theory on 'Materialist Film', also reinforcing the structuralist and self-reflexive practice by stating: 'Structural/Materialist film attempts to be non-illusionist. The process of the film's making deals with devices that result in demystification or attempted demystification of the film process'. Gidal (1996), p. 145, originally published in Gidal (1976).
46. My translation. Original quote: 'I formati suddetti sono stati alternativamente incollati con nastro adesivo trasparente, frammento su frammento'. Gioli (1969).
47. My translation. Original quote: 'Per conto mio la cinepresa deve integrarsi. Far parte del corpo, mentre si filma. Il pensiero resterà così estraneo al mezzo meccanico, dev'essere già spettatore della pellicola che man mano si impressiona. . . . Sono anche convinto che in futuro la cinecamera sarà usata da tutti come una comune PENNA A SFERA, ora però siamo ancora alla penna di struzzo'. Brebbia (2015), p. 157, emphasis in the original.
48. Rascaroli (2009), p. 21.
49. In a letter to Giovanna Brebbia, writer and friend Claudio Panini wrote about one of Brebbia's favourite topics: alchemy; 'Gianfranco was fascinated with alchemy. If I remember well, he frequently used this word in his public talks'. My translation. Original quote: 'Gianfranco era rimasto affascinato dall'alchimia. Se ricordo bene era un termine ricorrente nei suoi discorsi'. Brebbia (2015), p. 89.

50. All technical details concerning the films mentioned in this chapter are sourced from Gianfranco Brebbia's archive as published in Giovanna Brebbia's 2015 book. All images are published with Giovanna Brebbia's consent.

Works Cited

Aprà, Adriano, ed. (2013), *Fuori norma. La via sperimentale del cinema italiano*, Venice: Marsilio.
Aprà, Adriano (2006), 'Cinema Sperimentale e mezzi di massa in Italia', in Cosetta Saba ed., *Cinema Video Internet. Tecnologie e avanguardia in Italia dal futurismo alla Net.Art*, Bologna: CLUEB, pp. 177–91.
Aprà, Adriano (1976), *Cinema Sperimentale e mezzi di massa in Italia*, Milan: Fondazione Angelo Rizzoli.
Bacigalupo, Massimo, ed. (1974), *Il film sperimentale*, Special Issue of *Bianco e Nero*, 5.8 (maggio–agosto): 1–187.
Biondi, Rocco (1973), 'Neoavanguardia', *Rocco Biondi. Avanguardia e Kitsch nel cinema italiano fino al 1970*, <http://www.roccobiondi.it/Neoavanguardia.htm>, last accessed 8 October 2017.
Brebbia, Gianfranco (1974), 'Gianfranco Brebbia', in Massimo Bacigalupo ed., *Il film sperimentale*, Special Issue of *Bianco e Nero*, 5.8 (May–August): 58–62.
Brebbia, Giovanna, Mauro Gervasini, Fabio Minazzi, eds. (2016), *'Filmavo da indipendente, solo e contro tutti', Gianfranco Brebbia e la cultura internazionale a Varese negli anni sessanta-settanta*, Varese: Mimesis.
Brebbia, Giovanna (2015), *'Idea assurda per un filmaker', Gianfranco Brebbia e il cinema sperimentale degli anni sessanta-settanta*, Milan: Mimesis.
Bursi, Giulio (2013), '*La questione sperimentale (dalle origini agli anni Sessanta)*', in Aprà, Adriano ed., *Fuori norma. La via sperimentale del cinema italiano*, Venice: Marsilio.
Bursi, Giulio and Massimo Causo (2010), *'Occhio privato sul (vecchio e nuovo) mondo. Omaggio a Massimo Bacigalupo'*, in Giulio Bursi and Massimo Causo eds., *Massimo Bacigalupo*, in Catalogo Film Festival di Torino, in collaboration with: Cineteca Nazionale; Università degli Studi di Udine, Dams Gorizia/La Camera Ottica, Film and Video Restoration/Crea – Centro Ricerca Elaborazioni Audiovisivi, pp. 136–41.
Casetti, Francesco (2004), *Teorie del Cinema 1945–1990*, Milan: Studi Bompiani.
Celant, Germano (1969), *Arte Povera: Conceptual, Actual or Impossible?*, London: Studio Vista.
Celant, Germano (1969), 'Arte Povera: Notes for a guerilla war', *FlashArtonline.com*, <http://www.flashartonline.com/article/arte-povera/>, last accessed 28 May 2017.
Christov-Bakargiev, Carolyn (2001), 'Thrust into the Whirlwind: Italian Art Before Arte Povera', in Richard Flood and Morris Frances eds., *Zero to Infinity: Arte Povera 1962–1972*, Minneapolis: Walker Art Centre, pp. 29–40.

De Bernardi, Tonino (2016), 'Il Cinema Innocente. Per Giovanna Brebbia e il cinema di Gianfranco', in Giovanna Brebbia, Mauro Gervasini, Fabio Minazzi eds., *Filmavo da indipendente, solo e contro tutti*', *Gianfranco Brebbia e la cultura internazionale a Varese negli anni sessanta-settanta*, Varese: Mimesis, pp. 156–8.

Echaurren, Pablo, Claudia Salaris (1999), *Controcultura in Italia 1967–1977. Viaggio nell'underground*, Turin: Bollati Boringhieri.

Emmedi – incomplete name (1968). *Con tre pellicole di un varesino astrattismo cinematografico al Cine Club*', in *La Prealpina*, 20 April.

Fondazione Angelo Bozzola, 'Gli anni Cinquanta e il Movimento Arte Concreta', <http://www.fondazioneangelobozzola.it/angelo-bozzola/biografia/gli-anni-cinquanta-e-il-movimento-arte-concreta/>, last accessed 10 December 2016.

Flood, Richard, Frances Morris (2001), 'Introduction: Zero to Infinity', in *Zero to Infinity: Arte Povera 1962–1972*, Richard Flood and Frances Morris eds., Minneapolis: Walker Art Centre, pp. 9–20.

Gidal, Peter (1996), 'Theory and Definition of Structural/Materialist Film', in *Avant-Garde Film. An Anthology of Writing*, Michael O'Pray ed., London: The Arts Council of England/John Libbey Media/University of Luton Press.

Gidal, Peter (1976), *Structural Film Anthology*, London: BFI.

Gioli, Paolo (1969), '*Commutazioni con mutazione*', <http://www.paologioli.it/film1.php?page=film&id=1>, last accessed 10 December 2016.

Lumley, Robert (2001), 'Spaces of Arte Povera', in Richard Flood, Frances Morris eds., *Zero to Infinity: Arte Povera 1962–1972*, Minneapolis: Walker Art Centre, pp. 41–66.

Madesani, Angela (2002), *Le icone fluttuanti. Storia del cinema d'artista e della videoarte in Italia*, Milan: Bruno Mondadori.

Minazzi, Fabio (2015), 'Prefazione. La Cinepresa come mitragliatrice', in Giovanna Brebbia, '*Idea assurda per un filmaker*', *Gianfranco Brebbia e il cinema sperimentale degli anni sessanta-settanta*, Milan: Mimesis, pp. 11–20.

Morin, Edgar (1982), *Il cinema o l'uomo immaginario*, Milan: Feltrinelli.

Morin, Edgar (1963), *L'esprit du temps*, Paris: Grasset.

O'Pray, Michael (1996), *Avant-Garde Film. An Anthology of Writing*, London: The Arts Council of England/John Libbey Media/University of Luton Press.

Rascaroli, Laura (2009), *The Personal Camera. Subjective Cinema and the Essay Film*, London: Wallflower Press.

Studio di Monte Olimpino, Lo: <http://nuke.monteolimpino.it/icoloridellaluce/tabid/474/Default.aspx>, last accessed 10 December 2016.

Wees, William C. (1993), *Recycled Images*, New York: Anthology Film Archives.

Woods, Gaby (2004), 'Meet Marnie . . . ', *The Observer*, 18 July, <http://www.guardian.co.uk/theobserver/2004/jul/18/features.review7?INTCMP=SRCH>, last accessed 7 December 2005.

Youngblood, Gene (1970), *Expanded Cinema*, New York: P. Dutton & Co.

Filmography:

A Corpo (*Corporeality*), film, directed by Guido Lombardi and Anna Lojolo, 1968.
Amarsi a Marghera (*Love in Marghera*), film, directed by Sirio Luginbhül, 1970.
An Optical Poem, film, directed by Oskar Fischinger, Germany/U.S., 1938.
Anno 2000 (*Year 2000*) film, directed by Gianfranco Brebbia, Italy, 1969.
Bazar, film, directed by Gianfranco Brebbia, Italy, 1973.
BET film, directed by Gianfranco Brebbia, Italy, 1972.
Commutazioni con mutazione (*Commutation with Mutation*), film, directed by Paolo Gioli, Italy, 1969.
Deserto in luce solare (*Desert in the Sunlight*), film, directed by Gianfranco Brebbia, Italy, 1969.
Extremity 2, film, directed by Gianfranco Brebbia, Italy, 1968.
Fumus Art (*Smoke Art*), film, directed by Gianfranco Brebbia, Italy, 1969.
Go Kart, film, directed by Gianfranco Brebbia, Italy, 1962.
I colori della luce (*The Colours of Light*), film, directed by Bruno Munari and Marcello Piccardo, prod. Studio di Monte Olimpino, Italy, 1963.
Idea assurda per un filmaker. Luna (*An Absurd Idea for a Filmmaker. Moon*), film, directed by Gianfranco Brebbia, Italy, 1969.
Idea assurda per un filmaker. Matilde, *Idea assurda per un filmaker. Ester*, and *Idea assurda per un filmaker. Germana* (*An Absurd Idea for a Filmmaker: Matilde, An Absurd Idea for a Filmmaker. Ester, An Absurd Idea for a Filmmaker. Germana*), film, directed by Gianfranco Brebbia, Italy, 1969.
Identificazione (*Identification*), film, directed by Gianfranco Brebbia, Italy, 1965.
La legge è uguale per tutti (*All Are Equal before the Law*), film, directed by Gianfranco Brebbia, Italy, 1964.
Lichtspiel Opus 1–4, film, directed by Walther Ruttman, Germany, 1921–5.
Light-play: Black-White-Gray, art installation, by Làslò Moholy Nagy, Hungary, 1930.
Moiré, film, directed by Bruno Munari and Marcello Piccardo, prod. Studio di Monte Olimpino, Italy, 1964.
Mothlight, film, directed by Stan Brakhage, United States, 1963.
Polemizzando in bianco e nero (*Polemizing in Black and White*), film, directed by Gianfranco Brebbia, Italy, 1967.
Scusate il disturbo (*Apologies for the Interruption*), film, directed by Giorgio Turi, Italy, 1968.
Stein, film, directed by Gianfranco Brebbia, Italy, 1967.
Terra (*Earth*), film, directed by Gianfranco Brebbia, Italy, 1971.
The Garden of Earthly Delights, film, directed by Stan Brakhage, United States, 1981,
Trade Tattoo, film, directed by Len Lye, New Zealand, 1937.

Tutto, tutto nello stesso istante (*All, All at Once*), film, directed by Cooperativa del Cinema Indipendente, Italy, 1969.
Ufo, film, directed by Gianfranco Brebbia, Italy, 1968.
Voy-age, film, directed by Giorgio Turi and Roberto Capanna, Italy, 1964.
The DVD titled *Gianfranco Brebbia. Il Filmaker che cadde sulla terra* (*The Filmmaker Who Fell on Earth*) was authored by Giovanna Brebbia and distributed by MIC (Museo Interattivo del Cinema), 2016.

CHAPTER 5

Italian Family Films: The Case of the *Archivio Nazionale di Bologna*

Laura Ceccarelli

Introduction

The contemporary age is marked by a radical transformation of the modes of recording and transmitting one's memories – both within the public and private spheres. 'Family films' are a product of the private sphere, and are part of the broader universe of amateur filmmaking, which began in the mid-1920s, and has steadily developed since, also in Italy as a result of the introduction of non-professional and lighter filming equipment.[1] Moreover, as an amateur audiovisual practice it has developed, since its inception, its own codes, styles and an altogether alternative and autonomous language, in juxtaposition to institutionalised practices of conventional cinema. Amateur films have mainly portrayed marginal and atypical subject matter, which are oriented towards and influenced by personal interests, by domestic and social contexts to which the amateur cineaste belonged.

Roger Odin – the French scholar who first theorised amateur cinema – explains the specificity of family films ('home movies') as follows: 'By family films I mean films made by a member of the family about characters, events, or objects that are, in one way or another, linked to this family's history, and which are made for the privileged use of those family members'.[2] Family films are in fact chiefly made by a person who works alone and is therefore responsible for shooting, photography and oftentimes soundtrack and editing, and whose modes of consumption are far removed from conventional commercial circuits. It should also be noted that since its inception, recurring themes have emerged from this cine-amateuresque form of film-making: the filming of children, wives, parents, pets, home parties, private ceremonies, family trips, the product of which is characterised by spontaneity, freshness, naturalness, but also by the absence of technical and stylistic precision, the *mal fait* (badly / amateurly executed) according to Odin's own definition. What is of primary interest is to reaffirm the sense of cohesion of the family nucleus, rather than to retell the everyday life of the same in any poetic or artistic way.

One key feature of the genre is that these films act as a sort of repository of cultural and personal, memory. Anyone who makes a private film – the filming of surrounding people, places and objects – in some important way gives expression to their own memories. This in turn determines a profound transformation in the processing of matters of 'private memory', which is thus imprinted on audiovisual support. It triggers particular processes of representation and self-representation of one's own private experiences and, in some sort of renewed way, it becomes interesting to contemplate the hierarchical order of family relationships (their stability and permanence or their alteration).

Overview of *Film di famiglia* (Family Films)

In Italy, the collection and archiving of family films forms part of the broader work of recovering amateur films, and it is mainly carried out by regional film libraries, which maintain a greater bond with the territory and therefore with private film archives.[3]

The case of the Associazione Home Movies (Home Movies Association) stands out in particular. From the very beginning it has been oriented towards a very ambitious goal: to become a comprehensive national collection centre for family films in Italy. It was legally established in Bologna in 2002 as a cultural promotion association *per la creazione dell'archivio filmico della memoria familiare* (for the creation of the filmic archive of family memories). Home Movies immediately begun to survey, and collect film funds from, the national territory, and committed itself to the establishing of an archive devoted to the heritage of private and unknown audiovisual material, that is, of all audiovisual artefacts that had no commercial or documentary purpose. A characteristic example is the Archivio diaristico nazionale di Pieve Santo Stefano (National Diaristic Archive of Pieve Santo Stefano) – initially modelled after the ANFF, Archivio Nationale dei Film di Famiglia (National Archives of Family Films) – which, thanks to the initiative of Saverio Tutino, has been since 1984 the basis for a *Città del diario* (*City of the Diary*) housed in the premises of City Hall.[4]

Since 2005, the ANFF has been housed at the Istituto Storico Parri di Bologna (Parri Historical Institute of Bologna). The initial project began to immediately grow thanks to the possibility of creating a restoration lab for the preservation of film reels, in rooms with controlled temperature/humidity, and equipped with a film transfer and digitisation system. Since 2008 Home Movies has been part of the European network INEDITS.[5] In

2011, the Ministero per i Beni e le Attività Culturali (Ministry of Cultural Heritage and Activities), through the Direzione Regionale per i Beni Culturali e Paesaggistici dell'Emilia-Romagna (Regional Directorate for Cultural and Landscape Heritage of Emilia-Romagna) and after the proposal made by the Soprintendenza archivistica per l'Emilia-Romagna (Emilia-Romagna Archival Authority), declared the Archivio Nazionale del Film di Famiglia (National Archive of Family Films) of *interesse storico particolarmente importante* (particularly important historical interest), thus officially ratifying the value of the archive, which underscores its specific character as a storehouse of private memory and of individual visual histories of a given period by rediscovering the varied collection.

The Archive currently holds about 20,000 items, almost all of them on original media formats consisting of small gauge films and created between the 1920s and the 1980s. The formats are several: the classic 35mm, the specific amateur-cinema gauge of 17.5mm, the various formats used in the 1920s, such as the 16mm Kodak film and the 9.5mm Pathé Baby, in addition to the 8mm launched by Kodak in 1932 and the Super8 format released on the market in 1965. To the small amount of 35mm films are increasingly added audiovisual artefacts on magnetic media – video and audio supports. The total collection amounts to 5,000 hours of audiovisual material, sourced from all over Italy. Families, and other entities, have stored such documentary material for years in drawers, wardrobes, attics and cellars, a legacy of visual culture of enormous historical and social interest. The range of subject matter is rich and varied: from the celebration of family life in all its most ritual aspects down to the documentation of free-time and work activities, from the recording of public events to the chronicling of landscape transformations.

Noteworthy examples include the Mossina collection. From the collection emerged footage from the 1940s and 1950s, such as the casting of girls competing for title of 'beauty queens' and the 'Miss Cinema' ribbon, as well as footage from the archival series titled *Matrimonio all'italiana* (*Marriage Italian Style*), which consists of wedding movies from the 1930s, 1960s and 1980s. There is also a record of the Marcinelle tragedy, which took place in August 1956 and is partly retold 'live' by the miners themselves, who had migrated to Belgium. Finally, there is the Bologna of the 1990s, with the images of the Dipartimento universitario di Arti Musica e Spettacolo (University Department of Arts, Music, and Entertainment Arts) seized by the students of the Movimento della Pantera (Panther Movement).

Over the years, the Associazione Home Movies has thus worked extensively on recovering family films and entering into contractual agreements with the various donors of the filmic artefacts. Once the material becomes part of the archival collection, it is subjected to a careful review, followed by the filling out of an entry-form and the creation of an inventory, which are meant to register information relating to the origins of the film as well as information on the person depositing the same with the Archive. The most complex part of the entire process is the cataloguing of the material. The cataloguing is based on a system developed from the prototype proposed by the International Federation of Film Archives (FIAF),[6] but readapted on the basis of the descriptive requirements peculiar to the features of audiovisual artefacts. What follows is the digitisation, the conversion to digital format – after the footage has been manually unwound and its state of preservation carefully reviewed. If the conditions of the footage present no problem, or once this has been dealt with by suitable conservative film-restoration procedures, the film is placed into a specific scanner for reduced gauges. The digitised footage can then be transferred to DVD and DCP,[7] or finally uploaded onto designated online platforms.

Moreover, it is worth mentioning the successful crowdfunding campaign launched by the ANFF in 2018, the aim of which was to create a multilingual online platform for the publication of a part of the archive through innovative dissemination and access techniques. The overall goal has been that of providing a *dal basso* (bottom-up) self-portrait of the country, that is, from the point of view of ordinary people and their history.

The project includes, among other things, the geo-localisation of historical amateur images, and their inclusion into a cartographic context (based on Google Maps). The combination of historical and geographical data offers a new and effective means of reading and interpreting the visual data. Thanks to the characteristics of web cartography it enables one to intuitively appreciate the changes that the various places depicted in the amateur family-video recordings have undergone compared to the present day.

It ought to be emphasised that one of the peculiar facets of the work carried out by archivists dealing with the recovery of such materials, is that of directly contacting the amateur cineastes – *enti produttori* (production bodies) as referred to in the archival parlance – or the people who have had a direct contact with them, in order to reconstruct – also through targeted interviews – specific details pertaining to places, people and factual events. This constitutes a preliminary activity in order to contextualise, as far as possible, the specific details of the filmed event. The encounter gives rise to a particular relationship between archivists and film-owners, one made up of trust and appreciation, as informed by the various material containing depictions that carry strong emotional value. Thus, it becomes imperative for the archivists to be able to grasp the subtle and private nature of the depictions and reflections that emerge from the amateur films.

Over the years, the ANFF has promoted numerous activities aimed at disseminating knowledge of this particular type of film. Foremost among them is *Archivio aperto* (*Open Archive*), an annual review launched in 2008. It includes a program of guided tours, screenings with live music, video-installations, talks and workshops.

Home Movies, in collaboration with the Istituto Storico Parri (Parri Historical Institute), also offers professional development courses, for teachers working with secondary school students, on research activities and on the pedagogical use of unpublished and private audiovisual-material stored in the archive. It constitutes an effective way of responding to the increasing need to propose pathways that bring young people closer to the history of the twentieth century: the use of amateur films facilitates our encounter with history, thereby bringing the import of history closer to the everyday-life of the new generations. Furthermore, in collaboration with the Istituto Storico Parri, intensive courses have been created in the attractive form of Summer School Programmes. They are aimed at younger candidates, between the age of 18 and 35, who are interested in professional curatorial work pertaining to the artefacts of our audiovisual heritage, for the purpose of producing documentary cinema, even that exclusively sourced from archival materials.

Other noteworthy initiatives include *LostScapes*, which began in 2017 as a presentation of unusual depictions of the city of Bologna taken from the collection of family films of the ANFF, as well as the project *Sguardi in camera: Ravenna nei film di famiglia e amatoriali* (*Camera Glances: Ravenna in Family and Amateur Films*) begun in 2016 in collaboration with the eponymous association of social promotion in Ravenna.[8]

The ANFF also created the app *Play the City RE* in collaboration with Relabtv (Dipartimento di Comunicazione ed Economia, Università di Modena e Reggio Emilia – Department of Communication and Economics, University of Modena and Reggio Emilia). This application enables one to view on portable devices, such as one's smartphone, the transformations undergone by the city of Reggio Emilia through a selection of 120 clips sourced from the Reggio Emilia archive of amateur cineastes.

Numerous other projects are directly linked to the activities promoted by the Direzione Generale degli Archivi (General Directorate of Archives): in particular, the signing on to the *Antenati* (*Ancestry*) portal, *Gli Archivi per la ricerca anagrafica* (*Family-Registry Research Archives*). In the section *Storie di famiglia* (*Family Histories*) it is possible to explore some of the films preserved at the ANFF, which are particularly interesting for their ability to represent household histories, to document social constructs, to offer depictions of everyday-life moments and of aspects of local customs and mentality, from dominant decades of the twentieth-century. The editing and the video edition were realised with the Klynt software, a platform that allows the user to consult the filmic collections through innovative and interactive tools: following their chronological sequence or by generating alternative routes via the menu features. The digital video-clips offer a wide selection of sequences from the uploaded material of the archival collection and are accompanied by short texts, inserted as titles, captions, or superimposed on the images themselves, and which introduce, contextualise and give precise indications about, the people, places and situations depicted. The varied information was collected through a careful search and documentation work carried out during the cataloguing of the individual items.

The ANFF also collaborated with the Soprintendenza Archivistica per l'Emilia-Romagna (Emilia-Romagna Archival Authority) and the Archivio di Storia delle Donne (Women History Archive) – preserved at the Centro di Documentazione delle Donne della Città di Bologna (Women Documentation Centre of the City of Bologna) – both promoters of the *Censimento degli archivi femminili nella provincia di Bologna* (*Census of women archives in the province of Bologna*).[9] Among the Fondi (Collections) that belong to the Archivio nazionale (National Archive), the selection of family films included in the census offers a cross-section of the activity of different women amateur-cineastes, all of whom share, 'though the biographies are quite diverse . . ., the desire to narrate their life stories, to talk about oneself and tell one's story through film, to embrace, and re-convey their experience of, the world through their glances'.[10]

Among the most notable collections one finds the Famiglia Darix Togni films, which document the activity of the renowned circus-family and which consists of 15 reels, in the 8mm format, scrupulously gathered and restored.

It is noteworthy also to report the presence of the Archivio nazionale dei Film di famiglia (National Archive of Family Films) on the archIVI portal, which offers online users instrumental and informational resources on the most significant items of the archives pertaining to the history of the city of Bologna, during the nineteenth and twentieth centuries.

For a Historical and Artistic Use of Family Films

The activity promoted by the Archivio nazionale dei film di famiglia (National Archive of Family Films) undoubtedly raises important reflections about the new horizons within which the archivists, who work with this type of material, operate. First of all, the need arises for the archivists to acquire the necessary sensitivity which the treatment of private memories requires. In fact, the legacy of intensely emotional stories – made up of both pleasant and painfully-sad memories – is found on the varied media collected: reels, video tapes, as well as on the most recent digital supports. Another facet in need of careful attention pertains to the interviews carried out with the filmmakers themselves, or with those who can give detailed and contextual information about the various elements present in a given film in their stead. To this end, the ANFF has developed a sort of interview template.11 In addition to the direct personal testimonies documented and collected according to such procedures, the diaries and photo albums kept by the makers of the films have also proven to be extremely valuable – providing supplementary information to be added to the interviews.

An item worthy of investigation is the extent to which family films offer different venues for the dissemination of cultural traits. In fact, various types of initiatives pertaining to the filmic collection may be launched: public screenings of selected films – as per the presentation programmes mentioned above – their dissemination in thematic or chronological anthologies, the creation of a tableau of memories from a given family through a collage of video fragments, the realisation of artistic installations and the creation of documentaries via the practice known as 'found footage'.[12] Worthy of note in this regard is the production of the multi-authored film titled *Formato ridotto* (*Reduced Format*), curated by the Home Movies archive. The project required the authors to work on a selection of fragile and fragmentary footage and on single images, mostly dating back to the 1950s and 1970s. The images were deeply evocative and were therefore submitted to the gaze of five Italian storytellers: Ermanno Cavazzoni, Emidio Clementi, Enrico Brizzi, Wu Ming 2 and Ugo Cornia. Each of them subsequently began to write five original stories based on the experience. Their own voices narrate the texts of the five different episodes that make up the film, constructed thematically through the careful assembly of different materials: the summer and winter sea on the Adriatic coast during the 1960s, a romantic climb by the rocks of the Emilia Apennines, a Sunday spent at the stadium watching a soccer game, the festivals of the Unità (political movement associated with left-wing parties) and the sentimental network of old pathways and new highways. The result is an exceptional film, an 'archive film', a lively experimentation between cinema and literature: a lost world, which comes back to life thanks to the work of 'ancient' cineastes and the narrative inventiveness of five contemporary writers.[13]

It therefore seems evident that family films can and have played a formidable role in the context of contemporary communication strategies: they can be useful for fiction films and television programmes, to newscasts or investigative reporters (where they may be utilised as documentary evidence) and moreover in entertainment broadcasts where they may have a comedic function, as well as in advertising where the authenticity of such films is valued by marketing projects. They can also be the source of artistic ideas and creations. We are reminded of the well-known cases of *Un'ora sola ti vorrei* (*For One More Hour with You*, 2002)[14] by Alina Marazzi, and the most recent *I film di famiglia 1959–1974* (*Family Films 1959–1974*, 2018)[15] by Serena Nono. Thus, such materials possess a significant density and peculiar complexity, 'a developing interconnection between family history, socially shared iconography and the interpellation practices directed to the consumer by the tech industry',[16] which subsequently pose stimulating challenges to the archivists who curate, study and make such collections available to the general public.

Notes

1. The birth and development of amateur cinema, and thus family films, is in fact based on some basic assumptions: the use of non-reversible and non-flammable film, of considerable lower cost (no negative to print); the adoption of increasingly smaller and cheaper formats, from 35mm to 16mm, 9.5mm, 8mm and Super8; the several technological innovations that mark a transition from manual to automatic and mechanised processes: ready-to-load film cartridges in place of the manual loading of reels, the continual miniaturisation of bulky equipment and the development of various automatisms, including focus and shutter opening, and ultimately the transition from the heavier materials of corporate cameras to electronic components and video cameras.
2. Odin (1995), p. 27.
3. We recall the important project carried out by the Cineteca Sarda (Sardinian Film Library) titled *La tua memoria è la nostra storia* (*Your Memory Is Our History*); a regional campaign the goal of which has been to create an archival history of the private, and family, memories of the Sardinians.
4. It is a public archive that to this day collects the writings of ordinary people, and which, in its assortment of formats and styles, reflects the life of different individuals and the history of Italy: diaries, letters and autobiographical memoirs. In 1991, on the initiative of the Municipality, the Fondazione Archivio Diaristico Nazionale (National Diary-Archive Foundation) was established, which later became an 'Onlus' (non-profit organisation) and was ratified by Ministerial Decree on 7 June 2000. http://archiviodiari.org/.
5. The INEDITS (a clever use of the French *inédits* and/or morphing of the Italian plural word for 'unpublished' or 'unknown', *inediti*) association is a

European non-profit association, created in 1991 to encourage the collection, preservation, study and presentation, of amateur films.
6. The FIAF, Fédération internationale des archives du film (International Federation of Film Archives) was founded in Paris in 1938, by the British Film Institute (BFI), the Museum of Modern Art (MoMA) in New York, the Cinémathèque française and the Reichsfilmarchiv, and brings together the main world institutions in the field for the conservation and appreciation of one's film heritage. https://www.fiafnet.org/.
7. Digital Versatile Disk (DVD), and Digital Cinema Package (DCP).
8. The project was promoted by Comune di Ravenna (Municipality of Ravenna) – Assessorato alle politiche e culture di genere (Department of Genus Cultures and Policies) – and by Home Movies – Archivio Nazionale dei Film di Famiglia (National Archive of Family Films) – in collaboration with the Istituzione Biblioteca Classense (Classense Library Institution) and the Fondazione Casa Oriani (Casa Oriani Foundation).
9. The result is a mapping of the women's archives preserved in the municipal administration offices of the province of Bologna: the various conservation institutes (Parri, Gramsci, the Archiginnasio Library, the University Library and so forth), associations, women's groups and collectives, political parties, trade unions, trade associations and single individuals. The census can be accessed from the SIUSA-Archivi femminili in Emilia-Romagna (SIUSA-Emilia-Romagna's Women Archives portal).
10. My translation. Original quote: 'pur nella disparità delle biografie ... [il] desiderio di raccontare le proprie vite, di raccontarsi e dire di sé attraverso le pellicole, di abbracciare e restituire il mondo con il loro sguardo'. Lucia Cardone, in Filippelli (2012), p. 8.
11. Filippelli (2012), pp. 173–4.
12. The expression refers to films which are made, partially or entirely, with pre-existing footage reassembled and laid out into a new context.
13. The DVD release is part of the Cinemalibero series, published by the Cineteca di Bologna (Bologna Film Library), and the unabridged five original stories are published in the accompanying booklet.
14. The film leads viewers into the delicate and touching terrain of memory, through the reading of diaries, letters and medical records, from the nursing homes where Liseli Marazzi Hoepli spent long periods before her suicide – at a time when her daughter Alina was only seven years old. Through these texts and the images of the films, shot by her grandfather since 1926, the author comes to know her mother, reconstructs her face and celebrates her by documenting her life story.
15. A documentary film on the years 1959–74, taken from the 8mm and Super8 films of the Luigi Nono family.
16. My translation. Original quote: 'mutevole intersezione tra la storia di famiglia, l'iconografia socialmente condivisa e le politiche di interpellazione del consumatore da parte dell'industria tecnologica'. Zimmermann (1995), pp. 121–32.

Works Cited

Avantaggiato, Luigi (2010), *Home stories, Il filmino di famiglia nelle pratiche artistiche contemporanee*, Rome: Bulzoni.
Bertozzi, Marco (2018), *Documentario come arte. Riuso, performance, autobiografia nell'esperienza del cinema contemporaneo*, Venice: Marsilio.
Cardone, Lucia (2012), *Prefazione. Film di famiglia: altri sguardi*, in Sara Filippelli ed., *Le donne e gli home movies*, Pisa: ETS, pp. 8–9.
Cati, Alice (2013), *Immagini della memoria. Teorie e pratiche del ricordo tra testimonianze, genealogia, documentari*, Milan: Mimesis.
Cati, Alice (2009), *Pellicole di ricordi. Film di famiglia e memorie private (1926–1942)*, Milan: Vita e Pensiero.
Filippelli, Sara (2012), *Le donne e gli home movies. Il cinema di famiglia come scrittura del sé*, Pisa: ETS.
Odin, Roger (1995), *Le film de famille. Usage privé, usage public*, Paris: Meridiens Klincksieck.
Sapio, Giuseppina (2014), 'Homesick for Aged Home Movies: Why Do We Shoot Contemporary Family Videos in Old-Fashioned Ways?', in K. Niemeyer (ed.), *Media and Nostalgia*, London: Palgrave Macmillan.
Simoni, Paolo (2005), 'La nascita di un Archivio per il cinema amatoriale: il caso dell'Associazione Home Movies', *Comunicazioni sociali*, n. 3/2005.
Zimmermann, Patricia R. (1995), *Reel Families" A Social History of Amateur Film*, Bloomington: Indiana University Press.

Filmography

Formato ridotto (*Reduced Format*), film, directed by Ermanno Cavazzoni, Emidio Clementi, Enrico Brizzi, Wu Ming 2, and Ugo Cornia, Italy, 2012.
I film di famiglia 1959–1974 (*Family Films 1959–1974*), film, directed by Serena Noto, Italy, 2018.
Un'ora sola ti vorrei (*For One More Hour with You*), film, directed by Alina Marazzi, Italy, 2002.

Online Resources

<https://homemovies.it/>, last accessed 30 August 2019.
<http://www.sa-ero.archivi.beniculturali.it/index.php?id=757>, last accessed 30 August 2019.
<https://www.fiafnet.org>, last accessed 30 August 2019.
<http://www.lacinetecasarda.it/cinemadifamiglia/>, last accessed 30 August 2019.

CHAPTER 6

Independence as Opposition? Redefining Political Cinema through the Case of Mirko Locatelli

Gloria Dagnino

Introduction

Italian independent cinema, to which this timely anthology is devoted, is a doubly problematic construct. Such complexity derives, on the one hand, from the very notion of what constitutes independent cinema and, on the other hand, from its significance within the Italian context. Independent cinema is universally described by means of what may be named an 'oppositional paradigm'. The terms of the opposition vary according to the relevant national and historical contexts, but also according to the filmmaker's individual beliefs and sensibilities. In Italian discourse, however, there is a recurring motif that film scholars, critics, practitioners and filmmakers themselves use when describing independent cinema. This motif presents Italian independent cinema as a strong political and militant practice, the values and purposes of which are associated with those of the historical anti-fascist movement of the *Resistenza*. In the second half of this chapter I present and discuss this very aspect, which appears to be consistent with an Italian-specific theoretical phenomenon, known as 'Italian difference'. This latter notion has been conceptualised in recent years by philosophers of the so-called 'Italian theory', and particularly by Roberto Esposito. That which is being argued for is the existence of a specificity to Italian thought in general, which lies precisely in political conflict and antagonism.

The analysis of the present case study, which is presented in subsequent sections three, four and five, argues for a changed perspective. We proceed with a review of Italian independent filmmaker Mirko Locatelli's activities, both 'off set' and 'on set', an analysis of his cinematic style and reference models, as well as a discussion of his ideas as an Italian citizen and as an artist. All of the preceding points would suggest that the political component of his cinema ought to be interpreted more in terms of his ethical and aesthetic commitment to a coherent and authentic artistic expression. The case study mostly draws on a semi-structured interview with screenwriter, filmmaker and producer Mirko Locatelli and screenwriter and producer Giuditta Tarantelli, conducted in October 2016.

This conceptualisation of the filmmaker's peculiar political, social and cultural role goes back to the 'Golden age of Italian cinema'[1] and the prestigious tradition of *auteur* cinema, both national and European. In this sense, Locatelli's independence is not to be viewed as a disruptive practice, but rather as the return to the medium-specific values of cinematic expression. The analysis of Locatelli's case also reveals that independent cinema is not (only) an oppositional term to describe an alternative system of film production and creation, but is also a multilayered and ever evolving concept. It is continuously self-negotiated by filmmakers, and it assumes different connotations according to the specific career stage they find themselves immersed in.

Independence as Opposition: Cinema and the 'Italian Difference'

The idea of independent cinema is universally conceived and described – though some important distictions may apply – on the basis of what I will term an 'oppositional paradigm'. In the US, the notion of independent cinema is used in opposition to Hollywood mainstream productions. *Hollywood cinema* encapsulates a set of industrial and economic practices that define the ways in which films are produced and distributed: vertical and horizontal integration strategies, corporate synergies, product placement deals, saturation booking, as well as skyrocketing production and marketing costs.[2] Whether in opposition or not, however, mainstream vs. independent cinema is not only to be defined in industrial and economic terms, but also with regards to their respective aesthetic and narrative features, as well as their relation to the social, cultural, political and ideological landscape.[3] In this sense, throughout the years, a number of stylistic and narrative conventions have come to shape the 'norm' of Hollywood movies. These may include continuity editing, happy endings, moral unambiguity between heroes and villains and a general conservatism in approaching social and political matters. Some authors, such as Steiger[4] use the term *indie* to refer to narrative and stylistic traits, and *independent*, to refer to the financial and production-related features of non-Hollywood productions. In such a context, independent cinema embraces cinematic works that are conceived, developed, produced and distributed outside the industrial as well as creative framework of Hollywood's film industry.

Whereas Hollywood has come to represent the quintessence of US filmmaking, American independent cinema has traditionally been connected to foreign, and notably European,⁵ cinema: 'The values associated with foreign film-making – serious treatment of adult issues, self-conscious cinematic style, film seen as art – were taken over by American independent film-makers'.⁶ Naturally, not all European films are art films.⁷ Yet, if we look at film policies, Europe, unlike the US, does in fact define (and financially support) cinema as an artistic, rather than a commercial, endeavour. When compared to the original US-based meaning, European filmmaking, which includes the Italian case, can to an important extent be considered inherently independent. So, what defines Italian independent cinema? And, most importantly, what is it independent from?

In Italy, as well as in much of Europe, most independent cinema is conceptualised on the basis of one shared rationale, namely: the opposition to television broadcasters. Specific definitions vary slightly according to the relevant institution and to policy goals. Italian law defines 'independent film' as a film for which an independent production company holds proprietary rights for a minimum share of 60 per cent,⁸ while 'independent production companies' are those that 'are not controlled by, nor related to'⁹ a broadcaster, nor work exclusively for the latter. The same rationale, but with different percentages, is used by the European Commission in setting the eligibility criteria to access the MEDIA support scheme: independent film companies are those in which a single broadcaster holds no more than 25 per cent of the share capital (50 per cent when several broadcasters are involved).¹⁰ Thus, television broadcasters constitute the 'dominant system'¹¹ of industrial and cultural production in opposition to which independent filmmaking is officially defined.

If we look at discourses concerning Italian independent cinema, the oppositional paradigm is not specifically (nor exclusively) used in reference to television broadcasters. Michela Ardizzoni describes contemporary documentaries as 'counter-discourse', 'counter-culture' and 'alternative discourse',¹² in opposition to the conventional representations conveyed, not only by television, but by Italian mainstream media in general. Anita Angelone and Clarissa Clò represent Italian documentary as 'a counter-discourse, oppositional, alternative and antagonist' not to broadcasters, but 'to mainstream hegemonic cinematic practices'.¹³ Luca Caminati further broadens the scope, and gives it a stronger political connotation, by referencing French Marxist theorist Guy Debord: 'The films I will be analysing here (low budget, small-scale productions) position themselves in opposition to the mainstream dissemination of the values of the "society of spectacle"'.¹⁴

The oppositional paradigm, which commonly defines independent cinema in Italy, acquires political nuances of activism and militancy, regardless of whether the referenced films actually address political topics in the strict sense. Let us consider the following text excerpts from Italian film scholars, critics and film festival organisers, as well as filmmakers. In describing the role of independent cinema within Italy's current cultural, economic and political landscape, Pasquale Verdicchio argues that

> what was once run by a completely dictatorial Fascist state is now run by the manifestation of a neo-liberal, "developed" state. In this light, independent film emerged a while back as an attempt to wrest feature films out of the grasp of commercialism.[15]

In arguing in favour of new, 'unruly' forms of cinematic expressions, Adriano Aprà writes that these deserve 'critical attention and militancy that may function as propelling forces . . . It is now time to stand for a cinema of opposition and resistance'.[16] Film critics Daniela Persico and Alessandro Stellino define independent cinema as 'an act of resistance', which bears responsibility also from the viewers' side: 'Perhaps the revolution against those who have monopolised and depressed our gaze, moves from this kind of actions: going to the movie theatre . . . as an act of militancy, as an act of freedom'.[17] Film critic Gabriele Rizza, curator of the Florence-based film festival Visioni Off (Off Visions), describes the type of works featured in the festival as 'independent productions, mostly made with low-cost budgets, and yet evidences of a resistant and brave Italian cinema'.[18] The Milan Film Festival, dedicated to independent productions, in September 2015 organised a workshop on *critica cinematografica militante* (militant film criticism). As Italian independent filmmaker Edoardo Winspeare describes it, independent productions have a fighter's character of their own: 'mine is a kind of cinema of resistance, crafted without any slogans or manifestos'.[19]

The Italian words *resistenza* and *resistente* ('resistance' and 'resistant'), similarly to their English equivalents, generally refer to the quality of a person, or an object, in their ability to oppose an external action. When used in politically themed discourses, however, especially in association with words such as 'militancy' and 'freedom', they inevitably carry an Italian-specific historical reference: the Italian liberation movement against the Fascist regime and the Nazi occupation during the Second World War. The use of such vocabulary situates independent cinema within an Italian-specific context of revolution against an oppressive system and regime, in a way that goes well beyond the attribution of a generic political value. Such an ideological and historically situated conception of the oppositional paradigm defining independent cinema finds its root, I argue, in a broader theoretical construct, known as the 'Italian difference',[20] which was conceived and developed within the ever-growing philosophical debate of 'Italian theory'.[21] The 'Italian difference' embodies the idea that there is a specificity to Italian thought, in its various manifestations, which differentiates it from other national philosophical traditions. The core of this specificity lies in political conflict:

> This is precisely where the first paradigmatic axis of Italian thought is rooted, in the highly complex figure of the *immanentization of antagonism*. The idea that conflict is constitutive of order. The origin cannot be eliminated by an order that, in its factual concreteness, derives from conflict and that, indeed, continues incessantly to reproduce it. This assumption is one of the fundamental, recurring vectors of all Italian philosophy, and not only its political thought.[22] (Emphasis in the original)

As per the section that follows, filmmaker Mirko Locatelli's practices are a good example of the various film-related activities that contribute to the notion of independent cinema. Hereafter, Locatelli's conceptualisation of Italian independent cinema is specifically analysed in comparison to the above-described idea of independent cinema as a political, even resistant, practice.

Off-Set Activities: Independence as an Unconventional Path

Mirko Locatelli is an independent filmmaker based in Milan and Trieste born in 1974, a screenwriter and producer, with a background as a cultural contributor for different news outlets, including Italy's national daily newspaper *Corriere della Sera*. Locatelli shares a professional life with his wife, screenwriter and producer Giuditta Tarantelli. Locatelli and Tarantelli have been actively involved in the Italian independent cinema scene since the early 2000s. Their work has always been diverse, encompassing both on-set and off-set activities. This section deals with the latter, which include cultural and training initiatives, local community engagement, as well as production and distribution of works by emerging filmmakers.

In 2000 Locatelli and Tarantelli founded *Cinemaindipendente.it*, a web portal that rapidly became the go-to website for all sorts of news concerning Italian independent films. The website had two major target users: 'those who were already making independent films' and 'those who wanted to make films'.[23] To emerging filmmakers, *Cinemaindipendente.it* was a film festival database, providing information on where and how to submit short films, documentaries and first features. To aspiring filmmakers and actors, the website was mainly a networking platform, which helped them find possible coworkers. The portal also had a forum and the basic tools for live messaging, whereby users could chat in real time on specific topics. However, over a decade, such features were made redundant by the boom of global social networks like LinkedIn and Facebook, and *Cinemaindipendente.it* was eventually shut down by its founders in 2014.[24]

Through the dissemination of information and the services offered by a networking platform, *Cinemaindipendente.it* pursued socially engaged commitments: the democratisation of cinematic knowledge and cinema-related professions, and the empowerment of the independent filmmakers' community. After the portal's demise, Locatelli and Tarantelli relocated those activities from a virtual to a physical environment, opening *I 400 colpi-La Cineteca di Quartiere* (*The 400 Blows-The Local Film Library*). The name of the association, inspired by François Truffaut's masterpiece, reflects its vocation to promote *auteur* cinema; its location, in the northern outskirts of Milan, shows its commitment in favour of a decentralised and autonomous offer of cultural products and initiatives. La Cineteca functioned as a regular film library, where people could borrow film books and DVDs, but it also offered low budget professional training to screenwriters, filmmakers and producers. It organised screenings and Q&As with *auteurs* such as Michelangelo Frammartino (*Le quattro volte – The Four Times*, 2013), Massimiliano and Gianluca De Serio (*Sette opere di misericordia – Seven Acts of Mercy*, 2011), producers and distributors such as Gianluca Arcopinto (Pablo Distribuzione Indipendente – Pablo Independent Distribution); and finally, it provided co-working spaces and facilities for emerging filmmakers and film professionals. La Cineteca allowed Locatelli and Tarantelli to avoid the isolation connected with the screenwriting phase of their work. Moreover, to them the workshops and seminars held at the Cineteca constituted valuable opportunities for professional self-improvement as well as for meeting perspective co-workers – 'I learnt so much while teaching what I know to others, it's almost paradoxical!'[25]

Another field through which Locatelli and Tarantelli provide support to the Italian independent film scene is to assist with the production and distribution of films by other emerging filmmakers. After a few sporadic precedents, in 2013 Locatelli and Tarantelli partnered with two young entrepreneurs to found Strani Film (Strange Films), a company whose mission specifically includes the production of films written and directed by others. This has been the case of Fabio Bobbio's *I Cormorani* (*The Cormorants*, 2016) a cross-genre first feature, which premiered at the Swiss documentary festival Vision du Réel.

Locatelli and Tarantelli's decision to support young writers – despite themselves still encountering difficulties in having their own work produced and distributed – stems from two main reasons. The first is a sense of solidarity among peers:

Giuditta and I have been through the experience of being unheard authors. We know how hard it is to get started in the industry. And yet, we were two, most filmmakers are by themselves. Being two is good, because if one of us gives up, the other hangs in there. It's hard to stay positive when you're alone.[26]

The second motivation, given in the interview, is the will to preserve a fresh and authentic attitude towards filmmaking after gaining some recognition as *auteurs* in the Italian film industry:

Another reason is probably to give ourselves a chance to keep that fire alive. Otherwise, you risk forgetting it. When you direct an international co-production, you step into a system that is not "the" system, but is still a system. One in which you struggle a little less, although you keep struggling. So, this is probably what Giuditta refers to as "independent cinema": to keep the authenticity and the urgency alive.[27]

The off-set activities described so far, and the rationale motivating them, offer a first outline of the meaning and characteristics of Italian independent cinema, according to Mirko Locatelli and Giuditta Tarantelli. Being an independent filmmaker means following unconventional paths when pursuing one's own creative goals. Independence lies in choosing, and in giving others the opportunity to choose, not to have to enroll in Italy's major film schools, or to have to sign up with a talent agency. This also means deciding not to have to relocate to Rome, where both the National Film School and all the major Italian talent agencies are based. In this sense, the web portal *Cinemaindipendente.it* offered knowledge, industry insights, as well as job and networking opportunities to filmmakers, technicians and actors, outside the Cinecittà-centred system of film training and production. Similarly, thanks to the spread of affordable, high-quality digital equipment, the workshops and seminars of La Cineteca di Quartiere offered low cost professional-education in a non-institutionalised environment. Indeed, in Italy and elsewhere, film schools work as privileged sites for the creation and leverage of social networks that constitute the main, if not the only, means to access the film job market.[28] People outside such (institutionalised) networks often remain 'unheard' by the system. Locatelli and Tarantelli, after having themselves sought alternative ways for 'making it' in the industry, work to provide others with the same freedom of choice, and possibly reduced struggle.

In this case, on one side of the oppositional paradigm defining Italian independent cinema, one finds the Rome-based traditional film institutions and the exclusionary practices they foster within the industry, and on the other side, one finds a more geographically dispersed, socially diverse and economically democratic, conception of the film industry. Locatelli and Tarantelli claim the right to an individual, yet not 'isolated', way of making films. This is a political, as well as a creative, statement. For Locatelli and Tarantelli, being uncompromising about where and how to start a filmmaking career, is part of realising a more authentic form of artistic expression. This conceptualisation of independent cinema derives from Locatelli and Tarantelli's ethos as independent creators.

On-Set Activities: Independence as Negotiated Identity

Locatelli and Tarantelli started their careers as filmmakers in 2002, when they founded Officina Film (Workshop Films). Officina Film is a two person company in which Locatelli works as a screenwriter, director and producer, whereas Tarantelli is screenwriter and producer. For each film project, Officina Film collaborates with a number of freelance professionals, who sometimes reappear from one set to the next: director of photography, cinematographer, lighting and sound technicians, assistant director and so forth. Officina Film produces short features, social advertising videos and medium-length documentaries on the topics of teenagers and disability.[29] Among these early works, the 45 minutes-long fiction film *Come prima* (*Just Like Before*, 2004) won a special mention at the Bellaria Film Festival. In 2008, Officina Film produced Locatelli's first feature film, *Il primo giorno d'inverno* (*The First Day of Winter*), which premiered at the 65th edition of the Venice International Film Festival ('Orizzonti' first features section) and was later screened at twenty national and international film festivals. The film, which addresses the topics of high school bullying and homophobia, is set in a small village of the Po valley in Northern Italy, and almost exclusively cast first-time actors. The industrial cost of the film, around 100,000 Euros, was covered through personal funds, a small contribution by the Assessorato all'istruzione della Provincia di Milano (Department of Education of the Province of Milan) and free labour, such as the case of Italian composer Giovanni Sollima, who licensed the rights to use his music in the soundtrack for free. *Il primo giorno d'inverno* had a limited release in national art-house movie theatres.

Locatelli's second feature production, *I corpi estranei* (*Foreign Bodies*, 2013) was essentially self-funded, but could count on a higher budget – around 300,000 Euros – provided by the partners from the newly founded company Strani Film. The film tells the story of a low-class, dialect speaking father who leaves his wife and children in a rural area in Central Italy and relocates to Milan with his two-year-old son, who needs cancer treatment. In the hospital, his racist attitude is challenged by the friendly approaches of a North-African boy, who is there to assist a sick friend.

I corpi estranei, which premiered at the Rome International Film Festival, enjoyed greater press coverage, due among other things to its chief protagonist, the Italian popular film and stage actor Filippo Timi, who joined a cast of acting rookies.

Due to a series of decisions by the filmmakers, which include its Northern and peripheral locations, the predominant use of non-professional performers, as well as its realistic style, Locatelli's debut and second feature have been associated with the early works of the Italian *auteur* Ermanno Olmi. Olmi is in fact one of Locatelli's cinematic references, which also include Austrian directors Michael Haneke and Ulrich Seidl, and the Belgian Dardenne brothers. However, Locatelli's aesthetic model is to be found especially in the French film tradition of Robert Bresson, François Truffaut and the New Wave, Jacques Doillon and André Techiné. It is not surprising, then, that his third feature film *Isabelle* stars French actress, and *auteur* Robert Guédiguian's muse, Ariane Ascaride. The film, which received *ex-aequo* the Best Screenplay award at the 2018 Montreal World Film Festival, addresses the themes of guilt and truth behind appearances. *Isabelle* was shot in the summer of 2017, between the Italian Northeastern city of Trieste and the south of France. Production-wise *Isabelle* is Locatelli and Tarantelli's biggest project: it is an Italian-French co-production, with an industrial cost of around 1.3 million Euros. The Italian Ministry of Culture awarded *Isabelle* with 150,000 Euros under the *interesse culturale* (cultural interest) selective support scheme.[30] Additional funding came from the Italy-France bilateral fund for film co-productions, managed by the French *Centre National du Cinéma et de l'Image Animée* (CNC) and the Italian Cinema General Directorate of the Ministry of Cultural Heritage and Activities. Moreover, unprecedentedly for Locatelli and Tarantelli, the film had the financial backing of RAI Cinema, the film subsidiary of the Italian public service broadcaster.

Locatelli's three feature films span almost a decade. The production practices of his films have been progressively evolving from a fully self-funded film, shot with a mixed crew of professionals, film trainees and friends, to an international co-production, supported by Italy's major broadcaster. This progression towards an economically sounder production (although still low-budget), and the potential advantages it brings in terms of distribution and publicity, is positively embraced by Locatelli and Tarantelli, as it allows them to work 'with a little more security'.[31] However, at the same time, this progression challenges their identity and self-representation as independent filmmakers. As described in the second section, from a strictly policy point of view, the definition of independent cinema does not completely rule out the possibility of financing from a broadcaster, as long as its share of proprietary rights does not exceed 40 per cent.[32] However, for Locatelli and Tarantelli, such a definition contrasts with previous personal beliefs of what independent cinema is all about: 'We grew up with the idea that independent cinema was completely free, unaccountable to anything or anyone'.[33]

Locatelli and Tarantelli problematise the policy-based definition of independent cinema in different ways. Tarantelli aligns herself to more radical criteria of what constitutes independent cinema, although, by doing so, she excludes her most recent work from the definition: 'In my opinion, if a film is funded by the Ministry, or by RAI Cinema, that is not independent cinema'.[34] The reason is that both institutions can potentially intervene in the filmmakers' artistic vision, in order to make it more commercially attractive. Broadcasters can do it in a direct way: 'If we had submitted our second film to a broadcaster, they would have told us to change the style. It would have taken us two more years, and we could not have done it the way we wanted. We would have had to change some things'.[35] National and regional governing bodies can do it in an indirect, preemptive way, by setting funding parameters that reward the following: films which cast famous actors and actresses, films directed by award-winning filmmakers, films set in specific geographic locations and so forth. Tarantelli seems to adhere to a cross-national idea of independent cinema, one which excludes direct or indirect forms of engagement from not only television broadcasters, but also 'a variety of institutions from which filmmakers are independent, such as governments, corporations, financing entities, and traditional production centres'.[36] Locatelli, on the other hand, embraces the policy-based definition of independent cinema, but frames it within a more individually-based ethical and aesthetic discourse:

> A film with a 5 million budget, with one million funded by a broadcaster, can still be regarded as independent. I feel free to express myself the way I want to. I don't really agree with the idea that, if I apply for public funding, I am no longer independent. The challenge is to manage to express your own artistic vision both with a low, and with a higher budget. In other words, one should not make up things that are not part of their cinematic style. Stay true to yourself! If you can't do it, then it's you, not the system, who has a problem. I will defend my authorial voice.[37]

Thus, in Locatelli's words, independence means fidelity to a personal idea of filmmaking, whether or not this is endorsed by the Ministry, the broadcasters, or other funding bodies:

> When I write a script, I don't choose locations according to the wealthier film commission, nor do I cast an actor or an actress because he or she can earn me five or

ten points in the Ministry's funding assessment. If you do this kind of reasoning, and you do it in advance, you are somehow losing track of who you are. That is why I still consider myself an independent and free filmmaker: because I fight for the choices I make. I don't make choices according to the funding schemes. If I did, I'd be a money machine, and all the things that I still enjoy doing would turn into a routine. And we make films because we don't really like routines.[38]

The analysis of Locatelli and Tarantelli's various activities – as educators, as producers and distributers for others, as well as screenwriters, producers and director of their own films – speaks of Italian independent cinema as a multi-layered, time-related concept, whose meaning and implications are constantly questioned and negotiated by filmmakers. At an early career stage, being independent means learning to oppose the traditional, Cinecittà-centric system of education and access to the job market. Later, independent filmmakers oppose the economic and creative dominant system of broadcasters and government-funded cinema. Over the years, conceptualisations based on economic and industrial criteria lose part of their relevance, in favour of those based on personal ethical and aesthetic values: to be independent means being uncompromising about one's own authentic vision. In the next section I address Locatelli's artistic vision in further detail. It is discussed in reference to the theoretical framework based on the philosophical construct termed the 'Italian difference'.

Cinematic Politics: Independence as a Coherent Style

As an individual, Mirko Locatelli is fully aware of his political affiliation, and does not shy away from expressing it: 'I consider myself a communist, and as a communist, I don't appreciate people who never step forward, who don't express their beliefs'.[39] Locatelli's political identity is unaffected by Italy's current political landscape, where the communist party has no delegates in Parliament. Rather, he shares some of the constitutive values of the communist ideology – egalitarianism, social solidarity, non-religious morality – particularly those embodied in the socialist turn of figures such as Enrico Berlinguer, former secretary of the Italian Communist Party.

As a filmmaker, though, Locatelli's political thought does not translate into what is traditionally known as *cinema di impegno civile* (civic engagement cinema). The traditional notion of *impegno* 'was inseparable from the idea of political hegemony', which means that the 'filmmaker had to shape collective consciousness and co-opt individuals into a communal project for global transformation and revolutionary change'.[40] This ideological scheme of 'right vs. wrong', 'us vs. them', is consistent with the philosophical notion of 'Italian difference', and the resulting narrative of resistance, which is largely used to describe Italian independent cinema, as previously shown.

Locatelli refuses the idea of committed cinema as ideological opposition and adheres to a notion of independent filmmaking that is not political in the sense implied, and often explicitly referenced, in the narrative of resistance: 'Mine is not so-called civic cinema. Civic cinema, civic theatre, as they are called, assume to hold a "right" standpoint'.[41] This is particularly evident in Locatelli and Tarantelli's work as screenwriters:

> When I create a character, I feel free to give him or her features that transcend, that challenge my political vision of the world. I do it so that it is difficult for me, and for the audience to accept that we can love or hate the character regardless of our own political vision.[42]

> Our aim is not to create a character that the audience can't help but be sympathetic to. We want to surprise ourselves by siding with the unlikable character, or maybe by siding with the victim up to a certain point, and then switch to the tormentor's side without even realizing it. No clear-cut thesis, no a priori judgments.[43]

All the main characters in Locatelli and Tarantelli's movies are difficult to relate to, and are the authors of despicable actions: Valerio, the protagonist of *Il primo giorno d'inverno*, after discovering the homosexual relation between the two school bullies, blackmails them, eventually leading one to suicide. Antonio, the main character of *I corpi estranei* is a violent, racist man, who physically assaults a North-African teenager for having blessed his ill child with an Islamic ritual. Isabelle, the protagonist of the homonymous film, lies and manipulates her younger lover to prevent a terrible family secret from being revealed. All these characters appear stuck in their fears and weaknesses without chances of evolving in nature or disposition, thus, no actual redemption is reached in the end. Locatelli's political engagement is not expressed by means of stories and characters that thematise his ideological beliefs. The latter are instead regarded as a datum, as they contribute to shape his creative work, but only insofar as this is shaped by other personal features, such as his education and life experiences.

In Conclusion

Locatelli's work can be considered independent not only from the dominant production and narrative system of mainstream cinema, but also from the hegemonic critical discourse that frames Italian independent cinema as an expression of political opposition. So, is there a political side to Locatelli's cinema?

> All cinema is political cinema. There is no such thing as apolitical cinema: from *cinepanettoni*, to, say, a film about a blind storyteller in Uganda. It's all political cinema: because the filmmaker cannot escape his own political vision of the world. Everyone tells their own piece of reality, and they tell it in their own way. That is political. Politics describes, deconstructs, and then intervenes on reality: cinema, as all art forms, does the same.[44]

Rather than subscribing to an oppositional idea of *political cinema*, Locatelli's films constitute a form of *cinematic politics*, which have their ideological core in the elaboration and strict observance of a realistic style. Locatelli's notion of cinematic realism draws on the documentary genre in that it aims to minimise the distance between the viewer and what happens on screen: 'The aim is to make the audience believe that those things are really happening. Otherwise, why would you go sit on the movie theater chair and watch?' From a formal viewpoint, this is achieved by means of a humanist approach to the directing process. In terms of camera angles, for examples, this translates to the abolition of those positions which do not correspond to any 'real' point of view:

> A man's eyes are around 1.3-meter-high when he is seated, and 1.7-meter-high when he stands, so all the frames that deviate from those heights are inhuman, unreal. I care for a film language that is close to our gaze, not the one of the Martians, or the one of God.

Similarly, in terms of editing style, Locatelli tends to favour long-takes and *plan-séquence*: 'Cutting a scene into different takes is an inhuman practice. The *découpage* is unreal'.[45] Locatelli pursues these stylistic choices in a very consistent, almost dogmatic way, in an effort to be transparent with his audience:

> My cinematic models are those films in which I see honesty; films that display linguistic coherence throughout. As a filmmaker, for me it is important to bear in mind that what I film is anything but my own personal point of view. A filmmaker is not omniscient.[46]

Locatelli's words outline his cinema as a first-person expression, one in which the filmmaker's political role is not intended as antagonist to a given point of view, but rather as the registering of a commitment to ethic and aesthetic coherence and transparency with the viewers. In this sense, Locatelli retrieves the idea of the role of the *auteur* that thrived within the prestigious tradition of Italian art cinema of the mid-twentieth century: in the Neorealism of Vittorio De Sica and Roberto Rossellini, in the psychological realism of Michelangelo Antonioni, or in the genre-resistant cinema of Pier Paolo Pasolini. All these *auteurs*, while retaining strong personal beliefs, did not subscribe to any idea of political cinema as a 'monological illustration of ideology'.[47] This also points to a re-elaborated notion of *cinema di impegno* (socially engaged cinema), one that can be described 'simply as an ethical or political position channelled through specific cultural and artistic activities, against any restrictive ideological brace'.[48] Such a notion strongly echoes in Locatelli and Tarantelli's idea of independent cinema, as it emerges from their words, as well as from the analysis of their on-set and off-set activities.

In this chapter we have argued that the dominant critical discourse, which frames Italian independent cinema as an oppositional practice, rooted in the political tradition of *Resistenza*, falls short of capturing certain important features of this diverse cinematic movement. The case of Mirko Locatelli and his production company has shown that the meaning of 'Italian independent cinema' is nuanced, not only in terms of production and narrative features, but also in terms of political engagement and civic commitment. Despite the oppositional trend inherent to the 'Italian difference', the very notion of *cinema di impegno* has been shifting, from an ideologically rigid notion to one more individualised and more apt to a renewed context. It is time, we suggest, for a similar shift to affect also the notion of Italian independent cinema. To move beyond the conceptualisation of independence as political opposition, would allow scholars, but also critics and professionals, to better account for the strong individual and authorial dimension that characterises the work of many Italian independent filmmakers.

Notes

1. Bondanella and Pacchioni (2017), p. 271.
2. See McDonald and Wasko (2008).
3. See King (2005).
4. See Staiger (2013).
5. The New American Cinema group manifesto, issued in 1962, stated as foreign cinematic models for US independent filmmakers 'the Free cinema in England, the Nouvelle Vague in France, the young movements in Poland, Italy, and Russia' MacKenzie (2014), p. 58.
6. Allen (2003), p. 140.
7. Consider, for example, the critically despised but commercially profitable Italian film genre of *cinepanettoni*, which came to represent the very opposite of arthouse cinema. See O'Leary (2011), for an extended analysis.
8. See Article 1, provision 2-1 of the Ministry Decree 22 July 2015.
9. Ibid.
10. See the guidelines of the Creative Europe MEDIA sub-programme.

11. Kleinhans (1998), p. 308.
12. Ardizzoni (2013), pp. 312–13.
13. Angelone and Clò (2011), p. 85.
14. Caminati (2011), p. 124.
15. Verdicchio (2011), p. 109.
16. My translation. Original quote: 'Il cinema e il video "fuori norma" . . . A essi va dedicata un'attenzione e una "militanza" critiche che funzionino da forza propulsiva . . . È arrivato il momento di schierarsi per un cinema di opposizione e di resistenza'. Aprà (2013), p. 10.
17. My translation. Original quote: 'un atto di resistenza . . . Forse la rivoluzione, nei confronti di chi ha monopolizzato e avvilito il nostro sguardo, riparte da gesti come questi: andare in sala . . . come atto di militanza, come gesto di libertà'. Persico and Stellino (2016).
18. My translation. Original quote: 'produzioni indipendenti, spesso a basso costo, e tuttavia testimoni di un cinema italiano resistente e audace'. Rizza (2015).
19. Marrone (2016), p. 441.
20. Esposito (2012), p. 1.
21. Besides Roberto Esposito, other philosophers variously linked to the Italian Theory include Dario Gentili, Toni Negri, Giacomo Marramao, and Giorgio Agamben.
22. Esposito (2012), p. 24.
23. Locatelli (2016).
24. Locatelli and Tarantelli observe, in hindsight, that Cinemaindipendente. it could have simply abandoned its networking features, and turned into a specialised news website, but the promotion of a virtual community of independent filmmakers and *cinéphiles* was ultimately one of the portal's main goals. Thus, the founders felt that there was no point in continuing it, since 'the same people that used to animate that virtual space are now using social networks'. Locatelli (2016).
25. Ibid.
26. Locatelli and Tarantelli (2016).
27. Ibid.
28. Blair, Culkin and Randle, (2003).
29. These themes were partially inspired by Locatelli's own experience, being himself a wheelchair user since the age of seventeen, as a result of a motorbike accident.
30. See General Directorate of Cinema, Feature film Cultural interest resolution of 29 December 2016.
31. Locatelli (2016).
32. See Article 1, provision 2-1 of the Ministry decree 22 July 2015.
33. Locatelli and Tarantelli (2016).
34. Tarantelli (2016).
35. Ibid.
36. Baltruschat and Erickson (2015), p. 15.

37. Locatelli, 2016.
38. Ibid.
39. Ibid.
40. Antonello and Mussgnug (2009), p. 10.
41. Locatelli (2016).
42. Ibid.
43. Tarantelli (2016).
44. Locatelli (2016).
45. Ibid.
46. Ibid.
47. Antonello and Mussgnug (2009), p. 10.
48. Ibid., p. 11.

Works Cited

Allen, Michael (2003), *Contemporary US Cinema*, London: Pearson Education.
Angelone, Anita, Clarissa Clò (2011), 'Other visions: Contemporary Italian documentary cinema as counter-discourse', *Studies in Documentary Film*, 5.2–3: 83–9.
Antonello, Pierpaolo, Florian Mussgnug eds. (2009), *Postmodern Impegno: Ethics and Commitment in Contemporary Italian Culture*, Oxford: Peter Lang.
Aprà, Adriano ed. (2013), *Fuori norma. La via sperimentale del cinema italiano*, Venice: Marsilio.
Ardizzoni, Michela (2013), 'Narrative of Changes, Images for Changes: Contemporary Social Documentaries in Italy', *Journal of Italian Cinema and Media Studies*, 1.3: 311–26.
Baltruschat, Doris, Mary P. Erickson eds. (2015), *Independent Filmmaking Around the Globe*, Toronto: University of Toronto Press.
Blair, Helen, Nigel Culkin, Keith Randle (2003), 'From London to Los Angeles: a Comparison of Local Labour Market Processes in the US and UK Film Industries', *The International Journal of Human Resource Management*, 14.4: 619–33.
Bondanella, Peter and Federico Pacchioni (2017), *A History of Italian Cinema. 2nd Edition*, New York and London: Bloomsbury.
Caminati, Luca (2011). 'Narrative Non-fictions in Contemporary Italian Cinema: Roberto Munzi's *Saimir* (2002), Giorgio Diritti's *Il vento fa il suo giro* (2005), and Pietro Marcello's *La bocca del lupo* (2009)', *Studies in Documentary Film*, 5.2–3: 121–31.
Creative Europe – MEDIA Sub-Programme, Support for Development of Single Project and Slate Funding, Guidelines, <http://ec.europa.eu/culture/calls/media/s3013/guidelines_en.pdf>, last accessed 15 November 2016.
Esposito, Roberto (2012), *Living Thought: The Origins and Actuality of Italian Philosophy*, Stanford, CA: Stanford University Press.
King, Geoff (2005), *American Independent Cinema*, London: I.B. Tauris.
Kleinhans, Chuck (1998), 'Independent Features: Hopes and Dreams', in Jon Lewis ed., *The New American Cinema*, Durham, NC: Duke University Press, pp. 307–27.

Locatelli, Mirko (2016), Interview with the author, 23 October 2016.
MacKenzie, Scott ed. (2014), *Film Manifestos and Global Cinema Culture. A Critical Anthology*, Berkeley, CA: University of California Press.
Marrone, Gaetana (2016), 'The cinema of resistance: Interview with Edoardo Winspeare', *Journal of Italian Cinema & Media Studies*, 4.3: 439–53.
McDonald, Paul and Janet Wasko eds. (2008), *The Contemporary Hollywood Film Industry*, Boston, MA: Wiley-Blackwell.
O'Leary, Alan (2011), 'The Phenomenology of the Cinepanettone', *Italian Studies*, 66.3: 431–43.
Persico, Daniele and Alessandro Stellino (2016), 'Un atto di resistenza', *Filmidee* (22 September): <www.filmidee.it/2016/09/un-atto-di-resistenza/>, last accessed 9 December 2016.
Rizza, Gabriele (2015), Interview by Elettra Rizzotti, 'Al via allo Spazio Alfieri la nuova edizione di Visioni Off', Città di Firenze, Portale Giovani Firenze, 1 October, <https://portalegiovani.comune.fi.it/pogio/rubriche_publish/cineglobo_dettaglio.php?ID_REC=9401>, **last accessed** 18 October 2019.
Rizzotti, Elettra (2015), 'Al via allo Spazio Alfieri la nuova edizione di Visioni Off', Città di Firenze, Portale Giovani Firenze, 1 October, <https://portalegiovani.comune.fi.it/pogio/rubriche_publish/cineglobo_dettaglio.php?ID_REC=9401>, **last accessed** 18 October 2019.
Steiger, Janet (2013), 'Independent of What? Sorting Out Differences from Hollywood', in Geoff King, Clair Molloy, Yannis Tzioumakis eds., *American Independent Cinema. Indie, Indiewood and Beyond*, London and New York: Routledge, pp. 15–27.
Tarantelli, Giuditta (2016), Interview with the author, 23 October 2016.
Verdicchio, Pasquale (2011), 'Documentary on the Verge of Progress', *Studies in Documentary Film*, 5.2–3: 107–19.

Filmography

Come prima (*Just Like Before*), film, directed by Locatello Mirko, Italy, 2004. Officina Film DVD: 2007.
I Cormorani (*The Cormorants*), film, directed by Fabio Bobbio, Italy, 2016. Cecchi Gori Home Video DVD: 2018.
I Corpi Estranei (*Foreign Bodies*), film, directed by Locatelli Mirko, Italy, 2013. Cecchi Gori Home Video DVD: 2014.
Il Primo Giorno D'Inverno (*The First Day of Winter*), film, directed by Locatelli Mirko, Italy, 2008. Officina Film DVD: 2010.
Isabelle, fim, directed by Locatelli Mirko, Italy, 2018.
Le Quattro Volte (*The Four Times*), film, directed by Michelangelo Frammartino, Italy, 2010. Potemkin DVD: 2013.
Sette Opere Di Misericordia (*Seven Acts of Mercy*), film, directed by Massimiliano and Gianluca De Serio, Italy, 2011. Cecchi Gori Home Video DVD: 2016.

CHAPTER 7

Travelling the World: The Essay Films of Massimo Bacigalupo (1968–77)
Donatella Valente

Introduction

In first-person filmmaking, authorial subjectivity is essential. The personal camera of the diary, notebook or self-portrait film echoes subjective reflections on the world unfolding across a proliferation of fragmentary temporalities. As this chapter will attempt to demonstrate, some of the experimental films made by the Italian independent filmmaker Massimo Bacigalupo can be placed at the crossroads of a strand of artistic and experimental cinema defined by Laura Rascaroli as 'first-person filmmaking', which foregrounds autobiography and authorial subjectivity, 'the personal cinema of the avant-garde, that of *auteur* and art cinema; and that of the first-person documentary'.[1] Distinguished by a hybrid sensibility toward the arts, Bacigalupo's approach to filmmaking entailed a profound dedication to cinema as a life-long dream imbued with a quietly intense poetic towards both the old and new worlds.

This chapter aims to map the filmmaker's transformative journey of the self through his films made between 1968 and 1977. It draws on his years spent travelling whilst gleaning impressions of his experiences as an artist and a young man. His journeys range from the metaphorical to the otherworldly imaginary and the actuality of travelling. Bacigalupo's introspective and meditative style builds on the essay form, which is essentially speculative and lyrical. His films are based on an idiosyncratic formal combination of the autobiographical, documentary and experimental techniques, such as the collage of intertextual cultural references, ranging from poetry to myth and popular culture. I argue that through his personal camera Bacigalupo may have found a different mode of addressing his social, historical and cultural contexts. As Paul Arthur also notes, 'the essay film is galvanised by the intersection of personal, subjective and social history', and its definition 'rests somewhere in between fiction and nonfiction cinema. . . . One way to think about the essay film is that of a meeting ground for documentary, avant-garde and art film impulses'.[2]

Arguably, Bacigalupo's subjectivity lies in his peculiar use of different media, which give his films a polyphonic voice. In most of his essay films, he did not use the voice-over technique, which has often been considered as predominant, and provided instead either a verbal metacritical commentary or an omniscient narrative voice for his nonfictional films. Rascaroli writes that 'narration in the essay film has normally been linked to the expression of subjectivity and most directly to the narrating "I"'.[3] In this regard, Tim Corrigan also notes how

> an expressive subjectivity, commonly seen in the voice or actual presence of the filmmaker or a surrogate, has become one of the most recognizable signs of the essay film, sometimes quite visible in the film, sometimes not. Just as the first-person presence of the literary essay often springs from a personal voice and perspective, so essay films characteristically highlight a real or fictional persona whose quests and questionings shape and direct the film in lieu of a traditional narrative and frequently complicate the documentary look of the film with the presence of a pronounced subjectivity or enunciating position.[4]

Whilst the voice-over is regarded as one of the most pronounced formal expressions of the essay film, many film scholars have critiqued the assumed authority of this expressive technique in personal discourse and instead highlighted how its use might in fact debunk the narrator's authority. Rascaroli, for example, aims to consider the relationship between sound and image, as well as other elements that conspire to inscribe subjectivity in the texts: 'I will consider how authorial subjectivity is played out in the interstices between enunciator and narrator'.[5] I will deploy Rascaroli's argument to explore how Bacigalupo interweaves his authorial subjectivity amongst lyrical audio-visual forms, such as his sparse self-reflexive presence as enunciator and a montage of texts and images from a wide range of art materials, which take the place of the more conventional voice-over, as the narrator of his essay film. These creative poetic devices may be said to activate the viewer's engagement and prime a thoughtful sensibility for the themes evoked in his films, from mass migrations to fallen war heroes, to love and death.

Thus, the disembodied voice of a narrator is replaced with portions of written and printed text and imagery that his camera gleaned from a variety of sources, from modernist poetry books, to contemporary mass media and ancient religious scriptures, in order to evoke ideas and invoke meditations. This intricate over-layering of interconnected imagery, at times via paint-brushed text over specific frames, provided his films with a poetic internal rhythm. I argue that the filmmaker's interwoven visual fabric forms meta-narrative portals through which his audience could envision historical events taking place in different parts of the globe, and engage with cultural memory. This was one way for him to channel his – perhaps escapist – desire to travel elsewhere. Finally, I will argue that Bacigalupo's suggestive use of text allowed his authorial subjectivity, inscribed in his specific choice of media, the autonomy necessary to open up spaces of reflection and critical engagement on a phenomenological, experiential state of being-in-the-world.

A Historical Outline of Bacigalupo's Essay Films

Bacigalupo's imaginary filmic journeys started in 1968, with *60 metri per il 31 marzo* (*200 Feet for March 31st*), a Happening film shot in Rome and entirely edited in-camera. He juxtaposed text and images he sourced from the sacred ancient Indian text of *The Upanishads*, and from modernist Anglo-American poetry. Also, in 1968, Bacigalupo made the short *Her*, through which he shows his viewers the tragic events taking place at the Chicago Convention, and invokes reflections on society's responses to cases of human rights abuse. Between 1968 and 1975, he travelled across real foreign landscapes and places, realising his dreams of leaving behind the known for the unknown, opening his camera up to imaginary and real historical records, personal and collective memories from a distant past.

Between 1968 and 1970, he crossed the Middle East and India. In the film *Versus* (1968), a street in Jerusalem on the Mount of Olives provides the starting point for a meditation on the perception of the image; the film forms a diptych with *60 metri per il 31 marzo*. Bacigalupo provocatively reveals the double perspective of the 'I/eye' of the camera. Between 1969 and 1970, he made a tetralogy film cycle called *Fiore d'eringio* (*Eryngium*), which comprises four diary, notebook and self-portrait films, and which could be seen as an audio-visual lyrical composition of a young man's existential journey. With this film cycle, the filmmaker's camera traced the uncertain traits of interior and exterior spaces, of fantasy lands, and the real worlds, belonging to ancient and modern cultures. These films combine the sensibility of the first-person gaze documenting real events in the world undergoing profound cultural and social changes, with an avant-garde, experimental interest, in the ontology of film and the moving image.

Bacigalupo was one of the founders of the Cooperativa del Cinema independente (Co-operative of Italian Independent Cinema). His desire to build a transnational bridge between Italian experimental films and international film co-operatives resulted in his travelling across Northern

Europe – after taking part in the 1970 London Underground Film Festival held at the National Film Theatre. He divided his time between Italy and New York until 1973, when he made *Warming Up*, first screened at the Anthology Film Archives. Bacigalupo said that '*Warming Up* is the journal of a season of creativity',[6] gathering glimpses of the world as an imaginative place.

After presenting a season of Italian experimental films at the National Cineteques of Madrid and Barcelona, in 1975 the filmmaker went back to America and made a home movie, his diary film *Into the House*. The film is composed of found footage from his family film album, and the documentary images of a family gathering, and it taps into personal records and cultural memory. Finally, whilst in New York the same year, Bacigalupo also made *Postcards from America*, re-imagined through the Japanese poet Matsuo Basho's words, which describes his unresolved journeys of self-discovery, his poetics for travelling the world: 'Time is a century-old passenger, and so are months and years eternal travellers . . . for a very long time – how long I cannot precisely remember – I too, like a solitary wind-swept cloud, have constantly been inclined to a nomadic life'.[7] This encapsulates Bacigalupo's compelling ruminations on an existential and dream-like way of experiencing life through a subjective inner world found in movement.

Influences and Legacies

His experimental and visionary essayistic style was influenced by many of his New American Cinema associates, including Gregory Markopoulos and Jonas Mekas, and by his study of the modernists William Yeats, T. S. Eliot, and Ezra Pound; they helped him shape his impressions of a chaotic modernity experienced as a young man who attempted to engage with a changing world.

Because of his interest in travelling across inner spaces and exterior landscapes, some of Bacigalupo's films can be firmly positioned within an Italian tradition of essayistic cinema. Arguably, the lineage of this form of filmmaking, in Italy can be traced back to the late 1940s with Michelangelo Antonioni's meditation on the people living in the Po region in *Gente del Po* (*People of the Po Valley*, 1947), and Roberto Rossellini's television miniseries *L'India vista da Rossellini* (*India as Seen by Rossellini*, 1958), composed of ten notebook films he made while travelling to India. Also, throughout the Sixties, Cesare Zavattini made first-person documentary films such as *Cinegiornali della Pace* (*Cine-newsreels for Peace*, 1963) and *Cinegiornali Liberi* (*Free Cine-newsreels*, 1968–70), thus 're-writing' in the neo-realist vein the vocation of the 'newsreel', as did Federico Fellini with *A Director's Notebook* (1969), and Pier Paolo Pasolini with *Appunti per un film sull'India* (*Notes for a Film about India*, 1968) and *Notes Towards an African Orestes* (1970). Alongside these internationally renowned filmmakers there were, as in the case of Bacigalupo, other less known independent filmmakers who operated within a hybrid context, at the junction of art, cinema and essay writing, such as Alberto Grifi with his diptych *L'occhio è per così dire l'evoluzione biologica di una lacrima* (*The Eye Is, So-To-Speak, the Biological Evolution of a Tear*) and *Autoritratto Auschwitz* (*Self-Portrait Auschwitz*) (1968–70), and Mario Schifano with *Umano Non Umano* (*Human Not Human*, 1969). This strand of essayistic diary, notebook and self-portrait films, is close to the ethnographic and poetic cinema of Maya Deren, Jonas Mekas and Jean Rouch. It is for these reasons that Bacigalupo's essayistic films build on a tradition of both a transnational network and what could be regarded as a specifically *Italian* essay film tradition.

The Diary Film *60 metri per il 31 marzo* (1968) and the Notebook Film *Versus* (1968): An Essay Film Diptych8

Bacigalupo's film diptych, the diary *60 metri per il 31 marzo* (Figure 7.1) and notebook *Versus*, outlines the multi-layered dimensions of time, and translates his imaginary travelling over the course of one day in Rapallo, in *60 metri*, and over a longer period of time throughout the Middle-East, in *Versus* (Figures 7.2 and 7.3). However, despite their geographical and stylistic differences these two films complement each other.

For its distinct aesthetics, this film diptych draws attention to Bacigalupo's formal idiosyncrasies: while the diaristic style of *60 metri* was based on spontaneously testing his own ideas by recording daily life and

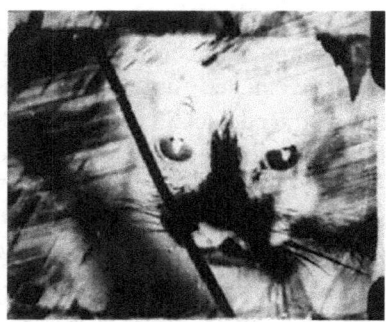

Figure 7.1 *60 metri per il 31 marzo* (*200 Feet for March 31ˢᵗ*, 1968).

Figures 7.2, 7.3 *Versus* (1968).

referencing tropes of popular culture, the notebook *Versus* became a more sombre text through which he ponders on photographic techniques – this latter film essentially consists of a series of notes and sketches on the ontology of the still image in relation to temporality and history. The diptych films complement each other because the filmmaker explored universal binary oppositions, such as life and death, youth and old age, and especially the separation between stillness and movement. His impressionistic and existentialist perspectives encompassed a concern, on the one hand, with the *a priori* ontology of the image *per se* at the moment of its being photo-chemically imprinted onto the film medium and before it translates into audio-visual representation, and on the other hand, with the subjective experience of foreign cultures and lands that the moving image finally represents.

Bacigalupo made *60 metri* as an in-camera edited 'film-Happening', filmed on 8mm, and mostly over the course of twenty-four hours (hence the date 31st March of the title). As Timothy Corrigan argues:

> Diaries map the expressions of an individual according to different temporal chronologies and rhythms, perhaps as detailed sequential organisations, sometimes with dramatic ellipses, and invariably according to various rhythms usually associated with daily life and experience.[9]

The authorial subjectivity of his personal camera creates a diary film which depicts an imaginary life in a day, as a euphoric and optimistic Happening; a metaphorical journey to India through an appreciation of the country's history of art. The film's 8mm format holds up a mirror to society's desire to politicise the arts by integrating them into everyday life. The mobility and lightness of such a format allows the filmmaker to contribute a spontaneous and unscripted tracing of events as they unfold, while the text from ancient Indian literature provides the over-layered, textual, commentary. Overall, this results in an insightful meditation on the year '68. The filmmaker provides a subjective, fictional, worldview with the structure of the sacred Indian philosophical scriptures of the Katha-Upanishad.[10] They are divided into six 'Vallis', or branches, and narrate the dialogue between the young man Nakiketa and Death, and they inspired Bacigalupo with a pre-historical vision of humanity. His camera creates literary and artistic quotations in multiple directions, as it gleans texts from modernist, and a variety of other, artists: the poet Ezra Pound, symbolist painter Kandinsky, going on from Stan Brakhage to E. E. Cummings and Botticelli, from John Donne to Hieronymus Bosch, and from The Katha-Upanishads and Piero della Francesca to Caravaggio.

Through montage and juxtaposition, the filmmaker gives expression to his perceptions of contemporary daily reality and depicts his personal impressionistic diary of events populated by archaic imagery and echoes of time immemorial, enmeshed as they are within the immediacy of an ephemeral present. While travelling across imaginary and real pleats of time, and testing creative ideas while experiencing different cultural dimensions, Bacigalupo's intertextualities amount to disembodied 'I's, the voice-over replaced by these media quotations: his subjective-objective self embedded within a dialogue between the 'I' of the camera and the 'other' of the referent. This form of thinking through visual quotations is reminiscent of Walter Benjamin's radical re-thinking of the intrinsic nature of the essay as a form founded on quotations that voice a subjective expression, and which 'inhabits and reformulates itself constantly as the expression of another or an other'.[11]

Otherness' is remediated in the notebook film *Versus* through the image of a street in Jerusalem, which provides the filmmaker with a philosophical objective for musing over reality and representation, his thinking visualised through his becoming 'other'. In an existentialist mode, *Versus* denounces the excessive happiness and euphoria of *60 metri* and argues that life and death are irreconcilable. Moreover, *Versus* reflexively studies the perception of the image through the mirroring point-of-view of the 'I/eye' of the camera/audience, which is visible from the start of the film, when the filmmaker is inside a bus on a street in Jerusalem, driving through the Mount of Olives. The desolation and poverty of this location are meant to reflect the 'poverty' of the image as a fading indexical trace. It is the result of Bacigalupo's study of the chasm separating the 'real', of the present, from its historical dimension, which acknowledges the presence of the image within a specific, temporal and located, subjective experience. Compared with the lighter and joyful tone of *30 metri*, *Versus* conveys a more sombre phenomenological response to the impact of history on society in present-day life.[12]

This diptych prompts further considerations on the photographic mise-en-abîme illustrated by the same photograph in *Versus*. By so doing, Bacigalupo questions, and enables us to think about representation *versus* (my emphasis) the subjective experience of the image. Thus, thinking through filmmaking turns into an attempt to engage with an 'abysmal' ontological fracture, seeking to bridge first-hand perception with the mediation of experience. The duality of 'I'/eye – objective and subjective view of the world – finds its articulation in the filmmaker positing the self as concretely existing in the 'real' world, however bound up with the 'I'/eye of the camera. Thus, he postulates a series of questions in relation to the shaping of the present by the past, and generates meditations for the individual as a consumer of images, and for viewers who may contribute to cultural transformations through their film-going experience.

Thus, although shot in a foreign land, this film undertakes a series of reflections between external and internal, physical and metaphysical, spaces. The opacity of both film and image becomes the metaphor for life itself, ambiguous and irresolute. Influenced by Sartre's claim that one makes art in order to be essential, Bacigalupo sees the filmic object as an essential part of life's spatio-temporal dimension, like a stream of volcanic lava, in continuous transformation.[13]

Thus, the porous boundaries in Bacigalupo's inner and outer landscapes can be read through Michael Renov's conclusions on essay writing and its 'borderline status', as he suggests that its subjectivity is not in contrast to its inquisitive attitude (which is actually that of its marker). According to Renov, 'descriptive and reflexive modalities are coupled; the representation of the historical real is consciously filtered through the flux of subjectivity'.[14] As I have exemplified through a close critical analysis of this essay film diptych, subjectivity and reflexivity are marks of both Bacigalupo and the audience's essayistic gaze, drawn inward, in parallel with the documentary gaze, which retains an interest in some portions of the world.

Her (1968)[15]

Bacigalupo's thoughts on. the worldwide events deeply affecting society during '68 were particularly focussed on a case of violence perpetrated by the police on a woman during the Chicago Convention riots. For *Her*

Figure 7.4 *Her* (1968).

(Figure 7.4), which is entirely edited in camera, he repurposed textual portions and photographic reportage sourced from the mass media. *Her* was also Bacigalupo's contribution to the larger collaborative project, the 'swansong film' of the Cooperativa del Cinema Independente, *Tutto, Tutto nello stesso istante* (*All, All at Once*, 1968–9) a compilation of short films by twelve of the Co-operative's filmmakers, and originally planned to form a long 'circular letter'. It formed part of a collective response to, and critical commentary on, police repression and violence during the historic riots of Valle Giulia in Rome, in March 1968, and at the 1968 Democratic Convention in Chicago.[16] Animated by the collective spirit of Happenings, these films were shot spontaneously – some on sixty metres of Ektrachrome film – on the spur of the moment, and circulated among the other filmmakers, hence prompting their immediate response.

Specifically, in *Her* Bacigalupo uses the collage and paintbrush style for his creative expression, and sensitive personal meditations, on time as an intricate series of layers of temporalities, from the subjective, to the historical, to the mythical. Although the film is based on documentary evidence sourced from the media, and its mode of storytelling is rooted in immediacy, *Her*'s narrative poetics unsettle the notion of a univocal and one-dimensional present of chronologically linear documentary narratives. The heterogeneous materials of this film, in fact, reflect a variety of cultural phenomena as they took place and were being discussed around the world through popular media. The main part of the film shows a collage of news-cuttings from the American magazine *Newsweek*'s reporting on the 1968 Chicago Convention riots, with images of police rallies and violent charges at students. Text, either printed on a paper strip or paint-brushed on the magazine's news-cuttings, shows portions of a reportage on a woman pushed against a wall and beaten-up by the police. It painstakingly evokes physical violence, and documents the tension between the police, wearing gas-masks, and the demonstrators, lined up and facing each other. The collage of text that is printed on a white strip, which in turn is cut-up and superimposed on the magazine's photographs, progresses throughout the film in a montage sequence. The text spells out the woman's and the demonstrators' dread: 'God: Pushed up against a wall by a / phalanx of cops, a pretty blonde begged / for mercy. No one listened. / A group of police prodded her in the stom(ach) / with their clubs, sending her to her / knees, her face in her hands, screaming: / Please God, help me. Please help me'.[17] Some of these words, such as 'her', 'God' and 'screaming', are painted in capital letters on top of other photographs, detailing the event.

As Bacigalupo explained in his imaginary self-conducted interview for the film magazine *Bianco e Nero*, he chose this text from *Newsweek* magazine so that he could subsequently transform it into a broader meditation on violence. The film is internally punctuated by the rhythm of black intervals between images; from the magazine article, one word at a time flashes as they are juxtaposed on images of the riots throughout the film. Then, a series of images of women sourced from classical paintings leads to the true, real, and central image of a body – perhaps female – clothed in a long Islamic tunic, abandoned on a rocky shore by the sea, tucked into a gorge, and made visible through a crane shot. Held for about thirty seconds, this image ends in series of convulsive flashes. These narrative shifts back and forth from previous texts superimposed on other images in the news, hence invoking new, yet parallel, stories of violence in the world. In this sense, Bacigalupo's authorial subjectivity is articulated via both text and images, which each comment on the other, thus both broadening and narrowing down the filmmaker's metacritical heterogeneous 'voice-over' as provided by his reflexive narrative techniques. Bacigalupo wonders whether the printed text changes its meaning according to the accompanying images. Subsequently, he explained that the meanings of the printed texts expand and resonate throughout the film. They shift from story to subjective experience, from fiction to nonfiction, from the fantastical to the metaphysical.[18] As Michael Renov observes:

> [T]he essay form, notable for its tendency towards complication (digression, fragmentation, repetition, and dispersion) rather than composition, has, in its four-hundred-years history, continued to resist the efforts of literary taxonomists, confounding the laws of genre and classification, challenging the very notion of text and textual economy.[19]

The direct depiction of violence through the deployment of lyrical compositions of quotations from the media – in the form of either stills from newsreel television footage, or photographic reportages from magazines and newspapers – demonstrates the ways in which this collage formed the filmmaker's personal viewpoint and narrative voice; the breadth and depth of a cinematic essay on violence, despite its being in fact a very short burst of ideas and thoughts, perhaps influenced by his travels to Cyprus and Israel during the same time. His critical 'writing' on film, by materially blemishing the filmic medium to create a strong analogy with the wounds inflicted on people, conveyed his phenomenological approach to the mediation, and immediacy 'effect', of forms of aggression and repression on civil and human rights.

As Adorno argued: 'the essay does not allow the idea of immediacy, postulated by the very concept of mediation, to disappear entirely. All levels of the mediated are immediate to the essay, before its reflection begins'.[20] I would argue that this is central to the notion of writing essaystically with the film camera, which can be seen in Bacigalupo's meditative personal camera, which is undoubtedly also influenced by Alexandre Astruc's theory on the 'camera-stylo'.[21]

Fiore d'eringio (*Eryngium*, 1969–70)

Fiore d'eringio (*Eryngium*) is a cycle of four film-diaries describing Bacigalupo's perceptions of his travels to Iran, Afghanistan and India during 1969 and 1970 (Figures 7.5–7.8). The whole tetralogy, clearly, is both a metaphorical journey through his selfhood as a young man and an actual journey through faraway lands. He drew the idea of the eryngium as a symbol of cultural memory from the thistle that the Dutch Master Albrecht Dürer holds in a self-portrait of 1493, which Bacigalupo saw at the Louvre. Thus, this film-cycle denotes the painterly sensibility of the self-portrait, a trait of the personal cinema of the avant-garde, which, as Raymond Bellour argued, corresponded most

Figure 7.5 *L'Ultima Estate* (*The Last Summer*, 1969).

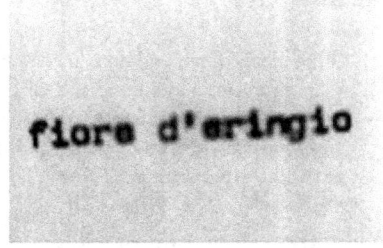

Figure 7.6 *Né Bosco (una conversazione)* (*Nor Wood (a love-dialogue)*, 1970).

Figure 7.7 *Migrazione* (*Migration*, 1970).

Figure 7.8 *Coda* (1970).

faithfully to the only autobiographical cinematic form which is unencumbered by any specific generic conventions or story-telling devices:

> The self-portrait clings to the analogical, the metaphorical, the poetic, far more than to the narrative. Its coherence lies in a system of remembrances, afterthoughts, superimpositions, correspondences. It thus takes on the appearance of discontinuity, of anachronistic juxtaposition, of montage. Where autobiography closes in on the life it recounts, the self-portrait opens itself up to a limitless totality.[22]

Thus, the whole the film hinges on the formal dichotomy between the personal and subjective and the poetic and mythical. It stands for an imaginary portrait of Bacigalupo as a twenty-three-year-old man and artist with the desire to carry forward the cultural legacies of the past, both personal and mythical, as the film is also heavily influenced by Greek mythology and other classical ancient texts. Its essayistic register denotes the style of travel diary-writing and evokes the 'I' of self-portraiture in painting.

Indeed, despite not having a camera with him for a while, Bacigalupo kept a diary, which he called 'Bamyan's News', after the name of a valley in Afghanistan. The 'News' inspired him with an Eastern soundtrack for the film section entitled *Migration*. The tetralogy starts as an intimate record of the director's personal experience and progresses to assume a more universal and existentialist perspective on life. As a whole, the film folds in on itself as a source of the progression of possibilities, a form of experience as if held within a pause before its complete realisation, and at times closer to a moment of absolute stillness. It affirms both the rational and the irrational, the responsible and the reckless side, of possible human actions.[23] This is where the tone of the essay film sets in, evoking Adorno's idea of the essay film as both 'self-reflective and self-reflexive'.[24]

Bacigalupo stated that this cycle of shorts should be projected as a whole film, in order to appreciate how its circularity meaningfully contributes to the idea of history transmitting cultural memory. All the sources from his personal art archive invoke meditations on binary oppositions such as life and death, and contemplation versus vital energy and kinesis – continually and metaphorically expanding and shifting in form and meaning.[25] In this sense, then, the subjective enunciator in the self-portrait and travel-diary film expands to borrow the objective third-person perspective of the archive in order to lend the whole film a meta-narrative reflexivity poised to open up a dialogical relation with its viewers. As Adorno reminds us:

> The essay is determined by the unity of its object, together with that of theory and experience which have migrated into the object. The essay's openness is not vaguely one of feeling and mood, but obtains its contour from its content.[26]

Consequently, as the content of the essay is based on conceptual, meaningful, mutations and alterations, occurring through multiple temporal folds, its form also takes the shape of indeterminacy and openness: the conceptual unity of its form, the circular shape of this film-tetralogy, doubtlessly porous and polyphonic.

The first film in this tetralogy *L'ultima Estate* (*The Last Summer*, 1969)[27] was shot before Bacigalupo left for India. He called it 'his Nepalese film'. It portrays his family, and their farewell and good wishes rituals, but also considers the decline of civilisation, which to the filmmaker is also an encounter with death:

> This is a moment of stillness in the course of the great migration. As the older family members are saying goodbye to life, the younger members are approaching it with gusto. Contemporary life is made to reveal an archaic substratum.[28]

Enthused by youthful feelings, in *L'ultima Estate* Bacigalupo traced his own rite-of-passage from a younger to a more mature consciousness – construing travelling as a personal journey. The existentialist worldview of 'the young man as artist' feeds into a more mature and lyrical vein in *Né Bosco: una conversazione* (*Nor Wood: a Conversation*, 1970).[29] Bacigalupo dedicated this film to the Greek poet Sappho; a fragment from her poetry ('And there was no meeting where we were separated, nor wood') provides the idea for the title, while this film provides the dialogues for the entire film cycle.[30] In the film the text alternates with images of paintings from both Indian and Western classical traditions. *Né Bosco* is a complex, lyrical textual tapestry, drawing from the *Song of Songs* in the Bible. It represents an amorous dialogue between a man and a woman, while positive and negative photographs provide the visual underpinning and counterpart to the couple's conversation. The filmmaker states that the film reveals the chasm existing between its textual abstractions and the documentary imagery from his travels, between the sacred and the profane, or between myth and 'reality'.

Cultural memory celebrates the life of women in *Migrazione* (*Migration*, 1970).[31] This could be seen as a feminist film, focussing on the representation of woman in the arts and throughout history, as it captures words and images from mythological, sacred and modernist literature. The female image is painted like a mighty character who can lead mass-migrations and movements. As Bacigalupo explained, the central myth is that of the Annunciation: the angel and the Madonna who is sometimes a virgin, sometimes a mother. It is also about the mystery and myth of Kore, or Persephone in Greek mythology, daughter of Zeus and queen of the underworld. A man's voice recites the text of the poem, while a girl interprets the text. For Bacigalupo, *Migrazione* represents the cyclical movement of history; the sacred and troubled universe traversed by the migrants becomes a metaphor for the students' daily clashes in the suddenly unsettled world of the late Sixties. While each sequence was rooted in the immediate present, composed of the sudden occurrence of situations, Bacigalupo imagined the whole film as if it were a sacred fresco populated by historical migrations, by people – not only from many centuries earlier – who were rather unaware of their historical circumstances.[32]

The concluding part of the film-cycle *Coda* (1970)[33] is about self-portraiture, and the various ways in which artists have approached the emptiness of life, both courageously and tragically. Bacigalupo's camera continues to avidly glean images from classical literary texts, as well as imagery from films and from Dürer's painting 'Self-portrait with Eryngium'.

Coda (1970) is the most intimately personal film of the tetralogy; it evokes an oneiric atmosphere and, in many sequences, depicts the individual set against vast natural landscapes. Again, the contrast between the past and present is starkly illustrated, maintaining the sombre tone, as at the end of a long panoramic take from a rooftop view of a town (perhaps the director's native Rapallo, where he resided and returned to) an epigraph is revealed: 'A Requiem for Soldiers lost in Ocean Transport'.

Hence the personal memories of such a long journey from Italy through Iran, India and Afghanistan, come to a close back in Italy, and with them a collision of images from both time immemorial and lost, and time re-found in 1970, through the allegories of life and death, his youthful enthusiastic yearning for a solution to a perceived deep social discontent and involution, the ongoing waging of imperialistic wars, natural disasters, and the epitaphs of fallen heroes. *Coda* dedicates an entire sequence to the film *Medea*, made in 1969 by one of the very few emerging female independent filmmakers, Pia Epremian, known as the 'girl with the H8 camera'.[34] Bacigalupo thought this sequence to be a natural follow up to the metaphorical representation of the flower in blossom.

Films on His Italo-American Heritage

The films Bacigalupo shot between 1973 and 1977 are representative of his Italo-American heritage. They build not only on a sense of rootlessness and a yearning for travel, but also on the desire to capture the past through the memories of family life, a personal cultural heritage. With *Warming up* (1973) (Figure 7.9),[35] an imaginative light-hearted film-journal shot with playful distance in New York and Italy, Bacigalupo pays tribute to creativity, spontaneity and imagination. He aimlessly wanders around city streets, graffitiing the walls and taking notes on made-up tales with his camera. His authorial subjectivity finds expression in an enquiry into gesture, both as a performed, culturally inflected expression, and as part of human behaviour, a natural utterance of language. For part of this film, the director recycled a 16mm film stock, which resulted in degraded moving-images. The film does not have a conventional storyline, nor does it provide any explanation other than clearly showing things and people in different environments, as local geographies are depicted as the external dimensions of inner lives and worlds.

For example, while a musical comedy is being shot by the Brooklyn Bridge, Bacigalupo approaches the director of this small film production to let him know that he has been shooting an even funnier movie. This sequence is intercut with shots from an imaginary, self-conducted interview, in which Bacigalupo explains his reasons for making this film. The overall effect is, on the one hand, a parody of structured meanings, where gestures are inferred as meaningless, and on the other hand, the gestures

Figure 7.9 *Warming Up* (1973).

that the film attempts to record and organise, are regarded, potentially, as the 'memory of the world', if there were one. By re-deploying one of his recurring formal narrative devices, the story within the story, or the present within myth and history, Bacigalupo stated that his intention was to call this film *The Planets' Mirror*. The film would partly form the memory of the world, based on a playful interplay between repetitions and coincidences of images and motifs, again as if they were mere empty vessels, having no meaning.[36] The filmmaker declared that: '*Warming Up* is an exercise in warming up the imaginary that is suspended on the moment which separates the wait from the starter, in a filmic economy of suspense that sets melancholy obliquely to euphoria, a perfect complement to the parsed time of *The Last Summer*'.[37]

In relation to travelling back to the past through personal memories and timeless gestures, Bacigalupo cites the English poet and painter William Blake, who said: 'Eternity is in love with the products of time', to suggest how, with irony, he wanted to reproduce the multi-layered sedimentations of memory which hold on to present-ness and timelessness.[38]

Into the House, 1975 (Figure 7.10),[39] interweaves the themes of memory and cultural heritage through Bacigalupo's use of found film footage called *The Family Album*, which is roughly three minutes long, from around 1939, and was shot on 16mm by a professional photographer, who was hired for the purpose of recoding family memories. This forms the beginning of the entire home movie, *Into the House*, which is about the wedding of Bacigalupo's cousin in the town of Elizabeth, Pennsylvania, in 1975.[40] The title refers to the child we see in the very last frame of the film about to enter the family home. This film is very different from *Warming Up*, and it denotes how particularly resonant the process of reconstructing memories became for him, especially those concerning his discovery of not only older family rituals of his Italo-American family, but also earlier methodologies of filming family portraits.

Figure 7.10 *Into the House* (1975).

The filmmaker added his mother's voice-over as it recalls her experience as a child growing up in an Italian family of immigrants in America between the wars: the difficulties of settling in a foreign country, the 1920s in a mining town, the onset of the war and her experience during it, her prolonged illness and her brother's death. The jarring element introduced by his mother's voice-over is its disconnection from the underlying images of the home movie portraying his cousin's wedding, though this recalls the same counterpunctual technique that Bacigalupo used in his previous essay films. This contributes to creating a meditative and evocative film about loss and survival. The misalignment of Bacigalupo's mother's voice with images from this home-movie evokes the 'family album' and echoes ancestral memories, while mobilising thoughts on diasporic lives.

During the course of an interview I conducted in July 2015, Bacigalupo talked about the family found film footage *The Family Album*, which only lasts three minutes and forms the opening of *Into the House*. It is a family-film-portrait and probably made, as was customary at the time, by a photographer who was hired for this purpose, and who used a static film camera to record family activities. When he came across the found footage, Bacigalupo initially thought they were a series of photographs on a film strip. Then he saw these were moving images of people who happened to be his great-grandparents and grandparents, posing still or moving ever so slightly as if for a photographic family shot. At the time, the photographer would film family members posing as if for photographic portraiture, looking into the camera, and greeting. On the whole, as a film *The Family Album* evokes both the photographic album, the aesthetics of stillness and movement and the illusion of seeing still images.

For Bacigalupo, this family found footage emphasises the value of the *Into the House* film, as a means to transmit personal cultural heritage, as well as a historically specific record of making home movies and family film portraits in the late 1930s – which followed a specific idiosyncratic custom. We find another recurrent film aesthetic, which also is a specific trait of the authorial subjectivity of the essay film, as stated at the beginning of this chapter: its being self-reflective insofar as it draws attention to its narrative techniques (the family film album and the home movie) and its core themes, such as personal memory, the experiences of displacement, trauma and war; and its being self-reflective insofar as it draws attention to its enunciators, Bacigalupo's mother and family members' poetic presence.

I would argue that the self-reflexivity of this film continues the legacy of the meditations started in the *Eryngium* cycle with the desire to transmit cultural memory and heritage. This is carried out through historical forms of film poetics informed by records and meditations: the patrimony of specifically resonant moments both at a personal level (the family album, the diary, the journal) and at a historical level (the records of displaced communities, diasporic memories).

His next American film shot on Ektrachrome, *Cartoline dall'America* (*Postcards from America*, 1975–77),[41] continues the themes related to travelling and personal journeys. In fact, Bacigalupo made this experimental notebook-film inspired by the Japanese poet Matsuo Basho's nomadic life and poetry, the *Narrow Road to the Deep North*, written in 1689. Arguably, the filmmaker made a series of short films that created a 'postcard aesthetic'. While on a coast-to-coast trip in America, he depicted sketches of the countryside as a remote land, reminiscent of his 1970 essay film *Migration*. For *Cartoline dall'America*, he imagined himself as an itinerant salesman of drawings and naïf paintings, sitting outside Columbia's Butler Library. He posthumously substituted the intricate magnetic sound compositions and lyrics, that originally accompanied these 'postcards', for a simplified digitised score, and brief excerpts from Walt Whitman's verses.[42]

Concluding Thoughts

This chapter has attempted to demonstrate how Bacigalupo's essay film output between 1968 and 1977 was the result of authorial subjectivity and first-person lyrical narratives. Through the diary, notebook, self-portrait film and home movie genres, Bacigalupo made ample use of his personal art and family archive. The resulting films demonstrated a concern with both temporality (the imaginary and actual personal experience of time) and space, both envisaged as a mindscape and a landscape.

This chapter has also seen that within the broader platform of Italian independent film productions from the 1960s and 1970s, a definition that includes other aspects of the essay-film aesthetic can contribute to replenishing a study of the overlooked legacies of this elusive and hybrid form. Bacigalupo's experimental personal cinema is made of idiosyncratic essayistic expressions that are both speculative and lyrical, founded on an internal consistency and coherence, based on recurrent threads and stylistic traits, such as self-reflexiveness, the story within the story motif, the present always inhabited by history and myth. I concur with Rascaroli's words on yet another elusive element of the hybrid character of the essay film, which is its lyricism:

> I refer to lyricism as counternarrative for its propensity to fragmentariness, incompleteness and lacuna and for it being a force that produces meanings associated not to story or rational discourse, but to affect. . . . Argumentation can be constructed also through poetic affect and aesthetic form'.[43]

The films' evocative texts and imageries embody the filmmaker's polyphonic voice. The empty space of an extra-diegetic disembodied voice-over lends itself to a consistently present authorial, intra-diegetic, evocative voice, as it invokes inquisitiveness and a dialogical relationship between the 'I' and the 'eye' of the camera – filmmaker's and viewers'. Moreover, the presence of a wide range of strong women, from the arts and ancient literature, and from his personal life, and that provide the underlying dialogues to many of his films, offer an interesting alternative voice. Overall, a variety of 'quotations' from the archive speak for the filmmaker's in-depth knowledge of, and love for, the arts, and are the essential testimony of cultural and personal memory.

Notes

1. Rascaroli (2009), p. 106.
2. Arthur (2003), p. 58.
3. Rascaroli (2017), p. 143
4. Corrigan (2011), p. 30.
5. Rascaroli (2009), p. 45.
6. Bursi and Causo (2010), p. 160
7. My translation. Original quote: 'Il tempo è un passeggero fra eoni di eoni, così come i mesi e gli anni sono eterni viaggiatori. . . da molto tempo a questa parte – quanto sia non ricordo con precisione – anch'io, come una nuvola solitaria spinta dal vento, sono stato costantemente soggetto a una disposizione al vagabondaggio'. Bursi and Causo (2010), p. 162.
8. *60 metri per il 31 marzo* (*200 Feet for March 31ˢᵗ*), 1968, 8mm/16mm, b/w, silent, 15'. Available at: <https://www.youtube.com/watch?v=KFFSg6dUmac>, last accessed 21 August 2019. *Versus* (1968, 16mm, b/w, silent, 14').
9. Corrigan (2011), p. 131.
10. 'Born at the end of the Middle Ages, established by the end of the Renaissance, as a result of this epoch's interest in individuality and the inner self, finally constituted as a literary genre in the nineteenth century, and currently in a phase of deep transformation and great expansion, the written diary is a multiform practice that takes many shapes (ledger, logbook, spiritual journal, pillow book, private diary, travelogue), and that accounts for the diarist's relationship with themselves, with others and with their epoch'. Rascaroli (2009), p. 115.
11. Lopate (1996), p. 246.
12. Bacigalupo (1974), p. 24.
13. Ibid., p. 26.
14. Rascaroli (2009), p. 31.
15. *Her*, 1968, 16mm, 3', colour, silent. *Her* was part of the collaborative, epistolary film *Tutto, Tutto nello stesso istante* (*All, All at Once*), 1969, 16mm, colour, sound, 25'.
16. Bacigalupo (1974), p. 9.

17. *Her*, 1968.
18. Bacigalupo (1974), p. 25.
19. Rascaroli (2009), p. 22.
20. Adorno (1984), p. 159.
21. 'In postwar France, perhaps the best-known pronouncement on the cinematic possibilities that would lay the groundwork for the essay film is Alexandre Astruc's 1948 "The Birth of the New Avant-garde: The Caméra-Stylo"'. Corrigan (2011), p. 64.
22. Bellour (1989), p. 7.
23. Bacigalupo (1974), pp. 26–7.
24. Adorno (1991), p. 171.
25. Bacigalupo (1974), p. 26.
26. Adorno (1954), p. 165.
27. *The Last Summer*, 1969, 8mm, colour, sound and silent, 30'.
28. Bacigalupo (2010), p. 156.
29. *Né Bosco: una conversazione* (*Nor Wood: A Conversation*), 1970, 16mm, b/w, silent, 20'.
30. Bacigalupo (2010), p. 157.
31. *Migration*, 1970, 16mm, b/w, 60'.
32. Bacigalupo (1974), p. 30.
33. *Coda*, 1970, 16mm, b/w, 15'.
34. '*Medea* gathers all my important relatives and friends. Above all, my daughter Alida as a child ... all of the characters somehow transmit the inner pains of birth, body, and life in a symbolic way'. My translation. Original quote: 'Medea raccoglie tutti i personaggi importanti della mia famiglia e dei miei amici. Soprattutto mia figlia Alida bambina ... Tutti i personaggi in qualche modo simbolicamente trasmettono le pene interiori della nascita, del corpo e della vita'. <http://www.fondazionecsc.it/events_detail.jsp?IDAREA=9&ID_EVENT=211&GTEMPLATE=events.jsp>, last accessed 30 August 2019.
35. *Warming Up*, 1973, 16mm, colour, 40'.
36. Bacigalupo (1974), p. 36.
37. Bursi and Causo (2010), p. 139.
38. Ibid.
39. The home movie *Into the House* is available at: <https://www.youtube.com/watch?v=qZZUlH8olUI>, last accessed 23 August 2019.
40. *Into the House* (1975, 16mm, b/w, 20').
41. *Cartoline dall'America* (*Postcards from America*), 1975–77, 16mm, colour, 25'.
42. Bursi and Causo (2010), p. 162.
43. Rascaroli (2017), pp. 144–5.

Works Cited

Adorno, Theodor (1991), *Notes to Literature*, volume 1, Rolf Tidermann ed., Shierry Weber Nicholsen trans., New York: Columbia University Press.

Adorno, Theodor W. (1984), 'The Essay as Form', *New German Critique*, 32 (Spring–Summer): 151–71. Originally published in 1958.
Arthur, Paul (2003), 'Essay Questions: from Alain Resnais to Michael Moore', *Film Comment*, 39.1: 58–63.
Bacigalupo, Massimo, ed. (1974), *Il film sperimentale*, Special Edition of *Bianco e Nero*, 5.8 (May–August): 1–187.
Bacigalupo, Massimo (1974), 'Introduzione', in Massimo Bacigalupo ed., *Il film sperimentale*, Special Edition of *Bianco e Nero*, 5.8 (May–August): 2–14.
Bacigalupo, Massimo (1974), in 'Massimo Bacigalupo: Intervista Immaginaria', in Massimo Bacigalupo ed., *Il film sperimentale*, Special Edition of *Bianco e Nero*, 5.8 (May–August): 20–36.
Bellour, Raymond (1989), 'Eye for I: Video Self-Portraits', in Raymond Bellour ed., *Eye for I: Video Self-Portraits*, New York: Independent Curators Incorporated, pp. 7–20.
Bursi, Giulio and Massimo Causo (2010), *Massimo Bacigalupo*, in Catalogo Film Festival di Torino, in collaboration with: Cineteca Nazionale; Università degli Studi di Udine, Dams Gorizia/La Camera Ottica, Film and Video Restoration/Crea – Centro Ricerca Elaborazioni Audiovisivi.
Corrigan, Timothy (2011), *The Essay Film. From Montaigne, after Marker*, Oxford: Oxford University Press.
Lopate, Phillip (1996), 'In Search of the Centaur: The Essay Film', in Warren, Charles ed., *Beyond Document: Essays on Nonfiction Film*, Hanover, N.H.: Wesleyan University Press.
Rascaroli, Laura (2017), *How the Essay Film Thinks*, Oxford: Oxford University Press.
Rascaroli, Laura (2009), *The Personal Camera. Subjective Cinema and the Essay Film*, London: Wallflower Press.

Internet Sources

Epremian, Pia, *Medea* available at: <http://www.fondazionecsc.it/events_detail.jsp?IDAREA=9&ID_EVENT=211&GTEMPLATE=events.jsp>, last accessed 23 August 2019.
Into the House is available at: <https://www.youtube.com/watch?v=qZZUlH8olUI>, last accessed 23 August 2019.

Filmography

60 metri per il 31 marzo (*200 Feet for March 31st*), film, directed by Massimo Bacigalupo, Italy, 1968.
Appunti per un film sull'India (*Notes for a Film about India*), film, directed by Pier Paolo Pasolini, Italy, 1968.
Appunti per un'Orestiade Africana (*Notes Towards an African Orestes*), television documentary, directed by Pier Paolo Pasolini, Italy, 1970.

Autoritratto Auschwitz (*Self-Portrait Auschwitz*), film, directed by Alberto Grifi, Italy, 1965–7.
Cartoline dall'America (*Postcards from America*), film, directed by Massimo Bacigalupo, Italy, 1975–7.
Cinegiornali della Pace (*Cine-newsreels for Peace*) film, directed by Cesare Zavattini, Italy, 1963.
Cinegiornali Liberi (*Free Cine-newsreels*), film, directed by Cesare Zavattini, Italy, 1968–70.
Fellini: A Director's Notebook, documentary for television, directed by Federico Fellini, Italy, 1969.
Fiore d'eringio (*Eryngium*), film, directed by Massimo Bacigalupo, Italy, 1969–70 – a four-film cycle:
1. *L'ultima estate* (*The Last Summer*), 1969;
2. *Né bosco (una conversazione)* (Nor *Wood: a Conversation*), 1970;
3. *Migrazione* (*Migration*), 1970;
4. *Coda*, 1970.
Gente del Po (*People of the Po Valley*), film, directed by Michelangelo Antonioni, Italy, 1947.
Her, film, directed by Massimo Bacigalupo, Italy, 1968.
Into the House, film, directed by Massimo Bacigalupo, Italy, 1975.
L'India vista da Rossellini (*India as Seen by Rossellini*), television series, directed by Roberto Rossellini, Italy, 1958.
L'occhio è per così dire l'evoluzione biologica di una lacrima (*The Eye Is, So-To-Speak, the Biological Evolution of a Tear*), film, directed by Alberto Grifi, Italy, 1965–7.
Tutto, Tutto nello stesso istante (*All, All at Once*), film, made by the Cooperativa del cinema indipendente – Cooperative of Independent Cinema, Italy, 1968–9.
Umano Non Umano (*Human Non-Human*), film, directed by Mario Schifano, Italy 1969.
Versus, film, directed by Massimo Bacigalupo, Italy 1968.
Warming Up, film, directed by Massimo Bacigalupo, Italy, 1973.

CHAPTER 8

Tales of Courage: Trade Stories of Italian Independent Cinema
Edward Bowen

> Instead of keeping the film in a drawer and showing it only at a few festivals, this choice [of self-distribution] was another act of courage. I believe that this film collected a record of acts of courage. A film that wasn't even expected to exist: that did not have the money to be shot and it was shot; that didn't have the possibility of being distributed and it was distributed door to door; that was not expected to be pleasing or to have a large audience and it had a large audience to the point of becoming the independent film of the year. If this is not a miracle . . . [1]
> Beppe Masengo Backstage video for *E fu sera e fu mattina*
> (*And There Was Evening and There Was Morning*, 2014)

Introduction

This chapter investigates trade stories of independent filmmaking in Italy in the new millennium as presented in DVD bonus materials and in documentaries on Italian cinema. In particular, it examines trade stories which feature 'against-all-odds'[2] narratives, including tales of success and/or frustration when facing a variety of challenges, such as: securing adequate funds for a film's production, shooting on a low-budget and in a short number of weeks, and initiating and promoting a film's theatrical run. Expanding upon recent scholarship by Jonathan Gray on media paratexts[3] and John Caldwell on trade stories in Hollywood, this chapter analyses the role that 'against-all-odds' tales play in the independent Italian film scene.

In *Production Culture*, Caldwell analyses different genres of trade stories and their cultural functions. He states that the different genres are not reserved for any particular production community, but he does note a tendency of 'below-the-line' workers (camera operators, editors, grips and the like) in Hollywood to utilise 'war stories' and 'against-all-odds allegories' in an effort to celebrate their strength, ingenuity and persistence.[4] Caldwell identifies four major themes in the 'against-all-odds' trade story genre. First, such narratives often highlight the 'humble, unexceptional origins [of film workers] needed to create the rising action and dramatic arc of the classical myth of heroism'.[5] Second, this genre places an emphasis on the 'tenacity of the worker' and how his or her persistence resulted in a 'well-earned success'.[6] Third, film workers emphasise how, early in their careers, their creative ingenuity on low-budget films helped them to earn respect and inclusion in a competitive industry. Fourth, this genre 'commonly serves as a form of cooperative griping about working conditions and lack of respect'.[7]

This chapter expands Caldwell's groundbreaking work to a new context and illustrates how the 'against-all-odds' story has an important role in the survival and persistence of Italian independent film culture. Such narratives are central to Italian independent film culture as they have the potential to add value to both the film texts and the directors' reputations, encourage the word-of-mouth promotion of films, advocate for improvements in government support for non-mainstream films and serve as pedagogical tools for aspiring indie filmmakers in a time of economic crisis.

Italian independent directors and producers share 'against-all-odds' stories in a wide range of contexts, both private and public. When shared in public, one must consider the role that these stories play in the film's marketing strategy. In order to create exposure, in Italy independent films, with limited budgets, need to pursue a far different promotional agenda when compared to major Hollywood productions.

Since they cannot afford expensive paratexts aimed at creating buzz, such as TV advertisements, merchandise, or billboards, contemporary indie films are heavily reliant on success at film festivals, low-cost social media campaigns and favourable newspaper and online reviews. Indie film directors, producers and cast members often find that they need to follow their films to theatres and engage in Q&A sessions in order to ensure a successful theatrical run. Such screenings are billed as 'special events' and they lend well to 'against-all-odds' stories given that spectators are often curious to know how directors got their start, found the money to make their film and how they overcame certain obstacles. Testimonies in which directors refer to their efforts as 'follies' or 'battles', and their successes as 'miracles' offer dramatic appeal to viewers: that of cheering for David (a director struggling to find funding for a non-mainstream film) against Goliath (a media industry in Italy controlled by Rai and Mediaset). The dissemination of these stories can play a role in conditioning reception and in how spectators talk about the film to others.

This process of circulating production stories with marketing aims is often replicated in a subsequent distribution window. Instead of organising a special event screening with a Q&A, a variant of this experience is made available in DVD bonus materials or in videos posted online. Watching a backstage video perhaps does not have the same effect as hearing a director speak in person, asking the director a question, or shaking his or her hand, but it can have its own persuasive potential through calculated editing. With so many opportunities to discuss their films at festivals and screenings, by the time directors arrive at an interview for a DVD bonus feature, many of them have become quite skilled in sharing dynamic production stories and positively spinning any weaknesses. In addition, editors can enhance trade stories with music and images in order to make them even more inspirational and compelling.

An interview containing an 'against-all-odds' narrative can be a way for a director to assert his or her career capital by mentioning awards, creative achievements, connections and so on. In turn, the 'behind-the-scenes' stories that directors share in public can be a way for spectators to develop cultural capital, given that such knowledge might have value in conversations, debates and publications. Barbara Klinger explains that special collector's editions on home video 'give viewers a still-mystified account of the cinema as a part of the cultural capital they possess as "masters" of the cinematic fact'.[8] In *Show Sold Separately* (2010), Jonathan Gray analyses a collector's edition DVD box set of *The Lord of the Rings* and argues that: 'the DVDs foster an intimate bond between cast, crew, and audience, one that combines with their construction of the film as Work of Art, and with their construction of the DVD audience as discerning and requiring art aficionados, cloaking the entire circuit of production, text, and consumption in an aura of artistry and excellence'.[9]

In no way am I claiming that all or most DVDs of independent Italian films feature 'against-all-odds' trade stories in the bonus materials. Some DVDs of well-known indie films do not feature extra materials at all. The DVD of *La capagira* (*The Head Spins*, 2001) only features a list of the cast and crew as bonus material, and the backstage for *Fame chimica* (*Chemical Hunger*, 2003) avoids discussion of any great hardships. In some DVD extras, directors might only make a brief comment on the obstacles. Alessandro Angelini, in the backstage for his *L'aria salata* (*Salty Air*, 2006), only spares a sentence on the tight funds and shooting schedule for the film. Guido Lombardi briefly discusses his difficult four-year search for funds to shoot *Là-bas - Educazione criminale* (*Là-bas: A Criminal Education*, 2011). Presumably, in some cases, directors, producers, or distributors, have preferred to avoid or limit such discussions on DVDs in order to not appear to be complaining nor to draw attention to budgetary shortcomings.

Micro-budget films in Italy, including those that are self-distributed, have more freedom in how they present their production and distribution stories. They have fewer people to answer to and fewer rules to follow. Indeed, some of the most comprehensive making-of videos for Italian films are those which cover micro-budget productions, citing obstacles and triumphs at all stages of the process: pre-production, production and distribution. In the following section, I present the major themes and functions of 'against-all-odds' narratives in the backstage materials of three microbudget films: *Fuga dal call center* (*Escape from the Call Centre*, 2008), *L'uomo fiammifero* (*The Thin Match Man*, 2009) and *E fu sera e fu mattina* (2014). I will expand upon the four major themes that Caldwell has identified in 'against-all-odds' stories – humble origins, tenacity, creative ingenuity and griping – and add discussion of two other plot points that often appear in this genre: moments of truth and crowning moments. On the first point, I refer to moments when tough and brave decisions need to be made, and on the second, to those moments of success that cap off a long struggle. It is worth mentioning that the *Fuga dal call center* backstage material is less dramatic than that relating to the other two films, perhaps because of the unassuming quality of the director Rizzo and also due to the fact that the film had a superior budget. Whereas *Fuga dal call center* had a budget of 400,000 euro,[10] teetering on the edge of what could be considered a microbudget film in Italy, *L'uomo fiammifero* and *E fu sera e fu mattina* both cost well under 100,000 euro to produce.

Themes of 'Against-all-odds' Narratives in DVD Bonus Materials for Micro-budget Films Setting the Dramatic Tension: Humble Origins and Fundraising Obstacles

The backstage videos for *E fu sera e fu mattina*, *L'uomo fiammifero* and *Fuga dal call center* all establish, early on, the 'humble origins' of the directors, or at least of the projects, and they do so whilst 'griping' about the difficulties of securing funding. Beyond setting the stage for an 'against-all-odds', heroic story,[11] these clips also educate viewers, including aspiring filmmakers, on the difficulties of funding a film. The attention granted to 'humble origins' and fundraising obstacles is also a way of encouraging spectators to reflect on the limitations that come with low-budget filmmaking, and to judge the finished product accordingly.

Emanuele Caruso, director of *E fu sera e fu mattina*, faced a 'series of rejections'[12] from producers for this debut film. He originally sought 500,000 euro for his film, but was only able to raise 70,000 euro, of which roughly half came from a crowdfunding campaign. He characterises his position as an 'outsider' or 'unknown' filmmaker and simultaneously presents crowdfunding as the only solution for someone 'in his shoes':

> No one would have given it [money] to me. No one. No public institution, no production company. No one would have invested 40,000 euro in *E fu sera e fu mattina* by the young unknown John Doe Caruso. This is the reality of the situation. Thus, crowdfunding opened up a new world for me.[13]

The emphasis placed on crowdfunding has an educational aim: to encourage aspiring filmmakers, who lack connections, to consider alternative funding sources.

Early in the backstage material for *L'uomo fiammifero*, screenwriter Giovanni De Feo discusses a humbling appointment that director Marco Chiarini had with a 'famous Roman producer'[14] who did not even grant Marco the courtesy of inviting him into his office. Instead, the unnamed producer met with the young director for five to ten minutes in the lobby, turned down the project and said goodbye. Similarly, the backstage video for *Fuga dal call center* begins with director Federico Rizzo's difficult search for funds. While at a co-production forum at the *Giornate Europee del Cinema* (*European-Days of Cinema*) in Turin, a tired and frustrated Rizzo addresses the camera in a somewhat joking voice: 'Will we succeed in leaving this co-production forum with a nice contract with Germany or England, or as usual, like at all the film markets where we have been, will we not accomplish a damn thing?'[15] Although these moments signal desperate beginnings for independent film projects, neither of the backstage videos dwell on these for long. Both bonus tracks quickly pass to the alternative steps that the directors and writers took to move their projects forward.

Moments of Truth: Deciding to Shoot on a Low-Budget

A difficult decision that many indie filmmakers face is whether to begin shooting a film with less money than expected, or whether to postpone or even abandon the project. Accounts of bold decision-making in trade stories are intended to demonstrate the bravery of directors to pursue a project against the odds. Boldness is a key character trait that workers highlight in their tales of 'self-affirmation' in order to assert their worthiness in the film industry.[16] The *E fu sera e fu mattina* backstage includes many 'moments of truth'. Assistant director Beppe Masengo refers to these tough decisions as 'acts of courage'. Masengo admits to having a practical mindset, and he narrates the moment when he questioned Caruso's plan to begin shooting a film on a shoe-string budget:

Carù, you are about to make a film that costs 500,000 euro and you only have 30,000 secured . . . and the rest, I have no idea. You can't pay anyone. You still lack several actors for the main roles. You lack a good number of locations. You don't know how you will move [the crew and actors around], how you will feed people, where you will have them sleep. Everything still needs to be decided, and in two months you want to begin shooting? Why? Why not postpone for a year?[17]

To this long list of questions, Caruso responded: 'Because I'm crazy'.[18] In this moment, Beppe, who wanted to see the film made on the subject that he originally came up with, gave in and stated: 'I trust you. You want to be a fool? Let's be fools'.[19] The importance of 'acts of courage' in life functions as the central narrative arc of this making-of video, and it builds toward a dramatic conclusion.

While told in less dramatic fashion, Michele Modaferri, the scenographer of *L'uomo fiammifero*, discusses the moment when director Marco Chiarini confessed to the set designers that he had very little money: 'Look, guys! There are limited funds. Almost nothing'.[20] To this claim, Modaferri asked 'Almost nothing? What does that mean?'[21] and Chiarini admitted to only having 1,500 euro on him. In order to lift the spirits of his scenographers, Chiarini explained that in the small town of Teramo it would be possible to increase the production value by soliciting donation of furniture and other materials. Likewise, a 'moment of truth' for the production of *Fuga dal call center* is presented early in the backstage video with the production team seated at a table, discussing the adjustments that they will need to make because of their tight budget. Such moments in backstage videos can play a role in conditioning the reception of the film by encouraging viewers to evaluate the film with new eyes and a different standard, understanding its budgetary limitations. In other words, discussion points or evaluation points of the film's quality can be guided by the paratexts; a viewer of *L'uomo fiammifero* might agree that the set design was superb given the circumstances. Viewers of the *E fu sera e fu mattina* backstage material might develop a strong admiration for the courage of the director and his team and be proud of the finished product. Narrating 'moments of truth' also has a pedagogical function as it sends a message to aspiring indie filmmakers that they will need to be flexible and have courage to accept the challenge of making a low-budget film.

Celebrating Sacrifice, Hard Work and Collaboration

Determination and fortitude are other important themes in 'against-all-odds' trade stories.[22] If a director or another film worker in a backstage video discusses his or her own tenacity, it is clear that the claim is self-congratulatory, but interviewees often speak of various members' sacrifices and their collaboration as the only way in which the film got made. Hence, this discussion found in DVD bonus materials can have the function of thanking workers for their contributions and sacrifices, which include working without remuneration.

The backstage of *E fu sera e fu mattina* celebrates the work of all who contributed. It states how many of the collaborators had day jobs but found a way to dedicate the necessary time to the production. The backstage clips detail the various extreme conditions under which both actors and crew worked, all due to the limited budget. The assistant directors not only juggled all the logistical tasks for shooting the film, but they also cooked for the crew and cleaned bathrooms in the makeshift living quarters in a school cafeteria, where actors and crew members slept on cots. Caruso insists that there would not be a film or backstage material without the 'enormous assistance that was given to me for this film'.[23] He adds that 'someone who sits in a cinema' does not think about all that it took to make the film, when 'in reality behind that film, there is a whole other story, always an intense effort'.[24] The backstage video delivers that 'other story' that is intended to improve one's evaluation of the film and one's respect for those who worked on it.

The DVD bonus materials for *L'uomo fiammifero* similarly celebrate the sacrifices of the production team from top to bottom. Producer Cico Diaz divulges that after the initial funds for the film were exhausted, he had to promise to take on great debts. The crew invested in the film, waiving their immediate pay for a promissory percentage of the film's profits instead. The backstage material also includes a segment in which the director of photography, Pierluigi Piredda, mentions all the members of his squad by name, with a sentence or two about the hard work and versatility of each of them. The most arduous task that the crew faced was shooting all the scenes with the actor who played the protagonist's father in two consecutive days of fourteen–fifteen hour-cycles each.

In the *Fuga dal call center* DVD extras, director of photography Luca Bigazzi maintains that it is possible to make a low-budget feature film; however, 'it must be done with great passion, with great commitment, and with total dedication'.[25] Milan, as the site of the film shoot, offered some challenges according to co-producer Enzo Coluccio, who claims that the Milanese are less team-oriented; yet, later in the video, associate producer Gabriella Pedranti affirms that the Milanese troupe overcame this obstacle and they worked well together.

The pedagogical value of discussing tenacity and sacrifice is twofold. First, it educates viewers at home who are not familiar with the work carried out on a film set. Second, this discussion is informative for aspiring indie filmmakers as it prepares them for the different types of financial, physical, and psychological, risks that they will need to take to complete a project.

Innovative/Creative Strategies Implemented to Overcome Obstacles

Independent Italian filmmakers often praise their own creative solutions to obstacles related to limited funds and resources. Caldwell states that this theme of the 'against-all-odds' trade story functions to establish 'craft mastery' as it emphasises how 'low budgets are the mother of invention'.[26] A bonus video which exhibits such innovation can function as a sort of demo-reel for crew workers and the director and may, in turn, help them secure future work. Indie filmmakers often discuss their artisanal solutions to obstacles in order to set their works apart from high budget commercial films. Jonathan Gray points out that even some DVD bonus materials for blockbusters, such as the *Lord of the Rings: The Two Towers* Platinum Series Special Extended Edition four-DVD, put forth such narratives of artistry to separate the film from typical Hollywood fare.[27] Gray notes that the *The Two Towers* DVD extras emphasise how the production staff opted for '"simple" and more "natural" answers for design dilemmas instead of technical CGI ones'.[28] Although the production story of *The Two Towers* is not an 'against-all-odds' tale, Gray's research on DVD bonus materials is illuminating for this study, which aims to show how such materials are used to construct films as works of art.

The *Fuga dal call center* backstage material includes numerous claims of the film's status as an independent work, and it praises the talents and experience of director of photography Luca Bigazzi above all production personnel, including the director. The focus on Bigazzi adds value to this low-budget production. Although Bigazzi is one of Italy's best-known directors of photography of the new millennium, in this clip he emphasises his humble origins of working on indie films decades prior to his being renowned, and how he learned to shoot without expensive lights. He affirms that it is possible to obtain a realistic and authentic look to a film using few lights. He also proclaims that having a small crew lends to innovation: 'Working with a team so small and with such reduced means is an even bigger incentive because one works by taking away instead of by adding'.[29] In a separate bonus video, Rizzo praises the ability of his actors to improvise, which was necessary with a fifteen-day shooting schedule. He puts a positive spin on this aspect of the production, calling the film an instant movie on precarity in Italy, and he argues that waiting around for years hoping to secure greater funds may have made the argument somewhat stale.

Along with highlighting artistic innovations on the set, both the backstage videos of *L'uomo fiammifero* and *E fu sera e fu mattina* underscore the creative marketing and logistical strategies that were implemented to complete and distribute the films. For instance, director Marco Chiarini first created and sold a book of illustrations titled *L'uomo fiammifero* in order to raise money for the film, and later, when funds were exhausted, he sold original drawings for 1,000 euro each. His team also utilised innovative techniques of self-distribution, which they refer to as 'social distribution'. This method included encouraging friends and spectators to promote the film in different cities and arrange for screenings in exchange for part of the profits of those screenings.

Similarly, Emanuele Caruso discusses how self-distribution saved *E fu sera e fu mattina* from invsibility. He and his production assistant Cinzia, both novices in distribution, implemented a distribution strategy that first focussed on the city of Alba, near the locality where the film was shot, and they then shifted their efforts to Turin and the Piedmont region, enlisting the help of the Turin-Piedmont Film Commission. Successful returns at cinemas in these cities paved the way for screenings throughout Italy. Caruso elaborates on the importance of this decision: 'After I self-distributed, I told myself "thank goodness" because any national distributor who would have taken this film, would have scorched me. It would have put the film in perhaps 100 theatres contemporaneously. Approximately ten people would have gone to each theatre. I would have had 1,000 to 2,000 total spectators. It would have been a flop'.[30] The DVD extras for *L'uomo fiammifero* and *E fu sera e fu mattina* could be viewed as manuals for microbudget filmmakers, full of do's and don'ts, and survival tactics with lessons on not giving up.

Crowning Moments: Sold-out Screenings, Enthusiastic Audiences and Awards

'Against-all-odds' stories in indie cinema often include a crescendo that features one or more crowning moments. In tales of self-affirmation, the storyteller needs to provide proof of success.[31] While indie directors might highlight financial returns as crowning moments, they typically emphasise various forms of career capital, such as awards, long theatrical runs, endorsements by famous people and festival appearances. A common hope is that an award-winning debut will lead to funding for a second, more ambitious project. When discussing the 'cultural economics of prizes', James English explains in *The Economy of Prestige* that the term 'capital' can be 'used to designate anything that registers as an asset, and can be put profitably to work, in one or another domain of human endeavor'.[32]

Even the presence of a film at a certain festival can be a way of asserting its quality and its indie film status.[33] Michael Newman, author of *Indie: An American Film Culture* asserts that film festivals and certain art cinemas have an 'exemplary' status:

> Within the community of an art world, members can identify new items as candidates for the category by matching them to those already recognized as exemplary. For American independent cinema in the indie era, the most salient exemplars tend to be films whose success arrived through alternative institutional channels, especially those of the film festival circuit and the alternative, independent, or art house theater.[34]

Comparing a film to another success story, or rather including it in the same conversation pertaining to an exemplary case from a previous year, is a way of marking its importance.

Indie directors in Italy strive to become one of the surprise success stories of the year by holding long theatrical runs in cinematic cities, such as Rome, Turin and Milan. A benchmark for most indie directors of the new millennium remains the story of Giorgio Diritti's self-distributed film *Il vento fa il suo giro* (*The Wind Blows Round*, 2005) which ran at the Cinema Mexico in Milan for nearly two years and was featured at over 130 festivals.[35] This exemplary case has been discussed extensively in at least three documentaries which largely focus on independent cinema in Italy: *Gli invisibili* (*The Invisibles*, 2009), *Di me cosa ne sai* (*What Do You Know about Me*, 2009) and *In via Savona al 57* (*At 57 Savona Street*, 2013). Even on a lower scale, a theatrical run of over a month at Sancassani's cinema for an indie film is a way of earning the respect of fellow Italian filmmakers and cinephiles.

The last section of the *E fu sera e fu mattina* backstage video celebrates multiple moments of success for the film's theatrical run, beginning with its sold-out premiere in Alba. A soft and uplifting music is added to images of spectators filling up the cinema Cine4 as Caruso announces that there was a 'collective awe'[36] at the film's premiere, even on the part of crew members. 'Against-all-odds' tales often emphasise how results exceeded expectations. Shortly after Caruso admits to having doubted the film would last in Alba for more than a few days, he exclaims that it ended up selling out Cine4 for 31 days over the course of six weeks. Beppe Masengo then asserts that the film became 'a cinematic event in the city of Turin'[37] where it lasted in theatres for six weeks. The film's most celebrated achievement in the backstage video was winning the FICE (Federazione Italiana Cinema d'Essai – Italian Federation of Essai Cinemas) 'Independent Film of the Year' award in 2014, a prize voted by the audience. Caruso's impassioned narration of the role that spectators played in the film's success is a form of positive feedback for viewers of the DVD to continue word-of-mouth promotion of the film and keep its success going. To conclude this dramatic story, Masengo, who had previously referred to himself as the 'practical one', reflects on acts of courage in life, stating: 'it truly became for me concrete proof that . . . you can allow yourself to do something crazy in life, to believe in it, to create something, to go off the tracks that you have already constructed for yourself and push yourself to do something that is extra'.[38] The narrative arc of the 'against-all-odds' story ends with an exciting and positive conclusion, with encouragement to aspiring artists to be bold, take risks and fulfill their dreams.

The backstage video of *L'uomo fiammifero* also praises the film's success in theatres, noting a positive opening run in Teramo, where the film was shot, and noting the subsequent three months of programming at Rome's Nuovo Cinema Aquila. Dimitri Bosi adds that this theatrical run caught the attention of the 'legendary Cinema Mexico' of Milan, where the film's success took off:

> In short, the film at this point left and literally took off until it arrived at the candidacy for the David di Donatello awards and at an encounter with the legendary Giorgio, not Giorgio Napolitano, not the President of the Republic, but the legendary Giorgio Diritti, who we met at the ceremony for the Davids, with whom we exchanged compliments and we told him that he was our beacon, our point of reference, with his fantastic and courageous distribution of *Il vento fa il suo giro*.[39]

This discussion of reaching certain national touchstones in indie cinema – being a candidate for a major award, being programmed at Italy's best known indie movie theatre, and receiving compliments from an affirmed indie director – caps off an 'against-all-odds' tale which is used to establish one's footing in the indie film scene.

Proving that audiences loved a film is another way of crowning a film's success. The bonus materials for *L'uomo fiammifero* demonstrate how director Marco Chiarini connected with spectators at the Isola del Cinema arena (Cinema Island arena) in Rome by sharing sound effects from the film using handmade instruments. The video shows a packed arena, with many spectators smiling, laughing and listening closely to Chiarini. To reward them, Chiarini told spectators that they would be taped and included in the DVD's bonus features. The backstage video presents Marco's ideas for interacting with the audience as a clever strategy and one important for the film's success. The video also shows how Marco filmed the audience every time he stepped on stages at festivals to receive awards: images that he would then post on YouTube as a thank you message. While these strategies could be viewed as gimmicks, in the backstage video they are championed as sincere links between the director and audiences.

The *Fuga dal call center* backstage video presents a briefer and more moderate celebration of a moment of success. It ends with images of crew members smiling on set and applauding at wrapping up the film shoot. Even if less dramatic than the other backstage videos, the goal here is to exude positivity to viewers at home and to encourage them to celebrate the hard work of the crew.

The fact that the *Fuga dal call center* backstage material does not feature all of the themes of the 'against-all-odds' tale in elaborate fashion does not exclude it from being an 'against-all-odds' tale. Most DVD extras do not feature such detailed and extensive 'against-all-odds' stories as *L'uomo fiammifero* and *E fu sera e fu mattina*, but it is common to find anecdotes and brief 'against-all-odds' testimonies in DVD bonus materials of indie films. For example, the 2014 DVD release for Ivano De Matteo's *La bella gente* (*Beautiful People*, 2009) features a brief interview with the director, who discusses his six-year struggle to distribute the film in Italian theatres and later on home video. Most likely for legal reasons, he avoids mentioning the names of those who blocked its national distribution; however, he explains that he suffered greatly during this struggle, and he even endured a lengthy lawsuit for organising a public screening. De Matteo's account shows hints of a war story. Affirming his tenacity, he states: 'I never threw myself to the ground. I never gave up'. He declares that his battle eventually paid off: 'The release of this DVD crowns this great battle that I fought'.[40] The function of this trade story is not simply a venting of frustration, or an attempt at self-affirmation, but it is also a bid to increase the viewer's appreciation of actually getting to watch the prohibited film. It is worth mentioning that scholar Umberto Berlenghini used an image from *La bella gente*'s poster on the cover of his book *Gli invisibili, 2000–2010: Dieci anni di cinema nascosto* (*The Invisibles, 2000–2010: Ten Years of Hidden Cinema*, 2012).[41] Consumers of indie film culture arguably value their own skills in discovering hidden gems and underdog productions in a marketplace in which high-budget films have an upperhand in publicity and distribution. Such activity could improve a cinephile's self-image as a talent scout or connoisseur. In the following section, I discuss how documentary filmmakers who focus on the state of indie cinema value this skill of discovering and sharing the trade stories of 'invisible' films.

'Against-all-odds' Trade Stories in Documentaries

The dramatic value of independent Italian trade stories explains why some documentary films, not simply backstage videos, focus on the difficult situations that filmmakers and exhibitors in Italy face today. This section illustrates how two documentaries, *Gli invisibili* (*The Invisibles*, 2007) and *In via Savona al 57* (*At 57 Savona Street*, 2013), utilise 'against-all-odds' accounts not only to report on crises in Italian cinema, but also to make their own documentaries more captivating, to bring greater visibility to Italian indie cinema and to add value to certain works. These documentaries also have pedagogical value as they present possible solutions to crises in film production, exhibition, and distribution.

The project *Gli invisibili: Esordi nel cinema italiano, 2000–2006* (*The Invisibles: Debuts in Italian Cinema, 2000–2006*, 2007),[42] curated by scholar and filmmaker Vito Zagarrio, consists of an edited volume and a documentary. The latter, directed by Christian Carmosino, Enrico Carocci, Pierpaolo DeSanctis and Francesco Del Grosso, presents the obstacles that young Italian filmmakers faced at the beginning of the twenty-first century with their debut films. Though the documentary does not focus entirely on independent cinema, many of the directors who are interviewed, worked on smaller budget films funded by MiBac and/or by independent production companies. The documentary *Gli invisibili* is divided into six sections that address: modes of production, distribution, narrating contemporary Italy, genres, authors and the most recent generation of directors. Beyond presenting accounts in which young filmmakers gripe about the obstacles they face, the documentary also features tales of tenacity, courageous filmmaking and a number of success stories.

In the first section, 'Modes of Production', several directors and actors respond to the question of what young filmmakers share in common, and the most prominent theme that emerges is the 'struggle' to make and distribute films. The following segment is peppered with words noting an 'against-all-odds' endeavour, such as 'struggle', 'effort', 'tenacity', 'titanic undertaking' and 'great difficulty':

Valentina Carnelutti:	There is a common trait and it has to do with the struggle we are forced to face in order to exist as filmmakers.
Francesco Patierno:	The effort, as unknowns, to succeed in convincing someone, a producer, to place some money, even if only a little bit, that will allow you to make a film.
Valentina Carnelutti:	It is the struggle that we undertake to counter pervasive television.
Michele Carrillo:	It is tenacity because this way of making films, above all for young people, is becoming a titanic undertaking.
Valentina Carnelutti:	It is the struggle that we undertake in order to be screened in a true movie theatre, rather than the smallest theatre of the most remote multiplex.
Catherine McGilvray:	We all experience a great difficulty in showing our films and to see our ideas produced.[43]

This section thus features a considerable dose of griping, which Caldwell explains having a cultural function as a plea for changes. Daniele Vicari and Andrea Porporati explain that the domination of the market by Rai and Medusa leads to conformism in film production, and does not leave room for an independent voice. Another complaint is that, because of funding obstacles, the gestation period for producing films is too long and can have adverse effects on the story. Alessandro Piva asserts that it is difficult to make a film about contemporary Italian society, when one starts writing the film in 2006 and may not complete it until 2010. Both the documentary and its accompanying volume on the state of film production and distribution could be used as a rallying call to the government to improve arts funding, or to create greater visibility for the films that it produces.[44]

Gli invisibili does not only seek to present the crisis, but to make suggestions for ways to overcome it. It underscores exemplary cases of films that either did well at the box office, such as Daniele Vicari's *Velocità massima* (*Maximum Velocity*, 2002), or on home video, such as Alex Infascelli's *H2Odio* (*H2Odium*, 2006), which was cleverly distributed in DVD format to newsstands while bypassing theatrical exhibition. Infascelli's innovative strategy is presented as a possible alternative path to beating the odds. Indeed, the documentary presents accounts which, as Caldwell highlights in his book, 'help practitioner communities weather change in the face of technological flux and economic instability'.[45]

Documentaries about indie film culture can also help increase the visibility of directors. In this sense, documentaries on cinema are not simply stand-alone films, but they also constitute paratexts for the films they mention. Jonathan Gray affirms that 'in a cluttered media environment, all texts need paratexts, if only to announce the text's presence'.[46] Section five of *Gli invisibili*, titled 'Authors', features montage sequences of clips from multiple films in a row, announcing their 'presence'. After watching this documentary, non-insiders, and perhaps even some insiders, of the indie film scene, could potentially have a new list of films and directors that they would like to check out. Given the early years of the twenty-first century in which it was made, the documentary also showcased certain films and directors over others. It begins with interviews in which directors name their other favourite young filmmakers from Italy: names such as Matteo Garrone, Paolo Sorrentino, Francesco Munzi and Saverio Costanzo, are repeated multiple times, and Munzi's indie film *Saimir* is highly valued. By making choices on which films and artists to present, documentaries on the film industry exhibit some parallels to literary anthologies in how they can contribute to canon promotion and/or reinforcement. Just as literary canons are often revisited by editors, curators and scholars who make space for overlooked or previously marginalised talents and works, a director of a documentary on independent cinema also assumes the role of a taste moderator. In the canon of recent independent cinema, the territory is ripe for discovery, and insiders like Vito Zagarrio (filmmaker, scholar and curator of *Gli invisibili*) can emphasise to viewers that directors such as Michelangelo Frammartino – who appears multiple times in *Gli invisibili* – also deserve attention. Even if the works of some of these directors, such as Frammartino's *Il dono* (*The Gift*, 2003), are hard to find because they were not distributed in DVD, documentaries such as *Gli invisibili* serve an important purpose in announcing the talent of certain directors and encouraging viewers to be on the lookout for other works by them.

Another documentary that showcases an 'against-all-odds' tale of independent Italian cinema, whilst also highlighting the presence of many gems of indie cinema, is Gregory Fusaro and Massimiliano Vergani's *In via Savona al 57*. This documentary presents the story of the Cinema Mexico, located in Milan's periphery, which is well-known for screening indie films that do not receive adequate exhibition. The documentary includes all the major themes of the 'against-all-odds' genre when discussing manager Antonio Sancassani's ability to turn the Cinema Mexico from a struggling cinema into a cherished venue for Italian indie films. The documentary opens with the narration of a crowning moment for Sancassani when he received the City of Milan's *Ambrogino d'oro* award for civic merit. It then describes the humble origins of both Sancassani and the cinema that he took over. Sancassani separates his background from that of many exhibitors: 'I don't have like my colleagues a grandfather or father or anyone who had movie theatres . . . My father was a farmer and he only had cows'.[47] He assumed management of the Cinema Mexico in the late 1970s in the middle of a serious exhibition crisis, sparked in part by the advent of private TV channels in 1976. Given that over half of Italy's cinemas closed between 1977 and 1989,[48] it is clear that Sancassani took on a serious challenge. All of his friends tried to talk him out of this endeavour, yet his decision to follow his passion and instinct was his moment of truth.

Sancassani has succeeded as an exhibitor because of his ability to innovate and find niche audiences. The documentary highlights three of his innovations, in particular. First, in a tough market in the late 1970s, Sancassani decided to improve his theatre's sound system and specialise in musicals and films on music. No other theater in Milan had this specialisation, and his decision to regularly programme *The Rocky Horror Picture Show* and to allow drama students to act out scenes on stage saved the cinema from closure and made it profitable. A more recent innovative practice was to specialise in independent films, primarily the works of young Italian filmmakers. Instead of being linked to a group of *cinema d'essai* and accepting their recommendations, Sancassani searches for films on his own. He states that multiplex cinemas 'have taken away oxygen' from the market, and his way of keeping this single-screen cinema open is to show films not featured elsewhere and bill the screenings as 'special events'.[49] Finally, he is known for his willingness to keep films programmed for long periods of time, allowing word-of-mouth to build up their visibility. This led him to perhaps his greatest achievement as an exhibitor, setting the national record of programming Giorgio Diritti's *Il vento fa il suo giro* for nearly two years.

The case of *In via Savona al 57* equally emphasises the importance of sacrifice, hard work and collaboration for the survival of indie cinema in Italy. Sancassani himself admits that his job is not easy and that his cinema would not have any success if he were passive. Despite being ill, he continues to work full-time. He avows that:

> It is hard to keep it open. It is difficult to manage. I also want to remain absolutely independent. There are some problems finding the right films to screen. There are some worries about keeping it open. This way, however, I do not think about my disease . . . and this helps me a lot . . . There's always a good attendance. I'm happy. In these years, approximately 350,000 people have passed through here, four times San Siro [stadium] full.[50]

In an interview, Giorgio Diritti claims that Sancassani's passion, conviction and skill in building relationships offer the type of 'authenticity'[51] that helps indie cinema thrive.

Similar to *Gli invisibili*, *In via Savona al 57* also contributes to a sort of canonisation of certain indie films from the new millennium. The bulk of praise is directed toward Giorgio Diritti, including his *Il vento fa il suo giro* for its record theatrical run and his subsequent award-wining film, *L'uomo che verrà* (*The Man Who Will Come*, 2009). The successes of Diritti and Sancassani are presented as intertwined: two underdogs who have proven that an alternative path, outside of multiplex cinemas and the typical *cinema d'essai* circuit, is possible. While *Gli invisibili* presents montage sequences of different films, listing their titles, *In via Savona al 57* features a slide show of posters for films screened at the Mexico. In one scene, film critic Morando Morandini declares that the Cinema Mexico is 'unique' and that it has greatly helped certain films, such as Marina Spada's *Il mio domani* (*My Tomorrow*, 2011), Marco Filiberti's *Il compleanno* (*David's Birthday*, 2009), Giorgia Cecere's *Il primo incarico* (*The First Assignment*, 2010) and Andrea Segre's *Mare chiuso* (*Closed Sea*, 2012). Directly after this list, the film cuts to a slide show of posters with the narrator's voice discussing the success of Antonio Bocola and Paolo Vari's *Fame chimica* (2003), Mirco Locatelli's *Il primo giorno d'inverno* (*The First Day of Winter*, 2008) and Federico Rizzo's *Fuga dal call center*. The narrator adds value to these films by calling them 'important works that, thanks to the Mexico, were able to find a theatre that screened them'.[52]

Concluding Thoughts

In sum, much of independent Italian cinema can be recounted as an 'against-all-odds' story. As evidenced by these media paratexts, it is common for 'above-the-line' artists of Italian indie films to utilise such narratives in an effort to add value to the films and to their own reputations. Just as Caldwell points out how 'below-the-line' workers in Hollywood use such narratives both to assert their belonging on sets and to help others improve their standing, a similar dynamic plays out in the Italian independent film scene. Indeed, the backstage videos analysed in this chapter are not solely aimed at praising a director, but they also serve as a way of thanking underpaid technicians and providing them with some publicity that may prove very helpful to find properly paid work in the near future.

'Against-all-odds' tales also play a crucial role in indie film culture as they often aim to condition the reception of films, drum up word-of-mouth support for films and satisfy cinephiles' desires to find out behind-the-scenes information on films. The DVD extras of *L'uomo fiammifero* and *E fu sera e fu mattina* repeatedly offer positive feedback to their audiences for crowning these films with achievements such as sold-out theatres and awards. Spectators are also told that audiences helped the films succeed through new methods such as social distribution channels. Sharing an 'against-all-odds' tale can go a long way in encouraging viewers to be more supportive, or at least more forgiving when it comes to offering criticism. With extremely limited funds for publicity, a dramatic tale of courage becomes an effective strategy in marketing a film. A film critic might insert the anecdote in a newspaper or online article, or a spectator might repeat the tale when talking about, and perhaps praising, the film to others.

The act of griping has a cultural function in the context of indie cinema trade stories. Associations of filmmakers in Italy regularly advocate for improvements in government funding for cinema. It is very telling that one of the outcomes of the activity of the group RING, an association of young indie filmmakers in Italy that met regularly from 2004 to 2006, was the production of the 'against-all-odds' documentary *Di me cosa ne sai* by Valerio Jalongo on the state of Italian cinema. Even though this film does not exclusively focus on indie film production, it dedicates considerable attention to the difficulties of maintaining an independent voice in Italian cinema. It includes a healthy mix of griping about obstacles and celebrating triumphs, just as *Gli invisibili*. Both documentaries appear to pressure the Italian government to better support young filmmakers and non-mainstream cinema, or at least not create conditions that stifle indie cinema.

By celebrating unlikely success stories and tales of innovation in indie cinema, documentaries can play a key role in canon formation. The exemplary case of Giorgio Diritti's *Il vento fa il suo giro* and its record theatrical run at the Cinema Mexico is told and retold in 'against-all-odds' trade stories. Documentaries (such as *Gli invisibili*) and other paratexts which announce the presence of 'invisible' works and relate anecdotes about their struggle perform the function of satiating cinephiles who value finding hidden gems. By learning more about these stories, the viewer can become an insider and develop cultural capital, which could be useful to them in certain social and professional circles, helping them earn the respect of others in conversations, blogs, job interviews and so forth. Moreover, one cannot discount the role that documentaries such as this one could play in selling more DVDs.

Indeed, 'against-all-odds' trade stories are part of the lifeblood of indie cinema in Italy, as they pervade so many aspects of film culture and play a role in its perpetuation. The struggle of overcoming numerous obstacles, related to limited funds, is a defining and ennobling characteristic of indie cinema and a key marker of difference when compared to commercial cinema. Recounting this dramatic struggle is not simply aimed at having viewers reevaluate films or a canon of indie films. Most of the objectives of 'against-all-odds' tales are forward-looking and growth-oriented, such as encouraging word-of-mouth promotion of a film, improving government support for non-mainstream cinema production, showcasing talents that will be useful for future work and educating aspiring filmmakers. 'Against-all-odds' tales also have the potential to create greater bonds between indie filmmakers and audience members; they have the dual aim of increasing a spectator's admiration for a film crew's struggle and celebrating the viewer's support for an independent voice in the world of cinema.

Notes

1. Beppe Masengo, 'Backstage "Un'altra storia" – Parte 3: Post-produzione e distribuzione', *E fu sera e fu mattina*, DVD, directed by Emanuele Caruso (Campi Bisenzio: CG Entertainment, 2014). Unless otherwise indicated, all translations from the original Italian are mine.

2. Caldwell (2008), pp. 37–47. Given that I am drawing this term from Caldwell's research, I will place it in quotes for the rest of this chapter.
3. Gray (2010).
4. Caldwell (2008), pp. 39–47. Some of the other trade story genres that Caldwell discusses include 'genesis myths' and 'paths-not-taken parables' which he claims are typically told by 'above-the-line' creative professionals (directors, directors of photography, producers, screenwriters) in order to highlight their pedigree, boast their contacts and mark their turf; ibid. pp. 47–51. Meanwhile, agents, personal assistants and clerical staff tend to tell 'making-it sagas' and 'cautionary tales' which underscore networking, mediating skills and efforts to save one's career; ibid. pp. 51–9.
5. Ibid., p. 40.
6. Ibid., p. 40.
7. Ibid., p. 43.
8. Klinger (2006), p. 75.
9. Gray (2010), p. 103.
10. *Fuga dal call center* (*Escape from the Call Centre*), at Internet Movie Database, <http://www.imdb.com/title/tt1331049/>, last accessed 24 February 2017.
11. Caldwell (2008), p. 40.
12. Beppe Masengo, 'Backstage "Un'altra storia" – Parte 1: Idea e sceneggiatura', *E fu sera e fu mattina* (*And There Was Evening and There Was Morning*), DVD, directed by Emanuele Caruso (Campi Bisenzio: CG Entertainment, 2014).
13. Emanuele Caruso, 'Backstage "Un'altra storia" – Parte 1: Idea e sceneggiatura', *E fu sera e fu mattina*, DVD, directed by Emanuele Caruso (Campi Bisenzio: CG Entertainment, 2014).
14. Giovanni De Feo, 'Dietro le quinte – La produzione (2005): dall'idea al set', disc 2, *L'uomo fiammifero* (*The Thin Match Man*), DVD, directed by Marco Chiarini (Campi Bisenzio: CG Entertainment, 2009).
15. Federico Rizzo, 'Backstage', *Fuga dal Call Center*, DVD, directed by Federico Rizzo (Campi Bisenzio: CG Entertainment, 2008).
16. Caldwell (2008), p. 68.
17. Beppe Masengo, 'Backstage "Un'altra storia" – Parte 2: Pre-produzione e riprese', *E fu sera e fu mattina*, DVD, directed by Emanuele Caruso (Campi Bisenzio: CG Entertainment, 2014).
18. Ibid.
19. Ibid.
20. Michele Modaferri, 'Dietro le quinte – La produzione (2005): dall'idea al set', disc 2, *L'uomo fiammifero*, DVD, directed by Marco Chiarini (Campi Bisenzio: CG Entertainment, 2009).
21. Ibid.
22. Caldwell (2008), p. 40.
23. Emanuele Caruso, 'Backstage "Un'altra storia" – Parte 2: Pre-produzione e riprese', *E fu sera e fu mattina*, DVD, directed by Emanuele Caruso (Campi Bisenzio: CG Entertainment, 2014).

24. Ibid.
25. Luca Bigazzi, 'Backstage', *Fuga dal Call Center*, DVD, directed by Federico Rizzo (Campi Bisenzio: CG Entertainment, 2008).
26. Ibid., p. 38, 42.
27. Gray (2010), p. 99.
28. Ibid., 99.
29. Luca Bigazzi, 'Backstage', *Fuga dal Call Center*, DVD, directed by Federico Rizzo (Campi Bisenzio: CG Entertainment, 2008).
30. Emanuele Caruso, 'Backstage "Un'altra storia" – Parte 3: Post-produzione e distribuzione', *E fu sera e fu mattina*, DVD, directed by Emanuele Caruso (Campi Bisenzio: CG Entertainment, 2014).
31. Caldwell (2008), p. 68.
32. English (2005), p. 9.
33. Newman (2011), p. 54.
34. Ibid., p. 51.
35. 'Il vento fa il suo giro: partecipazioni, premi, nomination', cinemaitaliano.info, <http://www.cinemaitaliano.info/film/00320/festival/il-vento-fa-il-suo-giro.html>, last accessed 12 February 2017.
36. Emanuele Caruso, 'Backstage "Un'altra storia" – Parte 3: Post-produzione e distribuzione', *E fu sera e fu mattina*, DVD, directed by Emanuele Caruso (Campi Bisenzio: CG Entertainment, 2014).
37. Beppe Masengo, 'Backstage "Un'altra storia" – Parte 3: Post-produzione e distribuzione', *E fu sera e fu mattina*, DVD, directed by Emanuele Caruso (Campi Bisenzio: CG Entertainment, 2014).
38. Ibid.
39. Dimitri Bosi, 'Dietro le quinte – La distribuzione (2010)', disc 2, *L'uomo fiammifero*, DVD, directed by Marco Chiarini (Campi Bisenzio: CG Entertainment, 2009).
40. Ivano De Matteo, 'Intervista al regista Ivano De Matteo', *La bella gente* (*The Beautiful People*), DVD, directed by Ivano De Matteo (Campi Bisenzio: CG Entertainment, 2016).
41. Berlenghini (2012).
42. *Gli invisibili: esordi italiani del nuovo millennio* (*The Invisibles: Italian Debuts of the New Millennium*), Documentary, directed by Christian Carmosino, Enrico Carocci, Francesco Del Grosso, and Pierpaolo De Sanctis (Rome: Dipartimento Comunicazione e Spettacolo Università degli Studi di Roma Tre, 2007).
43. Ibid.
44. Another documentary on the state of Italian cinema, *Di me cosa ne sai* (*What Do You Know about Me*), (2009) by Valerio Jalongo also features 'against-all-odds' stories of Italian cinema and identifies many of the factors leading to a decline in Italian film production and the closures of Italian cinemas in the 1970s and 1980s. The documentary denounces certain laws and cultural policies of the Italian government including the boom of multiplex cinemas, the

pervasion of advertising and others which have registered a negative impact on the freedom of expression in Italian cinema.
45. Caldwell (2008), p. 37.
46. Gray (2010), p. 39.
47. Antonio Sancassani, *In via Savona al 57* (*At 57 Savona Street*), Documentary, directed by Gregory Fusaro and Massimiliano Vergani (Milan: Officina Indie Milano, 2013).
48. Corsi (2001), p. 122.
49. Antonio Sancassani, *In via Savona al 57*, Documentary, directed by Gregory Fusaro and Massimiliano Vergani (Milan: Officina Indie Milano, 2013).
50. Ibid.
51. Giorgio Diritti, *In via Savona al 57*, Documentary, directed by Gregory Fusaro and Massimiliano Vergani (Milan: Officina Indie Milano, 2013).
52. William Angiuli, narrator, *In via Savona al 57*, Documentary, directed by Gregory Fusaro and Massimiliano Vergani (Milan: Officina Indie Milano, 2013).

Works Cited

Berlenghini, Umberto (2012), *Gli invisibili, 2000–2010: Dieci anni di cinema nascosto*, Piombino: Edizioni il Foglio.
Caldwell, John Thorton (2008), *Production Culture: Industrial Reflexivity and Critical Practice in Film and Television*, Durham, NC: Duke University Press.
Corsi, Barbara (2001), *Con qualche dollaro in meno: Storia economica del cinema italiano*, Rome: Editori Riuniti.
English, James F. (2005), *The Economy of Prestige: Prizes, Awards, and the Circulation of Cultural Value*, Cambridge, MA: Harvard University Press.
Gray, Jonathan (2010), *Show Sold Separately: Promos, Spoilers, and Other Media Paratexts*, New York: New York University Press.
Klinger, Barbara (2006), *Beyond the Multiplex: Cinema, New Technologies, and the Home*, Berkeley, CA; University of California Press.
Newman, Michael Z. (2011), *Indie: An American Film Culture*, New York: Columbia University Press.
Parker, Mark, and Deborah Parker (2011), *The DVD and the Study of Film: The Attainable Text*, New York: Palgrave Macmillan.
Zagarrio, Vito, ed. (2009), *Gli invisibili: esordi italiani del nuovo millennio*, Turin: Kaplan.

Filmography

Di me cosa ne sai (*What Do You Know about Me*), film, directed by Valerio Jalongo, Rome: Cinecittà Luce, 2009.
E fu sera e fu mattina (*And There Was Evening and There Was Morning*), film, directed by Emanuele Caruso, Campi Bisenzio: CG Entertainment, 2014.

Fame chimica (*Chemical Hunger*), film, directed by Antonio Bocola and Paolo Vari, Italy, 2003.
Fuga dal Call Center (*Escape from the Call Center*), film, directed by Federico Rizzo, Campi Bisenzio: CG Entertainment, 2008.
Gli invisibili: esordi italiani del nuovo millennio (*The Invisibles: Italian Debuts of the New Millennium*), film, directed by Christian Carmosino, Enrico Carocci, Francesco Del Grosso, and Pierpaolo De Sanctis, Rome: Dipartimento Comunicazione e Spettacolo Università degli Studi di Roma Tre, 2007.
H2Odio (*H2Odium*), film, directed by Alex Infascelli, Italy, 2006.
Il compleanno (*David's Birthday*), film, directed by Marco Filiberti, Italy, 2009.
Il dono (*The Gift*), film, directed by Michelangelo Frammartino, Italy, 2003.
Il mio domani (*My Tomorrow*), film, directed by Marina Spada, Italy, 2011.
In via Savona al 57 (*At 57 Savona Street*), film, directed by Gregory Fusaro and Massimiliano Vergani, Milan: Officina Indie Milano, 2013.
Il primo giorno d'inverno (*The First Day of Winter*), film, directed by Mirko Locatelli, Italy, 2008.
Il primo incarico (*The First Assignment*), film, directed by Giorgia Cecere, Italy, 2010.
Il vento fa il suo giro (*The Wind Blows Round*), film, directed by Giorgio Diritti, Italy, 2005.
Là-bas: Educazione criminale (*Là-bas: A Criminal Education*), film, directed by Guido Lombardi, Italy, 2011.
La bella gente (*The Beautiful People*), film, directed by Ivano De Matteo, Campi Bisenzio: CG Entertainment, 2016.
La capagira (*The Head Spins*), film, directed by Alessandro Piva, Italy, 2000.
L'aria salata (*Salty Air*), film, directed by Alessandro Angelini, Italy, 2006.
L'uomo che verrà (*The Man Who Will Come*), film, directed by Giorgio Diritti, Italy, 2009.
L'uomo fiammifero (*The Thin Match Man*), film, directed by Marco Chiarini, Campi Bisenzio: CG Entertainment, 2009.
Mare chiuso (*Closed Sea*), film, directed by Andrea Segre, Italy, 2012.
Velocità massima (*Maximum Velocity*), film, directed by Daniele Vicari, Italy, 2002.

CHAPTER 9

Niccolò Bruna's Ethical Process as Social Engagement: Upholding Human Stories against a Backdrop of Globalisation

David H. Fleming and Filippo Gilardi

The different perceptions of the same event are interesting. I like the idea that individuals manufacture of themselves or the image of themselves that they build to be shown to others.

Niccolò Bruna[1]

Introduction

Born in Turin, Italy, Niccolò Bruna is an independent filmmaker and producer who has been experimenting with the expressive tools of documentary-film since attending the EICTV (Escuela Internacional de Cine y Television) filmmaking School in Cuba in 1999. He moved to Barcelona in 2014 adding his name to the Italian phenomenon known as the 'fuga dei cervelli' (a 'brain drain').[2] Somewhat appropriately, his growing body of films highlights the effects of moving bodies and shifting identities undergoing, in one form or another, migration in-between different nation states. In this chapter we take the opportunity to view Bruna's documentary corpus holistically and investigate what it means to be an ethical documentary filmmaker in the epoch that the Mexican-Argentine philosopher Enrique Dussel calls the age of 'globalisation and exclusion'.[3]

The independent forms that Bruna's work assumes are informed by his formative experiences as well as by the topical subject-matter of his *impegno* (social engagement), which is characterised by a personal humanist approach, as discussed hereafter. Certainly, Bruna's work is that of a global itinerant, foregrounding human interest stories against the prejudicial and exploitative backdrop of globalisation. Although this demands that he research and film in a diverse range of global locations (which now includes Italy, Brazil, India, China, Cuba and Ethiopia), we can still identify a loose yet consistent series of themes, tropes and motifs that stitch together his expanding body of heterogeneous (and heteroglossic) work. These can be broadly adumbrated here as being linked to: (1) the director's preference for a dispersed or distributed mode of storytelling that leads to a multi-perspectival and polycentric view of a given situation, milieu, or event; (2) an ethically 'withdrawn' or absented *auteur* persona, that foregoes any authoritative 'voice-over' conventions, while allowing framing, editing and the characters themselves to build and convey the multi-aspectual stories; and (3) a tropological favouring of female perspectives and characters with regard to the various events and stories.

Modus operandi

Over the past fifteen years, Bruna has striven to produce quality films with a distinctive human interest that grant his viewers a variety of perspectives onto important global events and issues. During this time, he also honed his skills and praxis by studying with master filmmakers such as Abbas Kiarostami in 2003, and Werner Herzog in 2008. To date, Bruna's films have won several international accolades and awards, including a nomination for the David di Donatello award for *Dust: The Great Asbestos Trial* (2011). His more recent film *Magicarena* (2014), co-directed with Andrea Prandstraller, has received theatrical releases in Canada, mainland China and Taiwan. The film inspired a follow-up project, the co-directed *Hui He. The Soprano from the Silk Road* (2017), a film on the globally renowned Chinese opera singer Hui He, considered the best Aida and Butterfly in the world.

Bruna's first attempt at documentary filmmaking occurred when he was a student (he variously studied in Turin, Cuba and Rome). Arguably, the best way to approach Bruna as a filmmaker is in terms of what we might call an 'ethnographic documentarian': a label that helps account for his extended forms of covert participation in his subjects' daily lives, 'watching what happens, listening to what is said, and/or asking questions through formal or informal interviews . . . gathering whatever data are available to throw light on the issues that are the emerging focus of the inquiry'.[4] When asked, however, Bruna describes his own filmmaking practice in different terms. In a filmmaking workshop in China, for instance, he compared his filmmaking process to that of preparing a meal, and in such a context highlighted how Chinese and Italian gastronomic cultures were comparably renowned. In an interview with the authors of this chapter, he described his work in terms of an open and evolving process, informed by prior critical thought. Throughout his career the central idea or constant ideal informing his filmmaking has been his conviction that in order to remain true to life, filmmaking must be an ongoing process, because 'life itself is a process':

> As John Lennon said '*Life is what* happens while you are busy making other plans'. I am interested in showing these events in life that people are not probably

noticing at the moment they occur, but are interesting for me. Despite my goal being the final film, my interest is in the process of documenting what happens. If we were focussing more on the processes than on the results people would be happier. It is so boring when you have something achieved, fixed, finalised because . . . the process is the story to be told. I took that from Pirandello, an Italian writer. He was focussing on how things are changing and transforming and the impossibility of being there when things are getting fixed because . . . they die and [thus] creativity dies as well.[5]

Somewhat complicating the idea that his filmmaking should emerge from the organic process of life, as it unfolds before his camera, we must also recall that Bruna was educated at EICTV in Cuba, where he describes having learned to become a 'Marxist filmmaker'. He recalls benefitting from the pre-production sessions that were practiced there, where debate and dialectics with other crew members and filmmakers helped shape a theoretically sound pitch and plan. 'When I learned filmmaking in Cuba, the debates and arguments that happened before shooting were very productive. It was wonderful. We had to justify and think about everything'.[6] Here, the goal became to critically work through the entire filmmaking project in advance, before recording a single frame. Paradoxically, the ideal project thus informs and impacts the subsequent act of filmmaking, which is anterior to an encounter with the unfolding process of life that becomes the subject of the film. In this sense, the organic 'process' originates in the mind of the director, who then uses his camera – which Bruna describes as a 'democratic tool' for investigating and engaging with the world – and editing, to craft and sculpt this filmic idea out of the unfolding process of life.

If we noted above that Bruna typically absents himself as a voice of authority in his films – which would be ethically problematic for a white European director filming in post-colonial Africa, China and India – he does still recognise his directorial role as a privileged one with regard to documentary storytelling. In trying to explain this, Bruna says that, though there is a 'shared reality' everyone must confront, it is a reality on which we each have our own unique perspective. The role of a documentary filmmaker is to offer his or her perception of 'the truth', while trying to remain fair and true to their and others' visions. In this sense we can recognise parallels emerging between Bruna's multi-perspectival filmmaking techniques, his notions of documentary truth and the forms of *perspectivism* generated by Werner Herzog's work – a director with whom he studied in 2008. Indeed, as Katrina Mitcheson reminds us, rather than 'merely observing or recording' his characters, Herzog's films interweave their various different perspectives, along with the director's own characteristic worldview.[7] As such, she and others describe a 'Nietzschean' notion of truth emerging in Herzog's films, emerging from the manifold web of perspectives and vantages onto the story or event.[8] No doubt, we can locate echoes of these ideas in Bruna's (otherwise paradoxical) pedagogical advice to younger student filmmakers, when advising them to use the camera in a 'democratic' fashion, while simultaneously recognising that as filmmakers, they ultimately 'make reality in the editing room'.[9]

Panorama of Global Stories

Bruna's artistic film *Magicarena* (2014) may be regarded as a cypher that helps to make tangible the director's abstract or diagrammatic approach to documentary storytelling. This film gravitates around the magnificent 2000 year old *Arena di Verona*, capturing the trials and tribulations of the workers and artists as they prepare for a performance of Verdi's *Aida*, during the Centenary show of the most famous operatic festival in the world. Bruna consciously decided in advance not to focus on the story of the main divo or diva, and to instead foreground the collective effort: the experiences of a mime artist, a prop man, a trombone player, a background extra, a chorister and the assistant stage director. As such, the collective preparatory process leading up to the realisation of this spectacular show becomes the dynamic centre of the film. By offering the perspectives of so many remarkable individuals, who came together to make the event happen, the film – which, thus, one may regard as connotatively Marxist – allows life and art, fact and fiction, local and global, past, present and future, to overlap: the contemporary reality of the international production, the historical story of *Aida* set in ancient Egypt which is reinvigorated with a distinct futuristic science fictional aesthetic, Verdi's nineteenth-century opera which is housed and articulated within the magnificent setting of the imperial Roman amphitheatre.

At an abstract or symbolic level we can recognise how Bruna adopts a typically postmodern or postcolonial attitude in *Magicarena*, demonstrating that even if (to momentarily purloin a line from Shakespeare) 'all the world's a stage' or vice-versa, the ethical thing to do is to bring to the fore the stories of the typically backgrounded or less privileged 'off-stage' characters and players. For if the story of *Aida* itself focusses upon a 'transnational' struggle, important historical bodies – and their associated Leviathan-esque bodies politic – from Egypt and Ethiopia, the production of the contemporary show is also marked by countless transnational cooperations, including amongst others: the direction of the Catalan team *La Fura dels Baus*, the contributions of a Moldavian performer, and a Chinese opera singer star – who subsequently is the focus of Bruna's next co-directed documentary.

Recognition of *Magicarena*'s cross-border themes, alongside its foregrounding of multiple marginalised perspectives upon the grand events, allows us to use this artistic film as a key for identifying comparable themes, tropes and concepts at work in Bruna's other – arguably more politically and socially engaged – global filmmaking projects. For example, while it would be possible to (tenuously) geopolitically link together the historical Ethiopian character of *Aida* to the strong female subjects of *A Closed Mouth Catches no Flies* (2015) – filmed on location in the contemporary Federal Democratic Republic of Ethiopia – it is arguably the two films' interwoven multi-perspectival forms, and their privileging of otherwise peripheral characters, that makes them the most interesting from an auteurial perspective.

The latter documentary begins and ends with the lively sounds of Ethiopian jazz saxophonist Gétatchèw Mèkurya's track *Akalé wubé*. Although this is initially deployed as an extradiegetic score, the vibrant tune is soon-after diegetically grounded, so that it appears to emanate from the tinny speakers of a bajaj (a small taxi-tricycle), which literally leads the film's audience into the town of Wuchale, of a 'predominantly female' population – as dutifully conveyed by the bajaj's male driver. Thereafter, Bruna opts to zoom in on four different female characters: Tsehai, a police officer and single mother who deals with crimes against women and children (such as rape and domestic abuse); Asrebab, a domestic house cleaner; Toiba, a shopkeeper and mother of three, who escaped forced labour in Saudi Arabia; and Tringo, a student who walks two hours back and forth to school, each day, to pursue her dream of becoming a doctor.

Using his camera to frame and follow these four women as they go about their daily lives, Bruna manages to document various interactions, in and around their communities, and milieu. All the while each protagonist talks reflexively about their lives, hopes and dreams, directly to the director/audience. Such methods ultimately allow Bruna to open up a network of vistas into this marginalised world, and unearth a series of intersectional issues that make tangible a variety of overlapping social, geopolitical and biopolitical, problems related to poverty, unemployment, gender inequality, exclusion and the lack of opportunities. In this manner, the sum of *A Closed Mouth*'s four separate threads combine to become greater than its parts: the four complimentary biographical narratives draw the viewers' attention to broader patterns and in-forming events relevant to other contemporary Ethiopians, and toward a broadened geopolitical tapestry.

At the level of his oeuvre, we might recognise how the different geopolitical locations that Bruna opts to film both *Magicarena* and *A Closed Mouth* in allow for radically diverging and asymmetric vantage points upon the nature and realities of globalisation, and upon his pespective view of the Global North and Global South. Thus, those filmed in Italy can be seen to benefit from the flows of bodies and ideas coming together to create fantastic spectacles that enrich the cultural lives of many, while the excluded and marginalised women in the horn of Africa reveal the negative dimensions of these same processes from that particular geopolitical location. Similar thematic concerns become knitted together most overtly in the complex multidimensional story of *Dust* (2011), which demands that Bruna increasingly follow the tangle of different story threads all across the globe, interconnecting a multitude of worlds, characters and locations.

The Glocal Perspective

Dust begins by focussing on a key international court hearing taking place in Bruna's hometown of Turin, involving the multinational company Eternit, which faces claims of having caused the deaths of around 30,000 former Italian plant workers and members of the local population at Casale Monferrato. The film initially focusses on the stories and feelings of the victims and surviving family members of those affected by the poisonous material, which over a protracted period of time is known to slowly suffocate and overcome those exposed to it. In an early scene, Bruna invites the audience to ride along with the plaintiffs and witnesses in a bus, heading to the court room. There, a man shows the camera a two-page spread in a local newspaper, which is covering the trial he will later give evidence in. Later, viewers are introduced to other key figures, including Luisa Minazzi, who Bruna joins inside her home as she rakes through her own personal archive of press clippings. In her front room Minazzi speaks of being the founding member of the environmental association in Casale, in the 1980s. She subsequently became the town's environmental councillor between 1990 and 1995, and then an activist, who was responsible for kick-starting the asbestos decontamination process in Italy. Dealing with Eternit has been a colossal lifelong struggle, she explains, as the ongoing battle against them begins to unfold in court. Throughout the film the intimate access to personal experiences, which Minazzi offers Bruna, extends to her trips to the hospital for various scans and treatments, after she became diagnosed with mesothelioma in 2006 as a result of asbestos contamination. In this sense, Minazzi is traced fighting a battle on two fronts and scales: the biological and the political. Such ideas are reinforced by her comments – given to the camera whilst having her hair dyed in her bathroom – when she explains that after her diagnosis, she wanted to show other victims that sufferers can continue to live, uphold a positive attitude and fight for justice, despite their shortened life expectancy.

Undoubtedly, the recorded testimony of such characters grants the film an intense emotional texture, but on account of the deep historical nature of the story, and the complex politics surrounding the finances of the multinational market with its various 'bodies' – raw materials, industrial asbestos, transportation vessels, legal bodies, transnational labourers and contractors, and so on – mapping the boundaries of this complex story demanded that Bruna also zoom out, to direct his attention elsewhere, on events unfolding or transpiring in far-flung locations, including India, Brazil and Canada. Whatever the subject matter, Bruna encourages viewers to perceive the unfolding story on an ever-larger scale: while local Italian justice is sought for the deceased and still suffering, the struggle is not merely local in nature, but it is rather a struggle against a multimillion-dollar multinational corporation, that yields considerable lobbying power, is able to take advantage of various legal loopholes and can manipulate various international legal authorities. By opening his film up to these larger fractal dimensions – exploring the economics of an asbestos mine in Canada, the needs of builders and the homeless in India and so on – Bruna refuses to let go of the emotional trials and tribulations of the Italian individuals with whom the film began.

Later in the film, Bruna re-directs viewers' attention to the Italian bus on the way to court. This time, two eighty-year-old women erupt into a heated discussion, ignited by their shared frustrations at the slow pace of the trial. The first claims that the victims have ultimately 'obtained very little'. In response to this, Bruna then pans left to pick out another character, seated on the opposite aisle of the bus, and wearing an eye patch, who contests this idea: 'What? We have obtained a trial!' she retorts, and then continues, 'after thirty years of struggle we have made a big step: the most important trial in Europe!' The hand-held camera here zooms in on her visibly angered countenance, as she continues: 'So it's nothing!? How can you say we have achieved nothing?' Conceding some ground, the first woman now attributes her dissatisfaction to the other victims and plaintiffs, who chose to stay home, as the trial drags out. Her interlocutor then reminds her: 'But you do it for yourself, I do it for me, [and] for those who have died. And for my friends who have gone'. It is in this sense that we can grasp Bruna's work more generally, as offering a human (if not humanist) perspective upon the wider processes of globalisation.

The end of *Dust* delivers forth a mixed bag of emotions and feelings. For if the actual Turin trial is ultimately lost in the end – allowing companies such as Eternit to continue to expose around 70 per cent of the world's population to an incredibly dangerous (and highly profitable) carcinogenic material – Bruna ethically foregrounds many of the small battles won by the victims, whose struggles demonstrate that it is the very act of standing up against powerful opponents that is important, as this can inspire change and offer hope. The final information relayed to viewers before the film's credits roll is constituted by three screens of white text overlaying a silent black background. The first informs viewers that Minazzi sadly lost her fight to mesothelioma in 2010, before the trial reached its end. The second notes that: 'The asbestos industry is still growing in the world. The Government of Quebec is supporting the reopening of the second asbestos mine in the country, encouraged by new Indian investors'. Only the final message offers a glimpse of some form of future hope or justice:

> On 13 February 2012 the court of First Instance of Turin sentenced [the company's president] Stephan Schmidheiny and [the company's CEO] Jean-Louis Marie de Cartier de Marchienne to 16 years of prison and around 100 million Euro in compensation.

Global Migration and Exclusion

After *Dust*, Bruna's next feature-length documentary, *The Travel Agent* (2015), chose to focus on the human dimensions and consequences of US–Cuban geopolitical relations. Filmed on the streets of Cuba, this documentary foregrounds the life and work of a woman named Lourdes, a 58-year-old Cuban national, whose job involves counselling thousands of Cubans seeking out entry visas for travel to the US. Bruna's camera is drawn to Lourdes, constantly gravitating around her home and work as she coaches countless hopefuls on how to best answer the tricky US embassy visa questions. The film builds up an intense intimacy with Lourdes, as Bruna captures her expertly plying her trade, in a series of medium-close-ups, or in a close-up angle for the director/camera as she reflexively discusses her life and work with others. In key scenes, recorded in her small office or the surrounding street, Bruna's intimate framings manage to capture the shrewd and savvy practitioner helping to fine tune her customers' stories, so that they have the best chances of succeeding. By collaging together a series of such encounters, which blend the life stories of the visa seekers with the experiences and anecdotes of Lourdes, the film builds up a dynamic living picture of the broader contextual situation: the forced and painful separation of countless families and loved ones.

Ironically, despite helping many other Cubans to travel to the US, Lourdes tells Bruna that she has never been able to visit her own mother, son, five brothers, two grandsons and twenty-three nephews who now live in Florida: 'I quench the thirst of others every day', she says mournfully to the camera, 'yet there's not a drop of water for me'. Throughout the film, the focus upon human relations highlights how organic communities can spontaneously emerge, with people coming together to pool their knowledge, skills and resources, in order to help others. Capturing these moments of human connection results in a string of memorable scenes, including one where a group of friends and helpful strangers, band together to host a farewell party for a successful candidate, who will shortly depart for the US – presumably forever. After a long wait over the course of the film, Lourdes' own interview date is finally set. She thus switches roles from objective professional expert to subjective and vulnerable applicant.

As Lourdes' interview date grows nearer, Bruna's intimate access to her home and life makes her mounting excitement and anxiety palpable. Viewers thus become emotionally drawn in to her story, as she speaks of her heartfelt desire to visit her dying mother, who emigrated during the Sixties. In a series of memorable scenes Lourdes also locates, befriends and hires a traditional *Santería* healer, to help her petition supernatural beings, in order to positively influence the upcoming decision. At these moments Lourde's emotional investment is expertly relayed by close-ups that capture her affected speech, face and body language. On the day of the interview Bruna records Lourdes entering the embassy with many other hopefuls. His camera, though, remains outside with her partner, who frets and worries alone in her absence. Cutting to a later moment, after what seems an eternity, her partner appears framed alone on the street. When she finally spots Lourdes emerging from her bureaucratic ordeal, the perception of her flat dejected body language directly communicates the negative result of the decision. As she and her partner hug, we learn that the dejected Lourdes must continue to endure her indefinite separation.

The multiple sad stories, interwoven throughout the documentary with Lourdes' own story, make clear what is meant by the notion of 'exclusion and difference' in the era of globalisation. Indeed, the film not only allows the voice of multiple excluded Cubans from the Global South to be heard, but also makes us ask questions about the few who go on to become illegal or legal US migrants in the Global North. What realities and futures lie in wait for these poor Cuban migrants entering the US, where different forms of economic and cultural exclusion, exploitation, persecution and marginalisation surely await them?

The theme of migration, so central to *The Travel Agent*, also becomes an important thematic vector threading together Bruna's wider body of work. The social and human consequences of migration become the central subject of several other documentaries and shorts, including *Storie di paglia* (*Straw Stories*, 2003), *Verso casa* (*Homeward*, 2004), *My Nigerian Sisters* (2005) and *Taormina Taj Mahal* (2008). Common to these films is Bruna's focus on migrant and displaced communities that attempt to recapture or retake possession of ancient and traditional ways of life, including now forgotten rituals and practices. Among other things, these films capture and convey how permanent migrants and diasporas can come to idealise their native land, or how returning migrants often struggle to rediscover what they remember/imagined was once there and is now lost.

Storie di Paglia, for instance, focuses on a rural population forced to leave the Italian Alps at the beginning of the twentieth century in order to find employment in France, Switzerland and Germany. Bruna documents the consequences of depopulation upon the mountain villages surrounded by fields of rye, while also showing how a cereal crop, far from being a mere source of nutrition, plays a major role in defining a community's identity. *Storie di paglia* thus attempts to testify to a nearly lost culture and ecology, emerging from a trans-kingdom nexus of plants, animals, humans and habitat. In one of the short episodes entitled *L'orso di paglia* (*Rye Bear*) Bruna records the events of a traditional carnival, where villagers fashion bear costumes out of the rye straw, which is then worn by a male villager as he scares children and entertains the adults. Villagers openly discuss the figure of the rye bear, highlighting that although they have been performing such a ritual since they were little kids, they retain no memory of how the tradition started, or from what it derived. As one resident explains in a voice-over: 'During Carnival every possible kind of joke is made. I do not know who dreamed to make this one of the bear, though'.

A concomitant migration period becomes the focus of *Taormina Taj Mahal*, wherein Bruna explores the relocation of Italian peoples to the United States during the nineteenth and twntieth centuries. The Italian communities of Brooklyn and Atlantic City allow Bruna to investigate the idealisation of a lost native land, while interrogating the population's nostalgic feelings and desires to return to, or uphold, more traditional customs. The focus here is very much on the preservation of an imagined national identity within a different geopolitical space – albeit one that is itself based on symbolic objects bound up in the living memory of the past, rather than on the actual evolving state of the country and its organic relation to unfolding events. Such ideas are made overt in one scene where the owner of a record shop explains that he himself prefers the 'old America', in the same way that he prefers the 'old Italy', which he believes to be better than the contemporary one.

The idea of immigrant idealisation is investigated again by Bruna in *Verso casa* (*Homeward*) and in *My Nigerian Sisters*. In juxtaposition to the romanticising of Italy as a longed for 'home country', these documentaries paint a picture of Italy as a dreamed of geopolitical 'Promised Land'. In *Homeward*, for example, Bruna incorporates the story of nine people hailing from Morocco, Albania and Nigeria, who ended up being expelled by the Italian government[10] following their various and harrowing migratory experiences. The migratory process is here framed in terms of what we might call a deterritorialisation and reterritorialisation of unwelcomed people, who are torn between the impetus to seek a better future outside their homeland and their conscious (and/or self-conscious) re-routing and re-rooting back to their home countries. These include the stories of Khalid, a young Moroccan man who struggles to find employment; Edmond, a 29 year-old Albanian man who travelled to Italy to find a proper job in order to support his retired parents; Faith, a 25 year-old Nigerian woman who feels she has lost time by living outside Nigeria, and Becky, another Nigerian who thanks to the Alnima project learnt how to become an hairdresser in Italy, in order to then better reintegrate into her home country.

In these films Bruna blends ethics and aesthetics in an expressive manner. To take but one illustrative case in point, we might turn to when Bruna interviews Edmond, an Albanian topographic engineer. First, Bruna opts to frame Edmond in medium close-up standing in the streets of Albania. In an off-centre framing, Edmond speaks in Italian of working for the Albanian regime for over thirty years before moving to Italy. As he tells in voice-over his story of migration and spiralling return, Bruna inserts a montage of beautiful long shots depicting Edmond moving through, or seated within, beautiful and bucolic aestheticised landscapes. The first shot frames him jogging through fields and along a dilapidated train track, which is scored with melancholic music, as he speaks to the audience in voice-over: 'When the new party took power they wanted to put me in prison, because here politics operates on a system of revenge. People who work for one party cannot work for another'. The next scene shows him in silhouette, sat within an unusual wooden structure, which appears somewhat cage-like in its dark outlines. Being left without a job, and threatened with arrest, Edmond was forced to leave his family and country: first attaining a Greek visa in order to expatriate, and then move on to Italy. Returning several years later, Edmond voices his frustration that his prospects have not improved. 'Things only changed cosmetically', he says. As if to highlight this idea aesthetically, Bruna here opts to frame

Edmond standing in front of the old buildings where his parents live, and which have recently been painted over with bright new colours in an attempt to make them look more modern.

Unfortunately, many other characters appearing in the film also fail to be successfully reintegrated into their countries of origin. This also becomes an emotionally charged topic explored in *My Nigerian Sisters*, which relates the experiences of three Nigerian women – Rita, Rosemary and Joy (fictional names) – who were repatriated after working as prostitutes in Europe. In this film, Bruna opts to record interviews with his subjects, building relationships with the women as they tell of their experiences of prostitution in Italy, Spain and France. Throughout the course of the film, viewers are also shown their failed attempts to reintegrate back into Nigerian life, after having been forced to return in 2005. While *My Nigerian Sisters* highlights a range of comparable topics and themes to those which appeared in *Homeward* – including human trafficking, migration, repatriation from Europe and the double identity of migrants – the three protagonists here encounter uniquely incredible difficulties when they return to their homeland. Indeed, these women appear to be nearly destroyed by their migration experience, and left seemingly without any hopes for their future, in a country where their own kin initially encouraged them to take up the challenge of parting from. The latter are the very families and communities that invested in their emigration out of Nigeria in the first place. For various reasons, the three women do not want to travel again. One of them, now with child, has developed AIDS. Another is in a state of depression and had previously attempted suicide. The third had run away from her relatives in order not to succumb to their demands, and as a result feels deprived of any meaningful relationships.

Their shared perceptions of having hit-rock-bottom ultimately serve the purpose of bringing these three women together. In the interview they note that they now also recognise each other as 'sisters'. By bringing these women to viewers, through a series of shots that frame all three bodies together, the film aesthetically underscores how they created a new supportive community, held together by mutual solidarity forged by their shared experiences of globalisation's exclusion effect. This is the human story Bruna opts to salvage from this documentary excursion, showing his global audiences how strong women can come together to help each other survive. Once more Bruna manages to use his camera, framings and editing, to highlight how human dignity defies the contingency and catastrophe of a given situation. It conveys the message that it is these women's resilience, or what we might call their 'survival intelligence', that allows them to seize a future, whatever challenges this may involve.

Concluding Thoughts

Despite his having recently moved to Barcelona Bruna remains an important Italian filmmaker and documentarian whose work is instructively symptomatic of, and critically engaged with, processes of globalisation. Over the past fifteen years, Bruna has endeavoured to carry out quality film productions with an unique human interest for human plight, which concomitantly offers viewers a range of perspectives on various national and international social issues. As we have shown, his documentary films defy institutionalised formulas and invariably strive to open up the worlds of, and grant a voice to, those who for various economical (*Dust*), logistical (*Magicarena*), or political (*The Travel Agent, My Nigerian Sisters*) reasons are not normally heard, and are cast away from the limelight. Although his films often intercept the stories of people undergoing or enduring intense and exceptional hardship (including disease, legal fights, visas applications and international migration), the ethical and emotional motivation driving Bruna's work is the need to draw attention to human stories and crises, as they are catalysed by processes of globalisation, and which give us cause for concern but which are not completely deprived of hope. Our analysis of Bruna's documentaries has also shown how the filmmaker most often works to interweave his idiosyncratic and directorial point of view around a diverse range of stories and perspectives that collectively draw our attention to a range of political issues, which are pertinent to the era of globalisation and exclusion. By so doing, his films also demand that viewers in turn examine and question their own global situations and situatedness in relation to such unsettling depictions.

Notes

1. Fleming and Gilardi (2016).
2. The expression refers to the thousands of well-educated, creative and innovative Italian people leaving the country due to the lack of opportunities, poor working conditions and high living costs.
3. Dussel (2013), p. xv.
4. Hammersley and Atkinson (2007), p. 3.
5. Fleming and Gilardi (2016).
6. Ibid.
7. Mitcheson (2013), p. 348ff.
8. For example, see also Eldridge (2019).
9. Fleming and Gilardi (2016).
10. Under Article n.12 of the law of the 6 March 1998 Bill, n.40, allowing the Ministry of Interior to expel foreigners for reasons of public order or state security.

Works Cited

Dussel, Enrique (2013), *Ethics of Liberation in the Age of Globalization and Exclusion*, Durham, NC: Duke University Press.
Eldridge, Richard (2019), *Werner Herzog: Filmmaker as Philosopher*, London: Bloomsbury.
Fleming, David H. and Filippo Gilardi (2016), *We Make Reality in the Editing Room! Global Documentary Filmmaker Gives Workshops and Screenings at UNNC: An Interview with Niccolò Bruna*, Ningbo (China): unpublished.
Hammersley, Martyn and Paul Atkinson (2007), *Ethnography: Principles in Practice*, New York: Routledge.
Mitcheson, Katrina (2013), 'Perspectivism in Nietzsche and Herzog: The Documentary Film as a Perspectival truth Practice', *Film-Philosophy*, 17.1: 348ff.

Fimography

A Closed Mouth Catches no Flies, documentary, directed by Niccolò Bruna, Italy: CIFA Onlus, 2015.
Dust: The Great Asbestos Trial, documentary, directed by Niccolò Bruna and Andrea Prandstraller, Italy: GraffitiDoc, 2011.
Hui He. The Soprano from the Silk Road, documentary, directed by Niccolò Bruna and Andrea Prandstraller, Italy: Le Talee, 2017.
Magicarena, documentary, directed by Niccolò Bruna and Andrea Prandstraller, Italy: Le Talee, 2014.
My Nigerian Sisters, documentary, directed by Niccolò Bruna, Italy: Tampep Onlus, 2005.
Storie di paglia (Straw Stories), documentary, directed by Niccolò Bruna, Italy: Overfilm, 2003.
Taormina Taj Mahal, documentary, directed by Niccolò Bruna, Italy: Colombrefilm, 2008.
The Travel Agent, documentary, directed by Niccolò Bruna, Italy: Cataclisma Film, 2015.
Verso casa (Homeward), documentary, directed by Niccolò Bruna, Italy: Kinoetika, 2004.

CHAPTER 10

The Paradox of 'Independence' in Cyberspace: The Case of Italian Experimental and Independent Cinema
Anthony Cristiano

> Whoever controls the motion picture industry controls the most powerful medium of influence over the people.
> Thomas Alva Edison[1]

Introduction

Among the features of our common humanity, yearning to explore one's surroundings and engage reality via our sensorial, perceptual and cognitive faculties finds expression across various epistemological fields. These include the arts, the invention of computing systems and the new environment of cyberspace, which we inhabit via our communication practices and, increasinlgy, via the products of our artistic and/or professional lives. Indeed, a single propulsive yearning seems to underpin the story of representational media, whether it pertains to the art of cinema or to the management of entire socio-cultural network structures: the excersise of creativity and power. Throughout the twentieth century and into the twenty-first, Italian representational arts have been marked by surges in experimental activities. Since the birth of the new medium of moving images, an increasing number of artists have converted to visual, time-based, media. From the late 1960s onward – which is the period chiefly refered to in this chapter – the activities of the CCI, Studio Monte Olimpino, Filmmaker, Videobase, Gruppo Uno, Altrementi, Sudio Azzurro and other similar initiatives, were marked by both independent and experimental endeavours. They are the historical manifestations of creative and artistic attempts to organise one's cinematic output and various forms of social *impegno* (engagement). Though some groups may have had a very short lifespan – the CCI lasted only about three and a half years, from 1967 to 1970 – their activities were variously documented and have reached us in the forms of diaries, memoirs, booklets, articles or essays, exhibition catalogues, photographs, recorded interviews and personal testimonies, whole films or film and video 'fragments'.[2] From the perspective of the social sciences, anthropology, figurative arts, history of moving-images and so forth – thus, from a much valued interdisciplinary viewpoint – the appeal and contextualisation of such histories is compelling. They were not born in a vaccum or in total isolation from the socio-cultural *melieu* of their times. Their historical precedents and, thus, *continuum*, at the level of theory and praxis, have been attested to on several occasions by historians and critics such as Antonio Costa, Bruno Di Marino, Sandro Bernardi, Marco Meneguzzo and others.[3] As discussed in this chapter, the more urgent question of our times is not whether a given group of 'film artists' or *auteurs*' activities are classifiable as purely art or as conventional practices of cinema – or whether there is sufficient archival attestation to legitimise their history – but whether 'independence and experimentation' are at all possible, and tenable as epistemic discourse in the age of cyperspace and 'Internet of things'. The dominant quality of contemporary new media, is that it is characterised by umbelicality – a term intended to conjure up the idea of tethered dependency. In the twenty-first century, the nature of the digital algorithmic medium – increasingly employed by artists, filmmakers, intellectuals and the like – is embedded with the undetachable order to conform to strict protocols, thus, limiting, reshaping and redefining any exercise of creative output.

Experimentation and independence are not a mark of a single period, nor are they exclusive to a group of artists or *auteurs*. The character of Italian arts, including those pertaining to moving image, is umistakable throughout its variegated incarnations: it is marked by intellectualism, audacity, pathos/melancholy, exploration, buffoonery and joviality. The painterly, performative and stylistic virtuosity of the Italian artistic tradition is rooted in its cultural history, and its artefacts and paradigms have been successfully exported or emulated the world over. Before the emergence of contemporary digital media, there were virtually no doubts that the same held true for the art of moving image – including its pioneers and mavericks, from Pastrone to Rossellini, De Sica and Zavattini, Antonioni and Fellini, Olmi, Moretti, Soldini and beyond. In the tradition of the arts the Italian character has customarily favoured realism and immediacy over programmatic and structuralist approaches – though some important exceptions apply. True to the artistic verve of Italian talent, several well-known Italian filmmakers were independent cineastes at one point – some of whom remained so throughout their careers.

As was the case with narrative cinema,[4] in the late 1960s and into the '70s the American influence was also felt in Italian independent and experimental initiatives. Inspired partly by the North American model, as in other European cases,[5] the late 1960s saw the rise of collective art-centres in Italy, notably in the cities of Turin, Rome, Naples, Milan and other urban centres. In virtue of theoretical considerations, however, such initiatives are comparable to those driven by artistic and socio-cultural stimuli earlier in the century. It has been widely acknowledged that they (unofficially) share the legacies of forms of independence and experimentation in conjuction with the revolutionary approaches of vanguardist manifestos – such as the historical case of 1909 featuring the Italian Futurists. As Di Marino has observed, the oppositional trends of the Futurists are reflected in Italy and internationally: the venturing beyond traditional representational models, beyond the technical apparatus, the inseparable nexus of art and existence, the narrative use of the human body and so forth.[6] Across different eras the experimentation practices and independence enjoyed by visual artists and filmmakers – that is, the greater forms of autonomy they have enjoyed relative to institutionalised and commercial practices of cinema – bore a paradoxical mark: their survival depended on the financial support of private endeavours or public sectors, and on the access to the technology that made their practices possible. While the notoriously unstable Italian political and administrative state of affairs has challenged the sustainability of independent initiatives – often by issuing impractical definitions and creating impractical laws, unlike several other European nations – the ideal state of creative and productive freedom sought by filmmakers and visual artists has met with a growing paradox, one which appears to have reached its pinnacle in the new century with the emergence of online technologies.

The advancement of technology, and the tumultuous history of the twentieth and beginning of the twenty-first centuries, has seen the emergence of new forms of creative and consumption practices relating to film and video. Practices of cinema have particularly changed to a significant degree as dictated by the new technologies – such as compact and electronic equipment, and the political economy that aids their diffusion and use. The twenty-first century is ushering the new medium of the Internet into most parts of the world. Online practices offer a new space in which the means of production and habits of consumption meet in an unprecedented way – with their increasing dominance attesting to the ongoing convergence of technological and commercial developments. The result is a new and encompassing environment, referred to as 'cyberspace'– where the human and the medium 'merge' – and which increasingly transcends national borders. In it, one finds a horde of archival and novel material: well over a century of moving images, of varied type, genre and style, are found and consumed by increasingly greater parts of the globe. This new scenario raises a host of new questions. What impact are such developments having on practices of experimentation and independence? Are independent and experimental cinematic practices aided or weakened by the novel environment of cyberspace? Is Italian independent cinema enjoying a new renaissance online, or is it being met by a greater paradox that threatens its survival? Do the new technologies threaten to erase ethnic distinctiveness and impose a rigid and sterile model of use and consumption? The ensuing discussion of the socio-cultural and aesthetic features of practices of experimentation and independence is guided by a scrutiny of the (1) objectives, the (2) modalities and (3) the unexpected imperatives of the new trends.

Experimentalism: Legacies and Transformations

Transnationally, and particularly within Western traditions, independent and experimental practices have mainly been characterised by creative and productive autonomy: the exploration of new subject matters or untold stories, meta-cinematic concerns regarding aesthetic and technological procedures, non-linear narratives (if any), unconventional distribution and screening practices and the interdisciplinary nature of experimentalism and novel research paths. In Italy experimentation has also been read as a form of realism – a characteristically distinguishing feature from its early cinematic history.[7] Italian arts are traditionally marked by industriousness. To the Italian inventiveness are attributed primacy of form and style and the exploration of new frontiers since the early historical vanguard movements – in this regard, European, English and American experiments are, chronologically, later developments (Figure 10.1).

Brothers Arnaldo Ginna and Bruno Corra were among the first artists to use colour and hand drawn shapes directly on film frames, as described in Bruno Corra's essay 'Abstract Cinema – Chromatic Music 1912'.[8] The legacies of this development are indubitably strong, and have been revisited by multiple artists – even if only in tribute – including members of the underground end experimental scene from the 1960s onwards. *Futurismo rivisitato* (*Futurism Revisited*, 1965), by Mario Schifano is one such example. It has often been observed that the Futurists' activities, with their 'explosive' appeal to movement and energy, anticipated the digital age and digital culture in important ways. Today, while technological innovation and practices have the tendency to homogenise one's expressive (if not thematic) concerns, the legacy of the Italian tradition, and the distinctive nature of its filmic and artistic texture[9] across experimental, independent

Figure 10.1 From left to right: Futurists Luigi Russolo, Carlo Carrà, Filippo Tommaso Marinetti, Umberto Boccioni and Gino Severini. Paris, 9 February, 1912.

and commercial cinema, has begun to infiltrate the online world. It is an attempt to preserve and share a national cinematic legacy, thanks to the indefatigable work of various curators, which at the same time contributes to making this legacy 'exportable' to foreign lands and audiences. The 'transferability' and 'translatability' of Italian filmic and, now video, texture is informed by the long-held artistic traditions peculiar to Italy, its aesthetic and inter-disciplinary elasticity, even its socio-political exuberance. As Sandro Bernardi has observed:

> [T]he great pictorial tradition could not be ignored and clearly functioned as a reservoir of ideas, or as an almost inexhaustible "hunting reserve", for those who came to the cinema with artistic or cultural intentions, but there is also something deeper, which makes it so that this historical-artistic richness functions at the genetic level, so-to-speak, as an inspiring cromosome and deep-seated generative structure.[10]

The realistic, perfomative and immediate character of Italian filmmakers has been informed by the scope of its artistic traditions, and by personal talent. At the centre or periphery of such a tradition, any change in the notion of an 'independent' approach and style is contemporaneously informed by the affinities and talent of each individual filmmaker and the peculiar historical-political circumstances in which they find themselves. During the 1960s and 1970s a host of artists, intellectuals and creative minds have migrated from the canvas and the scriptorium to the new medium of film, and later to video. They may not have had commercial success, through industrial and institutional channels, but they nevertheless pursued with various degrees of success their personal artistic agendas, and contributed to the advancement of the art form in unexpected ways. Many were associated with the official co-ops of those pivotal years (particularly 1965–75). Several members kept contact with similar co-ops in Britain, France and the United States. Jonas Mekas' journeys to Italy amounted to a 'revelation', confirming many an artist's vision – though the distinctive socio-political panorama of Italy, and its characteristic instability, was soon reflected in Italian counterpart groups. The members' artistic verve and elasticity was unaffected by their budgetary constraints, as they made do with 'shoe-string budgets' and proceeded to produce their works. One English writer, in a typewritten report published in *Tate Film* journal, speaks of those years and gives advice to his compatriots:

> The Cooperativa del Cinema Independente was formed last year. The majority of its members lived in three cities: Rome, Naples, and Turin. (There is less centralization of most aspects of life in Italy than in England or France; a fact most obviously exemplified by the fact that almost every city has its own daily newspaper.) . . . Many members of the Italian Co-op work on 8mm since they cannot afford 16mm and, like Stan Brakhage's SONGS, the films I was shown demonstrated that entirely satisfactory visual quality (and sound) can be obtained on a bootlace. If a lack of money is the hang-up in your filmmaking, then think seriously about using 8mm – although it is perhaps hardly necessary while members in London can obtain process-paid 16mm colour film at under 30s per hundred feet.[11]

Film scholars and historians are gradually paying greater attention to the peculiar experimental and independent phenomena of those years. A number of promotional retrospectives in Italy and other parts of the world, such as those held at the Istituti di Cultura (Institutes of Italian Culture), or programmes such as the 'Cinema Sperimentale Italiano 1966–1973: Bacigalupo, Brebbia, De Bernardi', sponsored by the City of Venice, are signs of growing interest (Figure 10.2).[12]

In the English speaking world, however, Italian independent and experimental filmmakers are scarcely known, let alone spoken or written about in scholarly circles.[13] It is very surprising to see that the legacy (and primacy of) the Futurist filmmakers, along with the transformations of, and contributions made to, experimental filmmaking and independent practices by several Italian artists of the 1960s–70s, have struggled to find a place in English studies attempting to historicise the subject matter.[14]

Figure 10.2 CCI members photographed by Luca Maria Patella. From left to right: Gianfranco Baruchello, Rosa Foschi, Massimo Bacigalupo, Guido Lombardi, Luca Patella (at the moment of taking the fish-eye photograph), Giorgio Turi, Alfredo Leonardi, Celestino Elia, Antonio Vergine and Adamo Vergine.

The panorama of this period is rich. Italian art and independent film work (of the post-Futurist period) include the painterly shorts of Luigi Veronesi (1908–1998), the conceptual 'body art' of Cioni Carpi, the visual and cinematic 'explorations' of Bruno Munari (1907–1998) and Marcello Piccardo (1914–99), the documentarist and maverick films of Silvano Agosti, the experimental work of Gianfranco Brebbia (1923–74), Luca Patella, Ugo Nespolo, Pia Epremian, Adamo Vergine, Paolo Brunatto (1935–2010), Tonino De Bernardi, Gianni Castagnoli, Ugo La Pietra, Franco Vaccari, the documentaries of the Roman group Alfredo Leonardi, Guido Lombardi, Anna Lajolo,[15] the films of Massimo Bacigalupo, Gianfranco Baruchello, Mario Masini, Giorgio Turi (1925–2015), and Alberto Grifi (1938–2007), the installations of Marinella Pirelli (1925–2012), the archival-footage work of Angela Ricci Lucchi (1942–1918), the films of Piero Bargellini (1940–1982) – among several others.

The 'Immmigration' Online

In order to explore the online presence and 'success' of Italian experimental and independent cinema, we should examine the dissemination of

Figure 10.3 Fondazione Cineteca Italiana (Milano).

some of its key works online alongside the character and affordances of online technologies. The Internet provides digital platforms to museums and cinématiques to promote and exhibit their collections, histories and cultural traditions across transnational borders via the connected world of cyberspace at a comparably very low cost. The Cineteca di Milano – now Fondazione Cineteca Italiana, supported by the Italian government – hosts its own promotional site.[16] It announces that: 'Since 1947, the year in which it was founded in Milan, the Cineteca Italiana – Fondazione from 1996 onward – has been uninterruptedly carrying on activities related to film preservation, the valorisation of cinematic heritage and dissemination of film culture both in Italy and abroad' (Figure 10.3).[17]

Though it does not offer virtual tours, the Cineteca webpage contains a variety of detailed information on its screenings, its museum, library, archive and restoration programmes. It maintains active Twitter and Facebook accounts, and invites its users to follow them via social media. Currently the Cineteca holds 35,000 films on celluloid – including international works – in its archive; it is part of the FIAF (International Federation of Film Archives), and it offers borrowing services. Moreover, it offers extra services to subscribers, including the viewing of film trailers, and a selection of promotional video-clips on its YouTube channel 'Cineteca di Milano'. Its viewership is not very significant – given it must compete with a host of macro and micro entities and individual Internet users in an age of new, erratic and haphazard, media cultures. In 2016 the Cineteca hosted a retrospective on Tonino De Bernardi in its MIC (Museo Interattivo del Cinema).[18] The same filmmaker created an account a few years earlier on Vimeo,[19] on which are uploaded a total of three videos – one of which is the trailer of *Jour et nuit* (*Day and Night*, 2014) – with a list of about ten followers. The page appears to have been inactive since – the views of each numbering over 100. To De Bernardi is named also a YouTube channel – which appears inactive at present – with a single upload, the film *Accoltellati* (*Stabbed*, 2006), which received over 700 views in the course of two years. It is noteworthy to mention that none of his early films appear on these webpages. De Bernardi is also present via Facebook and other social sites and online blogs. Notably, the Cineteca appears not to offer online viewing or screening of full films via its social media platforms.

De Bernardi's cinema – which does not disdain amateurism as an approach and whose later work is made up of overly long shows – represents an Italian response to the New American Cinema, the artistic movements of the Beat Generation, Pop and Minimal Art. His personal view is that unlike the USA, Italy never supported nor believed in independent and underground cinema. In an interview given in 2016 he reflected on his career:

> How would you define failure? –
> It's hard to ascribe failure to oneself. Besides, I never thought of success as a viable goal, thus I never experienced a real failure. Sometimes, though, when I'm depressed, I tell myself: Tonino, you're a loser. But it's just a momentary thing. And it's gone. If I had to come up with a definition which could give a more accurate idea of me, I would say I'm a 'defeated one yet not defeated'.[20]

One expert viewer of his late 1960s work expressed admiration for a spontaneous 8mm film De Bernardi made – while on a school trip with his students – by superimposing the footage of the movement of children with those of the same children filmed one at a time as they held flowers: 'The result is one of the most beautiful films I have ever seen', the viewer writes.[21] Much of his work is a blend of documentarian and surrealist impulses. De Bernardi very much valued his freedom to make the type of films he wanted, without restrictions or demands dictated by production or distribution imperatives. While the cinematic language may appear stylistically 'crude' at times, and the subject of his films influenced by foreign genres, the formal character of his work is situated in the Italian artistic sensibility. In De Bernardi's case, it reflects the tones and modulations of the localised milieu of his socio-political context and ascendancy, that of Turin. The fringe-like boundaries of most Italian independent filmmakers may make their work not readily 'edible' to the mainstream viewer, yet Internet technologies contribute to making their presence and work visible, and viewable, and subsequently open to historical and theoretical critique and study.

The historical Centro Sperimentale di Cinematografia in Italy's capital, Rome, promotes its courses and programmes, as well as those run conjointly in the regions of Abruzzo, Lombardy, Piedmont and Sicily, via its official website.[22] The three main subsections of the site are devoted respectively to 'Cineteca Nazionale', which includes restoration and archive, the 'Scuola Nazionale di Cinema', the programme behind its historical pedagogical mandate, and 'CSC Production', where films of various genres and length are listed and promoted. The Centro seeks to expand its reach and audience via its website, which includes the promotion of *artistes polyvalents* of wider appeal such as David Bowie – unsurprisingly given the new media cultures. Yet, the relatively unknown independent cinema phenomenon of the 1960s–70s is also featured on its site – an example being that of the Anna Lajolo and Guido Lombardo Fund. It acknowledges the 'movement' and notifies its users of the bibliographic material and relative works stored in its archive, though the listing details do not currently appear online. The CSC does devote regular *rassegne* (film exhibitions) to the experimental cinema of those years, however, and lists the titles, synopsis and other details pertaining to such work on its schedules promoted online (Figure 10.4).

> A career started in the 1960s and characterised by a great consistency – given the multiplicity and variety of works: militant and counter-information films and videos, social-anthropological documentaries, experimental films. These are works that express a "critical use" of audiovisual media, always conceived as an investigative and political tool of engagement.[23]

The archive may be very useful for graduate research on the subject of Italian independent and experimental cinema. The website informs users

Figure 10.4 National Film Library, Rome. Archivio Fotografico Cineteca Nazionale. Centro Sperimentale di Cinematografia, Roma.

that the CSC stores valuable letters and other material, which documents the exchange between the filmmakers from the Roman Cooperativa del Cinema Indipendente (Cooperative of Independent Cinema). The correspondence includes those with other Italian groups and with the DAAD (Deutscher Akademischer Austauschdienst) in Berlin. The authors, artists and filmmakers of the archived material include: Alfredo and Silvana Leonardi, Massimo Bacigalupo, Piero Bargellini, Enzo Ungari, Mario Ferrero and Gregory J. Markopoulos. While the CSC stores important material which can be useful to a historiography of peculiar cinematic phenomena, its main focus appears to be the promotion of narrative cinema, and particularly Italian cinema, with new and younger audiences and with aspiring makers of film and videos.

The collage-style of animation artists Marcello Piccardo and Bruno Munari, whose films are scarcely found online, is an excellent example of independent cinema's versatility, and its ability to respond even to demands from the Italian industrial sector – namely entities such as Ferrania, Olivetti and Fiat, among others. *I colori della luce* (*The Colours of Light*, 1963) is one such rare video viewable on Vimeo.[24] The collaboration between Piccardo and Munari, of the Cooperativa di Monte Olimpino (Cooperative of Monte Olimpinio) is spoken about in *Marcello Piccardo ricorda Bruno Munari* (*Marcello Piccardo Remembers Bruno Munari*, 2011) – a documentary in which Piccardo narrates his reminiscences of Munari, and which is available on the Archivio Audiovisivo del Movimento Operaio e Democratico (Audiovisual Archive of the Labour and Democratic Movement) website.[25] The Olimpino Studio likewise kept in contact with their American counterparts, including Hans Richter and Andy Warhol. The figures of the Monte Olimpino are succinctly summarised in somewhat mythic yet lucid tones:

> *Marcello Piccardo*, pioneer of Cinema, is one of those atypical figures that left a mark in the culture of Italy of the 1960s. A filmmaker and an eclectic intellectual, he applied avant-garde linguistic approaches to industrial cinema, creating some of the most successful commercials in the history of advertising. His taste for discovery led him to participate in the first Italian television experiences and, with Bruno Munari, to bring about the original and utopian experience of the Monte Olimpino Cooperative.[26]

From the early 1960s and into the 1970s Marcello Piccardo and Bruno Munari have been visually exploring, with peculiar scientific acuity, human phenomena in the form of time-based studies of performative behaviours. *Tempo nel tempo* (*Time in Time*, 1964), is one such project, which is viewable online, on YouTube (Figure 10.5).[27]

Figure 10.5 *Tempo nel tempo* (*Time in Time*, 1964) by Bruno Munari, Marcello Piccardo.

Their experiments echo Eadweard Muybridge's seminal exploration of movement in the second half of the 1800s, but with a renewed interest in the kinetic potential of modern techniques. In 1969 the Venice Film Festival also screened a number of shorts created by children through an audiovisual initiative promoted by the Monte Olimpino Cooperative. The works of Piccardo and Munari have been screened at retrospectives in various Italian film festivals.[28] Documentarian Enrica Viola's debut work, *Se la vita è meglio, butti via la telecamera* (*If Life Is Better, Throw Away the Camera*, 1998), which was screened at the well-known Filmmaker Cooperative in Milan in 1998, is an insightful portrait of Marcello Piccardo.[29] At the end of the twentieth century Piccardo spoke about his media experience, and related his own life stories, via artsy videos, later uploaded onto YouTube.[30] One of them, titled *Marcello Piccardo: l'informazione capovolta* (*Marcello Piccardo: Information Upside-down*, 2009) and referred to as a *videoritratto* (video-portrait), shows him reading his notable book *The Collina del Cinema* (*The Hilltop of Cinema*) published by Nodo Libri in 1992.[31] He speaks of how he helped the young, through youth initiatives held at the Olimpino Studio, to express themselves through the art of moving image. The videos were created by Andrea Piccardo and uploaded on YouTube via the channel bearing his name, in the first decade of the twenty-first century. The Internet is an indubitably rich archive and important resource, affording a glimpse into the life and work of the indefatigable protagonists of unconventional, experimental and independent cinema. Had Marcello Piccardo – who worked as a sketch artist, animator for TV programmes and experimental filmmaker – lived on to work his magic through the age of the Internet, it would have been of great interest to observe his response to the new medium. Could such figures' 'utopic' outlook have helped re-direct the purpose of online platforms to better ends? The archival nature and the accessibility of platforms such as YouTube not only offer a glimpse into the peculiar history and work of such veteran artists, but the video artefacts themselves become samples of a peculiarly new experience of independent cinema online, one of 'immigration'. Characterised as it is by ease of access, fragmented viewership and fragmentary viewing, interruptions and data collection, it is an anomalous yet invaluable miniature cinema and one-on-one new experience – with the potential to be turned into a tool, suited for research and study of rare artefacts. In such a case it would appear that the online 'revolution' has in some respects improved the lot of experimentalists and independent artists, though there may be a paradox to abiding by and depending upon the terms and conditions of multinational corporations – such as Facebook or Google – which places into question the notion of independence on several fronts.

The same appears to be true with the documentary videos created by Lombardi, Lajolo and Leonardi – as recalled by Lombardi in the 2005 *Schegge di Utopia* video by Paolo Brunatto, and now available online on YouTube. Lombardi speaks of how in their 'underground' style their cameras were 'absorbing' as an *aspirapolvere* (vacuum cleaner) does the reality of the housing and labour crises of the 1970s rather then channelling their own cinematic dreams.[32] Guido Lombardi, Anna Lajolo and Alfredo Leonardi, who together co-directed a number of films, are listed along with their individual filmography on the BFI (British Film Institute) website.[33] Documentaries directed include *Carcere in Italia* (*Prison in Italy*, 1973), and *E nua ca simu a forza du mundu* (*And We Who Are the Force of the World*, 1971), the latter of which was taken up to be screened on the RAI3 national television network (Figure 10.6). The value of such documentary material is incalculable – which includes rare features such as original dialogues in the local dialect, and rare folk songs such as the one included in the 1971 film.[34] It constitutes an important artefact and documentation, and not merely for the social sciences and for anthropological oriented purposes, but also given the historial situatedness, the depiction of authentic people and locals, the unfranchised and spontaneous approach, the metacinematic import of its aesthetics, and

THE PARADOX OF 'INDEPENDENCE' IN CYBERSPACE   229

as part of the legacy of Italy's socio-cultural and visual memory. The efforts made by foundations and scholars to preserve, curate and make available such material in various cities – Bologna, Milan, Turin and Rome – is praiseworthy. The filmmakers' turn toward works that engage their sense of civic responsibility, hark back to Zavattinian lessons on 'truth' and to those of *cinéma verité*. Even in this respect, it is appropriate to refer to them as *auteurs*, the camera functioning as an amplifier of socio-political and aesthetic concerns. The documentary films are meant to call the public's attention to undefended people and unfought causes and rouse its interest and participation in activities of social *impegno* (engagement). A Gospel-like moment comes to the fore, however, when the filmic apparatus, along with the aesthetic endeavour and its celebration, become in themselves the end result of such operations – as in the notorious case of *Anna* (1972–75) and the outcome for the real person represented therein, the dubious segments of which are now found online – revealing the 'unhealthy eye' behind the camera and before the screen; 'if your eye is unhealthy, your whole body will be full of darkness'.[35] It is a case in which the human subject (the means) is turned into a vehicle of cinematic voyeurism (the ends). The 'online migration' appears to contribute to the same trend.

Anna Lajolo and Guido Lombardi are also the authors of the fictional work *L'isola in capo al mondo* (*The Island on Top of the World*), published by Nuova ERI in 1994. Alfredo Leonardi is also the author of the beguiling *Se l'incoscio si ribella* (*If the Subconscious Were to Rebel*, 1967),[36] which opens with a scene from the Living Theatre company – on tour in Italy at the time. Not

Figure 10.6 *E nua ca simu a forza du mundu* (*And We Who Are the Force of the World*, 1971) by Alfredo Leonardi, Anna Lajolo, Guido Lombardi.

all of the film artefacts of Italian artists have been digitised and uploaded online, though even segments would make a difference to their study and appreciation. Some artists and filmmakers rightly fear low quality rendition or damage/deterioration of precious rare copies, whilst others may show scepticism toward the unstable and 'vulgar' nature of several online platforms and their politics. No doubt the absence of English subtitles in addition to the original Italian, narrows the potential viewership in the 'global online village' of cyberspace, yet it suffices to make the item available to the Italian speaking community spread across foreign lands. It connects one single viewer – in their office, studio or home apartment – to another, across the Atlantic and beyond. What appears to remain is a sense of displacement, and an almost exotic relation to the filmic and video texture: a sense of being confronted with the depiction of issues and times – largely unrelated to the present – which are themselves turned into artefacts of art forms, and celebrated as part of a miniature and makeshift cinematic experience. The independence then becomes that of electing to upload such material, and the underground or (humanistically) subterrenean experience of its discovery and viewing.

Yet, the response of some viewers may amount to a strong sense of nostalgia: 'the remembrance of things past' in low quality video-art-form. The BFI webpage lists several Italian independent filmmakers, including Gianni Castagnoli, whose filmography on the site consists of a single film, the 1973 artistic work *La nott'el giorno* (*The Night an' Day*).[37] Excerpts of his Super8 work can also be found on Vimeo, such as his *Valentino Moon* (1974)[38] made in collaboration with the Collectif Jeune Cinema (Young Cinema Cooperative). He is also known for his work at the boundaries of theatre and experimental cinema. Throughout the last century and into the twenty-first, the different media the moving-image has 'travelled through' appear to be visual cousins – engenderd by an untameable *scopophilia* for the iconic artefact – to which artists and filmmakers have likewise periodically migrated and adapted. It is presumed that since the 1970s the *immagine filmica* (filmic image) and the (new) electronic image have been merging; particularly in the case of video art, research cinema and animation.[39] Though some historians and scholars may read the signs of 'cinema's crises' in terms of aesthetic curves, periodisations, industrial success, normative developments, the convergence of formal and technological innovations and so on, artists who have sought alternative forms of expression in new media may have been in practice unaffected by such historicising constructs.[40] Beginning in the late 1970s, Videobase and Studio Azzurro have remained as two remarkable initiatives and offshoots of the film cooperatives' impetus. Since the late 1970s, filmmakers such as Guido Lombardi have read in this transition a change of mode and style:

After the 1970s, with the dissemination in Italy of the first *portapack* (camcorder and portable recorder), the electronic medium is complemented by, or replaces, the film medium in the practice of many artists. An entire epoch is probably fading away, and the most poetic and unconscious facets of cinema (*If the unconscious were to rebel* is the title of one of Leonardi's short films) leave room for performative-political documentation. Thus, visionary poetry, slips into the conceptual.[41]

From an artistic standpoint, the mutations of perspectives and *modus operandi* into new media and expressive forms may be seen as extending rather then curtailing one's technique and aesthetic reach. Baruchello and Grifi's collaborative work is an exemplary case of the *sguardo espanso* (expanded gaze), a terminology used to qualify a form of independent cinema that incorporates new technologies and strategies that are meant to widen its approach and reach as theorised by Gene Youngblood in 1970.[42] In the middle of the last century Gianfranco Baruchello was in dialogue with a number of intellectuals and artists – including the artist and provocateur Marcel Duchamp – and he is the author, along with the documentary film- and video-maker Alberto Grifi, of the celebrated film *La verifica incerta* (*Disperse Exclamatory Phase*, 1964), which is available in its entirety online.[43] They have both been widely written about online on various sites, and are conspicuously present in digital videos and interviews.[44] Alberto Grifi is included in the Italian version of Wikipedia with a page created under his name, which describes him as a chief representative of Italian experimental cinema, an artist, a film director and the inventor of video-cinematographic devices.[45] On the YouTube channel 'AssociazioneGrifi' the thirty-minute film *La verifica incerta* is described as an incendiary and provocative work:

> A cinematic butchery of famous Hollywood movies' scenes re-edited while thinking of Dada; presented for the first time in Paris, it aroused the excitement of Marcel Duchamp, Man Ray, Max Ernst. It is the ostentatious contempt for many famous Italian film critics. John Cage, enthralled by the soundtrack, introduced it at the New York Museum of Modern Art. This editing method, this "detournement", was inherited by Blob [an Italian TV program] many years later.[46] (sic)

Cyberspace, however, has its own evaluation criteria and peculiar regime; immigration to its 'land of opportunities' introduces new policies and protocols. At the time of writing, the uploaded video has gathered over ten thousand views over seven years, ninety-two 'likes' and one 'dislike', and a single comment. The commenter evokes Marcel Duchamp's enthusiastic reaction to viewing the piece, reiterating and adding irony to a descriptive line on how the 'mutilating' montage is meant as a form of iconoclasm: 'It is the ostentatious contempt for many famous Italian film critics' (sic). 'No wonder. . . '.[47] The mishmash recalls the provocative art forms and iconoclastic avant-gardes of the past century – and, today, proposes the hotchpotch of the visual carnival served online. Its presence online, however wittingly or unwittingly, celebrates and becomes part of the art form of which it is meant to be both a *dénouement* and *detournement*. Grifi's militant video work is part of various scholarly discussions of the 'videotape' age in Italian filmmaking (Figure 10.7).[48]

The idea of extending the reach of the camera and with it that of the human gaze – a propulsive force in independent and experimental cinema – is remembered and reviewed in the documentary *Lo sguardo espanso: Tecniche Miste su Schermo: il cinema sperimentale di Roma, 1965–1975* (*The Expanded Gaze: Mixed Techniques on Screen: The Roman Experimental Cinema, 1965–1975*, 2012–13), which also includes short interviews with several independent filmmakers from those years.[49] The piece is viewable on YouTube, though it is interrupted by full-blown short video-commercials or superimposed with pernicious advertising banners that cover a conspicuous strip of frame. Scholars including Adriano Aprà,[50] Maurizio Calvesi and several filmmakers themselves speak to, and offer their own historiography of, the experimentations and independent efforts of the 1960s onward. The project was spearheaded by Bruno Di Marino, Claudio Del Signore and the Fondazione Rocco Guglielmo di Catanzaro (Foundation Rocco Guglielmo in Catanzaro), which hosted a retrospective under the same title on the artist-filmmakers of that period. Among others, cases such as the multitalented Luca Patella, whose art background includes *incisore* (graver),[51] support the idea that the Italian experimental practice is marked by artistic traditions and trades which have informed and shaped such generation's work in film.

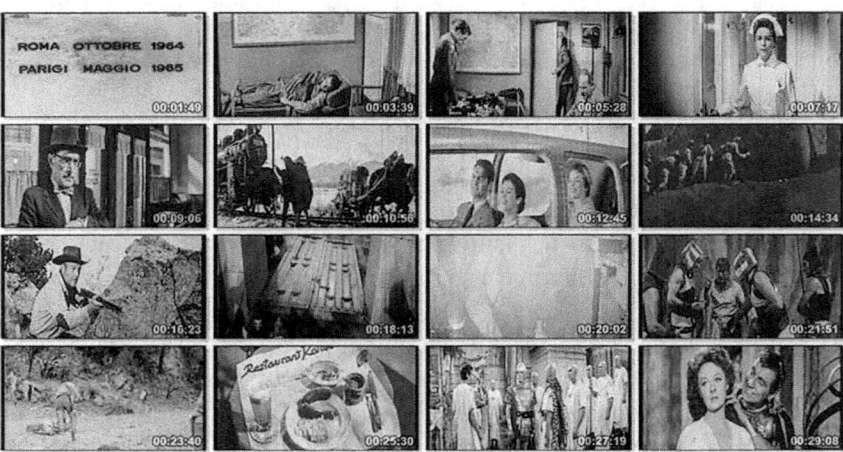

Figure 10.7 *Verifica incerta* (*Disperse Exclamatory Phase*, 1964) by Gianfranco Baruchello, Alberto Grifi.

Patella is known for his conceptual-art approach, and since the 1960s has explored the physical environment through a variety of disciplines including photography, text, graphic design and sound installations. His experimentation with mixed media and his inventive proclivity are further testimony to the Italic creative genius and tradition. His film work includes *Terra Animata* (*Animated Land*, 1967), and *SKMP2* (1968), screened at several international museums and festivals. He was a member of the CCI and made several films for Corona Cinematografica (Crown Cinematograph). The legacy and material related to the latter – a historical company – are now part of the 'filmarchives online' at the Cineteca del Comune di Bologna (City of Bologna Film Library).[52] Segments from his figurative and performative shorts are available to view in the *Lo sguardo espanso* collective documentary referred to above. The painter Ugo Nespolo, a graduate of the Accademia Albertina di Belle Arti (Albertina Academy of Fine Arts) in Turin, also known for his conceptual art, is likewise a distinguished heir of the rich Italian art tradition, and creator of experimental cinema since the '60s. Much of his art is viewable online. He has been written about on Wikipedia,[53] and several of his cinematic works – some of which date back to the 1960s – are available on YouTube in their entirety, such as his *Le gote in fiamme* (*The Cheeks Aflame*, 1967).[54] His diverse Torino Studio productions are emblematic of his eclectic artistry. Nespolo's arts and films span the textures of forms and genres, from painting to sculpture to art-design, and from slapstick to scripted narratives, with an eye to both structured compositions and Dadaist overtures. Another peculiar figure is that of architect and filmmaker Ugo La Pietra, who has given expression to forms of counter-art-cinema with a blend of styles informed by his expertise as a professional architect and artist. La Pietra issued a programmatic vision underpinning his film work. It posits the cinema as an instrument for urban reform and social change, the revelatory paradigm for re-appropriating one's living space and for improving the environment, as total ecology. The manifesto-like document 'Abitare è essere ovunque a casa propria' ('Dwelling Is Feeling at Home Everywhere') is conserved at the Fondazione Ugo La Pietra. It partly reads:

> The space within which we live and operate is the physical description of power ... by which usefulness and routine have created a very rigid behavioural structure ... which does not leave room for any *degree of freedom* and for intervening and participating in the definition and transformation of the same ... The deployment of "cinema" as an instrument of ambient analysis and codification, has become, for a number of years now, the means by which I am able to better develop the second phase of my research: "the critical investigation".[55]

In those years, La Pietra saw converging in the cinema, as a communicative tool, the ideal mix of his professional and artistic aspirations: his architectural urbanistic concerns and the aesthetic means to convey his philosophy of 'better living style'. The enjoyable and ironic *La riappropriazione della città* (*The Re-Appropriation of the City*, 1977), and several other short films, are available for viewing on Vimeo.[56] The 1977 film was made in association with the famous museum and exhibition venue, Centre Georges Pompidou in Paris (Figure 10.8). He is mentioned on Wikipedia and widely present on Vimeo and YouTube, with pieces that range from interviews to art installations.[57] Registering the artists' presence online is part of the introductory discourse on ingenuity and power. In cyberspace such works constitute unrecognised gems within a horde of consumerist trash. If it were not for the interactivity is provides, the online craze would make such material unsearchable. The language factor, however, along with the fact that it represents a rather unknown autochthonous and independent cinema, contributes to making such a presence online appear marginal and negligible, as a mere appendix. Yet, the potential for a grander scale of visibility is conspicuous. The same applies to cineastes who have gradually transitioned from small productions and independent efforts to mainstream products and audiences, from Ferrario to Garrone, to Diritti, to Marra and so on. While the new modalities contradict, and in some cases outright oppose, the underlying philosophy in practices of experimentation and independence, there is little doubt, however, that in some important sense the main objective has been reached: wider dissemination and exhibition.

Figure 10.8 *La riappropriazione della città* (*The Re-Appropriation of the City*, 1977) by Ugo La Pietra, Centre Pompidou Edition.

The Omnivorous Embrace of Cyberspace

Other material worthy of study includes the animations of Rosa Foschi[58] – Patella's partner – the work of artist Pino Pascali (1935–68) who is identified with the Arte Povera (Poor Art) movement, the graphic-alchemic work of Claudio Cintoli (1935–78), the positive-negative configurations of painter Umberto Bignardi, the 'iconoclastic' work, and psychoanalytical propositions, of the painter and scenographer Nato Frascà (1931–2006), the politically charged counter-narratives of Romano Scavolini (1940), and works by many others. Several of such works are characterised by their hybridism, which contributes to their alternative appeal and may draw attention to interdisciplinary study. The availability of such documentary projects online aids the possibility of study and research work into those experimental and unconventional phenomena of independent practices of filmmaking – and the addition of English subtitles in such cases could significantly extend the reach of the work to a broader number of Internet users. The 'omnivorous' nature of cyberspace makes the perusal of such videos possible and potentially enriching – given also their informative and pedagogical value – due to the number of players involved, and to practices of user-generated content and collaborations, which may contribute to 'improving' the level of intellectual exchange and engagement.

Works of so-called *impegno*, that is, of committed engagement with the socio-political milieu of the times, are exemplified in films by Mario Masini, Giorgio Turi and Roberto Capanna, among others. Masini is a graduate from the Centro Sperimentale di Cinematografia, and is also known as a cameraman and a documentarian.[59] Giorgio Turi is likewise known as a documentarian, and as a professional photographer, and has worked in the experimental scene since the 1960s having also contributed to RAI (Italian National Television) programmes.[60] A short biography of Giorgio Turi can be found on the Centro Sperimentale di Cinematografia's official website, as a Fondo (Fund) created at the 'Luigi Chiarini Library'.[61] Alongside Masini, the documentarian Paolo Brunatto[62] – to whom is credited the resourceful documentary *Schegge di Utopia: il cinema underground italiano* (*Utopian Splinters: Underground Italian Cinema*, 2005) – represent cases of filmmakers who did not belong to any co-op, a further statement of self-determination and independence. Like several others from those years, however, Brunatto kept in contact with his American counterparts.

Another important figure is that of Massimo Bacigalupo, spoken about online as a prominent protagonist of experimental and independent Italian cinema in various Italian cities, including Turin and Rome. The Turin Film Festival held a retrospective of his work in 2010 – the catalogue of which offers English translations of several related articles.[63] He is an indefatigable promoter of alternative and experimental cinema to this day, spearheading exhibition and other related cultural activities – and the author of the seminal piece *Il film sperimentale* (*The Experimental Film*), appeared in the journal *Bianco e Nero*, and concerning the decade from the mid Sixties to mid Seventies.[64] He is also a well-known expert on poetry, and taught English literature at the University of Genoa, the capital of his native province – having also studied at Columbia University. He is written about on Wikipedia and several other sites. His silent and 'literary' film *60 metri per il 31 marzo* (*200 Feet for March 31st*, 1968) is available for viewing in its entirety on YouTube (Figures 10.9 and 10.10).[65]

Figures 10.9, 10.10 *60 metri per il 31 marzo* (*200 Feet for March 31st*, 1968) by Massimo Bacigalupo. The representation with zoetrope is from Max Ernst's 1930 illustrated book *Rêve d'une petite fille qui voulut entrer au Carmel* (*Dream of a Girl Who Wanted to Join the Carmelites*).

In his peculiarly poetic way, his work attempts to break with the politicised environment of the later Sixties and onwards, as well as the *riporto* (carry over) pattern imported from overseas, to veer into inventive and erudite projects of his own outside any independent manifesto or programmatic proposition whatsoever. One such example is his film *Warming Up* (1972–3) – segments of which are also found online. How distinctive an experience a contemporary purview of cyberspace turns out to be when navigating from Bacigalupo's 'naturalistic' montage of outdoor camera-excursions to his English or American counterparts found on the same platform, and grouped anachronistically together by Google's algorithms, ultimately depends on the individual viewer. A contradiction felt by the need to break with the socio-politically oriented 'message-films' of the protest movements of those years, re-emerges in the form of a new paradox: video uploads of works, which are independent and unconventional by definition and inspiration, and subsequently get appropriated, reframed and reshaped by the priorities and semantics of Internet technologies' political-economic regime. Exposure is traded for aesthetic quality and purity of experience. There is indeed an ongoing trade-off, in which the multinational corporations increasingly have the 'upper hand', and by which the peculiarly distinctive characteristic of national and independent cinemas is gradually erased by increasing dross and bable. The 'sociability' economy of such online activities – often addictive in themselves – take centre stage in lieu of any artistic and expressive value of the uploaded material. The capital that matters is found in the number of 'clicks' according to the new technocratic giants – whether what is being clicked on are adverts or film frames.

The work and experience of the peculiar decades of experimental and independent Italian filmmaking is partly 'resuscitated' online; however, the viewing experience on cyberspace alters whatever *rapport* the viewer may be expecting to establish. Time may have aged many a perspective, and lack of acquaintance may estrange others. Forms of online conformity tend to flatten cultural traits and make experiences more illusory and cursory – unlike the theatre venues or indigenous event, which in some cases amounted to *happenings*. This paradox is made more conspicuous by the increasing impossibility of independence in cyberspace: its umbilical quality. The users must relinquish most of their will and power, that is, much of their autonomy and freedom. Yet, through so doing they acquire a greater, albeit false, sense of autonomy and independence by conforming 'internally' and 'pragmatically' to the requirements and regime of online protocols. These are pyramidally managed, directed top-down, from the individuals and entities who configure the system and intervene into it to reform its 'evolution' process, down to the self-managed users who are required to continually adapt and adhere to dogmatic directives. This umbilicality is made all the more invasive and suffocating through fingerprinting and tracking software. The imperative is clear: artistic aspirations and personal voice must likewise be legitimised through the same process. Forms of experimentation and independence are appropriated and constrained, if not altogether overridden, just as forms of cultural heritage are being displaced and poured into the undifferentiated environment of cyberculture. If the logic of the industry had ostracised many artists in the 1960s and 1970s, today's macro- and micro-managed neoliberal schemes have seen a reinvention of the tools of commodification and domination, whereby users are turned into new forms of 'human capital'. In the last century, many Italian experimental and independent filmmakers soon abandoned, or were forced to abandon, any aspiration they may have had to pursue a career in filmmaking. Adamo Vergine, a practicing psychiatrist, was an active experimental filmmaker during the 1960s and the founder, along with his brothers Antonio and Aldo, of the Centro di Filmologia e Cinema Sperimentale (Centre for Filmology and Experimental Cinema) and, with Alfredo Leonardi, also among the founders of the Cooperativa Cinema Indipendente (Cooperative of Independent Cinema) – which were both in Naples, before the CCI relocating to Rome. Adamo Vergine quit his filmmaking aspirations and career to devote himself to the medical profession. As a filmmaker he made both Super8 and 16mm film, and 'ideation projects' such as the 1968 *Es-pi'azione* (*Ex-pi'action*) described as 'unicamente una predisposizione registica' ('solely a directorial formulation or frame-of-mind'),[66] and which were never realised (Figure 10.11).[67]

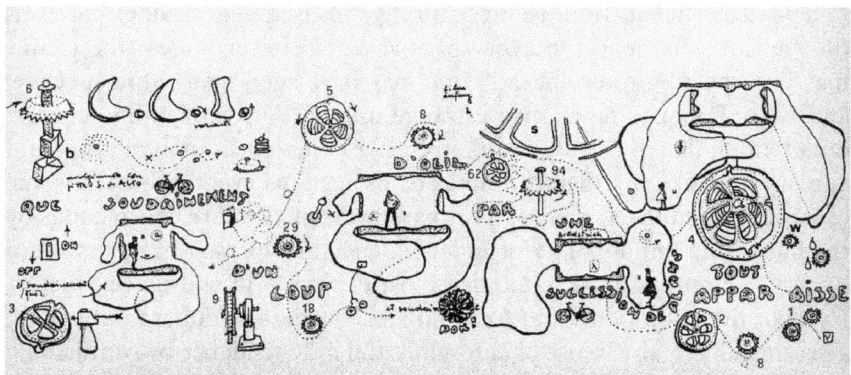

Figure 10.11 *Es-pi'azione* (*Ex-pi'action*, 1968), a directorial formulation by Adamo Vergine. The drawing is described and found in 'Adamo Vergine', in 'Il film sperimentale' by Bacigalupo

Adamo Vergine's short film *Ciao Ciao* (1967) is also available on YouTube.[68] His work was part of a rare screening of Italian independent filmmakers, which included Tonino De Bernardi and Pia Epremian, at the Los Angeles Istituto Italiano di Cultura.[69] The aforementioned documentary *Schegge di utopia* offers a portrait of him, alongside several other experimental and independent artist-filmmakers. The video is viewable on YouTube.[70] Likewise, Pia Epremian, the only woman in the CCI, was active into the 1970s and is the director of *Proussade* (1967), inspired by her own thesis work on Marcel Proust. She is also written about – along with her long-time friend Tonino De Bernardi – on the CSC website and in other online journals.[71] Antonella Porcelluzzi made a documentary film, *Vergine Roma* (*Virgin Rome*, 2017), in which she interviewed Pia Epremian in the spring of 2017, and asked about her 1960s film work.[72] Epremian's film *Pistoletto & Sotheby's* (1968) is viewable online at the LoSpettacolo.it webpage.[73] Though some had a short career, the prominent members of the Italian co-ops had strong profiles as experimental and independent artists. The co-ops functioned as catalysts and support centres for *débutants*, young filmmakers and artists, who sought alternative ways to get their work produced and seen. In many cases they amounted to the only production and distribution option for independent filmmakers, even for some of their maverick associates who hesitated to become supportive members.

> Beyond the good intentions, in factual terms even the cooperatives, often ended up gathering around the author figure. In short, the cooperative was automatically found to compensate for the absence of those "crazy" and courageous producers, who in the '60s allowed "controversial" and "difficult" authors to realize their works (an Alfredo Bini for Pier Paolo Pasolini, for example, or even an Enzo Doria for Marco Bellocchio).[74]

A particular case of 'independent devotion' to the craft is that of Paolo Gioli. He is one of the Italian experimental filmmakers most visible online with several film and videos on sites such as YouTube and much critical academic material on other sites. He was also a member of the CCI, having worked on 16mm projects, in original ways, since the 1960s. He is internationally renowned for pushing the boundaries of photography and camera procedures towards extreme forms of minimalism. He has been written about in scholarly books and journals, including David Bordwell's 'Observations on Film Art: Paolo Gioli, Maximal Minimalist'.[75] His optical experiments are written about in Patrick Rumble's critical essay 'Free Film Made Freely: Paolo Gioli and Experimental Filmmaking in Italy'.[76] The range of his experimentalism is rather broad, from intervention on

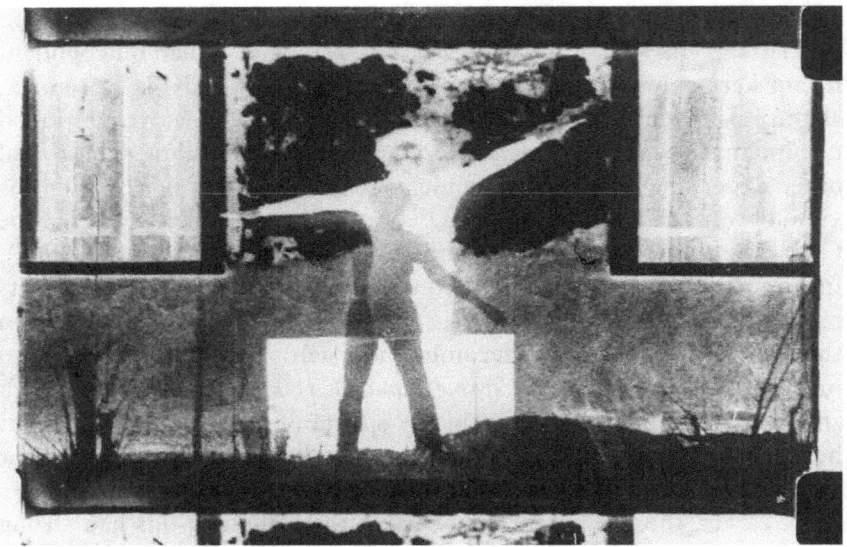

Figure 10.12 *Hilarisdoppio* (1973) by Paolo Gioli.

celluloid to camera techniques to visual subject matter – *Hilarisdoppio* (1973) being one such exemplary case (Figure 10.12).

In his short essay Rumble maintains that the two major periods of Italian independent filmmaking – the 1910s Futurist avant-garde period and the late 1960s artist-run film cooperatives – in many respects share a common drive, that of exploring the expressive potential of the medium of film. Gioli's work is discussed in terms of pressing forward the visual boundaries in photography:

> [Gioli. . .] makes films that call upon a tactile response in his viewers – we might call them "things of imprinted celluloid" – and to do so requires that he do battle, as Rothko did for painting, with the inherited "naturalist" and "illusionary" burdens of his medium—in this case, its photographic basis. And nowhere is the question of perception more central than in the films he made without a movie camera, using his own home-made pin-hole cameras . . . [77]

Other artists of the same period, who knew Gioli and shared ideas with him, were Marinella Pirelli and Piero Bargellini. Marinella Pirelli's official presence online is noted through the archive bearing her name, 'Archivio Marinella Pirelli'.[78] Several of her experimental installations are also viewable as videos on YouTube.[79] Her optical explorations and experimental work since the 1960s have attracted scholarly research in different fields.[80]

THE PARADOX OF 'INDEPENDENCE' IN CYBERSPACE

Though drawn to narrative hyperboles, the idiosyncratic and rather 'colourful' work of Piero Bargellini – also in dialogue with both Gioli and Pirelli – journeys along a similar paradigmatic trajectory. Bargellini joined the Roman CCI and made several films in the late 1960s and in the 1970s, and also worked for the RAI. He engages the cinematic apparatus in totally novel ways, manipulating colours and processes as an 'ingenious' alchemist would. Some of his shorts were aired on late night-hours shows on the 'leftist' station of Rai Tre. One such film is the eccentric silent work *Dove incominciano le gambe* (*Where the Legs Begin*, 1974) (Figure 10.13).[81]

He is also spoken about, alongside other Italian independent filmmakers on the online resource Experimental Cinema.org.[82] His 1969 short film *Nelda* is viewable in its entirety on YouTube.[83]

Some may hold the view that the purpose of experimental and independent cinema, regardless of the personalities and means involved, has remained quite the same across the various decades. They avow that it is the creative freedom that matters the most, the same freedom that underpinned the historical and revolutionary avant-gardes. In the words of one scholarly exponent:

> And perhaps this, most of all, is the task of avant-garde and experimental film artists from Futurism to today: to make films that take spectators to the very edge of

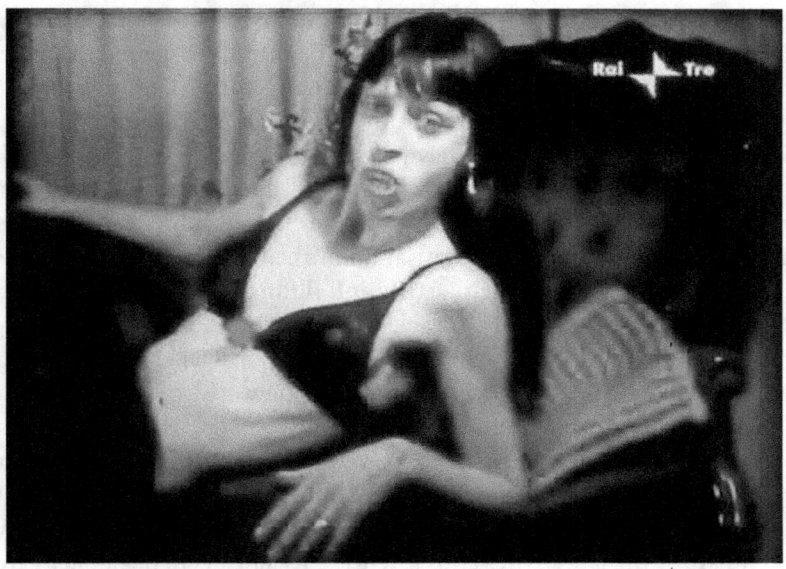

Figure 10.13 Frame from *Dove incominciano le gambe* (*Where the Legs Begin*, 1974) by Piero Bargellini.

human understanding, to the very limits of their own selves, where they can open their eyes, perhaps, and see what is there'.[84]

The same conclusion could be drawn from contemporary independent artist and video-makers were it not for the fact that they are anchored to established social and cultural tropes.[85] The activities artists engange in, within or through, the affordances offered by cyberspace – online editing, hypertextual options, and a host of other regimented choices – prioritise the viral effect over ethnic presence and cultural appreciation, which in most cases appear to be (totally, rather than virtually) absent. For example, within the new era of electronic means, Monica Bonvicini's work in video and photography explores performative paradigms, which carry a considerable historical valence and are culturally situated. They share similarities with other histories discussed herein:

> Monica Bonvicini's *Destroy She Said* (1998) involves the projection of sequences from auteurist cinema featuring women clinging to walls and other architectural elements onto sloping screens that look like unfinished plasterboard walls in a room lit with a red light. The viewer is enabled to re-enact the way in which in the historic avant-garde of cinema architectural space became psychic space, and how that space was gendered.[86]

This descriptive comment seems to amount also to a proposition and invitation, which may be tested by the viewer. Such 'tests', if indeed they are at all possible, may help ascertain the type of culturally oriented experience offered by the 2.0 and 3.0 Web and by the 3D turn. The only prohibition given by the Web is to dare not to know, that is, to be caught out by one's own inability to use and navigate it. Its omnivorous embrace takes on everything, from the most outrageous and horrific to the most banal and innocuous, irrespective of categories or ethnographic traits. The virtual presence online – via the digitisation of their works and recorded personal testimonies – of vanguard artists and filmmakers, such as Bergellini, Patella, Ricci-Lucchi, Piccardo, Bacigalupo and La Pietra, offers an inspirational template on which contemporary video artists can converge and sketch their creative vision in the ethereal online world.

Angela Ricci Lucchi and Yervant Gianikian's work is remarkable as it involves an aesthetic experiment conceived in term of 'clinical historiography'. They have a conspicuous presence online, and both have entries (in Italian) on Wikipedia.[87] They are also rooted in the electrifying and innovative climate of the late Sixties and Seventies. Ricci Lucchi began her career as an experimental filmmaker in the 1970s. In later years she shifted to documentaries, with an 'eye to the past', that is, she experimented in matter

THE PARADOX OF 'INDEPENDENCE' IN CYBERSPACE   243

of form and content with found footage. A number of the post WWI documentary series *Frammenti elettrici* (*Electric Fragments*, 2001–2013), made in collaboration with Yervant Gianikian, are available in their entirety on YouTube.[88] In the latter project they 'reframed' the propagandistic-like work of the historical cameraman Luca Comerio (1878–1940) – pioneer of Italian documentary – who filmed the Italian exploits of the nineteenth and early twentieth centuries for King Vittorio Emanuele III. Ricci Lucchi and her partner Gianikian speak of their film work and philosophy in the short documentary *Stop Forgetting: The Films of Yervant Gianikian and Angela Ricci Lucchi* (2015), uploaded on YouTube (Figure 10.14).[89]

In the *Millennium Film Journal* their work is spoken about as an intervention upon

> [o]rphaned film material. In this sense they become caretakers or custodians, such as when they stewarded the archive of the early documentarian Luca Comerio (1878–1940) – who's directed films include *L'avanzata di Tripolitania* (*The Tripolitania Advance*, 1912) and *Giovinezza, giovinezza, primavera di bellezza* (*Youth, Youth, Spring of Beauty*, 1922) – and by extension also his artistic legacy and reputation.[90]

In this respect, they stand as two extraordinary representatives of an ongoing tradition of retrival, preservation, and re-construction,

Figure 10.14 *Stop Forgetting: The Films of Yervant Gianikian and Angela Ricci Lucchi* (2015).

of filmic artefacts, and their work remains a source of inspiration to younger filmmakers, as well as archivists and curators, transnationally. Their works continue to be exhibited in important galleries and museums, including the Centre Georges Pompidou in Paris.

A conspicuous online presence is likewise that of Silvano Agosti; probably the epitome of the Italian independent filmmaker *per excellence*. He is indeed an emblematic figure in the history of Italian cinema, whose freedom of expression and production modes does not shy away from 'poverty of means' while exploring social, philosophical, or standard fictional narratives with pride and a peculiarly idiosyncratic style. His cinema stands in contraposition to institutionalised models of production, distribution and exhibition; a notable example of the power of micromanaged arts, in this case a practice of independent art cinema, and its ability to affect change in spite of its closure, or outright ostracism, from national industry channels and venues. Agosti has been a long-time curator and exhibitor of independent films and prefers to consider himself an *auteur* rather than a film director (Figure 10.15).

Agosti does not usually employ film crew personnel, and performs most of the film-work himself, from beginning to end. He is world-renowned and widely discussed online on various websites and blogs. *Il giardino delle delizie* (*Garden of Delights*, 1967), Agosti's first feature film, is probably also his best known and celebrated work:

Figure 10.15 Façade of 'Azzuro Scipioni Cinema' in Rome.

[That which...] makes *Il giardino delle delizie* truly remarkable for a viewer today is experiencing it as a loose string of quasi-autonomous images. As with many examples of modern European art cinema of the 1960s, this emphasis on disjointed imagery becomes both a self-conscious alternative to classical storytelling ... and a thematisation of an existentialist experience of the palpable yet mysterious presence of both living and inanimate things.[91]

Videos and clips from his work also abound on YouTube.[92] Moreover, Agosti is a writer and a novelist, the style of which is imbued with his love for moving images. In his interview on *660secondi, Silvano Agosti Il cinema indipendente* (*660seconds, Silvano Agosti The Independent Cinema*, 2012), available on YouTube, he elaborates on the meaning of cinema and gives a heroic, if somewhat startling, explanation of the notion of independence in the cinema:

A person doing independent cinema cannot have a fixed job, have a wife, seven children ... Being an independent filmmaker means to be free, not to depend on anyone or anything. First of all, not to depend on money and on contracts ... By now it's understood that drugs are not as toxic as dependence itself. ... Making independent cinema means above all that none of one's films are examined by the official apparatus of culture, as it has been the case with my own films. My films have never been exhibited in official channels in Italy, except through clandestine projections. But this is to be considered an honor, not a censure. ... I consider it a gift to have had a total of eight retrospectives of my films in Japan! Being independent means first of all being free, close to life and not submerged by existence.[93]

Agosti's radical views on the cinema, as a totalising way of life, underscore both his idealistic perspective on the religious-like meaning cast onto the art of moving-images and the self-sacrificing devotion, the 'devouring passion' or 'holy obsession', it demands in return. Agosti's conspicuous presence online, however, accentuates the paradox. If one's dependence on conventions and traditional industry have a *snaturante* (degenerating) effect on the independent filmmaker, what of the *dipendenza* (dependence or addiction) to new media and cyberspace? The countercultural trends, the alchemies of the materials, the exploration of new frontiers and styles, the revolutionasing times – from the historical avant-gardes to the 1970s and into the new century – appear to be appropriated, 'eugenised' and fed into media technology's autophagous cycle. Historical material undergoes 'homogenisation', is repackaged and then turned into an indistinguishable lump of files for a specific end: generate clicks and blinks. Regardless of filming resources and budgets, of creativity and talent, of subject matter and approaches, of socio-political concerns and cultural traits, the singular character of online material, whatever its origins or flaunted aesthetics, is being erased by new forms of *qualunquismo* (literally: whatever-ism), which stands for 'anything goes' as long as it is ruled by the policies of software and hardware protocols with its political-economic ends.

Not all artists and filmmakers, however, will necessarily take up Internet giants' gargantuan offers – Google, Facebook, Amazon and the like – of potentially uploading limitless hours of filming and videorecordings. The work of Cioni Carpi, a MoMA[94] exhibitor described as a conceptual and Body Art artist, is not easily found online. His video *Egg One Egg Zero* (1972), which was made for Studio46 is one rare artefact found online without registration or membership to a given platform.[95] The film is hosted by Piergiorgio Firinu's YouTube channel,[96] the description and directive of which is given as follows (Figure 10.16):

> The first portal of Italian art – www.artefutura.org – created in 1994. It contains thousands of works of painting, photographs, art books, graphics, posters, art magazines, artists' films, and art catalogs. The Portal is constantly updated and enriched with new content. You can publish news regarding events and exhibitions directly on the blog. Read criticism, and philosophy of art, texts. Follow us, we need your contribution to grow and improve.[97]

Firinu has taken up the challenge and confronted the paradox of independence online. He heads 'Artefutura', an online gallery and portal for visual arts, film and design,[98] and regularly uploads video-blogs on his namesake YouTube channel, alongside a growing gallery of performative art films.

Figure 10.16 Frame from *Egg One Egg Zero* (1972) by Cioni Carpi.

Likewise, the artist and photographer Franco Vaccari has continued to make films since the 1960s, yet his work is rarely found on online platforms. He began his career with Super8 and 16mm experimental films and has worked with video until recently. His biography and work are written about in Italian on Wikipedia and excerpts of his film, *Cani lenti* (*Slow Dogs*, 1971), as well as interviews about his work, are viewable on YouTube.[99] While the Internet may help to further the study, in the English language, of cases such as Vaccari – beyond the sporadic mention in encyclopedias[100] – it challenges artists and users to compete for attention as they rival each other. In some cases, they are also the only viewing public of each other's work. The modalities are not those of the co-ops, Film studio, La casa del cinema (The Cinema House), or supportive cinema-theatre owners, with their cultural promotion programmes, schedules, hosts and live encounters with artists and filmmakers. It is appropriate to wonder whether forms of independence and experimentation are still at all possible when the industry has metamorphosed and flattened its experience into sterile 'cinematic' conformism online. The dilemma persists: the advancement of technology with its relatively affordable use, has further complicated the definition of alternative and unconventional film practices, to the point of utter saturation. During the 1960s the *Ombre elettriche* magazine referred to independent cinema as a cinema of liberation and revolt.[101] Throughout the years, in various circles – including scholarly ones – terms such as experimental, artistic, independent, avantgarde, different, other, expanded, film-maker, video-maker, visual artist and the like are used without clear definitions or demarcations. As has been previously pointed out,[102] the subtle differentiation demanded by historical developments, not to mention the 'hues' of individual artists involved – who are quick to call out what they perceive as generalisations – yield a spectrum of disparate types and characteristics. Increasingly, the challenge is to differentiate and identify meaningful aesthetic and thematic features, and thus cultural forms, in the orgiastic-like glut of moving-images fed to the 'omnivorous' inhabitants of cyberspace.

Likewise, if it were not for the local initiatives of a few, film festivals, no matter how successful or obscure, may acquire meaning only if they are reproduced online. One example, among several others, is that of Ex-Dogana's 'Eterotopia – Linguaggi Ultra Contemporanei' (Heterotopia – Ultra Contemporary Idioms),[103] a travelling festival devoted to the representation and blending of performative action and space. The full video is available on YouTube.[104] Part of the explanatory blurb accompanying the video on YouTube reads:

> The artists are confronted with the interior of the space, with its soul which is trying to survive while its "body" crumbles and from the walls and the ceilings the instants

of the past and of the time keep falling. From the rest, from the absence, the artists develop their interventions conversing among themselves and with the records of the palace in order to create "a different space", of the internal, occupied by their vision which takes the form under the thrust of a thought and becomes sensible.[105] (sic)

It is difficult to make sense of such statements – while appreciating their sources without being distracted by their ungrammatical structure – if not by beginning to acknowledge the technology that made such a video-recording possible as well as its access online. This tendency to write and read poetic, or meta-narrative, patterns into the sensorial and perceptual experience offered by moving images, and into their electronic equivalents, appears to be approaching the breaking point of their illusory experience. The vanguard attempts to author new symbolisms through camera-stylo-like techniques, is now much part of the pseudo-life experience enjoyed on cyberspace; and it may amount to one of the major transformations of moving image arts. The new phenomenology presented to us by electronic technology is complicated by the chaotic jumble and exponential growth of its online players, humans or robots. The peculiar exploration of creative and cinematic language is superseded by, or else altogether loses its singular character in, a stiff, inhuman and computerised *mare dell'oggettività* (sea of objectivity)[106] – to borrow Calvino's conceptualisation of the phenomena of modernity with particular reference to man's rapport with the arts. It is a new mercurial-like 'sea' in which not merely habits and styles are drowned, but the integrity of our perceptual and cognitive faculties drawn, and lost, in it as well (Figures 10.17 and 10.18).

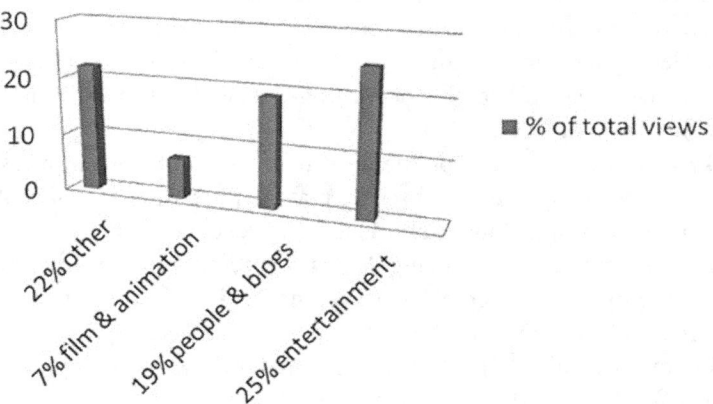

Figure 10.17 Distribution of YouTube video views, 2018. Sourced from Pex, Medium © Statista, <statista.com>.

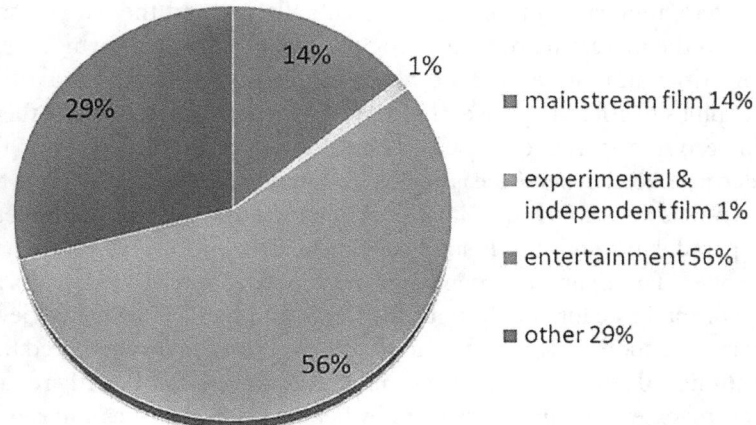

Figure 10.18 Distribution of Italian video views, 2018. Data is partly sourced from ISTAT 'Internet Italia 2018', and from average YouTube views over a 5-year period of several films reference in the anthology.

Concluding Thoughts

Cyberspace and Internet technologies are having a mixed effect on the legacies and transformations of Italian experimental and independent cinema. On the one hand it is partly aiding recognition and dissemination, and on the other it is challenging its development beyond recognition. For the most part Italian institutions, individual artists and users have embraced the new medium with alacrity and have garnered new viewers, and widened their reach, but the viewership is generally quite limited. The environment of cyberspace comes with fierce competition, stealthy operations and treacherous tactics – often the works of the corporations themselves – aided by the vertical management of computer protocols. While to some extent, it is surely contributing to the appreciation of the peculiar brand of Italian experimental cinema and independent practices, and to the dissemination of its rich legacy, it also dictates new forms of subjection and 'taxing' rules that threaten its relevance. It imposes imperatives that overide the modalities and objectives proper to ethnically diverse arts. As a result of the overarching philosophy of online corporations, forms of historicity and ethnicity undergo increasing standardisation and flattening. Archival material and contemporary users' uploads are appraised by the same criteria and receive 'special consideration' – that is, they are initiated into the 'partnership' pantheon – only when the posts or videos reach the required number of viewers' threshold and, thus, raise up the marketability scale. Individual filmmakers, renowned museums, national galleries, and the like, must all submit to the increasing overpowering regime of online platforms' corporate priorities and interests. If we were to apply the definitions and artistic philosophies proffered by several of the film artists reviewed above then it would become apparent that, rather than a renaissance of independent film or video practices, cyberspace is posing a new and formidable challenge that threatens the very survival of its independence and experimental impetus. It is a paradox which is increasingly laying bare the unsolvable conundrum borne by it. To be sure, independence must always be relative – just as any notion of total freedom ought to be illusory – and that is how many viewed the historical cooperatives and their offshoots. The existence tethered to an algorithmic 3.0 (and counting) environment, however, significantly reduces the natural extent of human freedom by bending it to the rules and rigidity of the machine. The versatility and inventiveness of Italian artists and filmmakers of all stripes must veer into different directions and leave the field open to alternatives. This is how Vito Zagarrio put it:

> After the utopian period of the cooperatives, which held a fascination between 1968 and the beginning of the 1970s, young filmmakers became small entrepreneurs of themselves and they founded limited liability companies that allowed productions with partial risk and access to governmental or regional funding.[107]

Niche and local, are not only still meaningful and relevant, they represent a haven in the growing clutter of on- and off-line space. They reaffirm the human over and beyond the technocratic space. The online experience may be viewed as a 'degenerated' form of the historical *cineclub* venue[108] where one's presence is teleported via pixelated frames and avataric options. The context, however, is quite different and the new paradigm and dynamics are such that they require acknowledgement and examination of, rather than remaining oblivious to, their orders and ulterior motives. Internet technologies and the environment of cyberspace can function as important tools, as a catalyst for dissemination and greater exposure; they can enhance the reach and aid the appreciation for practices of innovative forms of cinema, including cultural and national identities, only if the latter learn how to strategise new media's competencies. Importantly, they do pose a 'threat' to the sustainability of local industries, to cultural diversity, to ethnic and individual expression. Italian cinema must capitalise on its legacies and rein in unwanted transformations. Italian independent cinema must learn to take advantage of the new tools without letting the thorny paradox of the same compromise its identity and existence.

Notes

1. Thomas Edison in *The New York Times*, 16 May 1923.
2. Several items from such material are referenced throughout the bibliographies and endnotes of this anthology.
3. See the illustrated anthology of writings edited by D Marino, Meneguzzo, La Porta (2012).
4. See La Polla (2011), 170–91.
5. Jonas Mekas' New American Cinema initiative the 'Film-Makers Cooperative', the British 'London Filmmaker's Coop', and the French 'Paris Film Coop', some of the representatives of which included, respectively: Andy Warhol, Jack Smith, Stan Brakhage; Peter Gidal, Malcolm Le Grice, Stephen Dwoskin; Claudine Eizyk-man, Guy Fihman, Christian Lebrat, among many others.
6. Di Marino, Meneguzzo, La Porta (2012), p. 19.
7. See Bertetto (2011), p. 21.
8. See Bruno Corra's 'Abstract Cinema – Chromatic Music 1912', in Apollonio (1973), p. 67.
9. Here 'texture' refers to both the peculiar aesthetic and semantic quality of the work. See Cristiano (2007).
10. My translation. Original quote: '[L]a grande tradizione pittorica non poteva essere ignorata e chiaramente ha funzionato come serbatoio di idee o riserva di caccia quasi inesauribile per chi si sia proposto nel cinema intenzionalità artistiche o culturali, ma c'è anche qualcosa di più sotterraneo, che fa in modo che questa ricchezza storico-artistica funzioni per così dire a livello genetico, come un crormosoma ispiratore o come una struttura generative profonda'. Bernardi (2011), p. 279.
11. See Collins (2015), pp. 13–14.
12. 'Il cinema sperimentale italiano e la Cooperativa di Roma – Serata in IIC'. (Italian Experimental Cinema and the Roman Cooperative). Available online: <http://www.iicmarsiglia.esteri.it/iic_marsiglia/it/gli_eventi/calendario/2017/09/il-cinema-sperimentale-italiano_0.html>, last accessed September 2017. 'Cinema Sperimentale Italiano 1966–1973: Bacigalupo, Brebbia, De Bernardi', held 11 and 18 October 2019 at Casa del Cinema (Cinema House) Videoteca Panisetti, in Venice, and in collaboration with la Fondazione Cineteca Nazionale.
13. See Lischi (2017), pp. 340–60.
14. Dixon, Foster (2002).
15. Ibid.
16. Available online:<http://www.cinetecamilano.it/>, last accessed 9 May 2017.
17. My translation. Original quote: 'Dal 1947, anno della sua costituzione a Milano, la Cineteca Italiana – diventata fondazione dal 1996 – svolge un'ininterrotta attività di conservazione e valorizzazione del patrimonio filmico e di diffusione della cultura cinematografica sia in Italia che all'estero'. Fondazione wepage: <http://www.cinetecamilano.it/>, last accessed 9 May 2017.
18. English trans., MIC: Interactive Museum of Cinema.

19. Available online: <https://vimeo.com/user33464792>, last accessed May 2017.
20. My tranlsation. Original quote: 'Cos'è per lei il fallimento? / È una parola dura da attribuire a sé stessi. Oltretutto, non avendo mai pensato al successo come a un obiettivo condivisibile, non ho mai subito un vero fallimento. A volte, però, se sono depresso, mi capita di dire: Tonino sei un fallito. Ma è solo un momento. Passa. Se devo immaginare una definizione nella quale riconoscermi, penso di essere un vinto non vinto. Antonio Gnoli, 'Tonino De Bernardi: "Il mio cinema undergraound sparito, io ho perso, ma non mi sento un fallito"', *La Repubblica*, 5 June 2016.
21. Collins (2015), p. 14.
22. Available online: <http://www.fondazionecsc.it/>, last accessed 9 May 2017.
23. My translation. Original quote: 'Carriera iniziata negli anni '60 e caratterizzata da una grande coerenza pur nella molteplicità e varietà delle opere realizzate: film e video militanti e di controinformazione, documentari socio-antropologici, film di sperimentazione. Si tratta di lavori che esprimono un "uso critico" del mezzo audiovisivo, sempre concepito come strumento di indagine e di impegno politico'. Official website: <http://www.fondazionecsc.it/news.jsp?ID_NEWS=1926&areaNews=83&GTemplate>, last accessed 9 May 2017.
24. See *I colori della luce* (*The Colours of Light*, 1963) at: <https://vimeo.com/191166964>, last accessed 3 July 2017.
25. See AAMOD (Archivio Audiovisivo del Movimento Operaio e Democratico – Audiovisual Archive of the Labour and Democratic Movements) at: <http://patrimonio.aamod.it/aamod-web/film/detail/IL8000003246/22/marcello-piccardo-ricorda-bruno-munari.html>, last accessed 5 June 2017.
26. My translation. Original quote: '*Marcello Piccardo,* pioniere del Cinema, è una di quelle figure anomale che hanno lasciato un segno nella cultura dell'Italia degli anni Sessanta. Film-maker e intellettuale eclettico applicò i modi linguistici dell'avanguardia al cinema industriale, realizzando alcuni dei più riusciti commercials della storia della pubblicità. Il suo gusto per la scoperta lo portarono a partecipare alle prime esperienze televisive italiane e a dare vita all'originale e utopica esperienza del monte Olimpino assieme a Bruno Munari'. See Studio di Monte Olimpino: <http://www.noprofit.org/diapason/piccardo.html>, last accessed 5 June 2017. See official webpage at <http://nuke.monteolimpino.it/icoloridellaluce/tabid/474/Default.aspx>, last accessed 12 September 2017.
27. See *Tempo nel Tempo*, at: <https://www.youtube.com/watch?v=EkwpuZRCxmk>, last accessed 5 June 2017.
28. See a short biography of some of the pioneers of independent and experimental filmmaking and a chronohistory of the 1960s 'Studio di Monte Olimpino' at: <http://www.noprofit.org/diapason/piccardo.html>, last accessed 5 June 2017.
29. See a short biography on Enrica Viola at: <http://www.unafilm.it/about-us/>, last accessed 3 July 2017.

30. See 'Marcello Piccardo' and videos uploaded by Andrea Piccardo at: <https://www.youtube.com/results?search_query=Marcello+Piccardo>, last accessed 3 July 2017.
31. See 'Marcello Piccardo' at: <https://www.youtube.com/watch?v=rUG_Qv68sO4>, last accessed 3 July 2017.
32. See '*Schegge di utopia* – it cinema underground italiano' at: <https://www.youtube.com/watch?v=ObIXg0n2y6A>, last accessed 3 July 2017.
33. BFI (British Film Institute) at: <http://www.bfi.org.uk/films-tv-people/4ce2bbb921ef4>, last accessed 20 June 2017.
34. On traditional Calabrian folk music see Bronzini (1990), pp. 405–50.
35. NRSV Matthew 6.22-23: 'The eye is the lamp of the body. So, if your eye is healthy, your whole body will be full of light; but if your eye is unhealthy, your whole body will be full of darkness. . . ."
36. An excerpt of Leonardi's film is shown in the documentary Schegge di Utopia by Paolo Brunatto, in the series dedicated to Alfredo Leonardi and his film work – which is available to view online.
37. Gianni Castagnoli on BFI: <http://www.bfi.org.uk/films-tv-people/4ce2ba622af53>, last accessed 3 July 2017.
38. See Gianni Castangoli's *Valentino Moon* (Exceprt) at: <https://vimeo.com/93059147>, last accessed 3 July 2017.
39. Di Marino (2008), p. 422.
40. My translation: '[T]he ruling of the Constitutional Court on the radio and television monopoly . . . The historical-political context is that of the aftermath of the "historic compromise", of the emergence of the "Autonomy", the time of the Red Brigades, of the kidnapping and murder of Aldo Moro, and then, increasingly, of an Italy anemic in values, unable to construct new ideals on the ground of society and culture, and even incapable of representing one's own conflicts (such as terrorism) in its artistic expressions, particularly in the cinema. In short, at first sight the view appears desolate'. Original quote: '[L]a sentenza della Corte Costituzionale sul monopolio radiotelevisivo . . . Il contesto storico-politico è quello del dopo compromesso storico, dell'esplosione dell'Autonomia, delle Brigate Rosse, del delitto Moro, e poi di un'Italia via via sempre più anemica di valori, incapace di costruire nuovi ideali sul terreno della società e della cultura, e persino incapace di rappresentare i propri conflitti (come il terrorismo) nelle sue espressioni artistiche, il cinema su tutte. Insomma, si tratta a prima vista di un panorama desolante'. Zagarrio (2005b), p. 6.
41. My translation. Original quote: 'Dopo il 1970, con la diffusione anche in Italian dei primi *portapack* (videocamera e rigistratore portatili), il medium elettronico si affianca a, o sostituisce, quello filmico nella practica di molti artisti. Un'epoca sta probabilmente tramontando e il versante più poetico e inconscio del cinema (*Se l'inconscio si ribella* è il titolo di uno dei cortometraggi di Leonardi) lascia il posto alla documentazione performativo-politica. La poesia visionaria slitta nel concettuale'. Di Marino (2014), p. 6.

42. See Youngblood (1970).
43. See *La verifica incerta* (*Disperse Exclamatory Phase*, 1964) at: <https://www.youtube.com/watch?v=hmhvr3RbGnA>, last accessed 5 July 2017.
44. See 'Baruchello and Grifi' at: <https://www.youtube.com/results?search_query=Baruchello+%26+Grifi>, last accessed 5 July 2017.
45. See Alberto Grifi at: <https://it.wikipedia.org/wiki/Alberto_Grifi>, last accessed 5 July 2017.
46. My translation. Original quote: 'Un massacro cinematografico di film hollywoodiani famosi rimontati pensando al Dada; presentato per la prima volta a Parigi suscitò l'entusiasmo di Marcel Duchamp, Man Ray, Max Ernst. È l'ostentato disprezzo di molti famosi critici cinematografici italiani. John Cage, entusiasta della colonna sonora, lo presentò al New York Museum of Modern Art. Questo metodo di montaggio, questo "detournement", fu ereditato da "Blob" molti anni dopo'. *La verifica incerta*: <https://www.youtube.com/watch?v=hmhvr3RbGnA>, last accessed 5 July 2017.
47. Ibid. Original quote: '[D]isprezzo di molti famosi critici cinematografici italiani'. 'Chissà perché, la cosa non mi stupisce'.
48. Lischi (2005b), pp. 91–102.
49. See compilation of 'Tecniche Miste su Schermo: il cinema sperimentale di Roma, 1965–1975' in 'Lo sguardo Espanso: cinema d'artista italiano un antologia – rarovideo (The Expanded Gaze: Italian Art Cinema an Anthology – rarevideo', at: <https://www.youtube.com/watch?v=Xt-8AQ9YwT0>, last accessed 5 July 2017.
50. Adriano Aprà is the author of the eponymous searchable website devoted to the history of cinema <www.adrianoapra.it>, last accessed 15 September 2018. The site is devoted to the history of cinema and on it are also found pages dedicated to a number of independent and experimental filmmakers. The site includes articles, photographs and videorecordings.
51. A dedicated page on Patella's life and work is found on the 'The Galleria Il Ponte" site at: <http://www.galleriailponte.com/en/luca-maria-patella-en/>, last accessed 4 October 2017.
52. See Cineteca di Bologna at: <http://www.cinetecadibologna.it/archivi/corona>, last accessed 12 July 2017.
53. See Ugo Nespolo at: <https://en.wikipedia.org/wiki/Ugo_Nespolo>, last accessed 12 July 2017.
54. See *Le gote in fiamme* (*The Cheeks Aflame*, 1967) at: <https://www.youtube.com/watch?v=2XHsHFFae8U>, last accessed 12 July 2017.
55. My translation. Original quote: 'Lo spazio all'interno del quale ci troviamo a vivere ed a operare è la descrizione fisica del potere . . . in cui l'utilità e l'abitudine hanno creato una struttura di comportamento molto rigida. . . . che non lascia *nessun grado di libertà* e di intervento per la partecipazione alla definizione e trasformazione della stessa . . . L'uso del «cinema» come strumento di analisi ambientale e di codificazione, da alcuni anni, è diventato il mezzo con cui riesco meglio a sviluppare il secondo momento della mia ricerca: «la lettura critica»'. La Pietra (2019), pp. iii–iv.

56. See *La riappropriazione della città* (*The Re-Appropriation of the City*, 1977), at: <https://vimeo.com/11457755>, last accessed 12 July 2017.
57. See 'Ugo La Pietra' at: <https://www.youtube.com/results?search_query=Ugo+La++Pietra+cinema>, last accessed 12 July 2017.
58. Foschi's work is viewable at multimedia sites such as: <http://www.muspac.com/2017/11/28/foschi-rosa/> and, <http://www.hybridacontemporanea.it/artists/rosa-foschi/>, last accessed 4 October 2017.
59. See Mario Masini's cinematographic career span at: <http://www.imdb.com/name/nm0556415/>, last accessed 12 July 2017.
60. See 'Istituto il Fondo Giorgio Turi presso la Biblioteca "Luigi Chiarini" (Institution of Giorgio Turi Foundation at the "Luigi Chiarini" Library)' at: <http://www.fondazionecsc.it/news.jsp?ID_NEWS=2633&areaNews=8&GTemplate=news.jsp>, last accessed 12 July 2017.
61. See CSC: <http://www.fondazionecsc.it/news.jsp?ID_NEWS=2633&areaNews=8&GTemplate=news.jsp>, last accessed 5 June 2017.
62. See 'Paolo Brunatto' on BFI and Wikipedia: <http://www.bfi.org.uk/films-tv-people/4ce2ba3d05d88;https://it.wikipedia.org/wiki/Paolo_Brunatto>, last accessed 12 July 2017.
63. Bursi, Causo (2010), pp. 135–62.
64. Bacigalupo (1974), pp. 58–62.
65. See *60 metri per il 31 marzo* (*200 Feet for March 31st*, 1968) at: <https://www.youtube.com/watch?v=KFFSg6dUmac>, last accessed 12 July 2017.
66. See 'Adamo Vergine' in Bacigalupo (1974), pp. 179–81.
67. Ibid., p. 181.
68. See *Ciao Ciao* (1967) by Adamo Vergine at: <https://www.youtube.com/watch?v=9vMM-7eTNvE>, last accessed 12 July 2017.
69. See programme at the official website for the IIC: <http://www.iiclosangeles.esteri.it/iic_losangeles/en/gli_eventi/calendario/2017/07/part-ii-artists-and-experimental.html>, last accessed 12 July 2017.
70. See 'Schegge di utopia - Il cinema underground Italiano, Alfredo Leonardi' at: <https://www.youtube.com/watch?v=cMhO8H-b5I0>, last accessed 14 July 2017.
71. See Centro Sperimentale di Cinematografia at http://www.fondazionecsc.it/news.jsp?ID_NEWS=336&areaNews=10&GTemplate=news.jsp, and 'Pia Epremian, the 'ragazza col super8' (Pia Epremian, the girl with the super8 camera)' on the communist paper *Il Manifesto*, at: <https://ilmanifesto.it>, last accessed 14 July 2017.
72. See *Vergine Roma* (*Virgin Rome*, 2017) at: <https://www.youtube.com/watch?v=cABo_pYDvGE>, last accessed 14 July 2017.
73. See *Pistoletto & Sotheby's* (1968) at: <http://www.lospettacolo.it/persona/pia+epremian+de+silvestris/>, last accessed 14 July 2017.
74. My translation. Original quote: 'Al di là dei buoni propositi, nei fatti anche la cooperativa, sovente, finì con l'aggregarsi attorno alla figura e alla persona dell'*autore*. La cooperativa, in breve, si trovò automaticamente a supplire l'assenza di quei produttori "folli", coraggiosi, che negli anni '60 avevano consentito ad autori "scomodi" e "difficili" di realizzare le loro opere (un

Alfredo Bini per Pier Paolo Pasolini, per intendersi, o anche un Enzo Doria per Marco Bellocchio)'. De Bernardinis (2008a), p. 482.
75. See 'Paolo Gioli, maximal minimalist' at: <http://www.davidbordwell.net/blog/2016/04/19/paolo-gioli-maximal-minimalist/>, last accessed 14 July 2017.
76. Rumble (2009), pp. 10–16.
77. Ibid., pp. 13–14.
78. See Archivio Marinella Pirelli main page at: <http://www.marinellapirelli.org/>, last accessed 14 July 2017.
79. See 'Marinella Pirelli' at: <https://www.youtube.com/results?search_query=Marinella+Pirelli>, last accessed July 2017.
80. See Elwes (2015), pp. 172–80; 'Marinella Pirelli' at *Experimental Cinema: News and Resources on Experimental Film* at: <https://expcinema.org/site/en/tags/marinella-pirelli>, last accessed 14 July 2017. A chapter on her work is also found in the present anthology, written by Matilde Nardell.
81. See *Dove incominciano le gambe* (*Where the Legs Begin*, 1974) at: <https://www.youtube.com/watch?v=NTQSlrrnooA>, last accessed 14 July 2017.
82. See 'Piero Bargellini' at: <https://expcinema.org/site/en/tags/piero-bargellini>, last accessed 14 July 2017.
83. See Piero Bargellini's *Nelda* (1969), at: <https://www.youtube.com/watch?v=PbpAyXCXCTA>, last accessed 14 July2017.
84. Rumble, (2009), p. 16.
85. See Lischi (2005), pp. 457–71; and Cristiano (2015), pp. 415–22.
86. See Newman (2009), p. 121.
87. See Angela Ricci Lucchi at: <https://it.wikipedia.org/wiki/Angela_Ricci_Lucchi>, last accessed 14 July 2017.
88. See *Frammenti elettrici* (Electric Fragments, 2009) at: <https://www.youtube.com/watch?v=iRcRcFJU4X0>, last accessed 14 July 2017.
89. See *Stop Forgetting: The Films of Yervant Gianikian and Angela Ricci Lucchi* (2015) at: <https://www.youtube.com/watch?v=i1R2_7QeVVQ>, last accessed 14 July 2017.
90. De Cuir, De Rosa (2016), p. 69. Paolo Bertetto and Andrea Minuz also refer to their experimental turn in the 1990s; see Bertetto, Minuz (2011), p. 142.
91. Pethó (2014), p. 478.
92. See list of content at: <https://www.youtube.com/results?search_query=Silvano+Agosti>, last accessed 14 July 2017.
93. My translation. Original quote: 'Una persona che fa il cinema indipendente non può avere un lavoro fisso, avere la moglie, sette figli . . . Far cinema indipendente significa essere liberi, non dipendere da nessuno, e da nessuna cosa. Prima di tutto non dipendere dal denaro, non dipendere dai contratti . . . Ormai si è capito che non è tanto la droga a essere tossica ma la dipendenza. . . . Fare cinema indipendente significa soprattutto che nessuno dei tuoi film viene preso in esame dall'apparato ufficiale della cultura, come è accaduto ai miei. I miei film non sono mai usciti in Italia, se non attraverso proiezioni clandestine.

Ma questo è un honore che ti viene fatto, non una censura. . . . In Giappone ho avuto questo dono di otto rassegne totali dei miei film! Essere indipendenti vuol dire prima di tutto essere liberi e vicini alla vita e non sommersi nell'esistenza'. See *660secondi, Silvano Agosti Il cinema indipendente* (*660seconds, Silvano Agosti The Independent Cinema*, 2012), at: <https://www.youtube.com/watch?v=u0Vu-_ms0jk>, last accessed 14 July 2017.

94. See 'Cioni Carpi' at MoMA (Museum of Modern Art): <https://www.moma.org/artists/65922>, last accessed 16 May 2017.
95. 'Artefutura Film di Cioni Carpi' at: <https://www.youtube.com/watch?v=4EpjPdCi0Pk>, last accessed 16 May 2017.
96. Piergiorgio Firinu's YouTube channel: <https://www.youtube.com/user/artefuturafondazione>, last accessed 16 May 2017.
97. My translation. Original quote: 'Il portale dell'arte italiana www.artefutura.org creato nel 1994, primo portale dell'arte. Contiene migliaia di opere di pittura, fotografie, libri d'artista, grafiche, poster, riviste d'arte, film d'artista, cataloghi d'arte. Il Portale viene costantemente aggiornato e arricchito di nuovi contenuti. Puoi pubblicare direttamente sul blog notizie di eventi e mostre. Leggere i testi di critica e filosofia dell'arte. Seguici, abbiamo bisogno del tuo contributo per crescere e migliorare'. See 'About' page at: <https://www.youtube.com/user/artefuturafondazione>, last accessed 16 May 2017.
98. See 'Artefutura: Il portate italiano di arte contemporanea' ('The Italian Portal for Contemporary Arts') at: <http://www.artefutura.org/>, last accessed 7 June 2017.
99. See *Cani lenti* (*Slow Dogs*, 1971) at: <https://www.youtube.com/watch?v=GjUq4A30ymg>, last accessed 14 July 2017.
100. See 'Sperimentale, Cinema' in *Enciclopedia Treccani* at: <http://www.treccani.it/enciclopedia/cinema-sperimentale_%28Enciclopedia-del-Cinema%29/>, last accessed 14 July 2017. Studies which include Vaccari, in Italian, appear in the reference section.
101. 'Editorial' in *Ombre elettriche* (reprint 1974), pp. 152–3.
102. Lischi (2017), pp. 340–41.
103. See 'Eterotopia (Catanzaro) Full Video' at: <https://www.youtube.com/watch?v=FMHrR78uTEU>, last accessed 14 July 2017.
104. Ibid.
105. Ibid.
106. Calvino (1960), pp. 54–8. See Germini (2015).
107. My translation. Original quote: 'Finita l'utopia delle cooperative, che aveva avuto un certo fascino tra il 1968 e l'inizio degli anni '70, i giovani cineasti diventano piccoli imprenditori di se stessi e fondano delle società a responsabilità limitata che permettono di produrre con rischio parziale e di accedere ai finanziamenti governativi o regionali'. Zagarrio (2005b), p. 29.
108. See Zagarrio (2005c), pp. 601–22.

Works Cited

Agosti, Silvano (1987), *Uova di garofano: romanzo breve*, Rome: Edizioni L'immagine.
Agosti, Silvano (2003), *Il semplice oblio: romanzo*, Rome: L'immagine.
Apollonio, Umbro, ed. & trans. (1973), *Futurist Manifestos: The Documents of 20th Century Art*, New York: Viking Press.
Aprà, Adriano ed. (2013), *Fuori norma. La via sperimentale del cinema italiano*, Venice: Marsilio Editori.
Aprà, Adriano (2006), 'Cinema sperimentale e mezzi di massa in Italia', in Cosetta Saba ed., *Cinema video internet. Tecnologie e avanguardie in Italian dal Futurismo alla Net.art*, Bologna: CLUEB, pp. 177–91.
Aprà, Adriano (1986), *New American Cinema: il cinema indipendente americano degli anni Sessanta*, Milan: Ubulibri.
Aprà, Adriano (1976), *Cinema sperimentale e mezzi di massa in Italia*, Milan: Fondazione Angelo Rizzoli.
Bacigalupo, Massimo ed. (1974), *Il film sperimentale*, Special Edition of *Bianco e Nero*, 8.35 (May–August): 1–187.
Bacigalupo, Massimo ed. (2010), 'Dreaming a Life in Films', in Giulio Bursi, Massimo Causo eds., 'Massimo Bacigalupo' *28° Torino Film Festival* (Museo Nazionale del Cinema, Turin): 142–3.
Berghaus, Günter ed. (2000), International Futurism in Arts and Literature, Berlin: Walter de Gruyter.
Bernardi, Sandro (2011), 'L'inquadratura e il quadro. Presenza della pittura nel cinema italiano', in Paolo Bertetto ed., *Storia del cinema italiano. Uno sguardo d'insieme*, Venice: Marsilio, Edizioni di Bianco e Nero, pp. 279–300.
Bertetto, Paolo ed. (1983), *Il cinema d'avanguardia: 1910–1930*, Venice: Marsilio.
Bertetto, Paolo ed. (2011), *Storia del cinema italiano. Uno sguardo d'insieme*, Venice: Marsilio, Edizioni di Bianco e Nero.
Bertetto, Paolo, Andrea Minuz (2011), 'Le forme antirappresentative nel cinema italiano', in Paolo Bertetto, *Storia del cinema italiano. Uno sguardo d'insieme*, Venice: Marsilio, Edizioni di Bianco e Nero, pp. 117–46.
Bordwell, David, Kristin Thompson (1997), *Film Art. An Introduction*, New York: McGraw-Hill.
Brenez, Nicole, Christian Lebrat (2001), *Jeune, dure et pure! Une histoire du cinéma d'avant-garde et expérimental en France*, Cinémathèque Française: Paris-Milan.
Bronzini, Giovanni Battista (1990), 'Raffaele Lombardi Satriani e il piacere del folklore: Raccogliendo e commentando canti e racconti calabresi', *Lares*, 56.3 (luglio-settembre): 405–45.
Burke, Frank (2017), *A Companion to Italian Cinema*, Hoboken, NJ: John Wiley & Sons.
Bursi, Giulio, Massimo Causo, eds. (2010), 'Massimo Bacigalupo', *28° Torino Film Festival* (Museo Nazionale del Cinema, Turin): 135–62.

Calvino, Italo (1960), 'Il mare dell'oggettività', *Il menabò 2*, Turin: Giulio Einaudi Editore, pp. 54–8.
Cappabianca, Alessandro (2012), *Carmelo Bene: Il cinema oltre se stesso*, Cosenza: Luigi Pellegrini.
Censi, Rinaldo (2015), 'Tychic Motifs and Hidden Details: The Work of Yervant Gianikian & Angela Ricci Lucchi', *Journal of Film Preservation*, 93 (October): 33–40.
Collins, John (2015), 'Further Notes from Italy, 1970'. Extract, in *Tate Film. If Arte Povera Was Pop: Artists' and Experimental Cinema in Italy 1960s-70s*, Tate Modern Starr Auditorium, 23–5 (October): 13–14, <tate.org.uk/film>, last accessed 10 July 2017.
Comer, Stuart, ed. (2009), *Film and Video Art*, London: Tate Publishing.
Corra, Bruno (1912), 'Abstract Cinema – Chromatic Music 1912', in Umbro Apollonion ed. (1973), *Futurist Manifestos Futurist Manifestos: The Documents of 20th Century Art*, New York: Viking Press, p. 67.
Costa, Antonio (2002), *Il cinema e le arti visive*, Turin: Einaudi.
Costa, Antonio (2012), 'Otto frammenti di un discorso lacunoso: Il film d'artista nel contesto del cinema italiano', in Di Marino, Bruno, Marco Meneguzzo, Andrea La Porta, eds., *Lo sguardo espanso. Cinema d'artista italiano 1912–2012*, Cinesello Balsamo (Milan): Silvana Editoriale, pp. 42–5.
Cristiano, Anthony (2017), 'Appropriating the Film text in a Digital Age', *filmmaking.net* (17 April 2007), <https://www.filmmaking.net/blog/show_article.asp?id=53>, last accessed 10 May 2017.
Cristiano, Anthony (2015), 'Experimentations in Modern Media into the Twenty-first Century and Bongiò's Cilindro Raku: Numera una and Backstage (Formazione Radial, 1AmuLtimediA 2007–10:34, and 14:30)–Bongiò; Numera seconda and Backstage (1AmuLtimediA 2007–HD 14:38, and 12:38)–Marcello Bongiò', *Journal of Italian Cinema & Media Studies*, 3.3 (June): 415–22.
De Bernardinis, Flavio ed. (2008), *Storia del cinema italiano. Volume XII – 1970/1976*, Venice: Marsilio, Edizioni di Bianco e Nero.
De Bernardinis, Flavio ed. (2008), 'Ipotesi per nuovi modelli di produzione e distribuzione. 1970–1976: appunti per una mutazione', in Flavio De Bernardinis ed., *Storia del cinema italiano. Volume XII – 1970/1976*, Venice: Marsilio, Edizioni di Bianco e Nero, pp. 478–85.
De Cuir, Greg Jr., Miriam De Rosa (2016), 'A Treatise on the Apparatus and the Artistic Yield of Yervant Gianikian & Angela Ricci Lucchi', *Millennium Film Journal* 64 (Fall): 68–75.
Di Marino, Bruno (2002), *Interferenze dello sguardo. La sperimentazione audiovisiva tra analogico e digitale*, Rome: Bulzoni.
Di Marino, Bruno (2014), 'Lo sguardo, la tela, lo schermo. Gli anni Sessanta a Roma e dintorni ovvero: l'âge d'or del cinema d'artista italiano', *Flash Art* (maggio-giugno): 1–6, <http://www.flashartonline.it/article/lo-sguardo-la-tela-lo-schermo/>, last accessed 5 July 2017.

Di Marino, Bruno, Marco Meneguzzo, Andrea La Porta eds. (2012), *Lo sguardo espanso. Cinema d'artista italiano 1912–2012*, Cinesello Balsamo (Milan): Silvana Editoriale.

Di Marino, Bruno (2008), 'Oltre l'underground. Il cinema di ricerca, il videotape e l'animazione d'autore', in Fulvio De Bernardinis ed., *Storia del cinema italiano. Volume XII – 1970/1976*, Venice: Marsilio, Edizioni di Bianco e Nero, pp. 422–34.

Dixon, Wheeler W., Gwendolyn Audrey Foster (2002), *Experimental Cinema: The Film Reader*, New York: Routledge.

'Editorial' (1967), in *Ombre elettriche* (December), reprinted 1974, in *Bianco e Nero* (May-August): 152–3.

Elwes, Catherine (2015), *Installation and Moving Image*, New York: Columbia University Press.

Germini, Simone (2015), 'Italo Calvino – Il mare dell'oggettività', *Arti Umanistiche e Letteratura* (30 luglio), <http://freemaninrealworld.altervista.org/italo-calvino-il-mare-delloggettivita/> last accessed 5 July 2017.

Gnoli, Antonio (2016), 'Tonino De Bernardi: 'Il mio cinema undergraound sparito, io ho perso, ma non mi sento un fallito', *La Repubblica*, 5 June 2016.

Lajolo, Anna, and Guido Lombardo (1994), *L'isola in capo al mondo*, Turin: Nuova ERI.

Lane, John Francis (2002), 'Carmelo Bene: Actor and writer whose iconoclasm shocked Italy', *The Guardian*, 18 March 2002, <https://www.theguardian.com/culture/2002/mar/18/artsfeatures2> last accessed 5 July 2017.

La Pietra, Ugo (2019), 'Abitare è essere ovunque a casa propria', Fondazione Ugo La Pietra, pp. iii-vi.

La Polla, Franco (2011), 'L'americanizzazione del cinema italiano', in Paolo Bertetto ed., *Storia del cinema italiano. Uno sguardo d'insieme*, Venezia: Marsilio, Edizioni di Bianco e Nero, pp. 170–91.

Le Grice, Malcolm (2001), *Experimental Cinema in the Digital Age*, London: British Film Institute.

Lischi, Sandra (2017), 'Independents, Experimentalists: A Premise', in Frank Burke ed., *A Companion to Italian Cinema*, Hoboken, N.J.: John Wiley & Sons, pp. 340–60.

Lischi, Sandra (2005), 'Elettronica, videoarte e poetronica', in Vito Zagarrio ed., *Storia del cinema italiano. Volume XIII – 1977/1985*, Venice: Marsilio, Edizioni di Bianco e Nero, 457–71.

Lischi, Sandra (2005), 'Senza chiedere permesso: il videopate e il cinema militante', in Vito Zagarrio ed., *Storia del cinema italiano. Volume XIII – 1977/1985*, Venice: Marsilio, Edizioni di Bianco e Nero, pp. 91–102.

Magri, Lorenzo ed. (1995), *Centro Video Arte 1974–1994: videoarte performance partecipazioni*, Ferrara: Gabriele Corbo Editore.

Meneguzzo, Marco (2012), 'Il territorio mutante. Il film d'artista nel contesto dell'arte italiana: i primi cento anni', in Di Marino, Bruno, Marco Meneguzzo, Andrea La Porta, eds., *Lo sguardo espanso. Cinema d'artista italiano 1912–2012*, Cinesello Balsamo (Milan): Silvana Editoriale, pp. 36–41.

Mitry, Jean (2006), *Storia del cinema sperimentale*, Milan: CLUEB.
Newman, Michael (2009), 'Moving Image in the Gallery since the 1990s', in Stuart Comer ed., *Film and Video Art*, London: Tate Publishing, pp. 88–121.
Noguez, Dominique (1979), *Éloge du cinéma expérimental: définitions, jalons, perspectives*, Paris: Centre Georges Pompidou.
Panaro, Luca (2007), *L'occultamento dell'autore. La ricerca artistica di Franco Vaccari*, Carpi (MO): AMPedizioni.
Pendleton, David (2012), 'Inutile: The Cinema of Carmelo Bene', *Harvard Film Archive* (30 March – 2 April): 1, <http://hcl.harvard.edu/hfa/films/2012janmar/bene.html accessed 5 July 2017.
Pethó, Agnes (2014), 'The Garden of Intermedial Delights: Cinematic 'Adaptations' of Bosch, from Modernism to the Postmedia Age', *Screen* 55.4 (December): 471–89.
Piccardo, Marcello (1992), *La collina del cinema*, Como: Nodo Libri.
Rees, Alan Leonard (1999), *A History of Experimental Film and Video*, London: British Film Institute.
Rees, Alan Leonard (2009), 'Movements in art 1912–40', in Stuart Comer ed., *Film and Video Art*, London: Tate Publishing, pp. 26–65.
Rumble, Patrick (2009), 'Free Films Made Freely: Paolo Gioli and Experimental Filmmaking in Italy', *CineAction* 78 (Winter): 10–16.
Silvestri, Roberto ed. (1993), *Il cinema contro di Alberto Grifi*, Atripalda (AV): Edizioni Laceno.
Sitney, P. Adams (2000), '*Il cinema d'avanguardia*', in Gian Piero Brunetta ed., *Storia del cinema mondiale*, Vol. 2 Gli Stati Uniti, Turin: Einaudi, pp. 1569–603.
Subrizi, Carla ed. (2004), *Baruchello e Grifi. Verifica incerta. L'arte oltre i confini del cinema*, Rome: Derive Approdi.
Tempesta, Manuela ed. (2008), *Alberto Grifi: oltre le regole del cinema*, Atripalda (AV): Edizioni Laceno.
Tate Film. *If Arte Povera Was Pop: Artists' and Experimental Cinema in Italy 1960s–70s* (2015), Tate Modern Starr Auditorium (23–25 October): 1–32, <tate.org.uk/film>, last accessed 5 July 2017.
Youngblood, Gene (1970), *Expanded Cinema*, Buckminster Fuller intro., New York: Dutton.
Zagarrio, Vito (2011), 'I modi di produzione', in Paolo Bertetto ed., *Storia del cinema italiano. Uno sguardo d'insieme*, Venice: Marsilio, Edizioni di Bianco e Nero, pp. 147–66.
Zagarrio, Vito ed. (2005), *Storia del cinema italiano. Volume XIII – 1977/1985*, Venice: Marsilio, Edizioni di Bianco e Nero.
Zagarrio, Vito (2005), 'Dopo la morte dei padri. Dagli anni della crisi agli albori della rinascita', in Vito Zagarrio ed., *Storia del cinema italiano. Volume XIII – 1977/1985*, Venice: Marsilio, Edizioni di Bianco e Nero, pp. 3–42.
Zagarrio, Vito (2005), 'Nuove forme del consumo cinematografico: cineblub, cinema d'essai, massenzio', in Vito Zagarrio ed., *Storia del cinema italiano. Volume XIII – 1977/1985*, Venice: Marsilio, Edizioni di Bianco e Nero, pp. 601–22.

Filmography

Accoltellati (*Stabbed*), film, directed by Tonino De Bernardi, video, 85', 2006.
Cani lenti (*Slow Dogs*), film, directed by Franco Vaccari, 8mm, 8'38", 1971.
Carcere in Italia (*Prison in Italy*), documentary, directed by Alfredo Leonardi, Anna Lajolo, Guido Lombardi, ½ inch tape, 60', 1973.
Ciao Ciao, film, directed by Adamo Vergine, 16mm, 6', 1967.
Dove incominciano le gambe (*Where the Legs Begin*), film, directed by Piero Bargellini, 8mm, 1974.
Destroy She Said, film, directed by Monica Bonvicini, Video art, 1998.
Egg One Egg Zero, film, directed by Cioni Carpi, 16mm, 7'36", 1972.
E nua ca simu a forza du mundu (*And We Who Are the Force of the World*), documentary, directed by Alfredo Leonardi, Anna Lajolo, Guido Lombardi, 16mm, 58', 1971.
Es-pi'azione (*Ex-pi'action*), directorial formulation by Adamo Vergine, 1968.
Frammenti elettrici (*Electric Fragments*), film series 1–7, directed by Angela Ricci Lucchi and Yervant Gianikian, Digibeta. 60', 2001–2013.
Giovinezza, giovinezza, primavera di bellezza (*Youth, Youth, Spring of Beauty*), film, directed by Luca Comerio, 35mm. 51', 1922.
I colori della luce (*The Colours of Light*), film, directed by Bruno Munari and Marcello Piccardo, 16mm. 5'23", 1963.
Il giardino delle delizie (*Garden of Delights*), film, directed by Silvano Agosti, 35mm. 95', 1967.
La nott'el giorno (*The Night and Day*), film, directed by Gianni Castagnoli, 16mm, 40', 1973.
La riappropriazione della città (*The Re-Appropriation of the City*), film, directed by Ugo La Pietra, 16mm, 29'36", 1977.
L'avanzata di Tripolitania (*The Tripolitania Advance*), film, directed by Luca Comerio, 35mm, 1912.
La verifica incerta (*Disperse Exclamatory Phase*), film, directed by Gianfranco Baruchello, Alberto Grifi, 35mm. 30', 1964.
Le gote in fiamme (*The Cheeks Aflame*), film, directed by Ugo Nespolo, 16mm, 3', 1967.
Lo sguardo espanso: Tecniche Miste su Schermo: il cinema sperimentale di Roma, 1965–1975 (*The Expanded Gaze: Mixed Techniques on Screen: the Roman experimental cinema, 1965–1975*), film, directed by Bruno Di Marino and Marcello Del Signore, HD Video, 76', 2013.
Marcello Piccardo: l'informazione capovolta (*Marcello Piccardo: Information Upside-down*), film, directed by Andrea Piccardo, HD Video, 8'45", 2009.
Nelda, film, directed by Piero Bargellini, 16mm, 4', 1969.
Hilarisdoppio, film, directed by Paolo Gioli, 16mm, 19' 09", 1973.
Pistoletto & Sotheby's, film, directed by Pia Epremian, 8mm, 22', 1968.
Proussade, film, directed by Pia Epremian, Super8, 60', 1967.
Schegge di Utopia: *il cinema underground Italiano* (*Utopian Splinters: Underground Italian Cinema*), film series 1–12, directed by Paolo Brunatto, Video, 2005.

Se la vita è meglio, butti via la telecamera (*If Life Is Better, Throw Away the Camera*), film, directed by Enrica Viola, HD Video, 35', 1998.

Se l'inconscio si ribella (*If the Subconscious Were to Rebel*), film, directed by Alfredo Leonardi, 16mm, 21', 1967.

60 metri per il 31 marzo (*200 Feet for March 31st*), film, directed by Massimo Bacigalupo, 16mm, 17', 1968.

SKMP2, film, directed by Luca Maria Patella, 16mm, 30', 1968.

Stop Forgetting: The Films of Yervant Gianikian and Angela Ricci Lucchi, film, produced by Barbara Casavecchia, Jörg Heiser, Video, 10'58", 2015.

Tempo nel tempo (*Time in Time*), film, directed by Bruno Munari, Marcello Piccardo, 16mm, 3'30", 1964.

Terra Animata (*Animated Land*), film, directed by Luca Maria Patella in collaboration with Rosa Foschi, 16mm, 7', 1967.

Valentino Moon, film, directed by Gianni Castagnoli, Super8, 12', 1974.

Vergine Roma (*Virgin Rome*), documentary, directed by Antonella Porcelluzzi, Video, 54', 2017.

Warming Up, film, directed by Massimo Bacigalupo, 16mm, 40', 1972–1973.

Index

12 December 1969, 48
16mm, 7, 18, 54–5, 71–2, 93, 121, 133, 138, 172–3, 221, 238–9, 247
18 fps, 114
1900s, 2, 5–6, 80, 218, 222
1910s, 5–6, 80, 219–20, 222, 240, 243
1920s, 2, 33, 68, 73, 78, 114, 131, 133, 174, 222, 243
1930s, 2, 5, 20, 41, 56, 73, 84, 114, 117, 133, 173–4, 222, 235–6
1940s, 5, 12, 43, 50, 85–6, 94, 107, 120–1, 133, 161, 221–3
1950s, 2, 5, 27, 43–4, 47, 56, 71, 85, 88, 89–91, 94, 112, 133, 137–8, 161
1960s, 4–8, 10–15, 17–18, 21, 23, 25–7, 29–30, 32, 43–6, 48, 56, 68–75, 77–9, 91–3, 103–6, 108–11, 113–20, 133, 137, 158, 160–3, 165–6, 168, 170, 172, 175, 216–19, 221, 224–7, 229, 231–3, 235–36, 238–41, 244–5, 247, 250
1970s, 5–8, 10, 14–15, 17–21, 23, 25, 26, 30, 42–3, 46–53, 58, 69–73, 103, 110, 117, 122, 137–8, 145, 158, 160–1, 172–3, 175, 194, 221, 226, 228–32, 234, 237–42, 245–7, 250
1980s, 5, 9, 11–12, 15, 19, 21–2, 24–25, 41–7, 50–8, 73, 84–5, 109, 132–3, 194, 207, 222

1990s, 1, 12, 14, 18, 20–5, 41–7, 50, 52, 54–5, 57–8, 60, 133, 202, 207, 222–3, 227, 229, 242, 246
2000s, 9, 11–12, 18, 21–3, 25, 29, 31, 57, 68, 93, 132, 135, 138, 145, 148, 182–3, 189, 191–6, 203–4, 207, 211, 213, 222, 224, 227–8, 235, 243
2010s, 12, 15, 20, 22–3, 29, 31, 53, 69–70, 109, 122, 133–5, 138, 142, 144, 146, 148–9, 174, 180, 182–3, 189, 191–3, 195, 197, 202–3, 205–7, 209, 222–4, 226, 232, 235, 239, 243, 245, 248–9
2020s, 22
22 Dicembre (22 Decembre), 44–5, 56
35mm, 93, 121, 133, 138
3D, 242
55cm above Sea Level, 17
60 metri per il 31 marzo (*200 Feet for March 31ˢᵗ*), 13, 30, 160, 162, 236
660secondi, Silvano Agosti Il cinema indipendente (*660seconds, Silvano Agosti The Independent Cinema*), 245
8mm, 7, 17, 49, 93, 103, 133, 136, 163, 221, 224
9 Evenings: Theatre and Engineering, 75
A Closed Mouth Catches no Flies, 206

INDEX

A Director's Notebook, 162
A mosca cieca (*Blindman's Bluff*), 17
abolition, 153
Abruzzo, 225
absence, 32, 42, 56, 60, 131, 210, 230, 239, 248
abstract, 2, 4, 6, 8, 21, 23, 72, 76, 78, 107, 109–12, 114, 117, 120–1, 205, 219
  cinema, 78, 219
academic, 2, 10, 239
Academia di Belle Arti (Academy of Fine Arts–Naples), 23
Accademia Albertina di Belle Arti (Albertina Academy of Fine Arts), 233
Accademia di Brera (Brera Academy), 48, 58
accessibility, 11, 13, 18, 23, 44, 46, 70, 75, 134, 143, 147, 151, 207, 210, 218, 228, 248, 250
  inaccessible, 93
Accoltellati (*Stabbed*), 18, 224
Achtung banditi!(*Achtung: Bandits!*), 43, 85
acknowledgement, 250
acting, 149
action, 86–7, 144, 152, 169, 181, 247
activism, 14, 48–9, 143, 207
activity, 10, 14, 16, 24–5, 28, 30, 33, 45, 47–50, 54, 57, 105, 133–6, 141, 145–9, 151, 154, 174, 191, 196, 216–17, 219, 223, 229, 236–7, 242
  artistic, 154, 217, 242
  centres, 10, 14, 24–5, 45, 50, 54, 105, 216–17
  cultural, 49, 236
  family, 174
  film-preservation, 223
  free-time and work, 133
  Futurists, 219

Ministero per i Beni e le Attività Culturali (Ministry of Cultural Heritage and Activities), 133, 149
  online, 33, 237
  on-set and off-set, 141, 145–51
  political, 48
  research, 135
  social *impegno*, 229
  women, 28
actor, 18, 75, 118, 145, 147–50, 185–7, 192
actress, 149–50
adaptability, 3, 19, 238
  adaptation, 23, 59, 76, 80, 230
  readapted, 134
addictive, 237
administration, 57, 218
adolescents, 48
Adorno, Theodor, 75, 168–70
Adriatic Sea, 137
adult, 48, 52, 59, 143, 211
  adulthood, 12
advertising, 41, 43–4, 46, 51–2, 55–6, 118, 138, 148, 181, 226, 232, 237
  industry, 43–4, 46, 51–2, 56
aeroplane, 120
aesthetic, 2, 4–7, 9–10, 15, 16–17, 19, 21, 24–6, 29, 59, 61, 72, 89, 104, 141–2, 149–51, 153, 162, 174, 175, 205, 212–13, 219–20, 228–31, 234, 237, 242, 245, 247
  kinaesthetic, 78
  synaesthetic, 110, 113
affordance, 223, 242
Afghanistan, 168–9, 171
Africa, African, 148, 152, 162, 204, 207, 148, 152, 162
agency, 49, 147
agenda, 1, 16–17, 48, 181, 221
Agenzia matrimoniale (*Marriage Bureau*), 90

AGIS, 53
Agosti, Silvano, 3, 21, 222, 244–5
agreement, 133
Aida, 203, 205–6
AIDS, 213, 218, 235
Akalé wubé, 206
Al di Là della pittura (*Beyond Painting*), 70
Al primo soffio di vento (*At the First Breath of Wind*), 21
Alba, 188–9
Albania, Albanian, 212
alchemy, 103, 111, 120, 235, 245
algorithm, 32, 217, 237, 250
alienation, 16, 119
allegory, 31, 171, 180
Alpert, Jon, 56
Alps, 108, 211
alternative, 1–2, 8–11, 13, 15–16, 22, 24, 29, 32, 42, 44, 50, 52, 56, 61, 78, 85, 94, 103, 106, 110, 131, 136, 142–3, 147, 176, 184, 189, 193, 195, 230, 235–6, 239, 245, 247, 250
  art forms, 1–2, 16, 24, 52, 143, 147, 230, 235–6, 250
  cinema/film-practices, 8–11, 32, 42, 52, 110, 132, 136, 230, 235–6, 247, 250
  cinemas, 50
  discourse, 143, 147
  funding sources, 184
  means of production/distribution, 13, 15, 22, 42, 44, 50, 56, 61, 85, 94, 103, 142, 147, 184, 189, 193, 195, 239, 250
  perspective, 29, 230
  reality, 78
  to classical storytelling, 245
  to dominant cultural values, 106
  voice, 176
Altrementi, 216

Altri seguiranno (*More Will Follow*), 21
amalgam, 105
Amaro Ramazzotti, 51
Amarsi a Marghera (*Love in Marghera*), 117
amateur, 28, 108, 131–6
  cineastes, 28, 131, 135–6
  cinema, 131, 133
  film, 108, 131–2, 135
  filmmaking, 108, 131
amateuresque, 131
amateurism, 224
Amazon, 246
ambient (ambiente), 26, 68–80, 233
ambivalence, 80, 114, 116
Ambrogino d'oro award, 194
Ambrosino, Nuccio, 58
America, American, 1–2, 5, 7–8, 10, 13, 17–19, 21, 23, 27, 41, 49–50, 53, 56, 58, 106, 109–10, 142–3, 160–1, 166, 172–5, 189, 211, 217–18, 226, 235, 237
  cinema, 13, 54
  Anglo-American, 160
  New American Cinema, 27, 53, 103–6, 110, 161, 224
  North America, 23, 218
Amore in città (*Love in the City*), 27, 88–9
An Optical Poem, 117
analysis, 1, 8, 10, 12, 17, 24, 26–7, 30, 32, 41, 58, 86–7, 90, 103, 141–2, 151, 154, 165, 180, 182, 214, 233
ancient, 114, 137, 159–60, 164, 169, 176, 205, 211
anecdote, 191, 196–7, 209
ANFF, Archivio Nazionale Film di Famiglia (National Archives of Family Films), 132, 134–7
Angeli, Franco, 8, 13
Angelini, Alessandro, 182
Angelone, Anita, 143

Anger, Kenneth, 12
angle, 114, 153, 209
Anglo-American, 160
animation, 3, 14, 20, 55, 70, 72, 75, 112, 119, 166, 226, 230, 233, 235
animator, 228
Anna, 18–19, 225, 229
anni di piombo (years of the bullet), 48
Anno 2000 (*Year 2000*), 106
annual, 135
ANPI (Associazione Nazionale Partigiani d'Italia – National Association of Italian Partisans), 85
antagonism, 43, 120, 141, 143, 145, 153
Antenati (*Ancestry*), 135
Anthology Film Archives, 161
anthology, 2, 6, 15, 19, 24, 28, 137, 141, 161, 193, 249
anthropology, 1–2, 4, 9, 12, 28, 120, 217, 225, 228
anti-establishment, 13, 21
anti-fascist, 29, 141
Antonello, Pier Paolo, 48
Antonioni, Michelangelo, 17, 43, 60, 70, 88–90, 104, 153, 161, 217
Aperture Sweep, 72
app, 135
apparatus, 53, 72, 76, 80, 105–6, 121, 218, 229, 241, 245
appearance(s), 149, 169, 188
appendix, 234
approach, 2–5, 7, 9, 12–14, 16–24, 26–27, 30–1, 44–5, 47, 56–7, 70, 79, 87, 103–4, 111, 113, 118, 120–1, 142, 148, 153, 158, 168, 172, 202–3, 205, 217–18, 220, 224, 226, 228, 231, 233, 245
Appunti per un film sull'India (*Notes for a Film about India*), 162
Aprà, Adriano, 8–11, 20, 103, 144, 232
archaic, 164, 170
architect, 10–11, 19, 233

architecture, 6, 41, 45–7, 68–70, 72–3, 76, 233, 242
archive, 11–12, 28, 42, 105, 112, 116, 122, 132–7, 217–18, 222, 228, 249
Archivio aperto (Open Archive), 135
Archivio Audiovisivo del Movimento Operaio e Democratico (Audiovisual Archive of the Labour and Democratic Movement), 226
Archivio diaristico nazionale di Pieve Santo Stefano (National Diaristic Archive of Pieve Santo Stefano), 132
Archivio di Storia delle Donne (Women History Archive), 136
Archivio Marinella Pirelli, 240
Archivio Nazionale (National Archive), 28, 131–3, 136
Archivio Nazionale Film di Famiglia (National Archive of Family Films), 28, 132, 136
archivist, 28, 134–8, 244
Arcopinto, Gianluca, 146
Ardizzoni, Michela, 143
Arena di Verona, 205
Argentina, 50, 202
argument, 159, 187, 175, 204
Arianateo, 52
Aristarco, Guido, 88
'Art and Objecthood', 75
art, 1–16, 18–27, 30, 41–7, 49, 53–9, 68–70, 72, 75–6, 78, 85, 87, 104–9, 110–11, 114, 116–22, 121, 132–3, 136–8, 141, 143, 148, 150–4, 158–9, 162–5, 170–1, 176, 182, 187, 189, 193, 205–6, 216–22, 224, 227, 230–5, 237–8, 243–6, 247–50
artisanal, 2, 7, 12, 14, 26, 31, 71–2, 79, 109, 187
books, 246

art (*cont.*)
  cinema, 15, 42–3, 49–50, 55, 59, 70, 158, 233, 244–5
  criticism, 2, 75–6
  film, 2, 45, 54, 121, 143, 153, 246
  history, 26
  house, 16, 49–50, 59, 148, 189
  installation, 46, 55, 57, 234
  movement, 5, 14, 27, 107, 114, 235
  video, 3, 55, 230
  work, 107–8, 116
artist, 2–21, 23, 30, 32, 41, 46, 51–3, 56, 59, 68, 70–1, 73, 75–6, 78, 88, 103, 107, 110–12, 117–19, 121, 141, 143, 158, 164, 169–71, 182, 187–8, 190, 193, 196, 205, 216–19, 221, 225–6, 228, 230–2, 233–5, 238–42, 246–50
  filmmaker, 68, 70, 76, 239
  director/direction, 11, 53
  tradition, 4, 217, 220, 232
Arte Povera (Poor Art), 27, 78, 107–8, 119, 235
artefact, 5, 111, 132–5, 217, 228, 230, 244, 246
Artefutura, 246
Arthur, Paul, 121, 158
article, 84, 88, 90–1, 116, 121, 167, 196, 216, 236
articulation, 165
artificial, 107, 119
asbestos, 203, 207–9
Ascaride, Ariane, 149
ascendancy, 224
aspiration, 41–2, 46–7, 52, 57, 73, 233, 238
aspiring filmmakers, 145, 183–4, 197
assemblage, 13
Assessorato all'istruzione Prov. di Milano (Department of Education Province of Milan), 148

assistant director, 148, 184, 186
association, 41, 54, 85–6, 97, 132, 135, 144, 146, 196, 208, 234
Associazione Home Movies (Home Movies Association), 132, 134
Associazione Pandora, 58
assumption, 105, 146
astronomy, 110
Astruc, Alexandre, 26, 121, 168
Atlantic City, 211
Atlantic Ocean, 230
audacity, 217
audience, 16, 21, 25, 54–5, 61, 74–5, 84, 86, 88, 108, 111, 117, 152–3, 160, 164–5, 180, 182, 188–91, 194, 196–7, 206–7, 212–13, 220, 225–6, 234
audiovisual, 26–8, 52, 71, 88, 92–4, 120, 131–5, 159–60, 163, 225–7
  production, 52
August, 10, 133
Aurélia, 15
Auschwitz, 22, 162
Austria, 11, 149
Austrian Film Museum, 11
auteur, 3, 5–8, 10, 15, 17–18, 23, 84, 89, 142, 146–7, 149, 153, 158, 203, 206, 217, 229, 242, 244
authenticity, 15, 19, 110, 138,141, 147–8, 151, 187, 195, 228
author, 15, 21, 24, 28–9, 31–2, 84, 88–9, 92, 137, 142, 147, 150, 152, 154, 158–60, 163, 167, 172, 174–6, 189, 192–3, 203, 226, 229, 231, 236, 239, 248
authority, 51, 55, 57–8, 60, 133, 136, 159, 203–4, 208
autobiography, 158, 169
autonomy, 21, 24, 56, 75, 131, 146, 160, 218–19, 237, 245
autophagous, 245

INDEX

Autoritratto Auschwitz (*Self-Portrait Auschwitz*), 162
avant-garde, 1–2, 5, 20, 24, 27, 32, 53, 73, 86–7, 103–4, 106, 110–12, 117, 121, 122, 158–60, 168, 226, 232, 240–2, 245
   artist, 111–12, 121
   cinema, 53
   theories, 86
avataric, 250
average, 249
award, 23, 108, 149, 150, 182, 188–90, 194–6, 203
Azzuro Scipioni Cinema, 244

baby-boomers, 48
Bacigalupo, Massimo, 8, 13, 16, 19, 29–30, 158–176, 221–2, 226, 235–7, 242
background, 8, 23, 30, 46, 55, 116, 145, 194, 205, 209, 232
backstage, 180, 182–191, 196–7
   video, 181–6, 188–91, 196
bajaj, 206
Ballabio, Maurizio, 50
Bambú Cinematografica, 55
bank, 48, 51, 56, 60
Barcelona, 161, 202, 214
Bargellini, Piero, 8, 19–20, 33, 222, 226, 240–1
Barilli, Renato, 84
Barthes, Roland, 88
Baruchello, Gianfranco, 8, 13, 70, 106, 222, 231–2
Basho, Matsuo, 161, 175
Bauhaus, 107, 114
Bazar, 117
Beat Generation, 106, 224
Bechis, Marco, 56
Beck, Julian, 75
behaviour, 172, 226, 233
behind-the-scene, 11, 196

Belgium, 105, 133
belief, 47, 122, 141, 150–2, 154
Bella e perduta (*Lost and Beautiful*), 23
Bellaria Film Festival, 148
Bellocchio, Marco, 239
Bellour, Raymond, 168
Below Sea Level, 23
Bene, Carmelo, 17
benefit, 20, 204, 207
Benetton, 54
Benjamin, Walter, 164
Berardinelli, Alfonso, 47
Berlenghini, Umberto, 191
Berlin, 11, 56, 226
   Film Festival, 56
Berlinguer, Enrico, 151
Berlusconi, Silvio, 43–4, 52
   Finivest, 43
   Reteitalia, 43
   Silvio Berlusconi Communication, 43
Bernardi, Sandro, 5, 217, 220
Bertacchi, Armando, 46
Bertetto, Paolo, 3, 7–8
Bertolucci, Giuseppe, 56
Best Family Film, 108
best film, 58
best screenplay, 149
BFI (British Film Institute), 228, 230
Bianco e Nero (*Black and White*), 30, 106, 110, 112, 167, 236
Bible, 170
Bicycle Thieves, 94
Bigazzi, Luca, 55, 186–7
Bignardi, Umberto, 13, 235
Bigoni, Bruno, 53–5
Bilico (Monogatari), 55
billboards, 181
Bini, Alfredo, 239
biography, 28, 136, 235, 206, 247
   autobiography, 158, 169
   biographical narratives, 206

biological, 208, 262
blackmail, 152
Blake, William, 173
Blob, 231
blockbusters, 187
blog, 197, 224, 244, 246
Bobbio, Fabio, 146
Boccioni, Umberto, 220
Bocola, Antonio, 54, 57, 196
body, 1–2, 8, 20, 29, 68, 74, 76, 78, 118–19, 121, 134, 148, 150, 167, 202, 205, 207–8, 210, 213, 229, 247
  'body art', 20, 222, 246–7
  of work 1–2, 10, 25, 71, 84, 202, 211
Bolex Paillard Reflex, 108
Bologna, 28, 131–3, 135–6, 229, 233
Bolzoni, Francesco, 92
bonus features, 30, 181–3, 186–7, 190–1
Bonvicini, Monica, 242
book, 2, 104, 110, 122, 146, 159, 188, 191, 193, 227, 236, 239, 246
  booklet, 216
booking, 142
boom, 48, 145
  economic, 48
Bordwell, David, 20, 239
Bosch, Hieronymus, 164
Bosi, Dimitri, 190
Botticelli, Sandro, 164
boundaries, 69, 103, 165, 208, 224, 230, 239–40
Bowie, David, 225
Bragaglia, Anton Giulio, 5
Brakhage, Stan, 12, 27, 109, 112, 121, 164, 221
brand, 13, 24, 51, 249
Braque, Georges, 87
Brazil, 202, 208
Brebbia, Adele, 107

Brebbia, Gianfranco, 3, 27–8, 103–22, 221–2
Brebbia, Giovanna, 108–9, 118, 122
Brebbia, Paola, 108
Bresson, Robert, 149
Britain/UK, 7, 71, 105, 221
Brizzi, Enrico, 137
broadcast, 86, 138
  broadcaster, 18, 143, 149–51
Broodthaers, Marcel, 70
Brooklyn, 172, 211
  bridge, 172
Broughton, James, 12
Bruna, Niccolò, 31–2, 202–14
Brunatto, Paolo, 15, 17, 222, 228, 235
budget, 2–3, 9, 30, 43, 148, 150, 182, 185–6, 221, 245
  high-, 187, 191
  low-, 9 , 30, 43–5, 50, 54–6, 59, 94, 143–4, 146, 149–50, 180–1, 183–7, 192, 221
  microbudget, 183, 188
  'shoe-string', 184, 221
buffoonery, 217
bureaucratic, 210
Burns, Jennifer, 47, 103
Butler Library (Columbia University), 175

Cage, John, 231
Caldana, Alberto, 44
Caldwell, John, 30, 180–1, 183, 187, 193, 196
California, 23
Calvesi, Maurizio, 232
Calvino, Italo, 248
camcorder, 231
camera, 8, 13, 18–19, 32, 71, 86–8, 93, 103–4, 109, 111, 113–14, 116–19, 121, 135, 158–60, 163–5, 168–9, 171–2, 174, 176, 184, 204–10, 213, 227–9, 232, 237, 239–40

angle, 153
camera-eye, 30, 86, 88, 104, 118, 165
cameraless, 13, 27, 109, 111–12, 117, 122
cameraman, 235, 243
caméra-stylo, 18, 26, 121, 168, 248
cinecamera, 84
hand-held, 18, 119, 208
in-camera, 160, 163, 166
movement, 117, 119
operator, 180
techniques, 240
telecamera, 227
Caminati, Luca, 143
Canada, 17, 26, 86, 203, 208
Canal, Mario, 53, 247
Cani lenti (*Slow Dogs*), 247
canon, 4, 17, 20, 29, 193–5, 197
canvas, 6, 73, 87, 109, 221
Capanna, Roberto, 12, 120, 235
capital, 49, 143, 182, 188, 197, 237, 238, 250
cultural, 182, 197
human, 238
moral, 52
capital (city), 13, 18, 22, 24, 93, 225, 236
Cappelli (publisher), 92
caption, 136
Caravaggio (Michelangelo Merisi), 164
Carcere in Italia (*Prison in Italy*), 228
carcinogenic, 209
career, 18, 21–3, 25, 29–31, 59, 90, 142, 148, 151, 181–2, 188, 203, 217, 224–5, 238–9, 242, 247
Cariplo, 56
Carmosino, Christian, 192
Carnelutti, Valentina, 192
carnival, 211, 232
Carocci, Enrico, 192

Carosello, 43
Carpi, Cioni, 17, 222, 246
Carrà, Carlo, 220
Carrillo, Michele, 192
cartographic, 134
Cartoline dall'America (*Postcards from America*), 175
Caruso, Emanuele, 31, 183–6, 188–9
Casale Monferrato, 207
Casetti, Francesco, 50, 120
Cassavetes, John, 58
cast, 148–50, 133, 181–2
Castagnoli, Gianni, 222, 230
Catalan, 205
catalogue, 25, 103, 134, 136, 217, 235, 246
catalyst, 50, 107, 239, 250
category, 8, 22, 28, 45, 52, 69, 108, 189, 242
cathartic, 111
catholic, 48–9
circles, 49
liberalist, 49
Cavatorta, Salvatore, 42, 48, 50–1, 53–4, 60
Cavatorta, Silvano, 25, 52
Cavazzoni, Ermanno, 137
Cavell, Stanley, 73
CCI (Cooperative of Independent Cinema), 3, 13, 20, 216, 222, 233, 238–9, 241
Cecere, Giorgia, 195
Celant, Germano, 107
celluloid, 223, 240
Censimento archivi femminili provincia di Bologna (*Census of women archives in province of Bologna*), 136
censor, 17
censure, 245
census, 136
Central Italy, 148

INDEX

central, 24, 29, 41, 45, 47, 59, 88, 90, 114, 119, 221, 148, 167–8, 171, 181, 185, 203, 211, 240
  decentralised, 146
  Centre Georges Pompidou, 234, 244
  Centre National du Cinéma et de l'Image Animée (CNC), 149
  centre, 8, 10–16, 24–5, 28, 31, 49, 54, 56–8, 132, 136, 147, 149–50, 183, 212, 218, 234, 238–9, 244
    archival and curatorial, 28
    art, 14–15, 218
    Centre National du Cinéma et de l'Image Animée, 149
    Centre Pompidou (Paris), 11–12, 54, 56, 234, 244
    Centro di Filmologia e Cinema Sperimentale (Centre for Filmology and Experimental Cinema, 238
    Centro Studi Cinematografici (Centre for Studies of Cinema), 49
    Cinecittà-centred system, 147
    city, 58
    cultural, 49
    film, co-op/exhibition, 8, 10, 13–16, 24–5, 57, 239
    Fuga dal call center (*Escape from the Call Centre*, 31, 183
    institutional production, 56
    national collection, 132
    off-centre framing, 212
    traditional production, 150
  Centro di Documentazione delle Donne della Città di Bologna (Women Documentation Centre of the City of Bologna), 136
  Centro di Filmologia e Cinema Sperimentale (Centre for Filmology and Experimental Cinema), 238
  Centro S. Fedele, 49

Centro Sociale Autogestito Leoncavallo (Squat of Leoncavallo), 48
Centro Sociale Giambellino, 54
Centro Sperimentale di Cinematografia, 225, 235
Centro Studi Cinematografici (Centre for Studies of Cinema), 49
Cerri, Lionello, 50
Cézanne, 87
CGI, 187
change, 9, 15, 51, 53, 58–60, 90, 107, 122, 134, 141, 150–1, 160, 167, 193, 209, 212, 218, 220, 230, 233, 244
  exchanges, 12, 47, 56–7, 188, 190, 226, 235
channel, 11–12, 21–2, 44, 108, 154, 160, 189, 194, 196, 221, 223–4, 227–8, 231, 244–6
chaotic, 26, 161, 248
character, 1, 5–6, 10, 12, 21, 27, 31, 58, 90, 119, 131, 133, 144, 152, 171, 175, 184, 203–8, 213, 217, 220, 223–4, 245
  characteristic, 2, 4, 6, 16, 21, 27, 29, 54, 68, 70–1, 87, 90, 93, 107–10, 119–20, 131–2, 134, 147, 154, 159, 183, 197, 202, 204, 217, 219, 221, 225, 228, 235, 237, 247–8
Chiarini, Marco, 31, 184–5, 188, 190
Chicago, 160, 165–6
child, 14, 131, 148, 152, 173–4, 206, 211, 213, 224, 227, 245
childhood, 12
  Il cinema fatto dai bambini, 14
China, Chinese, 202–4, 206
choreography, 5, 119
Christian Democratic Party, 48

INDEX

chromaticism, 6, 112, 219
chronicle, 23, 30, 85, 90, 93
chronology, 136–7, 163, 166, 219
Ciao, 239
Cine4, 189
cineamatori (home-movie filmmaker), 108
cineaste, 2, 15, 21, 23, 28, 94–5, 131, 134–7, 217, 234
Cinecittà, 71, 147, 151
Cineclub Brera, 49
cineclub, 1, 8, 10–11, 16, 49–50, 58, 108, 250
cineforum, 49
Cinegiornali della Pace (*Cine-newsreels for Peace*), 161
Cinegiornali Liberi (*Free Cine-newsreels*), 161
Cinelandia Milanese, 42
Cinema Angelicum, 52
   Anteo, 50, 52, 56
   Arcobaleno, 52
   Argentina, 50
   Centrale, 52
   Cristallo, 50, 53
   Dal Verme, 52
   De Amicis, 52
   d'essai (Art house cinemas), 1, 11, 18, 49, 189, 195
   Mexico, 189–90, 194–5, 197
   Paris, 52
cinema exhibitors, 51
Cinema fatto dai bambini, Il, 14
Cinema General Directorate of the Ministry of Cultural Heritage and Activities, 149
Cinema sperimentale e mezzi di massa in Italia (*Experimental Cinema and the Mass Media in Italy*), 103
cinéma vérité, 20, 84, 87, 89, 229

cinemas, 4, 26, 29, 49–50, 52, 56, 59, 106, 188–9, 194–5, 237
   independent, 237
   national, 29
Cinemaindipendente.it, 145–7
Cinémathèque Française, 5
cinémathèque, 5, 56, 223
cinematic culture, 41–52, 58
   dreams, 228
   initiatives, 50
   language, 55, 57, 224, 248
   renaissance, 3
cinematography, 26, 46, 50, 90, 93, 104, 108–9, 231
cinematograph, 233
cinematographer, 17, 89, 148
cinepanettone, 43, 153
cinephile, 189, 191, 196–7
cinepitture, 6
cineteca, 146–7, 223–5, 233
Cineteca del Comune di Bologna (City of Bologna Film Library), 233
Cineteca di Milano, 223
Cineteca Nazionale, 225
ciné-verité, 87
Cintoli, Claudio, 235
circle, 11, 42, 44, 47, 49, 52, 56–8, 197, 221, 247
Circolo Creativo ISU (Creative Circle ISU), 58
Circolo del Cinema Mario Ferrari, 50
circularity, 169
circus, 136
Cirifino, Fabio, 46–7
citizen, 141
Città del diario (*City of the Diary*), 132
city, 11, 13, 18–19, 24–5, 27–8, 42, 44–6, 48–52, 54–60, 88, 90–1, 93, 132, 135–6, 149, 172, 188–9, 194, 211, 221, 233–4

civic, 58
  cinema, 151
  commitment, 154
  dissent, 49
  merit, 194
  responsibility. 229
  theatre, 152
civilisation, 24, 115, 170
clandestine, 245
classic, 5, 7, 24, 26, 133
classical, 6, 18, 104, 167, 169–71, 181, 245
  neoclassical, 31
Clementi, Emidio, 137
clicks, 237, 245
Clò, Clarissa, 143
close-up, 113–14, 116, 119, 209–10, 212
Club nuovo teatro (*New Theatre Club*), 110
Cocteau, Jean, 12
Coda, 169, 171
codification, 233
co-direction, 203, 206, 228
cognitive, 9, 17, 216, 248
  faculties, 216, 248
coherence, 26, 84, 90, 109, 141, 151, 153, 169, 175
cohesion, 90, 131
collaboration, 11, 14–15, 22, 41, 53–4, 57–8, 60, 120, 135, 166, 185–6, 195, 226, 230–1, 235, 243
  collaborator, 46, 91, 93, 106, 186
collage, 12, 137, 158, 166–8
  style, 226
Collectif Jeune Cinema (Young Cinema Cooperative), 230
collection, 2, 24, 28, 90, 132–8, 223, 228
collective, 7–9, 24, 27, 30, 45–50, 53, 56–7, 60, 85, 89, 151, 160, 166, 189, 205, 218, 233

Collettivo di Cinema Militante (Militant Cinema Collective), 49
Cologno Monzese, 42
Colombo, Gianni, 71
colour, 5–6, 14, 69, 72, 76, 78, 107, 109, 112–14, 116, 119, 213, 219, 221, 226, 241
  hand colouring, 5, 111–12, 117, 122
Coluccio, Enzo, 186
Come prima (*Just Like Before*), 148
comedy, 138, 172
Comencini, Luigi, 60
Comerio, Luca, 243
comics, 86
Comizi d'amore (*Love Meetings*), 92
commentary, 19, 90, 159, 164, 166
commercial, 14, 18, 22, 41–6, 50, 52–53, 59, 72, 90, 143, 150, 218, 221, 226, 232
  cinema, 18, 42–5, 50, 53, 187, 197, 220
  circles/circuits, 52, 131–2
  commercialism, 144
  content, 46
  non-commercial films, 45
  venture, 59,143, 218
commercials, 226, 232
commitment, 22, 26, 29, 32, 42, 47–8, 52, 60, 91, 107, 141, 146, 153–4, 186
commodification, 238
communication, 9, 24, 43–4, 86, 93, 95, 135, 138, 233
  practices, 216
  strategies, 138
communist, 151
  ideology, 151
  party, 151
community, 15, 28, 44, 91, 107, 145–6, 175, 180, 189, 193, 206, 210–1, 213, 230
  housing, 91

company, 5, 18, 42–6, 53, 55–7, 71, 75, 143, 146, 148, 154, 184, 192, 207, 209, 229, 233, 250
comparison, 92, 145
competencies, 56, 250
competition, 57, 108, 181, 249
compilation, 105, 166
complexity, 27, 31, 51–2, 68, 73, 76, 80, 91, 134, 138, 141, 170, 207–8
complexes, 21
component, 80, 141
composer, 148
   composition, 6, 27, 109, 112, 114, 117, 121, 160, 167, 175, 233
   de-composition, 87
compromise, 94, 250
   uncompromising, 148, 151
computer, 55, 217, 248–9
   graphic, 55
   protocols, 249
Comune di Bologna (City of Bologna), 233
Comune di Milano (City of Milano), 55
concept, 27, 31, 41, 47, 60, 86–7, 89, 95, 116, 119, 142, 144, 147, 151, 154, 168, 170, 206, 222, 231, 233
   conceptual film, 14
   conceptual-art, 119, 222, 233, 246
   conceptualisation, 59, 141–3, 145, 148, 151, 248
conclusion, 25, 30, 152, 165, 185, 190, 242
Concorso nazionale della federazione nazionale cineamatori di Torino il fotogramma d'oro (*National Competition of the National Home Movies Federation of Turin, The Golden Photogram*), 108
condemnation, 75
configurations, 107, 235
conflict, 12, 29, 53, 106, 141, 145

conformity, 4, 91, 193, 217, 237, 247
   nonconforming, 3, 6
connection, 24, 50, 110, 116, 182, 184, 210
   disconnection, 174
connoisseur, 191
connotation, 142–3
Conrad, Tony, 71
conscience, 17, 47
consciousness, 93, 110–11, 151, 170
consequence(s), 57, 209, 211
conservatory, 48, 134, 142
   conservatism, 142
   film-restoration, 134
consistency, 55, 141, 151, 153, 175–6, 202, 225
construct, 12, 29, 59, 136–7, 141, 144, 151, 175, 187, 190, 230
   construction, 6, 91, 182
   constructivism, 107
   deconstruct, 13, 153
   reconstruction, 72, 89–90, 95, 134, 173, 243
consumer, 12, 138, 165, 191, 234
   consumption, 9, 51, 131, 182, 218–19
contemporary, 5, 12, 25–6, 29, 31, 54, 69–70, 84, 92, 131, 137–8, 143, 159, 164, 170, 181, 192–3, 205–6, 212, 217, 237, 242, 247, 249
content, 3, 21, 44–6, 170, 235, 243, 246
context, 2, 16, 19, 23, 41, 47, 56, 70, 90, 92, 103, 131, 134, 137–8, 141–2, 144, 154, 158, 162, 181, 196, 203, 209, 224, 250
   contextualisation, 28, 134, 136, 217
   decontextualise, 41
continuity, 7, 59, 142
   editing, 142
   discontinuity, 90, 169
contract, 133, 184, 245
   contractor, 208

contradiction, 90, 94–5, 237
contribution, 4, 19, 27, 29, 31, 42, 74,
    84–6, 94–5, 148, 166, 186, 205,
    221, 246
  contributor, 145
controversial, 2, 7, 239
convention, 4, 22–3, 57, 60, 75, 94,
    108–9, 131, 142–3, 159–60, 165–6,
    169, 172, 203, 217, 245
  conventional practice, 60
  unconventional, 1–9, 29, 61, 116,
    145, 147, 219, 228, 235, 237, 247
convergence, 218, 230, 233
conversion, 134
co-op, 3, 6–8, 10, 13–17, 24, 27, 29,
    32, 53, 85, 103, 105–6, 120, 151,
    160, 166, 181, 221, 226–7, 230,
    235, 238–40, 247, 250
Cooperativa Cinema Indipendente
    (CCI), 106, 238
Cooperativa Spettatori Produttori
    Cinematografici (Cinema
    Spectators Producers
    Cooperative), 85
co-production, 147, 149, 184
copies, 230
Cornia, Ugo, 137
Corona Cinematografica (Crown
    Cinematograph), 233
corporate, 33, 142, 250
  corporation, 150, 208, 228, 237, 249
Corra, Bruno, 5–6, 219
correspondence, 104–5, 169, 226
Corriere della Sera, 145
Corrigan, Tim, 159, 163
cosmopolitan, 51
cosmos, 115
Costa, Antonio, 2, 8, 217
Costanzo, Saverio, 193
costume, 211
counter, 41, 44, 49, 51, 143, 192, 225
  art-cinema, 233
  counteract, 29

counterbalance, 4
countercultural-trend, 7, 245
counterculture, 6–7, 16, 106, 245
counterintuitive, 7
counterpart, 4–5, 7, 12, 18, 21–2,
    103, 120, 170, 221, 226, 235,
    237
counterpunctual, 174
  discourse, 143
  narrative, 175, 235
country, 4–5, 14, 21–3, 32, 41, 48, 92,
    134, 163, 174, 209, 211–13
countryside, 175
courage, 30–1, 92, 171, 180–1, 184–5,
    190, 192, 196, 239
course, 50, 135
court, 207–9
coworkers, 145
craft, 187, 204, 239
  craftsmanship, 4, 9, 20, 24
Craxi, Bettino, 51
  Craxismo, 51
creativity, 3, 13, 20–2, 29, 51, 54–6,
    58, 60, 103–4, 107–8, 110–11,
    113, 116–17, 119–21, 142, 147–8,
    151–2, 159, 161, 164, 166, 172,
    181–3, 187–8, 204, 216–19, 221,
    233, 241–2, 245, 248
creator, 18, 20, 93, 148, 233
creation, 7, 16, 20, 55, 111, 132,
    134, 137–8, 142, 147
  re-creation, 110
credits, 209
Crevani, Massimo, 120
crew, 21–2, 149, 182, 185–9, 191, 197,
    204, 244
  one-man-crew, 22
crisis, 1, 16, 23, 32, 51, 53, 60, 108,
    181, 192–4, 214, 228, 230
criteria, 13, 143, 150–1, 231, 249
critic, 23, 58, 70, 75–6, 108, 141, 144,
    154, 195–6, 217, 231
  criticism, 1–2, 89, 144, 196, 246

critique, 3, 8, 10, 25–6, 28, 30, 50, 57, 70, 72, 75–6, 85–7, 103–4, 107–8, 144, 152, 154, 160, 165–6, 168, 203–4, 214, 225, 233, 239
  metacritical, 159, 167
Cronache di poveri amanti (*Chronicles of Poor Lovers*), 85
cross-genre, 146
crowdfunding, 134, 183–4
CSC (Centro Sperimentale di Cinematografia), 225–6, 235, 239
Cuba, 202–4, 209
  Cuban, 209–10
cube, 68, 73, 77
Cubism, 87
culture, 11, 28, 31, 41–52, 55–6, 58, 69, 71, 75, 85, 95, 133, 143, 149, 158, 160, 163, 180–1, 189, 191, 193, 196–7, 203, 211, 219, 221, 223, 225–6, 245
  capital, 182, 197
  context, 16, 158
  countercultural context, 16
  countercultural trends, 7, 245
  fabric, 44
  history, 217
  memory, 48, 160–1, 168–9, 171, 174
  reference, 60, 158
  socio-cultural histories, 2
  surplus, 51
  traits, 10, 137, 237, 245
  transformation, 10, 55, 59, 165
  trend, 1
Cummings, E. E., 164
Curagi, Tonino, 54
curator, 14, 28, 135, 144, 193–4, 220, 244
curiosity, 50, 78, 84, 109
custom, 111, 136, 174, 211, 217
customers, 209

cyberspace, 32–3, 216, 218–19, 223, 230–1, 234–5, 237, 242, 245, 247–50
  cyberculture, 238
cycle, 6, 115, 120, 160, 168–71, 174, 186, 245

D'Agostini, Paolo, 3
d'essai, 1, 11, 18, 49, 106, 189, 195
DAAD (Deutscher Akademischer Austauschdienst), 226
Dadaist, 233
Dal Polo all'Equatore (*From the North Pole to the Equator*), 12
Damiani, Damiano, 44
Darix Togni (family), 136
data, 51, 93, 134, 203, 228, 249
database, 145
David di Donatello, 190, 203
DCP (Digital Cinema Package), 134
De Bernardi, Tonino, 8, 18, 221–4, 239
De Bernardinis, Flavio, 8
De Berti, Raffaele, 49, 56
De Bosio, Gianfranco, 44
de Cartier de Marchienne, Jean-Louis Marie, 209
De Feo, Giovanni, 184
De Giusti, Luciano, 90
de Kooning, Willem, 109
De Matteo, Ivano, 191
De Santis, Giuseppe, 85
De Serio, Gianluca, 146
De Serio, Massimiliano, 146
De Seta, Vittorio, 56
De Sica, Vittorio, 43, 91, 153, 217
death, 17, 84, 159, 163–4, 170–1, 174, 207
debate, 3, 8, 29, 41, 47, 49–50, 54, 86, 145, 182, 204
  cultural, 49
  philosophical, 145
  political, 49
  theoretical, 41, 47

Debord, Guy, 143
debts, 186
debut, 5, 22, 149, 183, 188, 192, 227, 239
decade, 1, 5–7, 10–11, 22, 25, 41–2, 45–52, 56–8, 70, 107, 136, 145, 149, 187, 228, 236–7, 241
decadence, 12
decoupage, 153
definition, 21–3, 29, 32, 58, 89, 110, 131, 143, 149–50, 158, 175, 218, 224, 233, 237, 247, 250
degeneration, 12, 245, 250
degrees, 77–8
Del Grosso, Francesco, 192
Del Signore, Claudio, 15, 19, 232
Delaunay, Robert, 87
democratic, 32, 48, 60, 85, 147, 166, 204–6
   Christian Democratic Party, 48
   convention, 166
   Labour and Democratic Movement, 226
demonstrations, 19, 48–9
demo-reel, 187
dependence, 217, 245
   interdependency, 75
depiction, 12, 134–7, 214, 228, 230
Deren, Maya, 162
Des Cinémas d'Art et D'Essai, 106
DeSanctis, Pierpaolo, 192
Deserto in luce solare (Desert in the Sunlight), 113–14
design, 6, 50, 185, 187, 246
   art, 233
   graphic, 233
designation, 2
desolation, 164
Destroy She Said, 242
determination, 24, 42, 185, 235
   self-, 24, 235

development, 3, 5, 7, 20, 24, 29, 31, 41–2, 48, 59, 73, 89, 135, 218–19, 247, 249
devices, 93, 135, 159, 169, 173, 231
devotion, 3, 239, 245
Di Marino, Bruno, 2–3, 8, 15–17, 19, 217–18, 232
Di me cosa ne sai (What Do You Know about Me), 31, 189, 196
di Sarro, Ernesto, 55
diagnosis, 207–8
diagram, 77, 205
dialectics, 204
dialogical, 170–6
dialogue, 69–71, 164, 168, 170, 176, 228, 231, 241
diary, 93, 132, 137, 158, 160–4, 168–70, 175, 216
   film-, 168
   travel-, 170
diaspora, 174–5, 211
Diaz, Cico, 186
dictatorial, 144
diegetic, 73, 206
   extra-, 176, 206
   intra-, 176
difficulty, 15, 146, 174, 183, 192, 197, 213
digital, 16, 32, 58, 70, 72, 94, 136–7, 147, 217, 223
   age, 219
   culture, 219
   digitisation, 132, 134, 242
   format, 58, 134
   media, 32, 70, 217
   revolution, 16, 223
   technologies, 32, 58
   video, 136, 231
dilemma, 187, 247
dimension, 6, 14, 25–6, 52, 68, 80, 88, 110, 112, 114, 117, 154, 162, 164–5, 172, 207–9

dimensionality, 25, 69
multidimensional, 55, 120, 207
one-dimensionality, 166
three-dimensionality, 25, 68, 73, 78, 87, 108
two-dimensionality, 69, 73
Dipartimento universitario di Arti Musica e Spettacolo (University Department of Arts, Music, and Entertainment Arts), 133
direct cinema, 89
direction, 11, 17, 50, 60, 116, 153, 164, 205, 250
directive, 238, 246
director of photography, 148, 186–7
director, 2, 5, 15, 17–18, 22–3, 25, 44–5, 47, 53–9, 87, 89–92, 148–9, 151, 162, 169, 171–2, 181–96, 202, 204–6, 209, 214, 231, 238–9, 244
Direzione Generale degli Archivi (General Directorate of Archives), 135
Direzione Regionale Beni Culturali e Paesaggistici dell'Emilia-Romagna (Regional Directorate for Cultural and Landscape Heritage of Emilia-Romagna), 133
Diritti, Giorgio, 22, 189–90, 195, 197, 234
discipline(s), 10, 28, 69–70, 72, 75, 109, 233
disclosure, 107
discontent, 171
discourse, 26, 28–9, 141, 143–4, 150, 152, 154, 159, 175, 217, 234
  counter-, 143
  epistemic, 217
discovery, 1, 50, 91, 116, 161, 173, 194, 226, 230
  rediscovery, 70
  self-, 161
disease, 195, 214

disruptive, 142
dissemination, 1, 32, 50, 134, 137, 143, 146, 181, 222–3, 231, 234, 249–50
dissolve, 104
distinction, 75, 91
distributor, 146, 182, 188
diversity, 250
division of labour, 59
diva, 205
divo, 205
doctor, 206
document, 12, 28, 78, 107, 117, 133, 135–7, 160, 166, 204, 206, 211, 216, 226, 228, 231, 233
documentary, 11–12, 15, 17–23, 25–6, 28, 30–1 42–6, 49–50, 53–5, 57, 89, 104–5, 107, 121, 132–3, 135, 137–8, 143, 145–6, 148, 153, 158–9, 161, 165–6, 170, 180, 189, 191–4, 196–7, 202–6, 209–214, 222, 225–6, 228–9, 231–3, 235, 239, 242–3
documentarian, 12, 54, 91, 203, 214, 224, 227, 235, 243
experimental, 120
festival, 146
filmmaker(s), 191, 202, 204
genre, 54, 57, 153
storytelling, 204–5
making, 117
dogmatic, 153, 238
Doillon, Jacques, 149
Dolce stil novo (Dolce Stil Novo), 54
domestic, 20, 104–5, 131, 206
dominant, 12–13, 23–4, 49, 72, 106, 136, 143, 151, 154, 217
  critical discourse, 154
  production, 152
  system, 143, 151
  predominant, 149, 159, 206
domination, 193, 238

Donne, John, 164
donor, 133
Dorfles, Gillo, 107
Doria, Enzo, 239
Dove incominciano le gambe (*Where the Legs Begin*), 241
drama, 94, 163, 181, 183, 185, 190–1, 194, 196–7
drawing, 94, 118, 170, 175, 188, 238
 redrawing, 69
dream, 27, 31, 84, 106, 119–20, 158, 160–1, 190, 206, 211–12, 228, 236
drugs, 245
duality, 165
Duchamp, Marcel, 231
duration, 88
Dürer, Albrecht, 168, 171
Dussel, Enrique, 202
Düsseldorf, 70
Dust: The Great Asbestos Trial, 203, 207, 209, 214
DVD, 30, 134, 146, 180, 182–3, 186–8, 190–1, 193–4, 196–7
Dwoskin, Stephen, 12
dynamism, 6–7, 25, 32, 57–9, 87, 104, 182, 196, 205, 209, 250

E fu sera e fu mattina (*And There Was Evening and There Was Morning*), 31, 180, 183–6, 188–91, 196–7
E nua ca simu a forza du mundu (*And We Who Are the Force of the World*), 15, 228–9
Eatherley, Gill, 71–2, 75
eclectic, 28, 55–6, 60, 121, 226, 233
 artistry, 233
 intellectual, 226
ecology, 116, 211, 233
 media ecology, 116
economy, 9, 23, 29, 32, 44, 48–9, 51, 59, 76, 135, 142, 144, 147, 149, 151, 167, 173, 188, 193, 208, 210, 214, 218, 237, 246
 boom, 48
 crisis, 181
 instability, 193
 political, 32, 218, 237, 246
 practices, 142
 structures, 49
ecosystem, 116
Edison Group, 44
Edison, Thomas, 44, 216
editing, 13, 15, 20, 46, 88, 131, 136, 153, 182, 203–5, 213, 231, 242
 continuity, 142
 style, 153
 online, 242
edition, 50, 53–4, 58, 136, 148, 182, 187, 234
 collector, 182
 video, 136
editor, 180, 182, 193
education, 147–9, 151–2, 182, 184
educator, 151
effort, 27–8, 31–2, 54, 56–7, 153, 167, 180–1, 186, 188, 192, 196, 205, 229, 232, 234
 collaborative, 57
 collective, 205
egalitarianism, 151
Egg One Egg Zero, 17, 246
Eggeling, Viking, 112
Egypt, 205
EICTV (Escuela Internacional de Cine y Televisión), 202, 204
Ektrachrome, 166, 175
 film, 166
elasticity, 220–1
Electric Film, 55
electric, 55, 111, 243
electronic, 70, 114, 218, 230–1, 242, 248
 image, 230
 music, 70, 114
 technology, 248
Elia, Celestino, 222
eligibility, 143

Eliot, T. S., 161
emancipatory politics, 48
embassy, 209–10
emerging, 10, 44, 49, 52, 60, 94, 145–6, 172, 203–5
  filmmakers, 145–6, 172
  new voices, 94
Emilia, 88
Emilia Apennines, 137
emotion, 6, 32, 137, 208–10, 213–14
  texture, 208
  value, 134
empirical, 107
employment, 21, 211–12
  unemployment, 206
emulation, 10
emulsion, 109, 111
encounters, 209, 247
encyclopedia, 247
ending, 108, 167
endorsement, 188
energy, 50, 103, 107, 111, 170, 219
engagement, 12, 21, 24, 31, 42, 47–8, 60, 108, 113, 145, 150–2, 154, 159–60, 202, 216, 225, 229, 235
  civic, 151
  critical, 160
  political, 31, 42, 47, 51, 60, 152, 154, 225
  sensorial, 113
  social, 12, 21, 24, 31, 202, 216, 229
England, 184, 221
English, 2, 25, 72, 76, 80, 110, 144, 173, 219, 221, 230, 235–7
  Free Cinema, 110
  language, 2, 25, 247
  literature, 236
  poet, 173
  studies, 221
  subtitles, 230, 235
English, James, 188
enlightenment, 76
entertainment, 5, 133, 138
  arts, 133

entrepreneur, 76 146, 250
entry-form, 134
enunciator, 159, 170, 174
environment, 19, 24, 26, 47, 57, 71, 73, 75, 80, 111, 119, 146, 172, 193, 207, 216, 218–19, 233, 237–8, 249–50
  adaptability, 19
  cultural, 56
  Environmental Screen, 26, 68, 72
  media, 193, 216, 219, 249–50
  natural, 119
  non-institutionalised, 147
  physical, 146, 233
  politicised, 237
  surroundings, 24
  theatre, 75
envision, 74, 76, 78, 95, 110, 112, 116, 160
epiphany, 86, 108
episode, 5, 90–2, 137, 211
  series, 91
epistemology, 104, 216
  approach, 104
epoch, 2–3, 202, 231
Epremian, Pia, 8, 172, 222, 239
equality, 106
  inequality, 206
equipment, 8–9, 15, 20, 42, 94, 131, 147, 218
Ernst, Max, 231, 236
escapism, 119
Es-pi'azione (*Ex-pi'action*), 238
epistemic, 29, 217
  discourse, 217
Esposito, Roberto, 141
Essay Film Diptych, 162, 165
essay, 2, 29, 54, 71, 73, 75, 89–90, 158–62, 164–5, 167–70, 174–5, 216, 219, 239–40
  film, 29, 54, 158–175
  cinema, 161
  style, 161

etchings, 111
Eternit, 173, 207, 209
eternity, 173, 210
ethereal, 68, 72, 242
ethics, 15, 29, 31, 106–7, 141, 148, 150–1, 154, 202–14
   commitments, 29, 141
   concerns, 15
   detachment, 31
   discourse, 150
   documentary, 202
   values, 151
Ethiopia, Ethiopian, 202, 205–6
ethnicity, 219, 242, 249–50
ethnographic, 10, 24, 28, 162, 203, 242
Eucharren, Pablo, 106
eugenise, 245
euphoria, 10, 163–4, 173
Euro(s), 54, 148–9, 183–5, 188, 209
Europe, 2, 7, 11–12, 22–4, 29, 48, 50, 70–1, 75, 105, 120, 132, 142–3, 161, 184, 204, 208, 213, 218–19, 245
   art film/cinema, 50, 54, 245
   cinema, 11, 29, 143
   Commission, 143
   countries, 22
   filmmakers, 56, 143
   galleries, 11
   immigrant, 23
evocation, 78, 80, 116
evolution of cinema, 42, 94
'evolution' process, 238
examination, 26, 250
exchange, 12, 47, 56–7, 188, 190, 226, 235
exclusion, 31, 78, 202, 206, 209–10, 213–14
   Ex-Dogana Eterotopia – Linguaggi Ultra Contemporanei (Heterotopia – Ultra Contemporary Idioms), 247
exhibitor, 51, 192, 194–5, 244, 246
exhibition, 3, 7–9, 11, 16, 18, 31, 70, 72, 103, 118, 192–4, 225, 234, 236, 244, 246
   catalogues, 216–17
   programmes, 16
   theatrical, 193
existence, 218, 245, 250
existentialim, 160–1, 163–4, 169–70, 245
exotic, 230
Expanded Gaze: Mixed Techniques on Screen: The Roman Experimental Cinema, 1965–1975), 232
expanded, 2–3, 9, 15, 27, 71–2, 103–122, 231–2, 247
   cinema, 71–2, 75–6, 107, 110–11, 121
   gaze, 15, 231–2
experience(s), 8, 16, 20–1, 26–7, 31, 48, 50, 57, 59, 69, 78, 86–7, 93–4, 104, 107–8, 110–12, 118–19, 132, 136–7, 147, 152, 158, 161, 163, 163, 167, 169–70, 174–5, 182, 187, 192, 202, 205, 207, 209, 212–13, 224, 226, 228, 230, 237, 242, 245, 247–8, 250
   avant-garde, 86
   cinematic, 20–1
   experiential, 160
   formative, 57
   haptic, 26
   illusory, 248
   kinaesthetic, 78
   life, 31
   media, 227
   optical, 112
   traditional, 68–69
   viewing, 237

INDEX

experimentation, 1–7, 9, 14, 18, 21, 23, 25–7, 45–6, 52, 55, 59–60, 85–7, 114, 116–17, 120, 137, 217–19, 232–4, 238–9, 247
Experimental Cinema.org, 241
expert, 1, 58, 209–10, 224, 236
  expertise, 56, 121, 233
explanatory, 247
exposure, 11, 107, 181, 237, 250
expression, 1–4, 6, 8, 18, 21, 71, 76, 80, 85, 93, 104, 106, 120, 132, 141–2, 144, 148, 152–3, 159, 163–4, 172, 175, 216, 230, 233, 244, 250
  artistic, 85, 141, 148
  cinematic, 142, 144
  creative, 13, 166
  expressionism, 6, 46
  freedom of, 106, 244
  idiomatic, 80
  subjective, 164
expressive, 6–7, 29, 45, 56, 86, 94, 103, 112, 116–17, 119, 121, 159, 202, 212, 219, 231, 237, 240
  conventions, 94
  forms, 231
  freedom, 29
  material, 112
  potential, 240
  technique(s), 119, 159
  tools, 202
  plurally, 6
extra-terrestrial, 111, 118
Extremity 2, 106
eye, 20, 24, 26, 30, 84, 86, 88, 104, 114, 116, 153, 160, 164–5, 176, 185, 208, 222, 229, 233, 242
  camera-eye, 30, 86, 88, 104, 160, 164–5, 176
  fish-eye, 222
  mind's, 114
  new, 185

  public, 70
  'unhealthy eye', 229

fabbriche (factories), 14
Fabrica of Benetton, 54
FAC (Film, Art and Culture), 49
Facce di Festa (Merry Faces), 46
Facebook, 146, 223–24, 228, 246
factories, 14, 49, 51
Fagone, Vittorio, 8
failure, 59–60, 91, 224
Fame chimica (Chemical Hunger), 25, 182, 196
Fame chimica 1 (Chemical Hunger 1), 54
Famiglia Darix Togni films, 136
Family Album, The, 173–5
family, 18, 28, 30, 70, 91, 108, 131–138, 152, 161, 170, 172–5, 207, 212
  album, 174, 161, 173–5
  archive, 175
  Best Family Film, 108
  circus-family, 136
  films, 18, 28, 30, 131–138, 161, 174
  history, 131, 135, 138
  members, 18, 131, 170, 174, 207
  memories, 132, 173
  rituals, 173
  secret, 152
  video, 134
Fantasia, 12
fantasy, 87, 160
Faro Film, 89
fascination, 78, 86, 250
Fascism, 85
feature film, 13, 29–31, 43–4, 55, 144–5, 148–9, 186, 244
  production, 31
  first, 145, 148, 244

features, 21, 24, 45, 91, 103, 134, 136, 142, 145, 148, 152, 154, 190, 216, 219, 228, 247
  aesthetic, 219
  narrative, 21, 142, 154
  thematic, 247
Feda Fargos, 49
Federal Democratic Republic of Ethiopia, 206
feedback, 190, 196
Fellini, Federico, 86, 89–90, 104, 162, 217
female, 25, 116, 167, 171–2, 203, 206
  independent filmmaker, 172
  perspective, 203
  portrait, 116
  protagonist, 25
  subject, 206
feminist, 41, 171
Ferrania (corp.), 226
Ferrania Home Movie Award, 108
Ferrario, Davide, 22, 25, 44, 234
Ferreri, Marco, 17, 89, 96
Ferrero, Mario, 11, 226
Ferroni, Giorgio, 85
Festival of Film and Video, 42, 52–8
festival, 1, 7, 10–12, 16, 18, 23, 25, 42, 52–60, 137, 144–6, 148–9, 161, 180–2, 188–90, 205, 227, 233, 235, 247
  circuit, 189
FIAF (International Federation of Film Archives), 134, 223
Fiat, 14–15, 226
  Fiat ricerca N° 1, 14
FICE (Federazione Italiana Cinema d'Essai – Italian Federation of Essai Cinemas), 189
fiction, 45–6, 55, 89, 93, 138, 148, 159, 164, 167, 205, 213, 229, 244
  film, 45–6, 138, 148
  narratives, 89, 244

nonfiction, 159, 167
  persona, 159
figure, 5–6, 28–9, 68, 84, 145, 151, 207, 211, 226, 228, 233, 235, 239, 244
  eclectic, 28
  emblematic, 5, 244
  geometric, 6
  human, 68
figurative, 13, 76, 107, 116–17, 217, 233
  arts, 217
Filiberti, Marco, 195
Film ambiente (Environmental Screen), 26, 68–80
Film Begets Film, 104
'film di denuncia', 11
film gauge, 7
film genres, 55
film industry, 22, 24, 41–4, 55–6, 60, 70, 142, 147, 184, 193
film installation, 70
film-journal, 172
film-restoration, 134
film school, 44, 147
film stock, 46, 172
filmic, 6, 28, 105, 111, 117, 132–3, 136–7, 160, 165, 168, 173, 204, 219–20, 229–30
  archive, 132
  artefacts, 133, 244
  arts, 6
  collection 136–7
  legacy, 32
  profilmic, 105, 117
  symphonies, 6
  texture, 219–20, 230
Film studio, 8, 110, 247
Film/a/TO, 12
Filmeco, 71
filmgoers, 51
Filmmaker, 41–61

filmography, 27, 29, 228, 230
Filmstudio '70, 10–11, 105
filter, 116
finance, 19, 46, 51, 85, 208, 142–3, 149, 187–8, 218
  crisis, 51
fine arts, 23, 70, 233
Finivest, 43
Fiore d'eringio (*Eryngium*), 30, 160, 168
Firinu, Piergiorgio, 246
first-person, 9, 14, 29–30, 153, 158, 160–1, 175
  filmmaking, 158
  narrator, 30
Fischinger, Oskar, 117
fish-eye photograph, 222
Flaherty, Robert, 26, 87
flash-film (film-lampo), 89, 91–3
flop, 188
Florence/Firenze, 15, 144
Florida, 210
Fluxus, 70, 108
folk, 10, 228
  song, 228
  character, 10
follower, 7, 88, 224
Fondazione (Foundation), 223, 232–3
Fondazione Cineteca Italiana, 223
Fondazione Rocco Guglielmo di Catanzaro (Foundation Rocco Guglielmo in Catanzaro), 232
Fondazione Ugo La Pietra, 233
Fontana, Lucio, 107, 114
footage, 12, 15, 104–5, 114, 116–17, 133–4, 137, 161, 167, 173–4, 222, 224, 243
  archival, 12, 105, 222
  digitised, 134
  found 104–5, 137, 161, 173–4, 243
  fragmentary, 137
  television, 116, 167

foreground, 111–13, 118, 158, 202, 205–6, 209
foreign, 7, 10–11, 15, 21–22, 29, 143, 148, 160, 163, 165, 174, 220, 224, 230
  artists, 10
  country, 174
  cultures, 163
  filmmaking, 143, 148
  genres, 224
  land, 21, 165, 220, 230
  landscapes, 160
formal, 3, 5, 7, 19, 71, 107, 112–13, 117, 120, 153, 159, 162, 169, 203, 224, 230
  approaches, 3
  compositions, 112
  experimentalism, 7, 45–58
  formalism, 5, 9
  innovation, 107, 230
  qualities, 5
  strategies, 46, 57, 173
  techniques, 158, 173
format, 1–2, 14, 55, 58, 121, 133–4, 136–7, 163–4, 193
formation, 57, 197
formative, 15, 30, 57, 202
  experience(s), 57, 202
  years, 30
Formato ridotto (*Reduced Format*), 137
Forties, 107
forum, 145, 184
Foschi, Rosa, 222, 235
fragmentary, 59, 71, 137, 158, 228
  viewing, 228
frame, 48, 51, 72–3, 118, 142, 150, 152–4, 159, 173, 204, 206, 212–13, 219, 232, 237, 241, 243, 246, 250
framework, 7, 47, 51, 57, 59–60, 151
frame-of-mind, 238

Frammartino, Michelangelo, 15, 25, 56–7, 61, 146, 194
Frammenti elettrici (*Electric Fragments*), 243
Frampton, Hollis, 70
France, 5, 7, 149, 211, 213, 221
Francesco Casetti, 50, 120
Francesco Maselli, 43, 89–90
Frascà, Fortunato (Nato), 11, 17, 235
Frattini, Vittore, 109
free, 15–16, 18, 21, 46, 50–1, 69, 78, 84, 93, 107–8, 110, 122, 133, 148, 150–1, 245
    freedom, 3, 10, 21–3, 69, 93, 106–7, 117, 144, 147, 183, 218, 224, 233, 237, 239, 241, 250
    of expression, 21, 29, 106, 150, 244
freelance, 148
French, 4, 26, 87, 94, 131, 143, 149
    cinema, 4, 26, 87
    film tradition, 149
    intellectuals, 94, 131, 143
    New Wave, 121
Fried, Michael, 75
frontiers, 46, 57, 219, 245
Fuga dal call center (*Escape from the Call Centre*), 31, 183–7, 191, 196
'fuga dei cervelli' (a 'brain drain'), 202
Fumagalli, Gianluca, 44, 50
Fumus Art (*Smoke Art*), 117, 119–20
function, 4, 6, 13, 25, 27, 31, 73, 75–6, 78, 92, 138, 144, 146, 180, 183, 185–7, 191, 193, 196–7, 220, 229, 239, 250
    cinematic, 4
    comedic, 138
    cultural, 31, 76, 180, 193, 196
    functionality, 9
    pedagogical, 185
    social, 25
    socio-cultural, 31

funding, 18, 22, 30, 41, 44, 55, 57–8, 60, 80, 85, 132, 134, 148–51, 180–8, 192–3, 196–7, 250
    alternative, 184
    crowdfunding, 134, 183–4
    governmental, 151, 196, 250
    self-funded, 148–9
fundamental, 8, 80, 88, 94, 145
    intermediary, 8
    role, 94
    to cinema, 80
    to the new vision, 88
    vector, 145
Fuocoammare (*Fire at Sea*), 23
Fuori Orario, 18
Fusaro, Gregory, 31, 194
future, 15, 71, 73, 84–6, 88, 92, 107, 121, 187, 196–7, 205, 209–10, 212–13
futuristic, 113, 205
Futurismo rivisitato (*Futurism Revisited*), 6, 219
Futurist, 218, 219–22
    filmmakers, 221
    films, 6

Gallery Denise René, 80
gallery, 1, 11, 16, 33, 244, 246, 250
Garrone, Matteo, 193, 234
gastronomic, 203
Gaudino, Giuseppe, 22–3
gauge, 7, 133–4
gaze, 12, 15, 88, 118, 137, 144, 153, 160, 165, 231–2
Gelmetti, Vittorio, 70
gender, 25, 28, 41, 72, 206, 242
generation, 41, 46–8, 52–8, 106, 112, 135, 192, 224, 232
    aspirations, 47
    beat, 106, 224
    footprint, 52
    gap, 57

new generation of filmmakers, 45, 54, 56–8, 192
of avant-garde filmmakers, 112, 232
older generation of experts, 58
younger, 41
generic, 7, 144, 169
conventions, 169
forms, 7
political value, 144
genesis, 47–8, 115
genre, 14, 22, 54–5, 57, 87, 132, 146, 153, 167, 175, 180–3, 192, 194, 218, 224–5, 233
'against-all-odds', 194
cross-genre, 146
documentary, 54, 57, 153
film, 55
foreign, 224
genre-resistant, 153
narrative, 22
trade story, 180–3, 192, 194
Gente del Po (*People of the Po Valley*), 43, 161
geographical, 19, 22, 60, 134, 147, 162
geometrical, 68, 107, 114
configurations, 107
patterns, 114
Germany, 7, 46, 184, 211
anti-German, 29
cinema, 4
expressionism, 6
New German cinema, 58
gestation, 193
gestuality, 118
Ghezzi, Enrico, 18
Ghione, Riccardo, 89
Gianikian, Yervant, 12, 242–3
Giannarelli, Ansano, 93
gift, 194, 245
Il dono (*The Gift*), 194
Ginna, Arnaldo, 5–6, 219
Gioli, Paolo, 8, 19–20, 71, 120–1, 239, 240–1

Giordana, Marco Tullio, 25, 44
Giornate del cinema privato (Days of Private Cinema), 9
Giornate Europee del Cinema (*European-Days of Cinema*), 184
Giorni di gloria (*Days of Glory*), 85
Giovinezza, giovinezza, primavera di bellezza (*Youth, Youth, Spring of Beauty*), 243
Giro di lune tra terra e mare (*Moons Spins between Land and Sea*), 23
Giulia in ottobre (*Giulia in October*), 25, 54
Gli Archivi per la ricerca anagrafica (*Family-Registry Research Archives*), 135
Gli invisibili, 2000–2010: Dieci anni di cinema nascosto (*The Invisibles, 2000–2010: Ten Years of Hidden Cinema*), 191
Gli sbandati (*The Wayward*), 43
globe, 58, 160, 207, 219
art cinema, 58
audiences, 213
audio-visual networks, 71
locations, 202
migration, 209
Global North, 207, 210
globalisation, 31, 202–14
Global South, 207, 210
'online village', 230
perspective, 59, 70
social networks, 146
stories, 205
transformation, 151
Go Kart, 108
goal, 10, 132, 134, 143, 147, 191, 204, 224
artistic, 10
creative, 147
pedagogic, 56
policy, 143

God, 153, 167
godfather, 53
golden age, 142
Google, 134, 228, 237, 246
Gospel, 229
government, 18, 150–1, 181, 193, 196–7, 209, 212, 223, 250
    funded cinema, 151, 181, 196–7, 250
    Italian, 212, 223
    of Quebec, 209
    sponsorship, 18
Graffiti, 172
grain, 113
    grainy, 107
Granchi, Andrea, 15
graphic, 55, 233, 235, 246
    computer, 55
    design, 233
Gray, Jonathan, 30, 180, 182, 187, 193
Greek, 169–71, 212
    mythology, 169, 171
    poet, 170
Greenberg, Clement, 70
Grierson, John, 26, 87
Grifi, Alberto, 13, 15, 18, 162, 222, 231–2
grips, 180
Gris, Juan, 87
groundwork, 107
group, 5, 8, 11, 14–15, 17, 24–5, 44, 48–9, 57, 60, 105–6, 167, 195–6, 210, 216–17, 221–2, 226, 237
    catholic, 49
    Edison Group, 44
    'Group One', 17
    leftist, 49
    Living Theatre, 8
    of artists, 217
    of *cinema d'essai*, 195
    online grouping, 237
    RING, 196
    Roman, 222

Gruppo Uno, 17, 216
Guazzoni, Enrico, 5
Guédiguian, Robert, 149
gusto, 170

H2Odio (*H2Odium*), 193
H8, 103, 108, 117, 172
habit, 4, 218, 248
    of consumption, 218
    conventional practices, 4
    surroundings, 27
habitat, 19, 107, 211
hallucinogenic, 119
hand-coloured, 6, 109, 111–12, 117, 122
hand-painted, 109
Haneke, Michael 149
happening, 13, 75, 108, 117, 119, 166, 237
happiness, 164
    happy endings, 142
hardship, 30, 182, 214
hardware, 46, 246
Harrington, Curtis, 12
He, Hui, 203
healer, 210
heavenly, 112
hegemonic, 42, 143, 152
    cinematic practices, 143
    discourse, 152
    film, 42
Her, 160, 165–8
heritage, 30, 33, 132, 135, 149, 172–5, 223, 238
    audiovisual, 135
    cinematic, 223
    cultural, 33, 133, 149, 172–4, 238
    Italo-American, 172–5
heroes, 31, 84, 93, 142, 159, 171, 183, 245
    heroism, 181
Herzog, Werner, 32, 203–5

heterogeneous, 53, 71, 89, 166–7, 202
　films, 53
heteroglossic, 202
Hidden Zavattini (*Zavattini sottotraccia*), 93
hierarchy, 89
　framework, 60
　model, 58
　order, 132
Higgins, Dick, 70
Hilarisdoppio, 240
historian, 1, 27–8, 59, 103, 108, 217, 221, 230
history, 1–7, 10, 12, 15, 42, 20, 23–6, 28–9, 30, 42–5, 47–8, 53, 58–9, 70, 84–5, 87, 90, 93, 103–4, 112, 131–8, 138, 144, 158, 160–1, 163, 165–7, 169, 171, 173–5, 205–6, 208, 216–20, 223–6, 228, 233, 241–5, 247, 250
　analysis, 24, 224
　anti-fascist movement, 141
　avant-garde, 1, 5, 20, 32, 87, 103, 112, 219, 241
　chronohistory of vision, 20
　cinematic history, 2, 219
　considerations, 42–5
　context, 2, 47, 141, 158, 220
　cooperatives, 15, 250
　data, 134
　dimension, 165
　family history, 131, 138
　forms, 174, 250
　historicity, 249
　historiography, 226, 232, 242
　household, 135
　interest, 133
　landscape, 104
　micro-histories, 42
　movement, 6
　music, 5
　of advertising, 226
　of art, 163
　of independent film centres, 24–5, 47, 53
　of Italian cinema/filmmaking, 1, 7, 26, 30, 84–5, 90, 95, 244
　of Italian experimental and independent cinema, 104
　of Milanese cinema, 45
　of moving images, 217–18
　of post-war Europe, 48
　of the audiovisual, 93
　of the country, 5, 23, 28
　of the medium, 30
　of the Resistance, 85
　of world cinema, 4–5
　outline of essay films, 160–1
　Parru Historical Institute of Bologna, 132, 135
　pre-historical vision of humanity, 164
　records, 160
　roots, 29
　social, 158
　Storia del cinema italiano (*History of Italian Cinema*), 90
　use of family films, 136–8
　Women History Archive, 136
Hollywood, 13, 22, 142, 180, 181, 187, 196, 231
Home Movie Award, 108
home movie, 28, 105, 108, 131–3, 135, 137, 161, 173–5
　video, 58, 182, 191, 193
homeland, 212–13
homeless, 18, 208
Homeward, 211–13
homogenise, 219, 245
homonymous, 152
homosexual relations, 152
honesty, 153
hope, 94, 188, 206, 209–10, 213–14
horizon, 27, 94, 110, 136

horizontal, 142
Horkheimer, Marx, 75
Horror Film 1, 72
hospital, 15, 19, 148, 207
   Policlinico Hospital's Struggle, 15
host, 11, 32, 50, 68, 210, 223, 232, 246–7
'hot autumn' 27, 93
household, 135
Hui He. The Soprano from the Silk Road, 203
Huillet, Danièle, 11
human, 164, 116, 217
   capital, 238
   rights, 160, 168
   trafficking, 213
humanism, 26, 31, 85, 94
hybridism, 89, 158, 162, 175, 235
hypertextual, 242

I 400 colpi—La Cineteca di Quartiere (The 400 Blows—The Local Film Library), 146
I basilischi (The Basilisks), 44
I colori della luce (The Colours of Light), 14, 113, 226
I Cormorani (The Cormorants), 146
I corpi estranei (Foreign Bodies), 29, 148–9, 152
I fidanzati (The Fiances), 45
I film di famiglia 1959–1974 (Family Films 1959–1974), 138
I misteri di Roma (The Mysteries of Rome), 27, 92
I ragazzi che si amano (Youngsters in Love), 44
Iannucci, Lorenzo, 48
ICET (Industrie Cinematiche e Teatrali – Cinema and Theatre Industries), 42–3, 56
iconic, 9, 230
   iconoclasm, 231, 232, 235
   iconography, 138

Idea assurda per un filmaker (book), 122
Idea assurda per un filmaker. Luna (An Absurd Idea for a Filmmaker. Moon), 111, 114, 116
Idea assurda per un filmaker. Ester (An Absurd Idea for a Filmmaker. Ester), 115
Idea assurda per un filmaker. Germana (An Absurd Idea for a Filmmaker. Germana), 115
Idea assurda per un filmaker. Matilde (An Absurd Idea for a Filmmaker. Matilde), 115
ideal, 3, 6, 71, 73, 78, 89–90, 104, 203, 218, 233
   development, 73, 89
   form, 6
   idealisation, 211–12
   perspective, 245
   project, 204
   state, 218
   views, 3
identity, 9, 24, 28, 31–3, 52, 57, 59, 148–51, 211, 213, 250
   artistic, 9
   'community', 211
   cultural, 33
   ethnographic, 24
   'Independence as Negotiated Identity' 148–51
   Italic, 24
   national, 211
   political, 151
ideology, 19, 20, 22–5, 31, 47–8, 51–2, 60, 72, 142, 144, 151–4
   categories, 52
   communist, 151
   dominant, 72
   freedom, 23
   landscape, 142
   locus, 22
   Marxist, 47, 60
   opposition, 152

orthodox, 51
scheme, 151
vision, 20
idiosyncratic, 1, 18, 103, 108, 158, 174–5, 214, 241, 244
  artworks, 108
  custom, 174
  point of view, 214
  style, 103, 244
  work, 241
Il capital (*The Capital*), 49
Il compleanno (*David's Birthday*), 195
Il deserto rosso (*Red Desert*), 70
Il dono (*The Gift*), 194
Il film sperimentale (*The Experimental Film*), 30, 236
Il fitto dei padroni non lo paghiamo più (*We Will No Longer Pay the Masters' Rent*), 15
Il gemello (*The Twin*), 23
Il giardino delle delizie (*Garden of Delights*), 21, 244–5
Il grande progetto (*The Big Project*), 23
Il mio domani (*My Tomorrow*), 195
Il pianeta azzurro (*The Blue Planet*), 21
Il prigioniero della montagna (*The Prisoner of the Mountain*), 43
Il primo giorno d'inverno (*The First Day of Winter*), 29, 148, 152, 196
Il primo incarico (*The First Assignment*), 195
Il rumore del sole (*The Noise of the Sun*), 29, 149
Il sole sorge ancora (*The Sun Rises Again*), 85
Il tempo dell'uomo (*The Time of Man*), 26, 71
Il terrorista (*The Terrorist*), 44
Il vento fa il suo giro (*The Wind Blows Round*), 22, 189–90, 195, 197
illusion, 78–80, 87, 174, 237, 240, 248, 250

illustration, 90, 114–16, 154, 165, 171, 181, 188, 192, 236
image, 3–4, 7, 9, 12–13, 16, 20, 24–6, 42, 51, 72–3, 78, 80, 88, 90, 92–3, 104–5, 107–9, 112, 114, 116–19, 133–4, 136–7, 149, 159–61, 163–7, 170–4, 182, 189–91, 202, 216–18, 227, 230, 245, 247–8
  abstract, 72–3
  amateur, 134
  chromatic, 112
  'concrete', 107
  documentary, 161
  electronic, 230
  filmic, 230
  imageless film, 72
  moving-, 4, 7, 9, 16, 24–6, 70, 116, 160, 163, 172, 174, 216–18, 227, 230, 245, 247–8
  self-, 191
  still, 117, 163, 174
  virtual, 78, 80
imagery, 76, 111, 116, 119, 159, 164, 171, 245
  abstract, 76, 111
  archaic, 164
  documentary, 171
  text and, 159
  textual, 119
imagination, 6, 109–11, 113, 116, 118–20, 158, 160–4, 167, 169, 172–3, 175
immediacy, 84, 91, 93, 64, 166, 168, 217
immigrant, 23, 174, 212
immigration, 32, 228, 231
  online, 32
impegno (engagement), 4, 11–12, 15, 21, 24, 31, 42, 47–8, 60, 151, 154, 202, 216, 229, 235
  film/cinema of social, 12, 15, 151, 154, 229
  ethics of, 31

impegno (engagement) (*cont.*)
  social/political, 4, 11–12, 21, 24, 31, 42, 47, 60, 202, 216
imperative, 47, 134, 219, 224, 238, 249
impression, 104, 108, 114, 158, 161
  impressionistic, 108–9, 163
improvise, 187
impulse, 4, 21, 121, 159, 224
In via Savona al 57 (*At 57 Savona Street*), 31, 189, 192, 194–5
inanimate, 245
incarnation, 72, 217
inclination, 43, 107
independence, 1–4, 6, 9, 18, 20–3, 29, 32–3, 108, 141–3, 145, 147–8, 150–1, 154, 216–19, 228, 230, 234–5, 237–8, 245–7, 250
indexical, 164
India, 111, 117, 120, 160–4, 168, 170–1, 202, 204, 208–9
  Appunti per un film sull'India (*Notes for a Film about India*), 162
  ink, 111, 117, 120
  Indian literature, 164
  Indian text, 160
indie, 142, 181–2, 184–97
  film/cinema, 181–2, 187–97
  film culture, 196–7
  filmmakers/directors, 181, 184–90, 196–7
Indigena, 42, 55
indigenous, 10, 18, 20, 25, 237
industry, 14, 17–18, 20–2, 24, 41–6, 51–2, 55–6, 59–60, 70, 72, 75, 79, 90, 94, 119, 138, 142–3, 147–9, 151, 181, 193, 208–9, 216, 221, 226, 230, 238, 244–5, 247
  advertising, 43–4, 46, 51–2, 56
  asbestos, 209
  autonomous, 56
  competitive, 181

creative, 60
culture, 75
film, 22, 24, 41–5, 55–6, 60, 70, 142, 147, 193
formula/model, 20–1
media, 181
music, 46
national cinema, 59, 244
self-sufficient, 59
tech, 138
television, 52
inequality, 206
Infascelli, Alex, 193
infinite, 80, 111, 120
information, 17, 28, 134, 136–7, 145–6, 186, 196, 209, 223, 225, 227, 235
Informazione Leitmotiv: L'informazione è ciò che conta (*Information Leitmotif: Information Is What Matters*), 17
infrastructure, 42
ingenuity, 32, 180–1, 183, 234
inhabit, 73, 112, 164, 175, 216
inhabitants, 247
  of cyberspace, 247
inhuman, 153, 248
initiative, 4, 7–8, 10, 14, 17, 22, 27, 30, 44, 49–51, 54, 57, 59–60, 105, 110, 132, 135, 137, 145–6, 216, 218, 227, 230, 247
innovation, 1, 4–6, 8, 14, 16, 24, 26, 44, 52–3, 56–7, 59, 103–4, 107, 112, 121–2, 134, 136, 187–8, 193–4, 197, 219, 230, 242, 250
inspiration, 5, 8, 15, 18, 30, 58, 68, 75, 104, 109, 182, 237, 242, 244
instability, 193, 221
installation, 26, 46–7, 55, 57, 69–72, 74, 76, 80, 135, 137, 222, 233–4, 240

instinct, 103, 108, 194
Institute of Contemporary Art, 70
institution, 1, 22, 28, 44–5, 56, 60, 71–2, 106, 131, 143, 147, 150, 184, 189, 214, 218, 221, 244, 249
instructions, 116
instrument, 10, 14, 59, 136, 190, 233
integration, 142
integrity, 248
intellectual, 9–11, 16, 41, 44, 48, 51–2, 56, 84, 87, 94, 103, 217, 221, 226, 231, 235
  intellectualism, 217
intelligentsia, 55
interaction, 42, 52, 107, 114, 206
  interactivity, 136, 190, 234
interconnection, 138
interdisciplinary, 16, 24, 41, 47, 217, 219, 235
interest, 3, 11, 17, 20, 28, 32–3, 44, 47, 50–1, 54, 56–7, 59–61, 70, 75, 79, 89, 91, 93, 107, 115, 119–20, 131–3, 135, 149, 160–1, 165, 176, 202–4, 206, 214, 221, 227–9, 250
  interesse culturale (cultural interest), 149
interior, 160, 247
intermediality, 68–9, 70–72
international, 1, 8, 12, 18, 24–6, 28, 31, 42, 44, 54, 56, 58–61, 108, 118, 121, 134, 147–9, 160–2, 203, 205, 207–8, 214, 218, 223, 233, 239
  accolades, 203
  appeal, 28, 56
  awards, 203
  careers, 25
  circulation, 59
  co-production, 147, 149
  counterparts, 12
  court, 207–8
  craftsmanship/practices, 24–5, 108, 121
  discourse, 26
  Federation of Film Archives (FIAF), 134, 223
  festivals/exhibition, 12, 18, 58–9, 118, 148–9, 233
  film, 1, 8, 24, 223
  film co-operatives, 160
  film practices, 1
  filmmakers, 162, 239
  legal authorities, 208
  migration, 214
  museums, 233
  practices, 25, 108, 121
  production, 205
  recognition/acclaim, 42, 44, 54
  social issues, 31, 214
International Federation of Film Archives (FIAF), 134, 223
'Internet Italia', 2018
Internet, 11, 217–18, 223–4, 228, 235, 246–7, 249–50
  'giants', 246
  of things, 217
  technologies, 11, 224, 237, 249–50
  users, 223, 235
interpellation, 138
interpretation, 6–7, 16, 89, 92, 134, 141
intertextual, 158, 164
Interventi pubblici per la città di Milano (*Public Works for the City of Milan*), 19
interview, 24–5, 29, 42, 52, 109, 134, 137, 141, 147, 167, 172, 174, 182, 186, 191–3, 195, 197, 203, 210, 212–13, 217, 224, 231–2, 234, 239, 245, 247
  interviewee, 186
Into the House, 30, 161, 173–4

invention, 26, 104, 187, 216, 233, 237
  approach, 104
  inventiveness, 5–6, 137, 219, 250
  proclivity, 233
  Recupero e reinvenzione (*Restoration and Reinvention*), 19
  reinvention, 20, 238
inventor, 19–20, 79, 231
inventory, 134
invisibility, 84, 191–2, 197
  Gli invisibili (*The Invisibles*), 189, 192
  Gli invisibili, 2000–2010: Dieci anni di cinema nascosto (*The Invisible, 2000–2010: Ten Years of Hidden Cinema*), 191
  Gli invisibili: Esordi nel cinema italiano, 2000–2006 (*The Invisibles: Debuts in Italian Cinema, 2000–2006*), 31, 192
  films, 191
Iran, 168, 171
irony, 19, 70, 75, 111, 116, 118–19, 173, 210, 231, 234
Isabelle, 149, 152
Islamic, 152, 167
Isola del Cinema Arena (Cinema Island Arena), 190
Israel, 168
ISTAT, 249
Istituti di Cultura (Institutes of Italian Culture), 221
Istituto Storico Parri di Bologna (Parri Historical Institute of Bologna), 132, 135
  Istituto Tecnico Statale a Ordinamento Speciale (State Technical Institute with Special Orientation), 58
Italic, 7, 24, 233
  arts, 7
  creative genius, 233

identity, 24
Latin stock, 4, 31
Italo-American, 172–5
Italy, 1–2, 7–8, 10–13, 16–19, 21–4, 26–7, 29, 31, 41, 48, 53, 61, 70, 72, 75–6, 86, 89, 91–2, 103–7, 131–3, 143–5, 147–9, 151, 161, 171–2, 180–1, 183, 187–90, 192–7, 202, 207, 212–13, 218–21, 223–6, 228–9, 231, 239, 245
  Central, 148
  Communist Party, 151
  'Italian difference', 29, 141–5, 151–2, 154
  Ministry of Culture, 149
  short films, 54
  Socialist Party, 51
itinerant, 175, 202

Jalongo, Valerio, 31, 196
Janni, Bruno, 44–5
Japan, Japanese, 21, 71, 161, 175, 245
Jerusalem, 160, 164
job, 147, 186, 195, 197, 209, 212, 245
  market, 147, 151
Jour et nuit (*Day and Night*), 223–4
journal, 26, 30, 41, 84, 89, 108, 110, 112, 161, 172, 175, 221, 236, 243
  cine-, 89
  film-, 110, 112, 172, 221, 236, 243
  online, 239
journalism, 86, 93
journey, 19, 22, 26, 48, 52, 84, 92, 158, 160–1, 163, 168, 170–1, 175, 221, 241
judge, 183
jump cuts, 119
June, 105
justice, 208–9
juxtaposition, 12, 17, 24, 27–8, 104, 114, 131, 164, 169, 212

Kandinsky, Vasilij Vasilevič, 164
Katha-Upanishad, 164
Kiarostami, Abbas, 203
kinetic, 13, 71, 78, 112, 117, 227
   installations, 71
   paintings, 117
   potential, 227
Kino-Glaz, 84
Kline, Franz, 109
Klinger, Barbara, 182
knowledge, 30, 85–7, 135, 146–7, 176, 182, 210
Kodak film, 133
Kracauer, Siegfried, 84
Kramer, Robert, 11
Kubelka, Peter, 12

L'alfabeto (*The Alphabet*), 14
L'amministratore (*The Administrator*), 23
L'amore in città (*Love in the City*), 27, 88–9
L'aria salata (*Salty Air*), 182
L'avanzata di Tripolitania (*The Tripolitania Advance*), 243
L'India vista da Rossellini (*India as Seen by Rossellini*), 161
L'isola in capo al mondo (*The Island on Top of the World*), 229
L'occhio è per così dire l'evoluzione biologica di una lacrima (*The Eye Is, So-To-Speak, the Biological Evolution of a Tear*), 162
L'orso di paglia (*Rye Bear*), 211
L'ultima Estate (*The Last Summer*), 168, 170
L'uomo che verrà (*The Man Who Will Come*), 22, 195
L'uomo fiammifero (*The Thin Match Man*), 31, 183–6, 188, 190–1, 196
L'uomo proiettile (*The Rocket Man*), 21
La bella gente (*Beautiful People*), 191
La bocca del lupo (*The Mouth of the Wolf*), 23
La capagira (*The Head Spins*), 182
La casa del cinema (The Cinema House), 247
La casa delle belle addormentate (*The Home of the Sleeping Beauties*), 25
La casa è un diritto non un privilegio (*Housing Is a Right and Not a Privilege*), 15
La casa telematica (*The Telematic House*), 19
La città del capitale (*The City of Capital*), 49
La fine della notte (*The End of the Night*), 22
La Fura dels Baus, 205
La Lega (The North League), 52
La legge è uguale per tutti (*All Are Equal before the Law*), 108
La mano nell'occhio (*A Hand in the Eye*), 15
La musica della danza (*The Music of Dance*), 6
La nott'el giorno (*The Night an' Day*), 230
La notte (*The Night*), 22, 42
La Pietra, Ugo, 8, 19, 33, 222, 233, 234, 242
La Porta, Andrea, 8
La Prealpina (*The Pre-Alps Journal*), 108
La prova generale (*The Dress Rehearsal*), 17
La riappropriazione della città (*The Re-Appropriation of the City*), 19, 234
La rimpatriata (*The Reunion*), 44
La strada, 22, 90
La strada di Levi (*Primo Levi's Journey*), 22

La terra trema (*The Earth Trembles*), 85
La verifica incerta (*Disperse Exclamatory Phase*), 13, 231
La veritaaaà (*The Truuuuth*), 85
La vita agra (*It's a Hard Life*), 43
lab, 1, 3, 7–8, 14–16, 42, 45, 50, 132
   art, 8
   experimentation, 3
   media-, 1
   Mount Olimpino Studio, 14
   of the Florence School, 15
   restoration, 132
   self-run, 7
Là-bas – Educazione criminale (*Là-bas: A Criminal Education*), 182
labyrinthine, 73
Lajolo, Anna, 8, 11, 14, 222, 225, 228–9
Lampedusa, 23
Land Art, 119
landscape, 6, 41, 49, 51–2, 58–60, 90, 104, 116, 119, 133, 142, 144, 160–1, 165, 171, 175, 212
   aestheticised, 212
   cinema, 58
   cinematic, 49
   financial/economic, 51
   historical, 104
   heritage, 133
   ideological, 142
   'mindscape and', 175
   natural, 116, 171
   political, 144, 151
   regional, 41
   technological, 58
   urban, 59, 90
language, 2, 7, 9, 13, 16, 25–6, 52–3, 55, 57, 93, 104, 107, 109, 114, 116, 131, 153, 172, 210, 224, 234, 247–8
   alternative, 131

   body, 210
   cinematic, 16, 53, 55, 57, 224, 248
   English, 2, 25, 247
   film, 13, 16, 114, 116, 153
   Italian, 234
   style and, 7, 9, 109
   visual, 16
   written, 26
Lattuada, Alberto, 60, 86, 89
Le amiche (*The Girlfriends*), 90
Le farfalle (*Butterflies*), 5
Le gote in fiamme (*The Cheeks Aflame*), 12, 233
Le Grice, Malcolm, 71–2, 75, 112
Le lotte di via Tibaldi (*Struggles in via Tibaldi*), 49
Le porte girevoli (*Revolving Doors*), 12
Le Prince, Louis, 78
Le quattro volte (*The Four Times*), 146
Le vie del cinema (*The Ways of Cinema*), 51
Left, the, 48–50, 137, 241
   the new, 52
legacy, 2, 4–11, 15, 24–6, 32, 91–4, 107, 133, 137–4, 161–2, 169, 175, 218–22, 229, 233, 249–50
   artistic, 243
   cinematic, 2, 10, 220
   filmic, 32
   Italian tradition, 219, 249
   of documentary, 15
   of Futurists, 221
   of Italian visual memory, 229
   of visual culture, 133
   Pirelli's, 26
   'Transformative Legacy', 91–4
legal, 29, 132, 191, 208, 210, 214
   illegal, 210
legitimise, 22, 217, 238
Lennon, John, 203
lens, 8, 93, 116

telephoto-, 93
zoom, 116
Leonardi, Alfredo, 8, 11, 13–15,
  19–20, 33, 104, 121, 222, 228–9,
  231, 238
Leonardi, Silvana, 226
Les Cahiers du Cinéma, 94
lessons, 188, 229
L'eta del ferro (*The Iron Age*), 45
letter, 88, 91–2, 104, 118, 166–7, 226
Leyda, Jay, 104
liability, 250
liberation, 9, 22, 24, 144, 247
  Cinegiornali Liberi (*Free Cine-
    newsreels*), 161
  cinema of, 247
  cultural, 9, 24
  Italian movement, 144
liberty, 161
library, 146, 175, 223, 233, 235
  City of Bologna Film Library, 233
  Columbia Butler's Library, 175
  film, 132, 146, 223, 233
  Luigi Chiarini Library, 235
  National Film Library, 223
licei (Lyceums), 48
Lichtspiel Opus 1–4, 114
life, 20, 23, 26–8, 30–1, 43, 59, 90, 92,
  104, 107–8, 110, 116, 118, 120–1,
  132–3, 135–7, 145, 152, 158,
  161–5, 169–72, 175–6, 185, 190,
  203–5, 207–11, 213, 216, 221,
  227–8, 245, 248
  afterlife, 120
  allegories of life and death, 171
  art, 56
  contemporary, 26, 170
  courage in, 185, 190
  documenting, 107
  emptiness of, 171
  everyday, 132, 135, 162–4
  expectancy, 208

experiences, 31, 108, 110, 152, 161
family, 133, 172
imaginary, 163
La vita agra (*It's a Hard Life*), 43
lifeblood of indie cinema, 197
lifelong struggle, 207
lifespan of co-ops, 216
Nigerian, 213
nomadic, 161, 175
political, 27
process of 204
professional, 145
pseudo-life experience, 248
story/stories, 28, 136, 209, 227
real, 92, 121
*Se la vita è meglio, butti via la
  telecamera* (*If Life Is Better,
  Throw Away the Camera*), 227
social, 118
true to, 203
way of, 59, 211, 245
Ligabue, Antonio, 23
light, 19, 25–6, 68, 71–6, 78, 80, 89,
  91, 104, 109, 111–14, 118, 120,
  148, 187, 242
  'and liminal', 25, 68–80
  'architecture', 73, 76
  'bath of', 75
  bulbs, 71
  cinematic, 78
  coloured, 68, 72, 76
  Deserto in luce solare (*Desert in the
    Sunlight*), 113
  etchings, 111
  experiments, 78
  I colori della luce (*The Colours of
    Light*), 14, 113–14
  lighting, 148, 187
  light-play, 114
  Light-play: Black-White-Gray, 114
  Luce e movimento (*Light and
    Movement*), 26

light (*cont.*)
    Luci del Varietà (*Variety Lights*), 86
    Mothlight, 109
    red, 242
    'sounds into light variations', 74
Light-play: Black-White-Gray, 114
liminality, 72
lineage, 161
LinkedIn, 146
Lira, 54
    post-, 54
Lischi, Sandra, 3, 8, 18
Lissitzky, El, 73
literal, 48, 73, 76, 87, 190, 206, 245
literary, 4, 11, 31, 47, 159, 164, 167, 171, 193, 236
literature, 2, 41, 85–6, 93, 104, 137, 164, 171, 176, 236
live, 74–5, 133, 135, 145, 247
    encounters, 247
    messaging, 145
    music, 135
    performance, 75
    're-told live', 133
    soundtrack, 74
Living Theatre, 8, 75, 108, 229
Lizzani, Carlo, 85, 89
Lo sguardo espanso: Tecniche Miste su Schermo: cinema sperimentale di Roma, 1965–1975 (*The Expanded Gaze: Mixed Techniques on Screen: Roman Experimental Cinema, 1965–1975*), 232
Lo svitato (*The Nut*), 43
local, 10, 25, 41–2, 44–6, 50–1, 54–8, 60, 115, 136, 145–6, 172, 205, 207–9, 228, 247, 250
    advertising industry, 44
    and foreign artists, 10
    'and global', 205
    authorities, 51, 55, 57–8, 60
    bank, 54–5, 60
    businesses, 45
    community, 145
    customs, 136
    dialect, 228
    factories, 51
    funding, 60
    geographies, 172
    glocal perspective, 207–9
    I 400 colpi-La Cineteca di Quartiere (*The 400 Blows-The Local Film Library*), 146
    industries, 41, 44–5, 55, 60, 250
    initiatives, 247
    institutions, 45
    left-wing radio, 50
    niche and, 250
    paper, 115, 207
    production companies, 46
location, 11, 42, 89, 112, 146, 149–50, 164, 185, 188, 202, 206–8, 211
    geo-localisation, 134
    localised milieu, 224
    people and locals, 228
    relocation, 58, 211
Locarno Film Festival, 54, 56
Locatelli, Mirko, 29, 141–54, 196
Loffredo, Silvio, 13
logic, 31, 47, 238
logistical, 22, 186, 188, 214
Lombardi, Guido, 8, 11, 13–15, 41, 106, 182, 222, 228–30
Lombardia (Lombardy), 51, 55
London, Jack, 23
London, 7, 70, 161, 221
    Underground Film Festival, 161
    Institute of Contemporary Arts (ICA), 70
long-takes, 153
Los Angeles Istituto Italiano di Cultura, 239
LoSpettacolo.it, 239

LostScapes, 135
Lotta di classe alla Fiat (*Class Struggle at Fiat*), 15
Lotte a Milano (*Struggles in Milan*), 49
Louvre, 168
love, 8, 21, 23, 27, 44, 50, 58, 85, 88, 90–2, 117, 152, 159, 168, 173, 176, 190, 209, 245
  Amarsi a Marghera (*Love in Marghera*), 117
  and death, 159
  Comizi d'amore (*Love Meetings*), 92
  Cronache di poveri amanti (*Chronicles of Poor Lovers*), 85
  D'amore si vive (*Living on Love*), 21
  I ragazzi che si amano (*Youngsters in Love*), 44
  'labour of love', 8
  L'amore in città (*Love in the City*), 27, 88, 90–1
  'dialogue', 168
  Milanese film lovers, 58
  Per amor Vostro (*For Your Love*), 23
  young cinema lovers, 50
  'younger lover', 152
low-budget, 2, 9, 44–5, 50, 54–6, 59, 94, 143, 146, 149, 180–1, 183–7
  low-cost/high-cost, 9, 49, 51, 144, 147, 181, 223
l.s.d., 17
Lucca Film Festival Europacinema, 11
Luce e Movimento (*Light and Movement*), 26, 78
Luci del Varietà (*Variety Lights*), 86
Luginbhül, Sirio, 117
Luigi Chiarini Library, 235
Lukàcs, György, 88
luminous, 77
Lye, Len, 112, 117

lyrical, 4, 8, 10, 13, 16, 18, 21, 30, 105, 112–13, 117, 121, 158–60, 167, 170, 175
  film, 13
  style, 8, 10, 21, 117, 159–60, 167, 170, 175

McCall, Anthony, 71
McGilvray, Catherine, 192
machine, 20, 79, 103, 151, 250
  -gun, 103
machinery, 22
microscope, 84
Made in Usa, 17
Maderna, Giovanni, 54
Madonna, 171
magazine(s), 11, 86, 88, 90, 118, 166–7, 246–7
Maggioni, Daniele, 50, 55
magic, 80, 120, 228
Magicarena, 203, 205–7, 214
magnetic media, 133
mainstream, 1–3, 12, 16, 18, 20–2, 31–2, 45, 49–50, 52, 55, 59, 61, 71, 142–3, 152, 181, 197, 224, 234
  audience, 21, 224, 234
  canons, 20
  cinema, 12, 16, 18, 21–2, 31–2, 45, 50, 52, 55, 59, 61, 142–3, 152, 234
  institutions, 71
  media, 143
  non-, 18, 181, 197
  vs. independent cinema, 142
making-of, 30, 57, 92, 119, 183, 185
Moldavian, 205
male, 25, 206, 211
  -dominated, 72
Malina, Judith, 75
man, 12, 20–2, 26, 31, 71, 87–8, 92, 94, 120, 152, 158, 160–1, 164, 168–71, 183, 195, 205, 212, 235, 243

man (*cont.*)
    Albanian, 212
    cameraman, 235, 243
    'eyes', 153
    Il tempo dell'uomo (*The Times of Man*), 26, 71
    L'uomo che verrà (*The Man Who Will Come*), 22, 195
    L'uomo fiammifero (*The Thin Match Man*), 31, 183
    L'uomo proiettile (*The Rocket Man*), 21
    Man of Aran, 87
    Moroccan, 212
    Oh! Uomo (*Oh! Man*), 12
    'one-man crew', 21–2
    'praying', 92
    'prop', 205
    'racist', 152
    'rapport with the arts', 248
    'sense of reality in', 120
    'single', 92
    'to machine', 20
    'unemployed', 88
    'voice', 171
    'young', 94
    'young artist', 158, 160–1, 164, 168–70
Man of Aran, 87
management, 194, 216, 249
manifestation, 144–5, 216
manifesto, 19, 29, 58, 144, 218, 233, 237
manipulation, 112
manuscript, 89
map, 70, 104, 116, 134, 158, 163, 208
Marazzi, Alina, 56–7, 138
Marcello Piccardo ricorda Bruno Munari (*Marcello Piccardo Remembers Bruno Munari*), 226
Marcello Piccardo: l'informazione capovolta (*Marcello Piccardo: Information Upside-down*), 227
Marcello, Pietro, 22–3
March, 13, 30, 105, 109, 160, 162–3, 166
    60 metri per il 31 marzo (*200 Meters for the 31st of March*), 13, 30, 160, 162–3, 236
Marcinelle tragedy, 133
Marcus, Millicent, 6
Mare chiuso (*Closed Sea*), 195
mare dell'oggettività (sea of objectivity), 248
Marghera (*Love in Marghera*), 117
marginalisation, 210
Marinetti, Filippo Tommaso, 220
market, 1, 55, 133, 138, 142, 147, 151, 181, 184, 188, 191, 193–6, 208, 249
Markopoulos, Gregory J., 7, 12, 161, 226
Marotta, Gino, 78
Marra, Vincenzo, 22–3, 234
Marshall Plan, 41
Martians, 153
Martin Eden, 23
Martuzzi, Gianni, 44
Marxism, 31, 47, 60, 143, 204–5
Maselli, Francesco, 43, 89–90
Masengo, Beppe, 180, 184, 189–90
Masini, Mario, 17, 222, 235
mass media, 12, 70, 75, 86, 103, 159, 166
Massenzio Rassegna Cinematografica, 10
master, 15, 54, 58, 73, 168, 182, 203
    Dutch Master Albrecht Dürer, 168
    Il fitto dei padroni non lo paghiamo più (*We Will No Longer Pay the Masters' Rent*), 15
mastery, 14, 187
masterpiece, 26, 94, 146
material(s), 12, 20, 27–30, 68, 71, 73, 76, 79–80, 103–5, 107–8, 110–13, 116, 119–21, 132–8, 159, 166, 168, 180, 182–7, 190–1, 207–9,

218, 225–6, 228–30, 233–5, 237, 239, 243, 245, 249
art, 110, 159
audiovisual, 28, 104–5, 116, 132–8, 229–30, 233–4, 235, 243
biographical, 225–6
bonus/backstage, 30, 180, 182–7, 190–1
critical, 104, 239, 245
documentary/archival, 28–9, 116, 133–5, 137–8, 218, 226, 228–9, 233, 235, 243, 245, 250
donations, 185
energy, 111
expressive, 112
materiality, 68, 71–2, 78–80, 103, 107, 120–1, 168, 245
ordinary/heterogeneous, 20, 76, 79, 107, 119, 121, 137, 166
plastic, 73, 119
poisonous, 207–9
preexisting, 12
recycled, 27, 108
specific, 71, 79, 107, 113, 116, 119–20, 245
sub-material forms, 14
uploaded/online, 136, 230, 234, 237, 245
world, 12
Matrimonio all'italiana (*Marriage Italian Style*), 133
Mattina (*Morning*), 80
maturity, 56, 116, 170
Mauri, Fabio, 71, 73
maverick, 3, 17, 217, 222, 239
Mazzoleni, Arcangelo, 15
Mazzucco, Massimo, 44
Mead, Taylor, 7
meaning, 32, 41, 60, 80, 87–8, 92, 95, 107, 113, 143, 147, 151, 154, 167, 169–70, 172–3, 175, 213, 245, 247, 250
meaningless, 172

mechanic, 71–2, 79, 121
mechanisms, 6–7, 22, 44, 121
Medea, 172
media, 1, 6, 12, 14, 17, 26, 30, 32, 47, 49, 70–1, 85–6, 89–90, 103–4, 107–8, 110, 116–17, 120, 133, 137, 143, 159–60, 164, 166–8, 180–1, 193, 196, 216–17, 223–5, 227, 230–1, 233, 245, 250
cultures, 223, 225
digital, 32, 70, 217
-ecology, 116
environment, 193
establishment, 49
experience, 227
'Experimenting with Media', 107–14
industry, 181
intermediality, 68–70, 72
-lab, 1
magnetic, 133
mainstream, 143
mass-, 12, 70, 75, 86, 103, 159, 166
Mediaset, 43, 181
mediated, 89, 168
mediation, 90, 165, 168
mixed, 233
modern, 117
multimediality, 26, 71
new, 14, 32, 217, 230–1, 245, 250
original formats, 133
paratexts, 30, 180, 196
technology, 245
remediated, 164
representational, 216
social, 181, 223–4
unconventional, 116
Mediaset, 43
meditation, 105, 121, 158–61, 164–8, 170, 174

medium, 3, 5–6, 8, 13–14, 16, 20, 24, 26–7, 30, 47, 71–3, 78, 80, 85–9, 93, 95, 103, 107, 109, 111–12, 120–1, 142, 163, 168, 216–18, 221, 228, 231, 240, 248–9
  algorithmic, 217
  arts, 6, 120
  electronic, 231
  expressive, 103, 142
  mechanical, 121
  new, 5–6, 9, 16, 78, 216, 218, 221, 228, 249
  of film, 13, 20, 24, 26, 80, 85–8, 93, 109, 111–12, 142, 163, 168, 221, 231, 240
  original, 47
medium-closeup, 209, 212
medium-length, 148
Medusa, 43, 193
Mekas, Jonas, 7, 12, 18, 53, 78, 104–5, 161–2, 221
Mèkurya, Gétatchèw, 206
Melancholy, 173, 217
Méliès, Georges, 78
membership, 246
memoir, 14, 216
memory, 28, 30, 48, 132–3, 137, 160–1, 168–9, 171–6, 211, 229
  ancestral, 174
  collective, 160
  cultural, 48, 160–1, 168–9, 171, 174
  family, 173
  living, 211
  personal, 28, 132, 174, 176
  private, 137
  sad, 137
  visual, 229
Meneguzzo, Marco, 8, 217
mentality, 76, 136
mentoring, 58
menu, 136
merchandise, 181

mercurial, 118, 248
Merz, Mario, 108
Merz, Marisa, 108
Mesothelioma, 207, 209
message, 13, 145, 185, 190, 209, 213, 237
Messina, 89
metacinematic, 4, 19, 219, 228
metacritical, 159, 167
Metamorphosi, 45–6, 55
metamorphosis, 9
meta-narrative, 48, 160, 170, 248
metaphysical, 24–6, 165, 167
Meteore, Pulsars (*Meteors, Pulsars*), 71
methodology, 3, 4, 94, 107, 109, 173, 188, 196, 206, 231
Mexico, Mexican, 189–90, 194–7, 202
  Cinema Mexico, 189–90, 194–7
MiBac, 192
Micciché, Lino, 27, 86–7, 90, 94–5
micro-budget, 183
micro entities, 223
micro-histories, 42
micro-managed, 238, 244
microscope, 84
  microscopic, 10
micro-society, 106
Middle-East, 162
migrant, 171, 210–11, 213, 171, 210–11
migration, 32, 159, 169–71, 175, 202, 209, 211–14
  'Global Migration', 209–13
  online, 32
  Migrazione (*Migration*), 169, 171, 175
migratory experience, 212–13
Migrazione (*Migration*), 169, 171
Milan (Milano), 19, 24, 41–6, 48–53, 55–6, 58–9
  cinema world of Milan, 50

City of Milan, 51, 55
culture, 44–5, 51, 56, 58–9
film industry, 43
Lotte a Milano (*Struggles in Milan*), 49
Milanese coop, 11, 15, 24–5, 41–61
Milan's film industry, 43
Province of Milan, 45, 53, 55
Questura of Milan, 48
Scuola Civica of Milan, 58
militancy, 8, 14, 19, 44, 49, 56–7, 141, 143–4, 225, 232
   Collettivo di Cinema Militante (Militant Cinema Collective), 49, 56
Militant Cinema Collective, 49, 56
millennium, 30, 55, 57, 180, 187, 189, 195
Millennium Film Journal, 243
mime artist, 205
Minazzi, Fabio, 111
Minazzi, Luisa, 207, 209
mind, 7, 16, 30, 54, 73, 75–6, 80, 88, 114, 153, 175, 184, 204, 238
miners, 133
minimalism, 19, 68, 71–2, 76, 91, 153, 224, 239
   art, 224
Ministero per i Beni e le Attività Culturali (Ministry of Cultural Heritage and Activities), 133
Minnie, Ferrara, 55
Minuz, Andrea, 7
miracle, 43, 111, 180–1
Miracolo a Milano (*Miracle in Milan*), 43
mirror, 1, 6, 22–3, 25, 51, 55, 114, 163–4
   The Planets' Mirror, 173
Miscuglio, Annabella, 10, 19
mise-en-abîme, 165
mission, 52, 146

Mitcheson, Katrina, 204
'mobile film', 93
Modaferri, Michele, 185
modalities, 32, 72, 165, 219, 234, 247, 249
model, 15, 18, 21, 43, 53, 58, 61, 105–7, 132, 141, 149, 153, 218–19, 244
modernity, 11, 14, 24, 48, 70, 75, 80, 86, 117, 122, 159–61, 164, 171, 213, 227, 231, 245, 248
   Museo d'arte moderna di Torino, 14
   Museum of Modern Art, 11, 231
   postmodern, 205
modulations, 224
modus operandi, 4–5, 9, 59, 203–5, 231
Moholy-Nagy, László, 73
Moiré, 114
MoMA, 11–12, 246
momentum, 105
money, 151, 180–1, 184–5, 188, 192, 221, 245
monograph, 2
monolithic, 47
monological, 154
monopoly, 44, 56, 144
montage, 12, 104, 115–16, 159, 164, 167, 169, 193, 195, 212, 231, 237
Monteleone, Enzo, 44
Monte Olimpino, 14, 113, 118, 216, 226–7
Montesacro Alto Cineclub, 10
Monti, Adriana, 44
Montreal World Film Festival, 149
mood, 6, 170
moon, 23, 105, 114–16, 230
   An Absurd Idea for a Filmmaker. Moon, 105, 111, 114–15
   Giro di lune tra terra e mare (*Moons Spins between Land and Sea*), 23
   -landing, 105, 114, 116
   Valentino Moon, 230

morality, 26, 52, 142, 151
Morandini, Morando, 58, 195
Moretti, Nanni, 2, 217
Morin, Edgar, 120
Moro, Aldo, 48
Morocco/Moroccan, 212
Morris, Errol, 56–7
Mossina collection, 133
Mostra del Cinema di Venezia, 52
Mostra di Pesaro 13
Mothlight, 109
motif, 5, 29, 141, 173, 175, 202
   leitmotif, 17
      Informazione Leitmotiv: L'informazione è ciò che conta (*Information Leitmotif: Information Is What Matters*), 17
Motion Vision, 13
motive, 250
Mount of Olives, 160, 164
movement, 3–7, 12, 14, 16, 20, 24, 26–7, 29, 41, 47, 49, 59, 71, 76, 78, 90, 83, 106–7, 109–11, 114, 116–19, 133, 137, 141, 144, 154, 161, 163, 171, 174, 219, 224–7, 235, 237
   anti-fascist, 29, 141
   Archivio Audiovisivo del Movimento Operaio e Democratico (Audiovisual Archive of the Labour and Democratic Movement), 226
   art, 5, 154, 224–5
   Arte Povera (Poor Art), 27, 235
   avant-garde/vanguard, 5, 7, 24, 29, 47, 219, 225
   Beat Generation, 106
   camera, 117, 119
   cyclical, 171
   'expanded cinema', 71, 76, 154
   historical, 6
   Italian experimental film, 20

Italian liberation, 144
   Luce e movimento (*Light and Movement*), 26, 78
   Milanese independent cinema, 41, 59
   Movimento arte concreta (Concrete Art Movement), 107
   Movimento della Pantera (Panther Movement), 133
   Movimento spazialista (Spatialist Movement), 27, 107, 114
   political, 137
   Pop Art, 14
   'projection and', 71
   protest, 237
   Resistance Fighters Movement, 29
   student, 49, 93
movie, 9, 18, 28, 43, 71, 93, 105, 108, 131–3, 135, 137, 142, 144, 148, 152–3, 161, 172–5, 187, 190, 192, 194, 231, 240
   Associazione Home Movies (Home Movies Association), 132–3, 137
   camera, 18
   high-cost, 9
   Hollywood, 142, 231
   home, 28, 105, 108, 131–3, 135, 137, 161, 173–5
   'home-movie filmmaker', 108
   indie, 190
   instant, 187
   Movie Drome, 71
   small-budget, 43
   theatre, 144, 148, 153, 192, 194
   wedding, 133
   'without a movie-camera', 240
Movimento arte concreta (Movement Concrete Art), 107
Movimento della Pantera (Panther Movement), 133

INDEX 305

Movimento Operaio e Democratico (Labour and Democratic Movement), 226
Movimento spazialista (Space Art Movement), 107
moving-image art, 4, 25, 70
multiform, 6, 120
multidimensional, 55, 120, 207
multilayered, 142
multimedia, 26, 71
multinational, 207–8, 228, 237
　company Eternit, 207
　corporation, 208, 228, 237
　market, 208
multiplex, 192, 195
multiplicity, 2, 24, 28, 78, 110, 225
Munari, Bruno, 8, 14, 33, 71, 107, 113, 118, 222, 226–7
Munzi, Francesco, 193
muse, 149
Museo d'arte moderna di Torino (Turin's Museum of Modern Art), 14
Museo del Cinema, 22
Museo del Novecento (Twentieth Century Museum), 70, 72
Museo Interattivo del Cinema (Interactive Museum of Cinema), 223
Museo Nazionale del Cinema, 5, 11
Museum of Modern Art, 11, 14, 231
museum, 11–12, 14–15, 22, 33, 45, 47, 70, 72, 103, 223, 231, 233–4, 244, 250
music, 5–6, 8, 45–6, 49–50, 86, 114, 117, 133, 135, 148, 172, 182, 189, 194, 212, 219
　Arti Musica e Spettacolo (University Department of Arts, Music, and Entertainment Arts), 133

'Chromatic Music', 219
　chromatism in, 6
　electronic, 70, 114
　La musica della danza (*The Music of Dance*), 6
　live, 135
　melancholic, 212
　companies, 45
　industry, 46
　history, 5
　and poetry, 8
　musical, 6, 172, 194
　musicalità (musicality), 6
　musicians, 70
　experimental, 70
　MusiCine Teatro (MusiCine Theatre), 50
　tribal, 117
MusiCine Teatro (MusiCine Theatre), 50
Mussgnug, Florian, 48
Mussolini, Benito, 41
mutation(s), 9, 120, 170, 231
　Commutazioni con mutazione (*Commutations with Mutation*), 120
Muybridge, Eadweard, 14, 227
My Italy, 91–2
My Nigerian Sisters, 211–14
mystery, 171, 245
mystical, 111
myth, 20, 26, 158, 166, 169, 171, 173, 175, 181, 226

naïf, 23, 175
　painter, 23
　painting, 175
'Naissance d'une nouvelle avant-garde: la caméra-stylo' ('The Birth of a New Avant-Garde: The Camera Stylo'), 121

name, 2, 53, 89, 91, 106, 141, 146, 169, 186, 191, 193, 202, 209, 213, 224, 228, 231, 240, 246
  unnamed, 184
Nanook of the North, 87
Naples, 13, 23, 92, 105, 218, 221, 238
  Neapolitan, 13
Narciso, 71
narrative, 1, 4, 6–9, 12–13, 17, 21–4, 31, 48, 7, 87, 89, 93–5, 109, 137, 142, 152, 154, 159–60, 166–70, 173–5, 180–3, 185, 187, 190, 196, 206, 217–19, 226, 233, 235, 241
  'against-all-odds', 181–97
  anti-, 12
  arc, 185, 190
  artistry, 187
  biographical, 206
  cinema/films, 7–9, 13, 22, 87, 94–5, 152, 217, 226
  contemporary forms, 12
  conventions, 142
  counternarrative, 175, 235
  documentary, 166
  features/approach, 21, 142, 154, 167, 173–4
  fictional, 89, 244
  hyperboles, 241
  inventiveness, 137
  lyrical, 175
  metanarrative, 48, 160, 170, 248
  non-linear, 219
  'of resistance', 152
  procedures, 17
  scripted, 233
  socio-cultural, 24
  traditional, 159
  use of body, 218
  voice, 23, 159, 168
narrator, 30, 159, 196
  authority, 159
  first-person, 30
  voice, 196

Narrow Road to the Deep, 175
nation, 1, 28, 85, 202–3, 218
  borders, 1
  European, 218
  Italian, 85
  'nucleic textures', 28
  states, 202
national, 1, 5, 14, 18, 25–6, 28–9, 31, 33, 41–3, 48, 54, 56, 60–1, 108, 121, 132–3, 136, 141–2, 145, 147–50, 161, 188, 190–1, 195, 207–9, 211, 214, 218, 220, 225, 228, 235, 237, 244, 250
  (and private) television, 14, 18, 228
  appeal, 28
  Archivio diaristico nazionale di Pieve Santo Stefano (National Diaristic Archive of Pieve Santo Stefano), 132
  borders, 218
  Carosello, 43
  Centre National du Cinéma et de l'Image Animée (CNC), 149
  Concorso nazionale della federazione nazionale cineamatori di Torino il fotogramma d'oro' ('National Competition of the National Home Movies Federation of Turin, The Golden Photogram'), 108
  cineclubs, 108
  cinema, 29, 59, 142, 237
  'cinematic legacy', 220
  'climate', 25
  contexts, 141
  'cross-national idea of independent cinema', 150
  Cuban national, 209
  daily newspaper, 145
  distributor/distribution, 188, 191
  European cinemas, 29, 142
  film festivals, 148
  film industry, 41, 56, 59–60
  film practices, 56, 121

gallery/galleries, 33, 250
governing bodies, 150
hegemony, 42
histories, 1
identity, 211, 250
industry channels, 244
Italian National Television (RAI), 235
nationhood, 28
philosophical tradition, 145
recognition/acclaim, 42, 54
record of programming, 195
social issues, 31, 214
territory, 132
National Agrarian Bank, 48
National Archive of Bologna, 28, 136
National Archive of Family Films, 28, 132–3, 136
National art-house movie theatres, 148
National Cineteques of Madrid and Barcelona, 161
National Film Board, 26
National Film Library (Rome), 225
National Film School, 147
National Film Theatre, 161
National Museum of Cinema, 5
National Television, 14, 228, 235
native, 21, 171, 211, 236
natural, 6, 12, 21, 107, 116, 118–19, 171–2, 187, 237, 240, 250
  naturalness, 131
  supernatural, 210
nature, 12, 14, 85, 116, 207
Nazism, 85
Né Bosco: una conversazione (*Nor Wood: a Conversation*), 170
Negri, Anna, 57
Nelda, 241
neo-classic, 5
  neo-liberal, 144, 238
neorealism, 20, 26, 84–6, 88–90, 153
Nepalese, 170

Nero più bianco fa legge (*Black Plus White Equals Law*), 17
Nespolo, Ugo, 8, 12–13, 32, 222, 233
Nettezza Urbana (*Sanitation Department*), 43
network, 18, 22, 44, 53, 57, 71, 132, 137, 146–7, 162, 206, 216, 228
  platform, 145–7
Nevrastenia, 6
New American Cinema, 7, 13, 27, 53, 58, 103–7, 110, 161, 224
new art, 5
new frontiers, 57, 219, 245
new generation, 46, 54, 56–8, 135
new Left, 52
new media, 14, 32, 217, 225, 230–1, 245, 250
new millennium, 30, 55, 57, 180, 187, 189, 195
new Right, 52
new technology, 10, 56, 59, 79, 218–19, 231
new wave, 8, 58–9, 121, 149
New York, 11, 71, 75, 104–5, 109, 161, 172, 231
New York Filmmakers' Co-operative, 105
Newman, Michael, 189
news magazines, 86, 90
newscasts, 138
newspaper, 116, 145, 168, 181, 196, 207, 221
newsreel, 27, 93, 161–2, 167
Newsweek, 166–7
niche, 21, 194, 250
Nichetti, Maurizio, 55
Nietzschean, 205
Nigeria, Nigerian, 211–13
  My Nigerian Sisters, 211–14
nineteenth-century, 205
No alla tregua (*No to Truce*), 49
Nodo Libri, 14, 227
nomadic, 161, 175

non-commercial film, 45
nonconforming, 3, 6
nonfictional, 159
non-linear, 219
non-mainstream, 18, 181, 197
Nono, Serena, 138
Non-permetterò (*I Will Not Permit It*), 12
non-professional, 53, 131, 149
non-realist, 94
norm, 142
  normative, 230
North African, 148, 152
North American, 2, 7, 218
northern, 106, 146, 148–9, 160
Northern Italy, 148
nostalgia, 57, 230
notebook, 30, 104, 158, 160–4, 175
Notes Towards an African Orestes, 162
notion, 3–4, 9, 18, 20, 27, 29, 32–3, 48, 107, 115, 141–2, 145, 151–4, 166–8, 204–5, 210, 220, 228, 245, 250
Nouvelle Vague, 20, 58
novelist, 245
novellas, 84
nuance, 24, 31, 143, 154
nucleus, 132
Nuova ERI, 229
'nuovi autori', 3
Nuovo Cinema Aquila, 190
Nuovo Paradiso (*New Paradise*), 78
nurturing, 44–5, 56, 59

Oberhausen manifesto, 58
objectivity, 9, 32, 89, 104, 107, 164–5, 170, 197, 210, 219, 234, 248–9
Obraz Cinestudio, 49, 58
October, 25, 142
  Giulia in ottobre (*Giulia in October*), 25, 54
ocular, 121

Odin, Roger, 131
official, 1, 16, 22, 25, 53, 57, 89, 93, 133, 143, 221, 225, 235, 240, 245
  unofficial, 29, 218
Officina Film (Workshop Films), 148
officine (workshops), 14
  'officina di ricerca', 3
  'officine artistiche', 8
off-line, 250
offshoot, 119, 230, 250
Oh! Uomo (*Oh! Man*), 12
Olimpino Studio, 14, 226–7
Olivetti, 226
Olmi, Ermanno, 2, 14, 44–5, 56, 60, 149, 217
Ombre elettriche, 11, 247
omniscient, 153, 159
omnivorous, 235, 242, 247
  'Omnivorous Embrace', 235–249
oneiric, 12, 28, 171
online, 11, 16, 32–3, 134, 136, 181–2, 196, 218–20, 222–6, 228–35, 237, 239–42, 244–50
  'Immigration Online', 222–234
  journals, 239
ontology, 73, 160, 163
opera, 205
  singer 203, 206
operation, 22, 89, 205, 229, 249
opposition, 2, 13, 24, 29, 141–4, 147, 152–4, 163, 170, 218
  'Independence as Opposition', 142–45
oppressive, 144
optical, 20, 73–4, 112, 239–40
  An Optical Poem, 117
option, 239, 242, 250
ordinary, 20, 23, 76, 87, 116, 118, 121, 134
  extraordinary, 14, 19–20, 112, 115–16, 118, 243
organiser, 26–7, 57, 93, 144

origin, 16, 20, 84, 86–7, 134, 145, 181, 183, 185, 204, 213, 245
original, 13, 16, 22–3, 47, 52, 54, 71–2, 94, 108, 113–14, 116, 133, 137, 143, 145, 166, 175, 183, 187–8, 194, 226, 228, 230, 239
  originalità (originality), 2, 4, 21
orphaned film, 243
orthodox, 51, 72
Oscar, 23
Osservatorio nucleare del Signor Nanof (*Mr. Nanof's Lunar Observatory*), 25, 54
ostracism, 244
Oursler, Tony, 73
outlet, 145
outline, 24, 71, 147, 153, 160, 162, 212
output, 24, 42, 175, 216–17
overture, 233

Pablo Distribuzione Indipendente (Pablo Independent Distribution), 146
Pagherete caro, pagherete tutto (*You Shall Pay Dearly, You Shall Pay All*), 49
Pagliero, Marcello, 85
paintbrush, 117, 166
painter, 5–6, 10–11, 13, 16–17, 19, 23, 109, 114, 119, 164, 173, 233, 235
painting, 5–6, 10, 12, 20–1, 23, 70, 73, 84, 87, 104, 108–9, 111, 117, 121, 167–71, 175, 217, 222, 233, 240, 246
  Al di Là della pittura (*Beyond Painting*), 70
Palazzoli, Daniela, 108, 118
Panini, Claudio, 111, 118, 120
panorama, 1–2, 18, 20, 26, 90, 205, 221–2

'Panorama of Global Stories', 205–7
pantheon, 249
paparazzi, 117
para-cinematic, 71
paradigm, 9, 26, 53, 58, 141–3, 144–5, 147, 217, 233, 241–2, 250
paradox, 6, 32, 60, 72, 80, 88, 147, 204–5, 216–50
paratext, 30, 180–1, 185, 193, 196–7
Parenti, Neri, 43
Paris, 5, 11, 52, 54, 56, 220, 231, 234, 244
Parliament, 49, 151
Parma, 11
parody, 172
participation, 20, 26, 55, 70, 75–6, 108, 119, 203, 229, 233
Partisans Association, 85
partnership, 249
parties (festive), 131
party, 48, 51–2, 137, 151, 210, 212
  Christian Democratic Party, 48
  Italian Communist Party, 151
  Italian Socialist Party, 51–2
  La Lega (The Northern League), 52
Pascali, Pino, 8, 235
Pasolini, Pier Paolo, 2, 92, 153, 162, 239
Pastrone, Giovanni, 2, 5, 217
Patella, Luca Maria, 13–14, 70, 119, 222, 232–3, 235, 242
patent, 79
Pathé Baby, 133
Pathé company, 5
pathos, 217
Patierno, Francesco, 192
pattern, 1, 4, 6, 26, 59, 68, 76–7, 85, 113–14, 206, 237, 248
Pavesi, Matteo, 51
Pays barbare, 12

pedagogical, 14, 135, 181, 185–6, 192, 205, 225, 235
Pedote, Gianfilippo, 25, 42, 48, 50–5, 57–60
Pedranti, Gabriella, 186
peers, 19, 48, 146
Pennsylvania, 173
Per amor Vostro (*For Your Love*), 23
percentage(s), 143, 186
perception, 8–9, 26, 108, 110, 112, 160, 164–5, 168, 203–4, 210, 213, 216, 240, 248
performance, 4, 6, 8, 10, 26, 14, 71–2, 74–5, 117–19, 205, 217, 226, 231, 233, 242, 246–7
performer, 74, 149, 206
periodisations, 230
Persephone, 171
Persico, Daniela, 144
personal, 6, 9, 12, 18–20, 28–9, 31, 53, 57, 103–4, 121, 131–2, 137, 148, 150–4, 156, 159–61, 163–4, 166, 168–76, 202, 207, 217, 220–1, 224, 238, 241–2
 and expressive freedom, 29, 221
 archive, 161, 170, 207
 artistic agenda, 19, 170, 175, 221
 beliefs/values, 150–1, 154
 camera, 121, 158, 163, 168
 cinema, 158, 168, 171, 175
 cultural heritage, 172, 174
 features, 152
 funds, 148
 humanistic approach, 202
 interests, 131, 169
 interpersonal, 57
 journey(s), 170, 175
 memory/sentiment, 28, 132, 160–1, 164, 166, 169–71, 173–4, 176, 207
 point-of-view, 18, 153, 168, 224
 talent, 220
 testimonies, 137, 217, 242, 217, 242
 vision, 12, 18–19, 104
 voice/discourse, 159, 175, 238
personality, 20, 103, 241
perspective, 2, 9, 12, 17, 25, 29–32, 70, 87, 107, 118–20, 141, 146, 159–60, 163, 169–70, 203–8, 214, 217, 231, 237, 245
 alternative, 29, 231
 anthropological, 12
 auteurial, 206, 231
 critical-theoretical, 30
 double, 160
 empirical, 107
 existentialist, 163, 169
 female, 203
 'Glocal Perspective', 207–9
 humanist, 208
 idealistic, 245
 indigenous, 25
 marginalised, 206
 of the social sciences, 217
 personal, 159
 perspectivism, 32, 204
 subjective, 119
 'The Glocal Perspective', 207–9
 third-person, 170
 transnational, 70
 unique, 204
 web of, 205
Pesaro, 7, 11, 13
 Mostra di Pesaro, 13
phantasmatic, 79–80
phenomena, 1, 2, 8, 10, 13, 20–1, 25, 43, 80, 84, 87, 107–8, 110, 116, 141, 160, 165–6, 168, 202, 221, 225–6, 235, 248
philosophy, 9, 13, 24, 32, 45, 58, 111, 145, 151, 164, 234, 243–4, 246, 249–50
photo albums, 137
photo-chemical, 163

photograph, 68, 72–3, 80, 88, 107, 109, 112, 116, 118–19, 163, 165–7, 170, 174, 217, 222, 240, 246
photographer, 19, 114, 173–4, 235, 247
photography, 47, 90, 93, 104, 131, 148, 186–7, 233, 239–40, 242
physicality, 19–20, 26, 76, 80, 84, 111, 146, 152, 165–6, 187, 233
metaphysical, 24–6, 165, 167
Pian delle Stelle (*The Plain of Stars*), 85
Piavoli, Franco, 21
Piazza Fontana, 48
Piazza Garibaldi, 22
Picasso, Pablo, 87
Piccardo, Andrea, 227
Piccardo, Marcello, 14, 32, 113, 222, 226–8, 242
Piccoli orrori (*Little Horrors*), 18
pictorial, 12, 220
Piedigrotta, 92
Piedmont, 188, 225
Piero della Francesca, 164
Pieve Santo Stefano, 132
pigments, 113
Pinelli, Giuseppe, 48
pinhole, 19
 -camera, 19
pioneer, 3–5, 12, 24, 78–9, 109, 111, 217, 226, 243
Pirandello, Luigi, 204
Piredda, Pierluigi, 186
Pirelli Hangar Bicocca, 12
Pirelli, Marinella, 19, 25–6, 68–80, 222, 240–1
Pistoletto & Sotheby's, 239
Piva, Alessandro, 193
pixel, 150
plaintiff, 207–8
planet, 21, 111, 173
 Il pianeta azzurro (*The Blue Planet*), 21
 The Planets' Mirror, 173

plan-séquence, 153
plasticity, 16–17, 73, 80, 93, 111–12, 116
 scenoplasticity, 6
 Voce della foresta di plastica (*The Plastic Forest's Voice*), 17
platform, 11, 32, 43, 46, 52–3, 60, 70, 134, 136, 145–6, 175, 223–4, 228, 230, 237, 246–7, 250
Play the City RE, 135
play, 72, 80, 114
 player, 52, 54, 205, 235, 248
 playful, 118–19, 172–3
 playing, 8, 11, 27, 30, 47, 55, 59, 90, 94, 138, 180–1, 185–6, 189, 196–7, 211
 interplay, 107, 118, 159, 173
 Light-play: Black-White-Gray, 114
 Play the City RE, 135
 screenplay, 149
pliability, 16, 24
plot, 183
Po, 43, 148, 161
 Gente del Po (*People of the Po Valley*), 43, 161
 valley, 148
poetry, 4, 8, 16, 80, 108–11, 115–17, 121, 158–62, 169–71, 174–5, 231, 236–7, 248
 poet, 10, 80, 111, 158, 161, 164, 170, 173, 175
 poetics, 3, 27, 161, 166, 174
 poetronica, 3
 An Optical Poem, 117
point of view, 9, 18, 21, 93, 134, 149, 153, 164, 214
polarisations, 48, 60
Polemizzando in bianco e nero (*Polemics in Black and White*), 106
police, 165–7, 206
Policlinico in lotta (*Policlinico Hospital's Struggle*), 15

policy, 41, 143, 149–50, 231, 246
political, 2–4, 6–9, 11–12, 14–15, 19, 22–7, 29, 32, 42, 46–53, 60, 85, 93, 137, 141–5, 148, 151–4, 206–7, 209, 211–12, 214, 218, 220–1, 224–5, 231, 235, 237, 246
   activism, 14, 31, 32, 42, 47–9, 51–2, 60, 93, 137, 141, 143, 152, 208
   background, 46
   biopolitical, 206
   cinema/films, 12, 15, 29, 49, 153–4, 225, 229
   collectives, 48, 86
   culture, 7–8, 15, 19, 23, 24–7, 31, 42, 48–9, 51–2, 60, 85, 137, 141–5, 148, 151–2, 235
   economy, 23, 32, 218, 237, 246
   geopolitical, 206–7, 209, 211–12
   hegemony, 151
   historical, 220
   impegno (engagement), 47–50
   imperative, 47
   literary conscience, 47
   newsreels, 27, 93
   opposition, 152–4
   performative, 231
   politicised, 4, 8–9, 164, 237
   socio-, 4, 6, 19, 22, 24–5, 32, 42, 48–9, 51–3, 60, 85, 93, 141–5, 151–2, 206, 214, 218, 220–1, 224, 229, 235, 245
   tradition, 154
   vision, 152–3
politics, 41, 48, 151, 153, 208, 212, 230
   'Cinematic Politics: Independence as a Coherent Style', 151–2
polycentric, 31, 203
polyphonic, 159, 170, 176
polysemic, 114
polyvalent, 6
   artistes polyvalents, 225

Poma, Andrea, 45, 55
Poma, Marco, 45, 55
Pop and Minimal Art, 224
Pop Art, 14, 108
popularity, 50, 91
   popular/popularise, 8, 12, 25, 49–50, 52, 91, 110, 149, 158, 163, 166
   Radio Popolare (Popular Radio), 50
Porcelluzzi, Antonella, 239
Porporati, Andrea, 193
Porta Romana, 58
portal, 135–6, 145–7, 160, 246
portrait, 93, 116, 134, 158, 160, 168–71, 173–5, 227, 239
   Autoritratto Auschwitz (*Self-Portrait Auschwitz*), 162
   family, 173–4
   self-, 134, 158, 160, 162, 168–71
   video-, 227
portrayal, 91, 119
post, 182, 190, 249
postcard, 161, 175
Postcards from America, 161, 175
postcolonial, 204–5
poster, 191, 195, 246
post-Futurist, 222
postindustrial, 51
post-Lira, 54
postmodern, 205
postproduction, 13, 46
postwar, 1, 26–7
   documentary, 243
   Europe, 48
   films, 1, 103
   French and Canadian cinema, 26
Pound, Ezra, 161, 164
poverty, 164, 206, 244
power, 6, 32, 43, 51, 88, 93, 118, 208–9, 212, 216, 233–4, 237, 244
   empowerment, 146
   overpowering, 250

Pozzi, Angelo, 109
practice(s), 1–9, 11–12, 16–17, 19, 21–8, 30–2, 43, 48, 58, 60, 68, 70–2, 78, 86, 104, 106, 108, 111, 119, 121–2, 131, 137–8, 141–3, 145, 147, 149, 153–4, 194, 203–4, 211, 216–19, 221, 230–2, 234–5, 244, 247, 249–50
  'against-all-odds' stories and, 30
  animation, 3
  communication, 216
  consumption, 218
  disruptive, 142
  documentary, 43, 137
  economic, 142
  elitist, 147
  hegemonic cinematic, 143
  international film/art, 1, 25, 108
  interpellation, 138
  mainstream/conventional, 2–4, 22–4, 28, 58, 60, 131, 217–18
  militant, 141, 145
  online, 218, 235
  oppositional, 154
  resistant, 145
  rituals and, 211
  scientific, 104
  self-determining, 4, 149, 203
  subjective, 104
  unconventional and alternative film/artistic, 2–8, 11–12, 16–17, 19, 21–2, 24, 26–7, 31–2, 68, 70–2, 78, 86, 104, 106, 111, 119, 121–2, 131, 194, 218–19, 221, 231–2, 234–5, 244, 247, 249–50
  unconventional distribution, 181, 195, 197, 219
  underground, 2
practitioner, 29, 108, 141, 193, 209
Prampolini, Enrico, 5
Prandstraller, Andrea, 203

Prealpina, La (The Pre-Alps Journal), 108, 115
precarity, 187
precedent, 146, 217
predominant, 149, 159, 206
preemptive, 150
prejudices, 78, 202
premiere, 146, 148–9, 189
presentation, 18, 73–4, 135, 137
preservation, 5, 132, 134, 211, 223, 243
prestige, 11, 142, 153, 188
  The Economy of Prestige, 188
priorities, 237, 250
Prisoners of War, 12
private, 9, 15, 18, 131–5, 137, 181, 194, 218
  'Giornate del cinema privato' (Days of Private Cinema), 9
  film, 132
  TV, 18, 194
prize, 53–4, 58, 108, 188–9
procedure(s), 2–3, 17, 28–9, 92, 134, 137, 219, 239
process, 3–4, 13, 17, 19, 26, 31, 51, 59, 69, 85, 87, 92, 107–8, 110–11, 113, 116, 119, 121, 132, 134, 153, 173, 181, 183, 202–5, 207–8, 212, 214, 221, 238, 241
proclivity, 233
producer, 18, 29, 44, 47–8, 51–3, 57, 60, 85, 142, 145–6, 148, 151, 181–4, 186, 192, 202, 239
product, 53, 131, 142, 146, 173, 183, 185, 216, 234
production, 3, 5, 9, 12–15, 17–18, 20, 22–3, 24–5, 30–2, 41–6, 49, 51–60, 71–3, 84–5, 90, 94, 134, 137, 142–50, 152, 154, 172, 175, 180–8, 191–3, 196–7, 204–5, 214, 218–19, 224–25, 233–4, 239, 244, 250

production (*cont.*)
　advertising, 43
　alternative model, 15
　assistant, 188
　autonomy, 219
　budget, 3, 55, 94, 143, 172, 180, 183, 187, 191, 234
　channels, 44
　company/companies, 18, 22, 42–5, 53–7, 71, 143, 146, 154
　conventions, 94
　co-production, 147, 149, 184
　costs, 142
　CSC Production, 225
　cultural, 143
　facilities, 44, 46, 60
　freedom, 218
　high-cost, 9, 148–9
　Hollywood, 181
　international, 205
　mainstream, 17, 22, 43–6, 49, 51–6, 60, 72, 142, 149–50, 152, 192, 224, 244
　mode, 22, 30, 41–2, 44, 49, 52, 57–60, 84–5, 94, 134–5, 137, 145–7, 154, 182, 184, 192–3, 196–7, 205, 214, 218, 224, 239, 244, 250
　modes and practices, 24
　non-Hollywood, 142
　of propaganda films, 49
　paths, 57
　postproduction, 13, 46
　pre-production, 183, 204
　Production Culture, 180
　reproduction, 73
　tales, 31, 181–3, 185–7
　Torino Studio, 233
　unconventional/innovative, 3, 5, 12–14, 22–3, 25, 31, 42, 45, 55–6, 72, 90, 134, 142–4, 154, 175, 192, 197, 239, 250
profession, 14, 146, 238
professional, 17, 28, 41, 53, 56, 131, 135, 145, 146–9, 154, 173, 197, 210, 216, 233, 235
professionalism, 19, 46, 56
professor, 111
profilmic, 105
profits, 186, 188, 194, 209
program/programme, 8, 10–11, 16, 18, 43, 50, 52–3, 57, 93, 106, 135, 137–8, 190, 194–5, 217, 221–5, 228, 231, 233, 235, 237, 247
progress, 86, 115–16, 149, 169
　progressive, 42–3, 46, 48, 90, 149
projector, 68, 72–3, 76–8, 80, 110–12
projection, 25, 69–73, 76–8, 80, 109, 112, 242, 245
　Prospekt 1971: Projection, 70
　'Screen/Projection', 76–80
Promised Land, 212
promoter, 26, 85, 136, 236
promotion, 8, 42, 44, 55–6, 59, 132, 135, 181, 190, 193, 197, 221, 223, 225–6, 247
prop, 119, 205
propaganda, 49, 243
propelling forces, 144
properties, 88, 107, 112–13, 120
proprietary, 143, 150, 175
　rights, 143, 150
propulsive, 6, 216, 232
　movement, 6
　yearning, 216
Prospekt 1971: Projection, 70
prostitution, 213
protagonist, 11, 19, 24–5, 89, 91–3, 108, 116, 149, 152, 186, 206, 213, 228, 235
　'The Different Protagonists and Forms', 11–23
protest, 14, 237
proto-cinema, 20
protocol, 32, 72, 217, 231, 237, 246, 249

prototype, 6, 59, 134
Proussade, 239
Proust, Marcel, 239
Provincia di Milano, 45, 53, 55, 148
provocateur, 231
   provocation, 1, 5–6, 13, 87, 118, 160, 231
pseudo-life, 248
psychedelic, 119
psychiatry, 19
   psychiatrist, 238
psychic, 242
psychoanalytical, 235
psychological, 19, 23, 153, 187
public, 9, 11, 16, 18–19, 22, 44, 46, 50–1, 55, 57, 60, 70, 75, 94, 131, 133, 137–8, 149–50, 181, 184, 218, 229, 247
   Interventi pubblici per la città di Milano (*Public Works for the City of Milan*), 19
   demonstrations, 19
   event, 133
   funds, 22, 150
   institution, 184
   investment, 57
   opinion, 48
   relations, 44, 46, 51, 137
   screening(s), 16, 137, 191
   sectors, 218
   service broadcaster, 149
   spheres, 131
publication, 134, 182
publicity, 149, 191, 196
pure, 15, 73, 78, 87, 107, 112
   art-cinema, 15
   expression, 6, 90
   cinema, 112
   colour, 114
   form, 73
   representation, 87
   visual and kinaesthetic experience, 78

purpose, 2, 8, 13–14, 28, 42, 71, 87–8, 132, 135, 141, 173–4, 194, 213, 228, 241
   repurpose, 60, 166

qualità formali (formal qualities), 5
quality, 4, 6, 10, 27, 30, 43–4, 46, 50, 52, 61, 68, 77–8, 103, 110, 117, 122, 144, 147, 183, 185, 189, 203, 214, 217, 221, 230, 237
   'The "Absurd", Expanded Quality of Experimental Cinema', 103–22
Quando l'occhio trema (*When the Eye Flutters*), 20
Quartieri popolari di Roma (*Community Housing Quarters in Rome*), 15
Questura of Milan, 48

Raban, William, 12, 71
racist, 148, 152
radical, 7–8, 21, 26, 51, 69, 75, 88, 93, 112, 131, 150, 164, 207, 245
   radicalisation, 88
radio, 45, 50, 53, 56, 86, 89
   broadcast, 86
   campaigns, 50
   Radio Popolare (Popular Radio), 50, 53, 56
   station, 50
   Swiss Radio Television, 45, 53
RAI (Italian National Television), 14, 18, 43, 53, 181, 193, 235, 241
   RAI Cinema, 149–50
   RAI3, 228, 241
   RAI's national Carosello, 43
Rapallo, 7, 162, 171
Rascaroli, Luca, 158–9, 175
Ravenna, 135
   Sguardi in camera: Ravenna nei film di famiglia e amatoriali (*Camera Glances: Ravenna in Family and Amateur Films*), 135

Ray, Man, 112, 231
reaction, 92, 120, 231
real, 18, 28, 69, 92, 105, 107, 114, 119–21, 145, 153, 159–60, 164–5, 167, 224, 229
  failure, 224
  freedom, 69
  life, 92, 121
  person, 229
  social change, 107
  world, 105, 160, 165
realism, 20, 78, 88, 90–1, 153, 217, 219
  cinematic, 153
  psychological, 153
  realist, 7, 94, 149, 153, 187, 220
    anti-, 7
    character, 220
    neo-, 161
    non-, 94
    style, 149, 153
reality, 8, 15, 26, 43, 47, 52, 78, 84, 86–8, 90–1, 93, 105, 118–20, 153, 164, 171, 184, 186, 204–5, 207, 210, 216, 228
  contemporary, 205
  crude, 15
  of globalisation, 207
  social, 47, 91, 93, 105
  unreal, 153
realisation, 13, 27, 73, 117, 137, 148, 152, 160, 169, 205, 238–9
  'never realised', 238
  'unrealised visions', 73
realm, 17, 72, 86, 112, 117
  visual, 17
reception, 26, 72, 120, 181, 185, 196
recognition, 15, 25, 42, 44, 88, 147, 206, 249
recorder, 231
recording, 9, 28, 114, 131, 133–4, 162, 204

recrimination, 94
Recupero e reinvenzione (*Restoration and Reinvention*), 19
recycle, 27, 105, 108, 172
Recycled Images, 105
redemption, 85, 152
  Theory of Film: The Redemption of Physical Reality, 84
reel, 132, 136–7, 146, 162, 167, 187
  Cinegiornali della Pace (*Cine-newsreels for Peace*), 161
  Cinegiornali Liberi (*Free Cine-newsreels*), 161
  demo-, 187
  newsreels, 27, 93
  Vision du Réel (festival), 146
reference, 7, 29, 49, 60, 86–7, 107, 142–4, 149, 151–2, 158, 190, 248–9
reflection, 53, 73, 76, 80, 89, 95, 134, 136, 158, 160, 165, 168–9, 174
  self-, 169, 174
  The World Viewed: Reflections on the Ontology of Film, 73
reflexivity, 165, 170
  self-, 174
Reggio Emilia, 135
Reggio, Goffrey, 54
regime(s), 9, 22, 24, 32, 144, 212, 231, 237, 250
region, 41, 108, 132–3, 150, 161, 188
  'Abruzzo, Lombardy, Piedmont, and Sicily', 225
  funding, 250
  governing bodies, 150
  Piedmont, 188
  Po, 161
  Regional Directorate for Cultural and Landscape Heritage of Emilia-Romagna, 133
  Regione Lombardia (Lombardy Region), 55

INDEX 317

rejection(s), 48, 183
Relabtv (Dipartimento di
    Comunicazione ed Economia,
    Università di Modena e Reggio
    Emilia – Department of
    Communication and Economics,
    University of Modena and
    Reggio Emilia), 135
relationship, 3, 27, 31, 43, 47, 57, 59,
    86, 109, 111, 119, 132, 134, 159,
    176, 195, 213
religion, 151, 159, 245
renaissance, 3, 32, 219, 250
Rendez-vous Des Cinémas d'Art et
    D'Essai, 106
Renov, Michael, 165, 167
renovation, 5
reportage, 105, 166–7
reporters, 138
representation, 7, 9, 14, 69, 76, 87, 105,
    117, 132, 143, 149, 163–5, 171–2,
    216, 218, 231, 236, 243, 247
  anti-, 7, 9
  The Anti-Representation
    Approaches/Forms of Italian
    Cinema, 7
  arts, 218
  film/media, 117, 216
  models, 218
  self-, 149
republic, 190, 206
  Federal Democratic Republic of
    Ethiopia, 206
  President of the Republic, 190
reputation, 181, 196, 243
'Requiem for Soldiers lost in Ocean
    Transport, A', 171
requirement(s), 3, 13, 72, 134, 237
research, 10, 14, 25, 28, 30, 42, 52,
    60, 71, 91, 108–10, 113, 120, 135,
    187, 202, 219, 225, 228, 230, 233,
    235, 240

*Gli Archivi per la ricerca anagrafica
    (Family-Registry Research
    Archives)*, 135
researcher(s), 8, 111
Resistenza (Resistance), 29, 141, 144, 154
resource, 21, 25, 136, 187, 210, 228,
    235, 241, 245
responsibility, 32, 107, 131, 144, 169,
    229
restoration, 19, 132, 134 225
  film, 134
  programmes, 223, 225
  Restoration and Reinvention, 19
Reteitalia, 43
retrospective, 10, 13, 49–50, 52, 54, 57,
    70, 72, 221, 223, 227, 232, 235, 245
*Rêve d'une petite fille qui voulut entrer
    au Carmel (Dream of a Girl Who
    Wanted to Join the Carmelites)*, 236
revenue, 45
review, 23, 25, 28, 30, 50, 75, 80,
    134–5, 141, 181, 232, 250
  previewed, 53
revolution, 1, 4, 6, 8, 16, 103, 144,
    151, 218, 228, 241, 245
  approaches, 218
  avant-gardes, 241
  'Before and After the Revolution:
    Experimental Cinema in Italy', 8
  digital, 16
rhetoric, 70
rhythm, 12, 107, 114, 117, 160, 163, 167
Ricci Lucchi, Angela, 12, 222, 242–3
Richter, Hans, 6, 12, 112, 226
right vs. wrong, 151
rights, 15, 143, 148, 150–2, 160, 168,
    195
  human, 160, 168
  *La casa è un diritto non un privilegio
    (Housing Is a Right and Not a
    Privilege)*, 15
  proprietary, 148, 150

Right, the, 48, 52
  the new, 52
Risi, Dino, 60, 89
risk(s), 147, 187, 190, 250
Rittmann, Walter, 6
ritual, 133, 152, 170, 173, 211
Rizza, Gabriele, 144
Rizzo, Federico, 31, 183–4, 187, 196
robots, 248
Rocco e i suoi fratelli (*Rocco and His Brothers*), 43
Rocco, Gianni, 46
romantic, 121, 137, 212
Rome (Roma), 5, 7, 10–11, 13, 15, 17–18, 22–4, 27, 41–4, 56, 59–60, 74, 90–3, 105–6, 147, 149, 160, 166, 184, 189–90, 203, 205, 218, 221–2, 225, 229, 232, 235, 238–9, 241
  amphitheatre, 205
  artists, 17
  Azzurro Scipioni Cinema, 244
  Cooperativa Cinema Indipendente, 106, 226, 238, 241
  Filmstudio, 10–11, 105
  I misteri di Roma (*The Mysteries of Rome*), 27, 91–3
  International Film Festival, 149
  Lontano da Roma (*Far from Rome*), 22
  Nuovo Cinema Aquila, 190
  Porta Romana, 58
  Quartieri popolari di Roma (*Community Housing Quarters in Rome*), 15
  Roman film industry, 42, 56
  Roman group, 222
  Roman monopoly, 44, 56
  The Roman Experimental Cinema, 1965–1975), 232
  Valle Giulia riots, 166
  Vergine Roma (*Virgin Rome*), 239
Rosa, Paolo, 25, 46, 53–4
Rosi, Gianfranco, 22–3
Rossellini, Roberto, 1–2, 45, 91–2, 94, 153, 161, 217
  L'India vista da Rossellini (*India as Seen by Rossellini*), 161
Rosso di sera (*Read Evening*), 54
Rothko, Mark, 240
Rouch, Jean, 162
routine, 23, 151, 233
rule(s), 13, 149, 183, 246, 249–50
Rumble, Patrick, 8, 20, 239–40
rupture, 108
rural, 148, 211
Russolo, Luigi, 220
Ruttman, Walther, 114

sacred, 17, 160, 164, 171
sacrifice, 186, 195
Sacro GRA, 23
Saimir, 193
Salsomaggiore Film Festival, 11
Salvatores, Gabriele, 60–1
San Marino, 106
San Siro, 195
Sancassani, Antonio, 194–5
Sancassani Cinema, 189
Sangiorgi, Leonardo, 46
Sappho, 170
Sarchielli, Massimo, 18
saturation, 17, 142, 247
Saudi Arabia, 206
Sbardella, Americo, 10
scanner, 134
Scavolini, Romano, 17, 235
scenographer, 17, 185, 235
scenoplasticity, 6
scepticism, 75, 230
Schechner, Richard, 75
schedule(s), 182, 187, 225, 247
Schegge di Utopia: il cinema underground italiano (*Utopian Splinters: Underground Italian Cinema*), 235

scheme, 143, 149, 151, 238
Schermi (*Screens*), 13
Schifano, Mario, 6, 8, 13, 17, 162, 219
Schmidheiny, Stephan, 209
scholar, 1–3, 6–9, 11, 16, 20, 32, 50, 52, 111, 131, 141, 144, 154, 159, 191–2, 194, 221, 229–30, 232, 239–41, 247
  scholarship, 180
school, 15, 44, 48–9, 58, 87, 107, 109, 135, 147–8, 152, 186, 202, 206, 224
Schoenberg, Susanna, 45–6
science(s), 1, 14, 104, 111, 115–16, 118, 120, 205, 217, 226, 228
Sciuscià (*Shoeshine*), 94
scope, 85, 104, 143, 220
scopophilia, 230
screen, 4–5, 11, 13, 15, 18, 26, 68–9, 71–3, 75–6, 78, 80, 87–8, 109, 153, 195, 209, 229, 232, 242
  -arts, 4–5
  Film Ambiente (*Environmental Screen*), 26, 68, 72
  Lo sguardo espanso: Tecniche Miste su Schermo: il cinema sperimentale di Roma, 1965–1975 (*The Expanded Gaze: Mixed Techniques on Screen: The Roman Experimental Cinema, 1965–1975*), 232
  re-screened, 10
  Schermi (*Screens*), 13
  'Screen/Projection', 76–80
  'Screen, Space and Performance', 72–76
  single-screen cinema, 195
screening, 7, 10–12, 15–16, 26, 50, 70, 75, 91, 106, 110, 116, 135, 137, 146, 148, 153, 161, 181–2, 188, 191–2, 194–6, 219, 223–4, 227–8, 233, 239

'Crowning Moments: Sold-out Screenings', 188
  programme, 50
screenwriter, 84–5, 93, 142, 145–6, 148, 151–2, 184
  Best Screenplay, 149
  screenwriting, 146
script, 54, 84, 92, 150, 233
  manuscript, 89
  scriptwriter, 29, 84
  unscripted, 164
scriptorium, 221
scriptures, 159, 164
sculpture, 11, 68, 69–71, 78, 109, 111, 233
  sculpting, 26, 68, 72, 78, 109, 204
  sculptor, 109
Scuola Civica of Milan, 58
Scuola di Firenze, 15
Scuola Nazionale di Cinema, 225
Scusate il disturbo (*Apologies for the Interruption*), 120
Se l'incoscio si ribella (*If the Subconscious Were to Rebel*), 229
Se la vita è meglio, butti via la telecamera (*If Life Is Better, Throw Away the Camera*), 227
sea, 17, 23, 137, 167, 195, 248
  Adriatic, 137
  55cm above Sea Level, 17
  Below Sea Level, 23
  Fuocoammare (*Fire at Sea*), 23
  Giro di lune tra terra e mare (*Moons Spins between Land and Sea*), 23
  Mare chiuso (*Closed Sea*), 195
  'mercurial-like', 248
  'sea of objectivity', 248
search, 8, 14, 85, 108, 136, 182, 184, 195
  unsearchable, 234
season, 10, 105, 161
Second World War, 29, 41, 144

secondary school, 135
Secondo il mio occhio di vetro (According to My Glass Eye), 20
secret, 152
secretary, 151
Segre, Andrea, 195
self-conscious, 143, 212, 245
self-determination, 24, 235
self-discovery, 161
self-distributed, 183, 188–9
self-portrait, 134, 159–60, 162, 168–71
   Autoritratto Auschwitz (Self-Portrait Auschwitz), 162
   films, 162
self-reflexive, 3, 9, 159, 169, 175
self-representation, 132, 149
self-sacrificing, 245
self-sufficient, 59
semantics, 116, 237
seminar, 146–7
Senaldi, Marco, 8
sensual, 113
sensibility, 12, 24, 29, 107–8, 114, 121, 141, 158–60, 168, 224
sensitivity, 137
sensory, 108, 110
   sensorial, 113, 216, 248
   sensorium, 113, 116
sentiment, 28
'sentimental network', 137
September, 106, 144
sequence, 76, 115, 118, 136, 153, 167, 171–2, 193, 195, 242
   plan-séquence, 153
series, 6, 14, 27, 71, 73, 84, 91–3, 106, 133, 149, 163, 165–7, 174–5, 183, 187, 202, 206, 209–10, 213, 243
   mini-, 161
service, 42, 146, 149, 223
set, 6, 22–3, 75, 141, 145–8, 150, 154, 185–6, 188, 191, 196, 205
'Off-Set Activities: Independence as an Unconventional Path', 145–148
On-Set Activities: Independence as Negotiated Identity', 148–151
setting, 25, 50, 72–3, 78, 84, 205
Sette opere di misericordia (Seven Acts of Mercy), 146
Seventies, 16, 121–2, 242
   Idea assurda per un filmaker. Gianfranco Brebbia e il cinema sperimentale degli anni sessanta-settanta (An Absurd Idea for a Filmmaker: Gianfranco Brebbia and Experimental Cinema of the Sixties and Seventies), 122
Severini, Gino, 220
Sguardi in camera: Ravenna nei film di famiglia e amatoriali (Camera Glances: Ravenna in Family and Amateur Films), 135
Shakespeare, William, 205
Sharits, Paul, 71
'shoe-string budget', 184, 221
short documentary, 243
short film, 6, 11, 54–5, 145, 148, 160, 166, 169, 175, 211, 222, 227, 231, 233–4, 239, 241
short interviews, 232
short stories, 84
short texts, 136
short video-commercials, 232
shortcoming, 182
Show Sold Separately, 182
showcase, 11, 53, 55, 119, 193–4
Sicily, 225
Siena, 9
silent film, 5, 236, 241
silent period, 1, 20
Silvio Berlusconi Communication, 43
simplicity, 18, 80, 91
simultaneity, 92

INDEX

site(s), 11, 91, 147, 186, 223–5, 230–1, 236, 239
Sitney, Adams, 1
Sixties, 10, 16, 29, 87, 108, 120–1, 161, 171, 210, 236–7, 242
  Idea assurda per un filmaker. Gianfranco Brebbia e il cinema sperimentale degli anni sessanta-settanta (*An Absurd Idea for a Filmmaker: Gianfranco Brebbia and Experimental Cinema of the Sixties and Seventies*), 122
sketch, 163, 175, 228, 242
SKMP2, 13, 233
slapstick, 233
slideshow, 72
slogans, 144
small production, 55, 94, 234
smartphone, 135
Smith, Jack, 7
Smithson, Robert, 70
Snow, Michael, 12
Soavi, Michele, 44
soccer, 137
sociability, 237
social advertising, 148
social agenda, 48
social change, 15, 53, 107, 160, 233
social circles, 197
social consciousness, 111
social context, 131, 147
social critique, 43, 50, 60
socio-cultural, 25, 27, 118, 142, 242
social discontent, 171
'social distribution', 188, 196
social documentary, 50, 225
social engagement, 4, 11–12, 21, 24, 31–2, 43, 52, 95, 135, 146, 154, 202, 206, 216, 229
social enterprise, 44
social history, 158
social iconography, 138
social impact, 44
social interactions, 42, 52
social interest, 133
social issues, 14, 26, 31, 41, 47, 211, 214
social landscape, 51, 54, 86, 135–6
social media, 181, 223–4
social narratives, 244
social networks, 146–7
socio-political, 27, 31, 85, 142, 206
socio-political tension, 49, 51
social protocol, 72
social reality, 47, 54, 91, 93, 105
social role, 90, 142
social sciences, 1, 217, 228
social solidarity, 151
social sphere, 49, 86, 147
social transformations, 55, 59
social viewpoint, 19
social vision, 17
Socialist Party, 51–2
Società Italiana Cines, 5
software, 136, 238, 246
Solaris, Claudia, 106
solarisation, 119
Soldi, Giancarlo, 53
Soldini, Silvio, 2, 15, 25, 54–6, 60–1, 217
Sole in mano (*Appropriazione, a propria azione, azione propria*) (*Sun in One's hand* (*Appropriation, A-Proper-Action, Action-Proper*)), 71
solidity, 68, 114
solidarity, 106, 146, 151, 213
Sollima, Giovanni, 148
Song of Songs, 170
song, 86
  folk, 228
  Song of Songs, 170
  Songs, 221
  swansong, 106, 166

Sontag, Susan, 75
Soprintendenza Archivistica per l'Emilia Romagna (Emilia Romagna Archival Authority), 136
Sordillo, Michele, 44
Sorrentino, Paolo, 193
Sotto le stelle, sotto il tendone (*Under the Stars, Under the Tent*), 15
soul, 17, 30, 247
sound, 12, 17, 29, 74, 84, 93, 117, 148, 159, 169, 175, 190, 206, 221, 233
   and image, 159
   effects, 190
   Il rumore del sole (*The Sound of the Sun*), 29
   installations, 233
   magnetic, 175
   of Ethiopian jazz saxophonist, 206
   of tribal music, 117
   quality, 221
   soundboard, 50
   soundtrack, 74–5, 131, 148, 169, 231
   system, 194
   technicians, 148
source(s), 21, 45, 55, 58, 72, 76, 78, 85, 87, 93, 104–5, 122, 133, 135, 138, 159–60, 166–7, 169, 184, 211, 244, 248–9
Space art movement, 107, 114
Spada, Marina, 195
Spain, 213
spatio-temporal, 14, 165
spectacle, 75–6, 112, 143, 207
spectator, 3, 12, 16–17, 21, 26, 73–5, 85, 87, 121, 181–3, 188–90, 196–7, 241
   Cooperativa Spettatori Produttori Cinematografici (Cinema Spectators Producers Cooperative), 85

spectrum, 85, 247
spiritual, 53, 111
Spoleto, 7
sponsorship, 18, 22, 44, 221
spontaneity, 17–18, 19, 21, 23, 49, 132, 162, 164, 166, 172, 210, 224, 228
squatting, 48–9
stadium, 137, 195
stage, 13, 20, 56, 59, 68, 92, 142, 149, 151, 183, 190, 194, 205, 237
   backstage, 180, 182–91, 196
standard, 2, 17–18, 22, 87, 185, 244, 249
star(s), 15, 85, 115–16, 120, 149, 206
   Pian delle Stelle (*The Plain of Stars*), 85
   Sotto le stelle, sotto il tendone (*Under the Stars, Under the Tent*), 15
station, 50, 91, 241
Statista (statista.com), 248
Steiger, Janet, 142
Stein, 111–12, 117
Stella, Kiko, 54–5
Stellino, Alessandro, 144
stock, 4, 31, 46, 172
   film, 46, 172
   Italian artistic, 4
   Italic/Latin, 31
Stop Forgetting: The Films of Yervant Gianikian and Angela Ricci Lucchi, 243
Storia del cinema italiano (*History of Italian Cinema*), 90
Storia di Caterina (*Caterina's Story*), 90
Storie di famiglia (*Family Histories*), 135
Storie di paglia (*Straw Stories*), 211
story, 18, 31, 73, 76, 89–92, 136, 148, 167, 173, 175, 180–1, 183, 186–7, 189–91, 193–4, 196, 204–5, 207–8, 210, 212–13, 216

Storia di Caterina (*Caterina's Story*), 90
storyline, 172
storyteller, 7, 11, 23, 137, 153, 188
storytelling, 4, 9, 166, 169, 203–5, 245
storyboard, 22
Strani Film (Strange Films), 146, 148
strategy, 46, 72, 80, 181, 188, 190, 193, 196
stratosphere, 112, 116
Straub, Jean Marie, 11
stroboscopic, 72
structure, 13, 49, 68, 72–4, 76–8, 80, 85, 89, 94, 114, 120–1, 141, 164, 172, 212, 216, 220, 233, 248
   infrastructure, 42
   structuralism, 13, 23, 217
struggle, 27, 49, 53, 60, 93, 147, 183, 191–2, 197, 205, 207–9, 211–12, 221
   Lotte a Milano (*Struggles in Milan*), 49
   Totem, Le lotte di via Tibaldi (*Struggles in via Tibaldi*), 49
student, 27, 49, 93, 133, 135, 166, 171, 194, 203, 205–6, 224
Studio Azzurro, 15, 24, 45–7, 53–6, 230
Studio di Monte Olimpino, 14, 113
Studio Equatore, 42, 53–4, 56
Studio46, 246
style, 2–4, 7, 9, 13–15, 21–2, 31, 51, 55, 85, 93, 103, 106, 108, 111, 117, 119, 121, 131, 133, 141–3, 149–51, 153, 158, 161–2, 166, 169, 175, 217, 219–20, 224, 226, 228, 230, 233–4, 244–5, 248
subconscious, 9, 14
   Se l'inconscio si ribella (*If the Subconscious Were to Rebel*), 13, 229

subject, 2, 23, 25, 78, 90, 92, 131, 133, 185, 202–4, 206, 208, 211, 213, 219, 221, 224–5, 229, 240, 245
subjection, 249
subjectivity, 9, 18, 30, 104, 112, 114, 119–20, 158–61, 163–7, 169–70, 172, 174–5, 210
subscribers, 223
substantial, 58
substitution, 175
substratum, 24, 170
subtitles, 230, 235
suicide, 90, 152, 213, 168, 170, 173
   Tentato suicidio (*Attempted Suicide*), 90
summer, 52, 135, 137, 149
   L'Ultima Estate (*The Last Summer*), 168, 170, 173
   Summer School, 135
Sunday, 137
Super8, 14, 17, 121, 133, 230, 238, 247
superimposition, 13, 20, 78, 116, 136, 167, 169, 232
supplementary, 137
surface, 26, 69, 73, 107, 109, 114, 117
surrealist, 7, 94, 224
sustainability, 19, 218, 250
Swedish cinema, 4
Switzerland, 45, 53, 105, 107, 146, 211
   Swiss documentary festival Vision du Réel, 146
   Swiss Radio Television, 45, 53
symbolism, 6, 49, 107, 113, 205, 211, 248
symphonies, 6
synaesthetic, 110, 113
synergies, 45, 142
synopsis, 225

system, 10, 22, 26, 53, 56, 58, 78, 86, 94, 132, 134, 142–4, 147, 150–2, 169, 194, 212, 216, 237
  ecosystem, 116
  systematic, 1–2, 7, 10, 95

tactile, 240
Taiwan, 203
talent, 13–14, 16, 18–19, 23–5, 29, 31–2, 42, 60, 147, 187, 191, 194, 197, 217, 220, 245
  multitalented, 85, 232
talk(s), 135–6, 206
Taormina Taj Mahal, 211
tape, 20, 121
  videotape, 14–15, 18, 137, 190, 232
tapestry, 170, 206
Tarantelli, Giuditta, 29, 142, 145–52, 154
Tate Film, 221
taxonomist, 167
teacher, 135
team work, 57
tech industry, 138
Techiné, André, 149
technician, 42, 147–8, 196
technique, 2, 4, 6, 9, 12–14, 20, 27, 30, 32, 93, 103, 107–9, 111, 119, 121–2, 134, 158–9, 163, 167, 174, 188, 204, 227, 231–2, 240, 248
  Lo sguardo espanso: Tecniche Miste su Schermo: il cinema sperimentale di Roma, 1965–1975 (The Expanded Gaze: Mixed Techniques on Screen: The Roman Experimental Cinema, 1965–1975), 232
technical, 4, 19, 26, 27, 29, 32, 46, 58, 78, 88, 92, 94, 121, 122, 131, 187, 218
  expertise, 121
  facet, 26, 29, 32, 78, 88, 92, 218

Istituto Tecnico Statale a Ordinamento Speciale (State Technical Institute with Special Orientation), 58
  processes, 4
  skill, 46
  strategies, 27
technocratic, 33, 237, 250
technology, 3–4, 9–11, 16, 32, 46–7, 49, 56, 58–9, 71, 79–80, 86, 104, 115–16, 120, 193, 218–19, 223–24, 231, 237, 245, 247–50
  artisanal, 71
  context, 56
  developments, 3, 193, 218
  experimentation, 59
  innovation, 16, 115, 219, 230
  landscaper, 58
  procedures, 219
  progress, 86, 116
  transformations, 9
teenager(s), 48, 148, 152
telephoto, 93
telescope, 84
television/TV, 11, 14, 18, 22, 26, 43, 45, 51, 53, 56–7, 86, 89, 92–3, 105, 114, 116, 120, 138, 143, 150, 161, 167, 181, 192, 194, 202, 204, 226, 228, 231, 235
  advertising, 43, 51, 56, 181
  archives, 105, 114, 116, 167, 226
  broadcasters, 86, 143, 150
  cinema/films, 43–4, 89, 92, 120
  Escuela Internacional de Cine y Television, 202, 204
  industry, 52
  miniseries, 161
  network, 18, 22, 228
  programmes, 11, 43, 138, 228, 231, 235
  reportage, 89, 105
  State TV, 22

studios, 43
Swiss Radio Television, 45
TV channels, 194
TV documentary, 45
Tempo nel tempo (*Time in Time*), 14, 226–7
temporality, 14, 158, 163, 165–6, 170, 175
tenacity, 181, 183, 186, 191–2
tendency, 7, 41, 85, 167, 180, 219, 248
Tentato suicidio (*Attempted Suicide*), 90
Teorie del cinema 1945–1990 (*Theories about Cinema 1945–1990*), 120
Teramo, 185, 190
terms and conditions 228
Terra Animata (*Animated Earth*), 119
territory, 16, 132, 194
terrorist, 44, 48
  Il terrorista (*The Terrorist*), 44
Tesi sul Neorealismo (Thesis on Neorealism), 88
testimony/testimonies, 16, 28–31, 137, 176, 181, 191, 208, 217, 233, 242
tethered, 217, 250
text(s), 86–7, 92, 103, 119–20, 136–7, 144, 159–60, 163–4, 166–7, 169–71, 176, 181–2, 193, 209, 233, 246
  hypertextual, 242
  intertextual, 158, 164
  paratexts, 30, 180–1, 185, 193, 196–7
  texture, 6, 12, 28, 107, 114, 208, 219–20, 230, 233
Thaïs, 5–6
The Collina del Cinema (*The Hilltop of Cinema*), 227
The Flicker, 71–2
The Garden of Earthly Delights, 109
The Last Summer, 168, 170, 173

The Lord of the Rings, Lord of the Rings: The Two Towers, 182, 187
The Mysteries of Rome, 27, 91–3
The Rocky Horror Picture Show, 194
The Travel Agent, 209, 211, 214
The Upanishads, 160
The World Viewed: Reflections on the Ontology of Film, 73
theatre, 5, 8, 30, 41–2, 49, 51, 56–7, 68–70, 72–3, 75, 108–1, 144, 148, 188–97, 203, 229–30, 237, 247
  amphitheatre, 205
  and architecture, 47, 69
  and cinema, 42, 68, 70, 75, 108, 230, 247
  arts, 8, 56–7, 68, 72, 75
  civic, 152
  Club nuovo teatro (*New Theatre Club*), 110
  critics, 108
  'environmental', 75
  Evenings: Theatre and Engineering, 75
  ICET (Industrie Cinematiche e Teatrali – Cinema and Theatre Industries), 42
  installations, 55, 72–3, 75
  Living Theatre, 8, 75, 108, 229
  National Film Theatre, 161
  sound system, 194
  venue, 49, 51, 144, 148, 180–1, 188–97, 203, 237
theme, 2, 5, 17, 26, 31, 41, 47, 52–3, 57, 59, 87, 90, 117, 119–20, 131, 137, 144, 149, 152, 159, 173–5, 180, 183, 185, 187, 191–2, 194, 202, 206–7 211, 213, 219, 245, 247
theorist, 84, 86, 120, 143
theory, 26, 29–30, 41, 84, 86–7, 89, 90–2, 94, 120, 141, 145, 168, 170, 217

theory (*cont.*)
  debates, 41, 47, 94
  discourse/notion, 27, 29–30, 95, 141, 144, 204, 218, 224
  history, 26
  perspective 30, 218, 224
  science, 27, 111, 144
  source, 87
  template/framework, 3, 28, 151
Teorie del cinema 1945–1990 (*Theories about Cinema 1945–1990*), 120
Theory of Film: The Redemption of Physical Reality, 84
thesis, 4, 41, 88, 152, 239
  antithesis, 4, 41
  'Tesi sul Neorealismo' (Thesis on Neorealism), 88
third-person, 9, 170
three-dimensional, 25, 68, 73, 78, 87
time-based, 226
Timi, Filippo, 149
Tinelli, Fausto, 48
titles, 15, 28, 136, 195, 225
  subtitles, 230, 235
Tivulandia, 43
Toffetti, Sergio, 8
Tognoli, Ugo, 51
tool, 14, 24, 32, 49, 75, 111, 121, 136, 145, 181, 202, 204, 225, 228, 233, 238, 250
topic, 2, 23, 28, 144–5, 148, 202, 213, 228
totalising, 3, 5, 245
Totem, 49
tour, 19, 28, 135, 223, 229
toxic, 245
tracking shot, 109
tracking software, 238
Trade Tattoo, 117
trademark, 47, 55, 110, 117
tradition, 2, 4
  aesthetic, 10, 21, 170, 243
  artistic, 4–7, 24, 41, 45, 59, 110, 142, 161, 217, 219–20, 223, 232, 233, 243
  canons, 4, 20, 223
  cinema/film, 13, 45, 49, 60, 68–9, 73, 78, 84–5, 95, 147, 150–1, 153, 159, 245
  cinematic, 2, 7, 11–12, 20, 41
  customs/ways, 211
  French film, 149
  healer, 210
  Italian, 5–7, 10, 41, 59–60, 161–2, 217, 219, 233, 243
  journalism, 93–4
  non-traditional, 7, 20
  notion of *impegno*, 151
  philosophical, 145
  political, 154
  representation models, 218
tragedy, 70, 94, 133
trailer, 223
trainees, 149
training, 56–7, 145–7
transcendence/transcending, 6, 68, 72, 86, 105, 152, 218
transformation, 4, 8–10, 24, 52, 55, 59, 91, 108, 131–3, 135, 151, 158, 165, 219, 221, 233, 248–50
  'A Transformative Legacy', 91–94
  'Experimentalism: Legacies and Transformations', 219–22
  'From Legacies to Transformations', 4–11
transition, 13, 51, 230, 234
translation, 236
transnational, 58–9, 70, 160–2, 205, 208, 219, 223, 244
  borders, 223
  cooperation, 205
  labourers, 208
  network, 162, 244
  New Waves, 58–9

perspective, 70
practices, 219
struggle, 205
transparency, 76, 116, 121, 153
Traumatografo (*Thaumatrope*), 20
travelling festival, 247
treatment, 2, 109, 137, 143, 148, 207
Trenker, Luis, 43
tribal, 114, 117
tribute, 6, 172, 219
Triennale Museum, 45
Trieste, 145, 149
Trini, Tommaso, 75–6, 80
tropes, 163, 202, 206, 242
troupe, 186
Truffaut, François, 146, 149
truth, 87–8, 93, 149, 183–5, 194, 204–5, 229
  'Moments of Truth: Deciding to Shoot on a Low-Budget', 184–5
Turi, Giorgio, 12, 106, 120, 222, 235
Turin (Torino), 5, 7, 11, 14, 22, 105, 108, 184, 188–9, 202–3, 207, 209, 218, 221, 224, 229, 233, 235
  Concorso nazionale della federazione nazionale cineamatori di Torino il fotogramma d'oro ('National Competition of the National Home Movies Federation of Turin, The Golden Photogram'), 108
  Film Festival, 235
  Museo d'arte moderna di Torino (Turin's Museum of Modern Art), 14
  Museo del Cinema, 22
  Turin-Piemonte Film Commission, 188
Tuscany, 11
Tutino, Saverio, 132
Tutti giù per terra (*We All Fall Down*), 22

Tutto, tutto nello stesso istante (*All, All at Once*), 13, 106, 166
twentieth century, 3–4, 6–7, 9, 11, 18–20, 24, 85, 87, 112, 135, 153, 211, 216, 227
twenty-first century, 11, 192, 217–18, 228
Twitter, 223
type, 16, 19, 22, 28, 54, 70, 72, 137, 144, 187, 195, 218, 224, 242, 247
  prototype, 59, 134–5
typewriter, 221

Uboldi, Sandro, 109
UFO, oggetti volanti (*UFO, Flying Objects*), 118
Uganda, 153
Umano Non Umano (*Human Not Human*), 17, 162
Umberto D., 94
umbilicality, 237–8
Un giorno un aereo (*A Day an Airplane*), 17
Un'ora sola ti vorrei (*For One More Hour with You*), 138
unambiguity, 142
unconscious, 231
unconventional, 1–9, 29, 61, 116, 145, 147, 219, 228, 235, 237, 247
underdog, 191, 195
underground, 2, 4, 7, 10–11, 16, 20, 84, 103, 110, 161, 219, 224, 228, 230
  Schegge di Utopia: il cinema underground italiano (*Utopian Splinters: Underground Italian Cinema*, 235
Underground Cinema Today, 103
Underground Film Festival, 161
underpaid, 196
underworld, 171
Ungaretti, Giuseppe, 80

Ungari, Enzo, 8, 226
ungrammatical, 248
union (labour), 93
Unità, 137
United States/USA/US, 17, 22, 71, 120, 142–3, 209–10, 211, 221, 224
   Made in USA, 17
   US–Cuban relations, 209
   US embassy, 209
universe, 92, 94, 110–11, 131, 171
universalim, 48, 141–2, 163, 169
Università Statale (State University), 48
University of Genoa, 236
upload(s), 134, 136, 223–4, 227, 230–1, 237, 243, 246, 249
urban, 19, 24–5, 41, 43, 59, 90, 218, 233–4
   art, 19
   centres, 218
   concerns, 234
   fabric, 24, 41
   landscape(s), 59, 90
   Nettezza Urbana (*Sanitation Department*), 43
   reform, 233
   setting, 25
   suburban, 42
US–Cuban relations, 209
user, 136, 145, 223, 225, 235, 237–8, 247, 249
   -generated, 235
utopia, 14, 16, 85, 226, 228, 235, 239, 250
   Schegge di Utopia: il cinema underground italiano (*Utopian Splinters: Underground Italian Cinema*), 228, 235, 239

Vaccari, Franco, 222, 247
Valentino Moon, 230
Valle Giulia, 166
values, 106, 142–3, 151
van Doesburg, Theo, 73–4, 76, 78
Vanderbeek, Stan, 71
vanguardism, 5, 7, 17, 19, 218–19, 242, 248
Vanzina, Carlo, 43
Varese, 106, 108
Vari, Paolo, 54, 57, 196
variation(s), 74, 93, 119
Vaso Etrusco (*Etruscan Vase*), 18
Velocità massima (*Maximum Velocity*), 193
Venice, 18, 92, 148, 221, 227
   International Film Festival, 18, 148, 227
Vento di Terra (*Earthbound Wind*), 23
venue, 1, 16, 31, 70, 103, 137, 194, 234, 237, 244, 250
Verdi, Giuseppe, 205
Verdicchio, Pasquale, 144
Vergani, Massimiliano, 31, 194
Vergano, Aldo, 85
Vergine Roma (*Virgin Rome*), 239
Vergine, Adamo, 13, 105, 222, 238–9
Vergine, Aldo, 13
Vergine, Antonio, 13, 105, 222
Veronesi, Luigi, 8, 12, 32, 222
versatility, 16, 186, 226, 250
Verso casa (*Homeward*), 211–12
Versus, 30, 160, 162–5, 170
vertical, 142, 249
Vertov, Dziga, 26, 84, 86–7, 104
veteran, 228
VHS, 58
Via degli Orti d'Alibert, 11
Vicari, Daniele, 913
victims, 152, 207–9
video, 3, 11, 14–15, 18, 25, 28, 42, 45–7, 49, 52–8, 133–7, 148, 180, 182–91, 193, 196, 217–18, 220–1, 223, 225–8, 230–3, 235, 237, 239–40, 242, 245–50

advertising, 148
and cinema, 42, 47, 53, 58, 136, 218, 225–6, 228, 239, 247
art, 3, 42, 45–6, 53, 55, 217, 221, 225, 227, 230, 232, 242, 250
artefacts, 228
artist, 46, 242
backstage, 180, 182–6, 188–91, 196
-blogs, 246
bonus, 187
centres, 25, 56
-clip, 135–7, 183, 186–7, 193, 223, 245
commercial, 46, 53, 232
digital, 231, 235
documentary, 228
family-video-recordings, 134
Festival of Film and Video, 42, 52–8
home-, 58, 182, 191, 193
installations, 47, 55, 135
-maker, 226, 231, 242, 247
militant, 232
-portrait, 227
practices, 250
recordings, 28, 134, 217, 227, 246, 248
-sharing platform, 11, 182, 223, 226–7, 231, 235, 237, 239–40, 247, 249
tape, 14–15, 18, 137, 190, 232
technologies, 49, 56, 58, 133, 221, 231, 235
texture, 220–1, 230
views, 248–9
Videobase, 14, 216, 230
Vieni, dolce morte (*Come Sweet Death*), 17
Vienna, 11
Vietnam, 17
view(s), 3, 9, 11, 16–17, 21–2, 31, 70, 80, 86, 93, 134–5, 137, 142, 149, 153, 165, 190, 202–3, 207, 214, 223–4, 228, 230–1, 233–4, 236–7, 241, 245, 247–50
point-of-view, 18–20, 29, 31, 87, 153, 164, 168, 217
previewed, 53
purview, 237
viewable, 224, 226, 232–3, 239–41, 247
viewer, 20, 41, 73–6, 78, 80, 144, 153, 159–60, 165, 170–1, 176, 181–3, 185–6, 188, 190–1, 194, 196–7, 203, 206–10, 213–14, 224, 230, 237, 240, 242, 245, 249
viewership, 16, 223, 228, 230, 249
The World Viewed: Reflections on the Ontology of Film, 73
village, 91–2, 148, 211
villager, 211, 230
villain, 142
Vimeo, 11, 223, 226, 230, 234
Vincennes, 5
Viola, Enrica, 227
violence, 48, 88, 152, 165–8
virtuality, 78, 120, 217, 242
    environment, 146
    images, 78, 80
    presence, 242
    tours, 223
virtue, 59, 70, 75, 218
virtuosity, 217
visa, 209, 212, 214
Visconti, Luchino, 17, 43, 85–6
visibility, 19, 68, 70, 84, 90, 116, 159, 164, 167, 193, 195, 208, 224, 234, 239
Vision du Réel, 146
vision, 3–5, 8–10, 12–14, 17–21, 26–7, 29, 71, 73, 85–6, 88, 90, 94, 103–4, 108–9, 111–14, 117, 150–3, 164, 204, 221, 233, 242, 248
    field-of-, 19

vision (cont.)
  Motion Vision, 13
  visionary, 12, 71, 92, 104, 116–17, 121, 161, 231
  Vision du Réel, 146
  Visioni Off (Off Visions), 144
  'Zavattini's New Vision of the Cinema', 86–90
Visioni Off (Off Visions), 144
visual, 1, 4–7, 10, 12, 16–17, 19, 26–8, 52, 71, 78, 84, 87–8, 90, 92–4, 108, 120, 131–5, 159–60, 163–4, 170, 222, 225–7, 229–30, 232, 240, 246–7
  and kinaesthetic experience, 78
  approach, 12, 226
  arts, 1, 4–6, 10, 19, 78, 87, 90, 163, 222, 227, 246
  artefacts, 132–4
  artist, 7, 10, 12, 218, 222, 247
  carnival, 232
  culture, 84, 88, 92, 94, 131, 133
  data/archive, 134, 226
  heritage, 135
  history, 28, 93, 133
  language, 16, 120, 159–60, 163–4, 170, 222, 240
  media, 17, 26, 52, 71, 131–2, 216, 225, 230
  memory, 229
  perceptions, 108
  quality, 221
  realm, 17
Vitella, Federico, 90
Vittorio Emanuele III, 243
Vivo e glorioso (Living and Glorious), 8
vocation, 24, 146, 162
Voce della foresta di plastica (The Plastic Forest's Voice), 17
Voci nel tempo (Voices in Time), 21
voice, 9, 17, 21, 23–4, 28, 31, 45, 50, 71, 85, 94, 137, 150, 159, 164, 167–8, 171, 174, 176, 184, 193, 196–7, 203–4, 210–12, 214, 238
Voce della foresta di plastica (The Plastic Forest's Voice), 17
Voci nel tempo (Voices in Time), 21
voiceless, 85
voice-over, 159, 164, 167, 174, 176, 203, 211–12
Volevo nascondermi (I Wanted to Hide), 22
Voy-age, 120
voyeurism, 229

Warhol, Andy, 14, 70, 226
Warming Up, 30, 161, 172–3, 237
web, 94, 134, 145, 147, 205, 242
  webpage, 11, 223–4, 230, 235, 239
  website, 145, 225–6, 228, 239, 244
wedding movies, 133
Wees, William C., 105
Wenders, Wim, 56
Wertmuller, Lina, 44
Western, 4, 19, 170, 219
  peers, 19
  tradition, 4, 170, 219
Whitman, Walt, 175
wife, 107, 145, 148, 245
Wikipedia, 231, 233–4, 236, 242, 247
Winspeare, Edoardo, 144
winter, 29, 137, 148, 196
  Il primo giorno d'inverno (The First Day of Winter), 29, 148, 196
Wiseman, Frederick, 57
witness, 48, 90, 207
woman, 28, 70, 90, 115–16, 136, 165–7, 170–1, 176, 206–9, 213, 242
  activities, 28
  amateur cineastes, 28, 136
  archivi femminili (women archives), 28
  Archivio di Storia delle Donne (Women History Archive), 136

artists, 70
Centro di Documentazione delle Donne della Città di Bologna (Women Documentation Centre of the City of Bologna), 136
'crimes against', 206
'dialogue between a man and', 170
'eighty-year-old', 208
'featuring', 242
films dedicated to, 115
'four', 206
images of, 167
in court proceedings, 208
'life of', 171
'marginalised', 207
named Lourdes, 209
Nigerian, 212–13
'only woman in the CCI', 239
'poor', 90
'portrait-films of three', 116
representation of, 171
'resilience', 213
'strong', 176, 213
'three', 213
'violence perpetrated on', 165–7
'woman's face', 116
word-of-mouth, 181, 195, 197
worldview, 1, 164, 170, 204
Work of Art, 182
working conditions, 181
workshop, 54, 57–8, 135, 144, 146–8, 203
    Officina Film (Workshop Films), 148
World Wide Web, 94
writer, 7–8, 22, 26, 30, 54, 137, 146, 184, 204, 221, 245
    writing, 1, 22, 26, 46, 86–7, 90, 92–3, 108, 110–12, 121, 137, 144, 146, 150, 159, 162, 165, 168, 175, 193, 221, 224, 231, 233, 236, 239, 247–8
        diary-, 169
        re-, 161
        typewritten, 221

Wu, Ming 2, 137
Wuchale, 206
WWI, 243
WWII, 103
www.artefutura.org, 246

Yeats, T. S., 161
young, 18, 41–2, 44, 47–8, 50, 55, 59–60, 91, 94, 108, 135, 146, 152, 158, 160–1, 164, 168, 170, 184, 192–3, 195–7, 205, 212, 227, 230, 244, 250
    adult, 48, 52, 59–60, 94, 135, 158, 160–1, 164, 168, 170, 192, 205, 212
    'and homeless single mother', 18
    audiences, 226
    cinema, 50
    Collectif Jeune Cinema (Young Cinema Cooperative), 230
    entrepreneurs, 146
    French intellectuals, 94
    generation, 41, 227
    I ragazzi che si amano (*Youngsters in Love*), 44
    lover, 152
    members, 57, 170
    talent/directors, 42, 44, 47, 55, 59, 108, 135, 184, 192–3, 195–7, 205, 239, 244, 250
    writers, 146
Youngblood, Gene, 110, 231
YouTube, 11, 190, 223–4, 226–8, 231–4, 236, 239–41, 243, 245–9
yuppies, 51

Zaccaro, Maurizio, 44
Zagarrio, Vito, 3, 8, 31, 192, 194, 250
Zavattini, Cesare, 2, 14, 26–7, 84–95, 161, 217
Zavattinian, 90–2, 94, 229
Zeus, 171
zoetrope, 236
zoom, 116, 118, 206, 208

EU representative:
Easy Access System Europe
Mustamäe tee 50, 10621 Tallinn, Estonia
Gpsr.requests@easproject.com